Ernest Gellner

Ernest Gellner

An Intellectual Biography

JOHN A. HALL

VERSO

London • New York

First published by Verso 2010
Copyright © John A. Hall 2010

1 3 5 7 9 10 8 6 4 2

Verso
UK: 6 Meard Street, London W1F 0EG
US: 20 Jay Street, Suite 1010, Brooklyn, NY 11201
www.versobooks.com

Verso is the imprint of New Left Books

ISBN-13: 978-1-84467-602-6

British Library Cataloguing in Publication Data
A catalogue record for this book is available from the British Library

Library of Congress Cataloging-in-Publication Data
A catalog record for this book is available from the Library of Congress

Typeset by Hewer Text UK Ltd, Edinburgh
Printed in the US by Maple Vail

Contents

Preface

When Ernest Gellner died in December 1995, the flags of the University of Cambridge, where he had taught from 1984 to 1992, were set at half mast. This reflected the status he had achieved in the last years of his life, as a public intellectual able to comment on a very wide range of issues. It did not mean, however, that his views had lost their bite. If Gellner's name had been made during the scandal surrounding his early attack on Oxford linguistic philosophy, his late essays – not least his attack on Isaiah Berlin as a 'Savile Row postmodernist' – were capable of causing just as much outrage.[1] Still, many felt affection for Gellner, with whose voice they had become familiar, and to whom they often turned for guidance and insight. All the same, very few people knew what to make of him. He *was* hard to pin down. For two decades he had the curious title of Professor of Sociology with special reference to philosophy at the London School of Economics and Political Science (LSE) – held, it should be noted, in two different departments: first Sociology, then Philosophy, Logic and Scientific Method – before taking up the William Wyse Professorship of Social Anthropology at the University of Cambridge. He had separate reputations as scholar of Islam, theorist of nationalism, philosopher of history, and historian of ideas. He ended his career in Prague, the city in which he had grown up as a boy, though in his final years he was most interested in developments in Russia. His status as public intellectual rested on this background, that of a multilingual polymath, a modern *philosophe*. He was sometimes cited as one of the last great thinkers from Central Europe whose Jewish background meant a direct experience of the twentieth century's horrors.

It is possible to hint at what follows by noting the very particular way in which Gellner fits into this last category. The contours of his formative experiences are clear, and were pungently expressed by Gellner himself

---

1 'The Savile Row Postmodernist', *Guardian Weekly*, 19 February 1995.

when discussing the work of Hannah Arendt. The rise of nationalist sentiment at the end of the nineteenth century created a dilemma for Jews,
especially those who had experienced the Enlightenment and an end to
anti-Jewish discrimination by the state. Gellner insisted that the return to
cultural roots was always an illusion, a piece of pure romanticism he neatly
illustrated by noting sardonically that 'it was the great ladies at the Budapest
Opera who really went to town in peasant dresses, or dresses claimed to
be such'.[2] Illusion or no, the Jews felt the pull of belonging just as much as
others did – perhaps even more. But the romantic call to belong affected
the minority Jewish community and the demographic majority in two very
different ways.

> [T]he minority had no illusion *of its own* to go back to. It only had the
> recollection of the ghetto, which by definition was not a self-sufficient
> community or culture at all, but an unromantically (commercially)
> specialized sub-community of a wider world within which it was
> pejoratively defined. Although in fact a literary populist nostalgia for the
> *shtetl* does exist nevertheless, Jewish populist romanticism is in the end a
> contradiction in terms . . .
>
> So the romantic reaction placed the Jews in a dilemma . . . They were
> largely deprived of the illusion of a possible return to the roots, an illusion
> indulged by their gentile neighbours with enthusiasm and conviction.
> Thou shalt not covet thy neighbour's *Gemeinschaft*! But, of course, one
> does. So what's to be done? The options which were logically open were
> either to infiltrate the Other's *Gemeinschaft*, or to create a new one of
> one's own, whether or not there had been any peasants available for the
> past two millennia, who could define its folk culture.[3]

But the desire to enter does not mean that one will be permitted to do so –
or, even worse, permitted to remain within, as relatively assimilated German
Jews were to discover. In consequence, a third option arose, rejecting the
similarly homogenizing forces of assimilation and Zionism, namely that of
pure cosmopolitanism. A political version of this cosmopolitanism which
had world-historical consequences was that of the Jewish-born activists and
intellectuals who became the key stratum of the early Bolshevik leadership,

---

2 *Nations and Nationalism*, Oxford, 1983, p. 57. He went on to say that 'ethnic' gramophone
records were consumed in the Soviet Union by sophisticated urban dwellers.

3 'Accounting for the Horror', *Times Literary Supplement*, 6 August 1982, reprinted as 'From
Königsberg to Manhattan (or Hannah, Rahel, Martin and Elfriede or Thy Neighbour's
Gemeinschaft)', in *Culture, Identity and Politics*, Cambridge, 1987, p. 79.

and sought to create a left-wing empire in the East in which they would be safe.[4] An intellectual version of this cosmopolitanism that held equal power was Karl Popper's famous call for an open society, in which tribal yearnings for the womb – including those of Zionists – would not be tolerated.[5] Thinkers of this sort were prone to a romanticism of their own, liable to forget that the empires from which they came were sites of ethnic antagonism more often than they were arenas of benign multicultural-ism.[6] Allegiance to cosmopolitanism could also be demanding, potentially homogenizing into a single model, for all its emphasis on the universality of human values.

Thinkers of Jewish background lived the tension between cosmopoli-tanism and ethnonationalism in a variety of ways, and their ambivalence was in many cases intensified by the creation of the state of Israel. The uniqueness of Gellner's thought derives from his acceptance of this tension, acknowledging each position's weaknesses, whilst continuing to recog-nize both the power of universalism and the importance of nationalism. Accordingly, Ludwig Wittgenstein, whose thought Gellner had disliked from the start, became the great 'bête noire' in the book he was writing at the time of his death. The Austrian philosopher had moved from a total endorsement of universalism to the uncritical acceptance of a *völkisch* relativism, thereby, in Gellner's view, being utterly wrong twice.[7] The particularity of Gellner's intellectual achievement can be further illustrated by the briefest of comparisons with Popper, the contemporary thinker who influenced him the most. The immediate contrast concerns nationalism: Gellner took this protean force much more seriously, principally by empa-thizing with its proponents and attempting to understand its emotional appeal. A childhood in interwar Prague rather than Vienna helps to explain this, but far more fundamental differences are at issue. Gellner did not think that nationalism could simply be usurped by cosmopolitan ideals. For one thing, good ideas alone were unlikely to have that much power. For another, Gellner differed from Popper and other liberals in believing that Enlightenment values were not fully grounded, that universalism could not justify itself in purely philosophical terms. Consider his views on Julien

---

4   L. Riga, 'Ethnonationalism, Assimilation and the Worlds of the Jewish Bolsheviks in Fin de Siècle Tsarist Russia', *Comparative Studies in Society and History*, vol. 48, 2006.

5   M. Hacohen, 'Karl Popper in Exile: The Viennese Progressive Imagination and the Making of *The Open Society*', *Philosophy of the Social Sciences*, vol. 26, 1996.

6   M. Hacohen, 'Dilemmas of Cosmopolitianism: Karl Popper, Jewish Identity and "Central European Culture"', *Journal of Modern History*, vol. 71, 1999.

7   *Language and Solitude: Wittgenstein, Malinowski and the Habsburg Dilemma*, Cambridge, 1998.

Benda's famous argument that modernity had witnessed a '*trahison des clercs*'.[8] One might well expect a thinker with a Central European Jewish background, all too aware of Bolshevism and fascism, to heartily endorse the thesis of a betrayal by intellectuals of their heritage. But Gellner did nothing of the kind. To the contrary, he turned the tables on Benda — choosing to speak of '*la trahison de la trahison des clercs*'. For Gellner, a thinker such as Nietzsche had not betrayed intellectual values: rather, his honesty and rigour were almost unbearably painful to observe, and certainly worthy of the highest moral approbation. Gellner instead saw Benda as the traitor, because of his unjustified complacency about the solidity of liberal and rationalist values. The liberal's position is in many ways precarious rather than secure, and to deny this is to falsify modern intellectual history.

Gellner's own strategy was to ground his thought — partially yet powerfully — in a particular outcome of historical development, namely that of the higher standard of living and increased life expectancy brought about by modern science. But that is only one half of his position. Philosophical considerations are equally useful for understanding the nature of modern society. Gellner is thus the philosopher of industrialism and the sociologist of philosophy — a very particular mix of a highly integrated mind. This is reflected in his intellectual toolbox. Key themes, figures and ideas appear in rather different contexts. Thus Weber is seen as the sociologist of the rise of the West, but also as the best guide to modern epistemology. Hume has centre stage when the theory of knowledge is under discussion, but his arguments about enthusiasm and superstition are used as a key to understanding European development and the sociology of Islam, and as a vital clue to the genealogy of civil society. Gellner's mind was equipped with a broad range of intellectual resources, the versatility of which was surprising and elegant. It is crucial to stress as forcefully as possible that he was, to use the well-known opposition made famous by Isaiah Berlin, a hedgehog, even though his contributions in different fields made some think of him as a fox.

What concerned Gellner most was simply the nature of modernity. His son David once suggested that his father wanted to produce a philosophy of modernity. This is helpful, but it misses something. Gellner's brute definition of modernity, industry and nationalism, established an agenda: his concern was not just to explain the emergence of 'soft' and rational society and the contours of feeling that it allows us, but also to ask whether it might spread beyond the particular location in which it originated. He joined normative to social-scientific concerns. He did not merely define modernity, but also sought to defend and even to extend it.

---

8 '*La trahison de la trahison des clercs*', in *Encounters with Nationalism*, Oxford, 1994.

This is the appropriate point at which to explain my own personal connection with Gellner. In the academic year 1972–3, as a young graduate student at the LSE, I attended twenty lectures by him on 'Modern Ideologies', effectively drawn from *Legitimation of Belief* (1974). It was a thrilling experience. For one thing, nothing less than a new model of the world, with its central ideas and institutions specified and analysed, was on offer, challenging the listener to accept or to reject it. Quite simply, this provocation made me think for myself for the first time. Later on, from about 1977, I came to know Gellner personally. I gave classes at the LSE to supplement his lectures in social philosophy during the years when he was a member of its Department of Philosophy, Logic and Scientific Method. Subsequently I taught at the Prague campus of the Central European University in Prague, to which Gellner moved after the collapse of communism – an experience which allowed me to gain some sense of his background and what it meant to him. I found him to be an exceptionally attractive human being: witty, extremely kind, modest, and blessed with a genius for creating something of a tribe around himself, cemented by an endless stream of postcards – sent, one felt, to counteract a sense of loneliness. Despite my warm feelings for the man, this book is not a hagiography, which he certainly would have hated. Due perhaps to his influence I share some of his dislikes, but I do not accept all of his positive arguments or normative stances. Differently put, I am no self-appointed guardian of his life and thought, and so I take care to point out where his theories and arguments are, in my judgement, problematic or wrong. More generally, I seek to explain the pattern of his thought, to place it within the context already noted, rather than simply to list and describe every argument that he made.

Still, this personal link allows me at times to draw on my own memories. Though there may be dangers in this, in the end it is an advantage. For the materials available to a biographer are severely limited. Gellner was able to publish most of his thoughts. The Gellner Archive deposited at the LSE does contain some material, notably: a manuscript on 'Conservatism and Ideology'; a huge mass of detailed fieldwork notes from Morocco; short pieces from the world-transforming year that Gellner spent in Moscow watching *perestroika* and *glasnost* open the doors to the strange and sudden death of the Soviet Union; some important correspondence, notably an exchange of views with Noam Chomsky; and, above all, what will be termed 'The Notes', written from the late 1950s to the early 1960s, in which he worked out his central intellectual positions, often by means of distilling his thoughts into aphorisms. In addition, the LSE kindly allowed me to examine another useful source, Gellner's personnel file. This, in combination with nearly all of his passports, now in the possession of his family, allowed me to reconstruct his movements with a fair degree of accuracy.

It is a great pleasure to be able to acknowledge a great deal of support from very many quarters. The Gellner family has allowed me to quote from his papers, and its members have always been available for discussion and sometimes simply to look after me. Still, this book is not official in any sense and I am responsible for what it says, although I hope that Gellner's relations find its portrait veridical. Scholars of central Europe – Jiří Musil, Peter Bugge, Malachi Hacohen, Anatoly Khazanov and Roman Szporluk – were generous with their advice. I have also learnt a great deal from comments provided by Wolfgang Kraus, Al Stepan, Dominique Colas, Perry Anderson, Aviel Roshwald, Dominique Arel, Tom Nairn, Pierre Birnbaum, Siniša Malešević, Lilli Riga and Bill Kissane. At one time the book was to have been written with Brendan O'Leary. Though his other pressing concerns in Northern Ireland and Iraq prevented joint authorship, there are many traces of our discussions in what follows; his comments on a final draft of this book were invaluable. Another major debt is owed to Ian Jarvie, not least for his marvellous complete bibliography of Gellner's works.[9] I have reminisced about Gellner with many people since he died, and thank them all – especially those who gave the formal interviews noted in the text. I am grateful to Noam Chomsky for letting me cite his letter to Gellner, in chapter eleven, and to Mrs Melitta Mew for permission to cite two letters from Karl Popper, in chapters two and five. Csaba Szilagyi, librarian of the Central European University, helped locate material related to Gellner's years with that institution. Research was vitally supported by a STICERD Fellowship at the LSE, the Swedish Collegium for Advanced Study in Social Science, a Fowler Hamilton Fellowship at Christ Church College, Oxford, a grant from the Social Science and Humanities Research Council, a Fellowship from the National Endowment of the Humanities, and by my own university.

---

9   This is available online at http://www.yorku.ca/jarvie/ErnestGellner.htm. Many of Gellner's essays have been collected, and my citations are to those volumes unless changes to dates or names are significant, in which cases the original version is noted.

I

Malign Fates

History has no single gear, no set speed. Long periods of stability oscillate with moments of trauma, capable of sending societies in new directions. History was certainly on the move, to use Arnold Toynbee's expression, in the Bohemia from which Ernest Gellner came. Once ruled by the Hapsburgs, it saw in his lifetime the interwar Czechoslovak democracy dominated by Tomáš Masaryk; a short period of ethnic tension and political stalemate after Munich; incorporation (without Slovakia) into the Third Reich; and a further short period of putative Czechoslovak independence followed by effective rule by Moscow between 1948 and 1989, leading in turn to renewed independence for Czechoslovakia and ultimately the creation of separate Czech and Slovak Republics. Gellner's childhood was spent in Prague, and he returned to the city in 1945 after, as he put it, a first period of exile.[1] A long second period of exile followed when he left again in 1946, convinced that communist rule would condemn Bohemia to a period of darkness as long as that which had followed the imposition of the Counter-Reformation after the Battle of the White Mountain in 1620.

This chapter describes the formative period of Gellner's life, leaving for later the evolution of his views about Czechoslovakia and the Czechs – in which lack of interest turned to engagement followed by return. The Hapsburg world from which his parents came needs to be evoked here. Memories of that world were part of his childhood, and some of its tensions – above all those to do with nationalism – were also present in the Czechoslovakia of his youth. Gellner's brilliant parable about the character of nationalism, as the conflict between Megalomania and Ruritania, clearly derived from the late Hapsburg empire.[2] Gellner's theory will later be

---

1   J. Davis, 'An Interview with Ernest Gellner', *Current Anthropology*, vol. 32, 1991, p. 65.
2   *Nations and Nationalism*, Oxford, 1983, pp. 58–62.

confronted with evidence drawn from late-nineteenth-century Bohemia, but my initial intention is simpler: to put his theory to one side in order to describe a social world as it appeared to him in his early years.

Family Background

Identities were in flux in late nineteenth-century Bohemia. Two particular social forces need to be mentioned. First, industrialization utterly changed the character of social life. By 1914 Bohemia was producing fully half of the industrial output of the Empire, thereby turning peasants into urban industrial workers. But another force pointed in a different direction. Nationalist leaders sought to cage people vertically within national communities, preventing them from making lateral connections across them. This is a very careful formulation. Nationalist leaders were trying to *create* national identities; they were 'nationalizers' rather than representatives of pre-existing communities. It is important in this regard to stress that the use of a given language did not necessarily determine one's sense of belonging. German in particular was a language of social mobility, given its status in Vienna, for anyone who became fluent. German speakers had initially felt that the language transcended national identity, imagining that there would be some general movement towards the use of German, at once the language of a high culture and that employed at the heart of the imperial state. But this did not happen. Czech nationalist activists sought rather to create an alternative community. They turned Czech from a peasant dialect into a medium of high culture, thereby seeking to transform rather than merely to protect Czech speakers. Once they had achieved some success, a rationale for German nationalism developed in turn, that is, nationalist activists amongst German speakers sought to create a German-identified community capable of making its own demands.[3] The general point can be put in a different way. Feelings of national belonging had been, and often remained, very weak. In areas of mixed language use people's declared national identities switched back and forth in decennial censuses, deeply irritating nationalist militants.[4] The censuses in question did not allow the reporting of multiple identities, nor did they provide the option of claiming an identity based merely on political loyalty to the Hapsburg state. Further, it was not possible to report a Jewish national identity. A word of warning

---

3   P. Judson, *Exclusive Revolutionaries: Liberal Politics, Social Experience and National Identity in the Austrian Empire, 1848–1914*, Ann Arbor, 1996.
4   P. Judson, *Guardians of the Nation: Activists on the Language Frontiers of Imperial Austria*, Cambridge, (MA), 2006.

should be issued at this point: both German and Czech nationalist movements were in fact loyal to the state, seeking to change its character rather
than to destroy it.[5] And by the turn of the century they had at least partial
success, as Vienna partly abandoned its hopes of remaining a supranational
entity by explicitly recognizing national group loyalties.[6] This did not,
however, prevent many Jews and socialists from remaining loyal to the
ideal of a polity that would include or supersede all national affiliations.

The Jews of Bohemia, including Gellner's forebears, faced unique
difficulties. As the struggle between Czech and German nationalizers
intensified, not least because state funds were often allocated based on the
size of purportedly solid national communities, Jews were under pressure
to choose sides. The more educated and urban among them were German
speakers, many of whom were loyal to the empire. Because of the limited
options provided by the census form, the crucial question was whether
Jews would identify themselves with what might be termed the German or
Czech 'communities-in-formation'. If some Czech militants wanted Jews to
assimilate completely, others resisted this – and Masaryk, despite his fundamental liberalism, was sufficiently ill-at-ease with Jews to reject assimilation
in favour of integration, that is, to allow Jews civil rights while preferring
that they remain a distinct cultural group. Many developments followed
from this, including the creation of new Zionist politics, with intellectuals who felt especially 'de-territorialized' often moving between different
positions in short order.[7] Nonetheless, a generalization can be made: Jews
slowly moved, under pressure, towards the Czech side, calculating that
they had little choice given the demographic weight of Czech speakers in
Bohemia.[8] Some indication of the situation can be seen in 1921 figures for

---

5   Judson, in *Exclusive Revolutionaries*, gives details of some of the ambitions of German activists; the
situation of Czech activists is brilliantly analysed by P. Bugge, *Czech Nation-Building, National Self-
Perception and Politics, 1780–1914*, Doctoral Dissertation, Aarhus University, 1994 (revised edition
forthcoming from Harvard University Press). Bugge's book is exemplary in demonstrating that
no Czech nationalist militant sought secession from the Hapsburgs in the late nineteenth century.
6   Analysis of various plans can be found in J. King, *Budweisers into Germans: A Local History
of Bohemian Politics, 1848–1948*, Princeton, 2002.
7   S. Spector, *Prague Territories: National Conflict and Cultural Innovation in Franz Kafka's Fin de
Siècle*, Berkeley, 2000. Spector offers a brilliant account of a de-territorialized group of intellectuals
– whose numbers included Kafka, Egon Erwin Kisch, Max Brod, Franz Werfel, Hans Kohn,
Alfred Fuchs, Pavel Eisner and Hugo Bergmann – moving between Czech identity, populist
Judaism, high German culture, Zionism, and Catholicism. Kohn is one of the most well-known
theorists of nationalism, but most of these thinkers had distinctive ideas about the national question.
8   H. Kieval, *The Making of Czech Jewry: National Conflict and Jewish Society in Bohemia,
1870–1918*, Oxford, 1988; and *Languages of Community: The Jewish Experience in the Czech
Lands*, Berkeley, 2000.

Prague: 94.2 per cent of Prague, as measured by mother tongue, claimed to be Czech, highlighting the absolute end of German-speakers' hegemony in the city.[9] Within the Jewish community 5,900 claimed Jewish national identity (the new census form allowed this religion, but no others, to be selected as a nationality), 7,426 chose German, and fully 16,342 opted for Czech identity. This last figure may well have been exaggerated, as many sought to hide their links to the German community.[10] While Jews agreed to schooling in Czech, many took care to ensure that their children also gained German cultural capital. Gellner's parents exemplify this situation.

Gellner's father, Rudolf, came from the northern part of Bohemia, the area that became known as the Sudetenland. Rudolf's maternal grandmother was born Friederike Meltzer and later married William Lobl. A family memoir by Julius Gellner, the younger brother of Rudolf, describes their marriage in these terms:

> Mr Lobl was happy in his life in a small village: he got on well with all the peasants, though being a Jew and a very true believer – he ran the village shop, had a cow, a field and a little schnapps distillery, he was happy in his unlimited and unconditional belief in the goodness of God. Not so Friederike his wife: the strongest person I ever experienced (in direct contact) in my life, most powerful and dictatorial. She said one day, after having given birth to three children: 'enough is enough – I want to go to the big town of Saaz' . . . she wanted to live an intellectual life; indeed she did; she was not only a free thinker and an atheist, she believed in the rights of women . . . [11]

Their daughter, Anna Lobl, married Max Gellner, and the family initially lived in Kadan before moving, as the result of anti-Semitic riots, to Saaz in 1897 and to Prague in 1910. There were nine children; Rudolf was the eighth, born on 13 August 1897, and the fourth of five sons. The family was German speaking, and the names of the children – Hedwig, Toni, Otto, Elsa, Rosa, Fritz, Wilhelm, Rudolf and Julius – demonstrated, not

---

9   The classic analysis of this process remains G. Cohen, *The Politics of Ethnic Survival: Germans in Prague, 1861–1914*, Second Edition, West Lafayette, 2006.

10   Kieval, *The Making of Czech Jewry*, chapter 7.

11   J. Gellner, 'England Receives Me as a Human Being', unpublished memoir written in the 1970s. Julius Gellner appears in T. Ambrose, *Hitler's Loss: What Britain and America Gained from Europe's Cultural Exiles*, London, 2001, pp. 99–100. This memoir is the main source for the information in this paragraph. Ernest Gellner's son David possesses two family trees, one drawn up with his father in 1984, the other with his grandfather a year later, which contain a good deal of further detailed information.

least to Gellner at a later date, that the family's fundamental loyalty was to Vienna.[12] The dominant influence upon the children was that of the grandmother and mother; the latter came from a well-educated and affluent family, and surely gained centrality when Max's two business ventures failed. The two parents and nine children initially lived in two rooms, and slept on mattresses held up by chairs. Poverty was counteracted by cultural capital for 'literature was the substitute for luxury'. The eldest sister Hedwig would soothe the younger children to sleep by reciting the great monologues of Schiller's *Maria Stuart* and *Don Carlos*, and especially Goethe's *Faust*. The two eldest brothers later lived with rich local families, offering tuition for their children in exchange for room and board. If this helped the family to move to a slightly larger apartment, the character of family life did not much change: both Rudolf and Julius learnt great set pieces from *Faust* which they had to declaim to neighbours and visitors. The family made up for its lack of affluence by means of this emphasis on intellectual achievement, and through dramatic social mobility. Most of the brothers and at least one of the sisters gained doctorates in the professions. Hedwig ran the Zionist offices in Prague for many years, and then became a civil servant in Israel of sufficient seniority to embarrass her nephew by arranging for his transport by tank for a visit to the desert on what was probably his first journey to Israel in 1951. The two oldest brothers were lawyers; they started a law journal specializing in translation. Wilhelm became a medical doctor, eventually settling in Paris to work for agencies linked to the United Nations. Julius became a producer for the German Theatre in Prague before achieving fame as a theatrical producer in London. All Rudolf's siblings were to escape the Holocaust by moving to Palestine or to England, with the exception of Otto who refused to leave the successful international law firm he had established, a decision that led to his family's deaths, including his own, at the hands of the Nazis.

Rudolf ran away from home to fight as a volunteer in the First World War. 'The state of mind in which he did it must have been strange and contradictory', in the later judgement of his son, 'because he was at the same time some kind of pacifist'.[13] He was wounded, saved by Russian soldiers after lying in the snow for two days, and imprisoned near Lake Baikal – where, with prisoners giving lectures to each other, he received, in

12 Jiří Musil, 'The Prague Roots of Ernest Gellner's Thinking', in J. A. Hall and I. C. Jarvie (eds), *The Social Philosophy of Ernest Gellner*, Amsterdam, 1995, p. 31.
13 Asked by his son whether he had killed anyone in the war, Rudi replied that he had always taken care to shoot into thin air, not wishing to be responsible for the death of another human being. These details come from Gellner's address at the funeral of his father in December 1987, in the possession of David Gellner.

his son's estimation, an education in what must then have been one of the greatest universities in the world.[14] The young Rudolf developed a fascination with Russian culture and language; it seems that he visited Russia two or three times in the interwar period.[15] These sentiments were passed on to his son, who in his own turn loved to speak Russian and spent a sabbatical year in Moscow in 1988–89.[16] Rudolf was sympathetic to the Bolshevik revolution. Amongst his fellow prisoners was Arnošt Kolman (1892–1979), a cultural Zionist who became a communist in Russia during the war, and who was later something of an official mouthpiece of the regime in Prague.[17] Rudolf eventually left aboard a ship from Vladivostock and passed through Yokohama, perhaps receiving help from the Jewish community in the latter city. His intellectual interests then led him to Berlin to find out more about Max Weber, who had recently died and whom he came to admire greatly.[18] He then returned to Prague to gain further qualification in law at the German university.[19] He married on 30 January 1923. The marriage took place against the wishes of his eldest sister, who had extremely high expectations of her siblings. There is a sense in which she was right. Ernest André Gellner was born in Paris, on 9 December 1925,

---

14   Ibid.

15   Musil, 'The Prague Roots', pp. 31–2.

16   He started to learn the language, without much respect for grammatical rules, from the late 1960s, working at it first by listening to records, and later by going to Russian films. In the last decade of his life he liked to listen to Chekhov on records that he had brought back from one of his visits there.

17   Kolman was imprisoned in Germany for six months in 1922 before living in the Soviet Union until 1945. His return to Prague lasted only until 1948 when he was arrested and taken to the Soviet Union, where he spent three and a half years in prison. He returned to Prague in 1959. Ernest Gellner went out of his way to meet him, and wrote an essay about him in 1958 which showed how Kolman was testing the waters after de-Stalinization, and trying to reconcile contemporary physics with an improved version of dialectical materialism ('Ernst Kolman: or, knowledge and communism', Social Survey, vol. 23, 1958). Musil observes that 'Kolman was very proud of the amount of time that he spent in prison' under diverse regimes ('The Prague Roots', p. 31). Apparently Rudolf also knew Rudolf Slánský, executed in 1948 after a Stalinist show trial made particularly infamous on account of its open anti-Semitism. Kolman eventually protested against the invasion of Czechoslovakia in 1968, but he was not arrested, and left for Sweden in 1976 never to return. It is worth noting here in passing Gellner's considerable linguistic abilities, including the ability to read Russian at this time, though his oral skills were learned much later.

18   Weber was not well known in Czechoslovakia at the time, so this interest probably reflects the influence of his time in prison.

19   It is not clear whether this was a diploma or a doctorate. Rudolf was always known as Dr Gellner, and the first doctorate seems to have been earned either in Prague or Berlin before his son was born.

because Rudolf was undertaking research for a second doctorate on the works of the anti-revolutionary thinkers De Maistre and Lamennais. This project had to be abandoned, and Rudolf became a frustrated intellectual.[20] The birth of a second child in 1929, Marianne Rita, doubtless made an academic career still less likely. There was genuine poverty in the early years of the marriage, survival on one occasion dependent on the selling of books. Thereafter Rudolf gained employment in a chemical firm, and eventually established one of his own with a partner, Arnošt Taussig. Rudolf was the brains behind the business while his partner excelled at 'salesmanship', a formula they would reproduce successfully in England.[21] Rudolf's continuing intellectual interests found an outlet when he became the publisher of *Právo Československé* (which means both 'Czechoslovak Law' and 'Czechoslovak Right'), a legal journal that was close to the official ideology of the republic and which offered commentaries on new legislation. The young Ernest would see the proofs in the apartment, often with the title page badly printed. He would joke that the journal should have been called 'Czechoslovak Right with Crooked Letters'. 'The symbolism of Czechoslovak Right having wobbly letters was not lost on me, even at the time'.[22]

Ernest's mother, Anna Fantl, came from Krumlov, a beautiful medieval town in the south of Bohemia, much patronized by Viennese artists in the years before the First World War. Her family, comprised of the parents and three daughters, was predominantly German speaking. Anna was born on 13 November 1894, and so was slightly older than her husband. Her family had been more economically secure than Rudolf's, although it suffered badly due to the decision to invest in Imperial War Bonds in 1914 – on the mistaken grounds that these would be secure. But the family was never much more than lower middle class. It seems likely that the family had liberal leanings. The young Ernest was upset by a copy of a locally famous painting showing the arrest by Austrian police of Karel Havlíček, the outspoken Czech nationalist militant and journalist, that hung in the family house, and asked about its meaning.[23] Secularization had taken place

---

20 Ernest later said in private conversation that he felt blamed for the end of his father's intellectual career. This may have been so, but it seems to have been exacerbated by Rudolf witnessing the son having the career that he had himself wanted – something which made Rudolf at once proud and envious. (Information on this point comes from several sources, notably Michael McMullen, interviewed in February 2003).

21 J. Gellner, 'England Receives Me as a Human Being', p. 44.

22 'Funeral Address'.

23 Musil, 'The Prague Roots', p. 32. Gellner did not specify exactly why he found the picture disturbing.

in Anna's family a generation before it had in Rudolf's. Anna herself had Zionist leanings. In 1921 she worked for the twelfth Zionist Congress in Karlovy Vary.[24] She too moved to Prague, and worked as a secretary in the Zionist offices together with Hedwig. There she met Rudolf. Her Zionism, her considerable gift for languages (amplified sometime before the marriage by a year spent in England), and the fact that she married into an exceptionally intellectual family might indicate some concern with ideas. But Anna was not an intellectual; indeed, by common assent she was not very well educated. She was extremely warm and was remembered with great affection by Eric Hošek, whose mother was a friend of Anna's. The boys, too, became friends, and their mothers decided to send them to the same primary school.[25]

Gellner was much impressed with Perry Anderson's powerful argument that the exiles and émigrés who came to Britain from Central and Eastern Europe tended to adopt conservative views, while those with more radical opinions moved to the United States.[26] But Gellner was not always careful with the details of particular texts, and attributed an interpretation to Anderson − that the difference can be explained by the fact that the former but not the latter had lost their estates − that the essay does not in fact contain. This reading lies behind Gellner's insistence, at the end of his life, that his family had never enjoyed privilege:

> Both families I spring from were unambiguously petty bourgeois, and provincial to boot. The family only became very precariously middle class in culture (but not yet economically) during my father's generation and in the course of my youth. My father had a degree and so even did some of his sisters, but my mother had only pretty elementary education.[27]

This somewhat downplays the cultural development and educational achievements of Rudolf's family: it was unusual, for example, for women to obtain degrees. Further, Rudolf and Anna were able to establish a niche in the intellectual life of the city. The family lived in the Dejvice district and their longest residency was in an apartment on Veverková, the street on which Prague's modern art gallery was then found. This location is revealing. It was a new middle-class area, far removed from more

24   A copy of a letter furnished by the bureau in Karlovy Vary, asking the central organization to enter her name into their books as a member of Congress staff, attests to this.
25   A great deal of information about Gellner's Prague years was given by Hošek in an interview in January 1999.
26   P. Anderson, 'Components of the National Culture', New Left Review, no. 50, 1968.
27   'Reply to Critics', in Hall and Jarvie, The Social Philosophy of Ernest Gellner, p. 624.

recognizably Jewish areas of the city. Gellner remembered the meetings of many Czech intellectuals in the apartment. Amongst them were the sociologists Josef Navrátil, the last pre-war director of the Masaryk Institute; Karel Kupka, who worked in the Institut d'Études Slaves in Paris and wrote several articles on Max Weber; the architect and painter Arne Hošek; and Moritz Winternitz, an Indologist at the German university in Prague. An interview with Gellner late in his life led his friend, the sociologist Jiří Musil, to portray the parents as patriots of the first Czechoslovakia, deeply supportive of Masaryk's ideals, and integrated into the new local high culture.[28]

This was a deeply prosaic culture: social democratic and liberal, anti-fascist and opposed to irrational tendencies of all kinds.[29] The most general characterization of the family must be that it was 'Czechoslovakifying', but with knowledge of a Jewish cultural background and of Zionism. They were happy to take the holidays allowed to Jewish students – although these were used for picnics and other family outings. Jewish cultural identity emphatically did not translate into any Jewish religious observances, not even the minimal ones of circumcision or bar mitzvahs. Gellner was profoundly ignorant of the details of Jewish religious observances to the end of his days.

The census return of 1930 supports this view, but adds a little complexity. The law required people to identify their birthplace, their date of arrival in Prague, the district in which their legal records were kept, their nationality by mother tongue, their religion, and their profession. One element of the Gellner census return perhaps gives evidence of loyalty to Masaryk's world, and certainly to parental desire for their children to function successfully within it. A Roman Catholic Czech maid, Božena Krudičkova, lived with the family so as to ensure that the children would be fluent in Czech, which was indeed used between them, while the parents spoke together in German despite the fact that they had also learned Czech. Beyond that there are interesting complexities. A German-speaking governess of Jewish religion, Paula Gutmann, lived with the family, to ensure familiarity with German language and culture.[30] Then the father claimed German as nationality by mother tongue for himself and for the two children. In contrast, Anna's nationality was

---

28   Musil, 'The Prague Roots', passim. The relations between Gellner and Musil are described below, principally in chapter 6.

29   Musil, 'The Prague Roots', p. 36.

30   Paula Gutmann left at some point, but she was replaced by another German-speaking governess (interview with Marianne Sigmon, February 2003).

declared to be Jewish. Both the parents and children were accorded a
Jewish background in the religion column. This census return suggests
that there may have been some difference of opinion within the family,
given that Anna's nationality is reported as Jewish. This view may also
be supported by her earlier work for the Zionist bureau, as well as by a
passport application of 1938 in which her religion is given as 'Israel' – a
term somewhat stronger than 'Jewish'.[31] One reason for this change was
the clear understanding on the part of the Jewish community of Masaryk's
desire to diminish the size of the German population. Nonetheless
Rudolf identified himself as German, despite the family's admiration for
Masaryk.[32]

There were obvious reasons for the admiration of Masaryk. Czechoslovakia
was the only new democracy east of the Rhine to endure after the Great War.
It proved to be an exceptionally vibrant society. The republic was radically
democratic, instituting a mass of social reform programmes – from the right of
women to vote to tenant protection, from the removal of all aristocratic privilege to varied acts ensuring the protection of labour rights. Czechoslovakia
attracted thousands of students from Yugoslavia and Bulgaria, while many
Jewish students from Hungary and Poland came either for university or for
technical training. Prague boasted not just German and Czech universities, but
also a Ukrainian one. The German university was particularly distinguished,
numbering amongst its staff Rudolf Carnap.[33] Ukrainian and Russian émigrés
and exiles flocked there, including Roman Jakobson who did a great deal to
create the celebrated Czech school of linguistics, noting when he left for the
United States in 1939 that he felt more Czech than anything else. French and
Russian gymnasia and an English grammar school were opened, adding to
the four German gymnasia already in existence. If intellectuals of the right
moved to Belgrade and many of the left to Berlin, Prague tended to attract
social democrats. The culture of the city at that time looked resolutely to the
West, and particularly to the United States, whose powerful avant-garde art
was much admired.

One should not idealize this world. The weakness of the Second Republic
established after Munich showed that liberal democracy had not taken very

---

31   The 'may' in this sentence is deliberate. Ernest's sister has no memory of Anna's
support for Zionist causes being stronger than Rudolf's, noting that the father considered
giving money to Israel (interview with Marianne Sigmon, February 2003).

32   Jiří Musil worked hard to obtain the census return; help in interpreting it was given by
Roman Szporluk and Hillel Kieval.

33   The young Willard van Orman Quine, later Harvard's most distinguished twentieth-
century philosopher of logic, was tutored by Carnap in Prague in the years just before the
war, and spoke to Gellner of their meetings during a visit to Prague in the early 1990s.

deep root. Crucially, national groupings failed to reach any final form of political accommodation. Czech nationalists occupied the German theatre in the early 1920s, and they protested vehemently against the showing of German films in Prague cinemas in the 1930s. This is one element that lies behind the Republic's notable democratic deficit. A form of power-sharing between the major political interests, the *petka*, prevented full popular participation, not least because the Sudeten Germans were excluded for a long period. Perhaps this was inevitable; it seemed to allow the country to function. There was also a second element to consider. Masaryk and Edvard Beneš tended to see politics as a science rather than as an arena for competing interests, thereby creating what was very much a 'guided' democracy, in which the ruling forces never lost an election.[34] Still, one should not judge a democracy by timeless, Platonic standards. Prague in those years was a vibrant success, especially when seen in comparative terms.

Childhood and Youth

Gellner was a particularly handsome and mischievous child, often getting into scrapes as the result of 'dares'. The family was apparently a peaceful one, however, and there was little outward sign of differences between the parents.[35] At the weekends the family would visit Rudolf's father Max, who lived in the old town, and close relations were maintained with Anna's sisters.[36] Winter holidays were taken in the Reichenberg mountains in northern Bohemia. Some part of summer holidays were spent in Příbram, a small town to the south of Prague, where Anna's sister Ida helped her husband, Bergmann, run an ironmonger's shop.[37] The importance of the periods spent in Příbram needs to be underlined: Gellner was as aware of rural life as he was of the extreme poverty in Prague, whose population and industrial power both grew rapidly in the interwar period. Further, the young boy attended summer camps, then highly popular in Central Europe: he learnt Czech songs, became a fine skater, and gained a proficiency in canoeing that he retained thereafter.[38] Beneath this pleasant upbringing, however, there were tensions within the family, which sometimes strained relations. Gellner himself apparently felt that the father was closer to the

---

34 P. Bugge, 'Czech Democracy 1918–39 – Paragon or Parody?', *Bohemia*, vol. 47, 2006–7.
35 This point was stressed by Hošek in an interview in January 1999.
36 Interview with Marianne Sigmon, February 2003.
37 Gellner made a point of taking a long detour to Příbram, probably in 1992, when returning from a Central European University student outing to Krumlov.
38 Miroslav Hroch once claimed that at least some of the songs Gellner still knew late in life were in fact Slovak.

daughter, and later claimed, as previously noted, that he was blamed for curtailing his father's intellectual career. Equally, he felt suffocated by the mother, who habitually opened his mail even when he was an adult. Her desire to 'feed him up' apparently explained his near-vegetarian diet.[39] He certainly felt that his childhood had been unhappy and made this clear to his own children, who were well aware of his desire to give them the sort of upbringing of which he felt deprived. It is hard to weigh these psychological dynamics against the disorientation and sense of loss resulting from exile. Both elements contributed to his sentiments and character.

Gellner went to two schools in Prague. His primary school, which he entered in 1931, was 'amiably named "By the Little Fountain", which suggests an inn rather than a school . . . [It was on] the edge of the park where one might meet the President on his rides if one was lucky'.[40] It was within walking distance from his home, and he attended lessons with Eric Hošek who remained a friend thereafter. The school was Czech, and this led to a particular scene that Gellner would recount in later life. After the singing of a popular song, he put his hand up in class and said that he knew a different set of words, and then sang a German version. This was received with sufficient coldness that he never made the same mistake again. One detail of the school reports – repeated in his next school – is worth noting. Despite a lack of religious upbringing he was classified as Jewish or Hebrew, and thereby exempted from religious instruction.

In 1935 Ernest transferred to the Prague English Grammar School. One of his classmates was Otto Pick, who later also escaped to England, before pursuing an academic career, first in the United States and then in England.[41] Pick's parents had sent him to the school because they could see the writing on the wall. They had relatives in England, and felt that an English education might help emigration. Perhaps a similar calculation motivated Ernest's parents. Rudolf's sister Elsa had married an Englishman who worked in a shipping firm, and with whom she had three daughters; this happy fact

39   These last sentences draw upon Gellner's own account as given to many people, notably to members of his own family. Some of his friends – notably Hošek and McMullen – were mystified by Gellner's tense relationship with his mother, not least because she was particularly warm toward them.

40   'Foreword' to E. Schmidt-Hartmann's *Thomas G. Masaryk's Realism: Origins of a Czech Political Concept*, Munich, 1984, p. 7.

41   Interview with Otto Pick, January 1999. Gellner maintained contact with Pick – as he did with other exiles from Czechoslovakia – in England, inviting him on at least one occasion to a dinner at the LSE. Pick had a distinguished career at the University of Surrey before returning to Prague in 1993 to become Director of the Institute of International Relations. He was later Deputy Foreign Minister.

made the acquisition of a visa much more likely.[42] The school was also attractive, however, solely for the quality of the education it provided, and Gellner was sufficiently fond of it that he later went to some trouble to track down former pupils of whom he was aware, from before and after his time there.[43] In later life he described being taught by figures resembling Auden and Isherwood, that is, by casually dressed and relaxed young men who had attended public schools and Oxbridge. This was a happy contrast to the strict formalism of both Czech and German education. Indeed, one of his first assignments was to learn how to tell a joke in English. His school reports show that his progress was superior, with 'very good' marks sustained for more than half the subjects studied.

This did not mean that his intellectual formation was English in character. Very much to the contrary, his sentimental education at this time was overwhelmingly Czech. Several indications of the depth of this early identity can be seen from Gellner's later behaviour. He was in the habit of singing Czech songs with Peter Stern (who had married the sister of Michael McMullen, a close friend Gellner made at Oxford).[44] Then there is his declaration late in life about his fondness for Czech folk songs, responding to the charge made by critics of his theory of nationalism that he was insensible to nationalism's emotional appeal:

> . . . I *am* deeply sensitive to the spell of nationalism. I can play about thirty Bohemian folk songs (or songs presented as such in my youth) on my mouth organ. My oldest friend, whom I have known since the age of three or four and who is Czech and a patriot, cannot bear to hear me play them because he says I do it in such a schmaltzy way, 'crying into the mouth organ'. I do not think I could have written the book on nationalism which I did write, were I not capable of crying, with the help of a little alcohol, over folk songs, which happen to be my favourite form of music.[45]

---

42   There was another English connection. One of Rudolf's great-uncles settled in England, and one of this relative's daughters married into the Du Vergier family. This name was later given by Rudolf and Taussig to the firm they established in England. .

43   For instance, in a letter to Gellner dated 22 December 1976, Dr. Jan Tumlir, an economist several years his junior, responded, 'Yes, our paths must have crossed in the Prague English Grammar School'. Gellner also attended a ceremony to mark the reopening of the school after the collapse of communism.

44   Stern had a similar background to Gellner's, although he served in the air force during the war. He became a successful academic, writing powerfully on Kafka, Junger and on Hitler's relationship with German culture.

45   'Reply to Critics', pp. 624–5. The friend in question is Eric Hošek. I can attest to the fact that Gellner did sometimes take out a mouth organ and play these songs.

This is the appropriate moment to reiterate that, while he knew the tricultural world of Kafka, he was part of a different generation which was able to envision belonging – 're-territorialization' – within a world which was, especially in comparative perspective, manifestly attractive. It was precisely the abandonment of a potential site of belonging that was so painful for Gellner, and which led him to classify his periods away as those of exile. Two elements of identification are relevant here.

The most obvious element was simply that the presence of Masaryk symbolized the possibility of entrance into mainstream society. The presence of the Founder-President of Czechoslovakia was absolutely pervasive in the new state's public life, not least in schoolrooms where his picture was displayed. He had been a professional philosopher and sociologist before becoming the 'President-Liberator'. He maintained that the Czechs were returning to the path upon which they had set out before the Battle of the White Mountain in 1620. Czech democracy and Czech liberalism had been foreshadowed by the Hussite proto-Reformation of the fifteenth century, the socially radical practice of the Taborites, and the elective monarchy of George of Poděbrady with its plans for a novel and peaceful international order. Their incipient progress was brutally halted by the triumph of the Hapsburg Counter-Reformation.[46] Further, Masaryk was internationalist in his intellectual sources, and provided a philosophical justification for Czech state formation. In his *World Revolution*, published in 1925, the year of Gellner's birth, he argued that the Czech national revolution was vindicated as part of a wider global triumph of democracy and liberal national self-determination that was displacing theocratic and absolutist modes of governance, which were locally represented by the decaying Hapsburg Empire.[47] Gellner late in life described the impact of Masaryk's general credo on his fellow citizens in these terms:

> The West is democratic, the West is strong, it is democratic because
> it is strong and strong because democratic, and because this is the way
> world history is going. We had been in on this splendid movement
> sooner than most, as early as the fifteenth century, we had been
> unjustly deprived of our birthright, but now we are safely back where

---

46   Gellner enjoyed pointing out with Masaryk's critics that it was a 'good job we did indeed lose on the White Mountain, for otherwise the Prussians would have Germanized us in the course of using us as their Protestant allies' ('The Price of Velvet: Tomáš Masaryk and Václav Havel', in *Encounters with Nationalism*, Oxford, 1994, p. 119).

47   It was translated into English as *The Making of a State*, a more accurate reflection of the bulk of its contents than the original Czech title, but an appalling mistranslation of its central message which was, in Gellner's view, that the Czech democratic and national revolution was an inevitable part of the wider triumph of the West ('The Price of Velvet', p. 117).

we belong, and so we are indeed safe . . . I have had my primary education, and two and a half years of secondary education, in Prague schools, and I can only say that this message emanated, unambiguously and confidently, from the portraits of the President-Liberator which adorned every classroom. Major premise: world history is our guide and guarantor. Minor premise: world history has chosen democracy and the West as its agents, and therefore they are irresistible, and their allies (notably ourselves) are safe.[48]

There was much to admire in the life of this philosopher-president, including his debunking of fraudulent manuscripts intended to demonstrate Czech medieval glories and his brave public stance in defence of Rudolf Hilsner, a Jew falsely accused of ritual murder. Masaryk was a nationalist for whom Gellner had a lifelong appreciation, a man who did not knowingly embrace ethnic fictions and who resisted the anti-Semitism of many of his co-nationals. When Masaryk died in 1937, the young Gellner was one of those who walked past his coffin at the great national ceremony.[49]

Quite as important were the books that influenced the young schoolboy. He particularly enjoyed the works of Karel Čapek, Egon Erwin Kisch, Jaroslav Žak, Jaroslav Hašek, František Kopta and Vitezslav Nezval.[50] Čapek was probably the most important humanist Czech writer in the 1920s and 1930s, and a close friend of Masaryk. He warned against the dangers of modern civilization, and in his work, mainly his plays, he was anti-fascist – dying after Munich, popular myth had it, of a broken heart. Kisch was a committed journalist who wrote in German about his travels and about the lives of Prague people on the margin of society. Žak was a teacher writing witty stories from the grammar school milieu. Hašek was perhaps the best-known Czech writer internationally, thanks to his hero *The Good Soldier Švejk*. An indication of the distance of Gellner's generation from that of Kafka's is contained in a 1975 review of a new edition of the novel – in which Gellner claimed that the low humour and cunning compromises of *Švejk* were quite as much part of the Czech character as were the metaphysical mysteries of Kafka. Gellner further claimed that one of the characters in *Švejk* was based on a distant relation, the superb but drunken

---

48   Ibid., p. 122. There are curious echoes of Masaryk in Francis Fukuyama's thesis in *The End of History and the Last Man*, London, 1992. Fukuyama argues that we are at the end of history with the triumph of the West, liberalism, and democracy. Gellner had a good deal of sympathy for this book.

49   'Foreword', p. 7.

50   These were the names given by Gellner himself. See Musil, 'The Prague Roots', p. 32 and passim, on which the rest of this paragraph draws.

poet František Gellner, drawings of whose public readings hung in his house in Hampshire in later years.[51] Kopta was the author of novels about the Czech legions in Siberia – that is, the legions which fought briefly against the Bolsheviks in 1919. Gellner particularly remembered being impressed by Nezval's *Fifty-Two Bitter Ballads*: these Villon-like poems were for a time his favourite reading.[52] To this portrait of long-run background intellectual influences can be added the political satires of Jiří Voskovec and Jan Werich, which came to the fore in the 1930s. Gellner apparently particularly liked their 'Heavy Barbara' sketch, which involved a struggle between two mythical countries, Eidam and Yberland, the latter of which resembled Nazi Germany.

If there was a prospect of genuine belonging, it was not automatic or unconscious. At the age of eleven he would, he later remembered, systematically miss out one word at random from the national oath taken as the Czechoslovak flag was raised at his summer camp, not out of disloyalty, but because he felt it too early to commit himself until he had 'figured it all out'.[53] This element of contingency in his identity was surely exacerbated by storm clouds in the political sky.[54] The happy decade of the 1920s for the multinational Czechoslovakian state came into question in the 1930s. Deep tensions came to characterize Prague life. With unemployment came an exacerbation of poverty, and there were a few pro-fascist demonstrations and many anti-fascist ones – unsurprisingly, given that Prague had become the home of the exiled organizations of both Austrian and German social democracy. Edvard Beneš, another professorial president, uncritically absorbed from Masaryk a facile liberal historicism – the belief that history was patterned, and that democracy was its *telos*. This led Beneš to believe at the time of the *Anschluss* in 1938 that the Nazis were doomed, and left the new Republic's leaders insufficiently

---

51   'Review of Jaroslav Hašek, *The Good Soldier Švejk*', *The Political Quarterly*, 1975, pp. 358–9. Interestingly, Gellner's private papers contain the poet's family tree – although there is no indication as to the nature of the exact relation to Gellner himself.

52   Musil, 'The Prague Roots', p. 32.

53   Davis, 'An Interview with Ernest Gellner', p. 63.

54   When living in Hampshire, Gellner used to play 'Categories' with local friends. A list of categories, perhaps 'painters' or 'countries' or 'philosophers' was chosen (one by each contestant). Then a letter of the alphabet was selected at random. Contestants gained points when they gave examples, starting with the given letter. One is more likely to win if one can guess the obvious examples and avoid them. Not content with this, Gellner was famous for the obscurity of the categories which he chose. One of them was 'political assassinations of the 1930s'. There were many such, and they comprised his earliest political memories – as he made clear at LSE in the 1980s when casual conversation turned to this topic.

alarmed by the rise of Hitler.[55] Many Sudeten German speakers turned to
the Third Reich. Konrad Heinlein, their leader, increasingly took instruc-
tions directly from the Nazis, and sought to make it impossible for Prague
to govern the Sudetenland.[56] Appallingly ignorant British intervention, first
by Lord Runciman and then by Neville Chamberlain, encouraged France
to abandon its defence treaty obligations to Czechoslovakia. This led to
the handing over on a plate of the Sudetenland to Hitler in the Munich
agreement signed on 29 September 1938. Czechoslovakia lost 86 per cent
of its glass production, 80 per cent of its textiles, and 70 per cent of its iron
and steel industries. Still more important, it lost its defensive lines, allowing
Hitler easy entry six months later.

Throughout the late 1930s the adults in Ernest's family could not
have been unaware of increased danger to themselves and to the state.
'As Munich time approached, the anticipation of war and of the bombing
of Prague which, it was thought, would certainly accompany it, caused
my mother to take me and my sister to a small town in central Bohemia
where her kin (one of only two Jewish families in the community) ran
an ironmonger shop'.[57] He recalled President Beneš announcing that he
had a plan to cope with the crisis, but subsequently resigning and flying
off to Switzerland: 'In Czech, the word plan is the same as the final part
of the word aeroplane, and the joke went around – yes, he had a plan,
an aeroplane.'[58] After Munich, the returning Gellners had to prove they

---

55   I. Lukes, *Czechoslovakia between Stalin and Hitler: The Diplomacy of Edvard Beneš in
the 1930s*, New York, 1996, p. 200. This remarkable piece of revisionism makes readers
appreciate the pressures under which Beneš laboured, even if it does not exonerate him.
Gellner himself always considered Beneš a disastrous figure, not least in a late discussion
with Popper in which both stated firmly that they believed that Masaryk would have fought
rather than capitulated. The conversation is recorded in *In Memoriam: Karl Popper in Prague*,
a booklet prepared and printed by the Central European University in 1994, when Popper
received an honorary doctorate at Charles University.

56   R. M. Smelser, *The Sudeten Problem, 1933–38: Volkstumpolitik and the Formation of Nazi
Foreign Policy*, Middletown, 1975.

57   'Munich in Prague', *The National Interest*, vol. 13, 1988, p. 117. The town in question
is Příbram, as mentioned above.

58   Ibid., p. 118. A second short piece remembering Munich – 'Contribution' to '*Worin
sehen sie den sinn des Gedenkens an die Ereignisse vom September 1938*', *Bohemia*, vol. 29,
1988 – records both change and constancy in Gellner's views. He came to feel that British
behaviour, given the horrors of the First World War and honourable conduct in the Second
World War, was excusable:

My gut reaction to Beneš's surrender has remained the same over the years. Had Beneš
refused to surrender, no doubt that would have been the end of me and my family . . . All
the same I regret that surrender. No doubt it is very easy to make brave recommendations

were residents of Prague when the authorities tried to stop an influx of refugees from the Sudetenland, fearing that if too many German speakers came into the diminished Czechoslovakia they might endanger the new state by giving Hitler a new irredentist argument.[59] Any lingering optimism the Gellners may have had would have received a salutary blow from the speed with which the Nazis rounded up political opponents and Jews as soon as they entered the Sudetenland. Catholic anti-Semitism also became a much more palpable force in Czechoslovakia. It had always been vigorous in neighbouring Austria, and was legitimated there as government policy after the *Anschluss* with the German Reich. Gellner recalled that his teacher of Czech literature, who would abandon membership in the League Against Bolshevism to become a member of the Communist Party after the war, 'just happened to select, for reading aloud, a passage from a novel about peasant life in which the main character indulged in an anti-Semitic expletive'.[60] The Second Republic itself was witness to intensifying conflict between Slovaks and Czechs. 'Masaryk had hoped that the Czechs and Slovaks would come together as the English and Scotch had done; the Slovaks turned out to be the Irish'.[61] The Slovaks found Czech talk of their 'little brother' patronizing, and their growing self-assertion prefigured future crises.[62] In these circumstances it was not surprising that the dictum often repeated in the last years of the republic was that there were Czechs and Slovaks, but the only real Czechoslovaks were the Jews.[63]

Rudolf traveled to England twice in 1938 to make arrangements for a life abroad. But the family was still living in Prague on 15 March 1939 when the Nazis marched in, perhaps because Rudolf and Taussig had had

---

for hypothetical situations . . . I plead guilty to the charge of such facility, such cheap pseudo-fortitude.

We will see that Gellner felt that Beneš's surrender established a pattern whereby Czechs would continue to give in, time and again.

59   'Munich in Prague', p. 118.
60   Ibid., p. 119. The same teacher once asked the class to remember important sayings of Masaryk. Gellner suggested to his neighbour 'a state which betrays the ideas on which it is founded will perish'. The neighbour understood his meaning, but the teacher found the saying – in fact Roman, although attributed to Masaryk – to be of little interest ('Contribution').
61   A. J. P. Taylor, *The Habsburg Monarchy, 1809–1918: A History of the Austrian Empire and Austro-Hungary*, Chicago, 1976, p. 255.
62   See L. C. Skalnik, *National Conflict in Czechoslovakia*, Princeton, 1968; and A. Innes, *Czechoslovakia: The Short Good-Bye*, New Haven, 2001.
63   E. Mendelsohn, *The Jews of East Central Europe Between the World Wars*, Bloomington, 1983, p. 149.

difficulty in selling their small chemical firm. The family was in a perilous situation. It was, however, possible for Anna and her two children to leave by train, though this required Rudolf overruling Anna's sisters, who felt it irresponsible to leave given that Ernest's sister Marianne had a severe cold.[64] They eventually reached England on 9 April 1939, after a difficult journey through Belgium, apparently escaping inspection on one occasion because someone had written on the door of their carriage that the inmates had diphtheria. But Rudolf and Taussig were twice turned back at the Polish border. Otto Pick's father was shot dead while trying to cross the border illegally, but Rudolf and Taussig were luckier, and entered Poland illegally and clandestinely on their third attempt.[65] There they made contact with some old friends of Rudolf's from his period of imprisonment near Lake Baikal. They were well-placed inside the Communist Party, and this somehow enabled them to provide documents allowing the two Czechs to reach England through Sweden. Rudolf arrived in England on 23 May 1939.

London, Oxford and Prague

The family was reunited in London. Initially they joined Rudolf's brother Wilhelm on Parliament Hill in North London, but in short order were able to find their own place in nearby Highgate at 11 Makepeace Avenue, London N6. This remained Ernest's home until he married, except for two years spent evacuated at St Albans and time spent on active service and at Edinburgh University. Rudolf and Taussig went into business again, and began to make money immediately through a process that turned waste plastic chips and cuttings into plastic sheets.[66] The family was financially secure, and Ernest was even somewhat spoiled by his parents according to one of his university friends.[67] At a later date, Rudolf was able to support

---

64 The mistake was theirs, for they died in the Holocaust. However, Ida's son Karel survived the camps, and Gellner would later visit Karel's son Pavel who became a surgeon, and had two children of his own. These were Gellner's only relations remaining in Czechoslovakia.

65 Julius's ordeals and escape were as dramatic as Rudolf's. He was robbed three times, duped by a young innocent-eyed girl, and betrayed by both Czechs and Poles. He nevertheless talked his way out of an SS arrest on one occasion, demonstrating his acting skills in a life-threatening encounter ('England Receives Me as a Human Being', pp. 7–17).

66 When David Gellner visited the firm in the early 1980s there was evidence also of some moulding, of toilet seats and other bathroom fittings.

67 Interview with Michael McMullen, February 2003. Gellner never received a formal allowance, although Susan Gellner remembers that he did occasionally receive envelopes containing as much as a thousand pounds.

his son's initial fieldwork expenses as an anthropology doctoral student.[68] During the course of the 1960s the firm became very successful, with a turn-over of perhaps more than a million pounds. The social scene in Highgate reproduced part of the world from which the parents had come. Rudolf and Anna continued to speak together in German, to the embarrassment of their daughter when she brought home friends during the war. Intellectual life was taken seriously, with Rudolf soon showing considerable knowl-edge of English literature. Ernest's friends from university were welcomed into the Gellner home, but family tensions remained. The parents did visit Prague once after the war, but showed no desire to return: their world had gone.[69] Anna died in 1954. The father then married Olga Koerbel, a widow of similar background who had two children of her own.[70] Rudolf's political views were apparently middle of the road, veering from support for the Labour Party to enthusiasm for the Social Democrats. It is possible that some monies were sent to Israel, but there was no evidence of any fervent Zionism. Rudolf died in 1987. Marianne Gellner married in the early 1960s and lived thereafter in Hampstead, dying a decade after her brother.

Gellner's family has retained his school reports in England. He spent a year at Highgate School. Some of his teachers' comments about him are revealing. In early 1940 the headmaster noted that he was 'probably the most able boy in this division. He is contra-suggestive and to some extent anti-social. He works at subjects which interest him and scamps every-thing else'. His form master added that he was 'able but awkward. Affects a cynical indifference'. His English history teacher was irritated: 'He has done no work, and made no progress', but then had second thoughts and added in different ink, 'He is able'. Despite these misgivings, there was a

---

68   'My first trip [to the High Atlas] was possible thanks mainly to my father, and in this respect at any rate this study belongs to the nineteenth-century tradition of middle-class scholarship' ('Acknowledgements', *Saints of the Atlas*, London, 1969, p. xii).

69   Interview with Marianne Sigmon, February 2003.

70   Her first husband was the paternal uncle of Madeleine Albright, Bill Clinton's Secretary of State. Members of the Gellner family had difficulty believing Albright's claim that she had been unaware of her Jewish background. The Gellners' relations with Taussig did not survive Rudolf's second marriage. From 1985 Ernest was heavily involved in the firm's business, first in mediating difficulties between the partners (Taussig came to feel that he was doing all the work and suggested lesser remuneration for Rudolf, a position rejected by Rudolf on the grounds that both partners had built the firm) and then in selling it – or rather in selling parts of it to different companies. Some of the monies from these sales came to Ernest and Marianne. This certainly made life easier for the Gellner family in the last decade of his life, not least by allowing him to keep the Hampshire and London houses while buying new ones in Cambridge.

good deal of sympathy for him, with the headmaster noting in his final report that 'he is a silent boy, but would seem to have plenty of character'. Gellner completed his schooling between 1941 and 1943 at the St Albans's County School for Boys, which he described later as 'not-quite-a-grammar school'.[71] He enjoyed sports and began to do well academically, with comments being made that he was 'fertile in his views', and with regard to his studies in history, 'Ideas brilliant. But he needs to work harder on the facts'. In 1941 he took School Certificate exams, gaining high grades in English, Czech and German, with passes in Elementary Maths, European History, British History and Geography; he failed French, and would later joke about his success in mediating the translation of Claude Lévi-Strauss's *The Savage Mind*.[72] In 1942 he took four subjects in the Higher School Certificate: English, Mathematics, History and Advanced German. He was able to win an open scholarship to Balliol College in Oxford, aided both by the academic character of the school, and by Balliol's desire to recruit outside the normal private-school milieu. Gellner later described himself as the beneficiary of the 'Portuguese colonial policy' of A. D. Lindsay, the Master of Balliol, who wanted to 'keep the natives peaceful by getting the able ones from below into Balliol. . . . [he aimed at] one third upper class, one third grammar school, one third Scotsmen and foreigners. The upper class were to teach the others manners, the grammar school to introduce some brains into the upper class. He put it as brutally as that'.[73] The description suggests that Gellner was bound to be something of an outsider: Jewish but not really Jewish, far from completely English, and a grammar school boy to boot.

He arrived at the age of eighteen in the Michaelmas term of 1943. He had decided to study 'Modern Greats', the combined course in Philosophy, Politics and Economics which Oxford had introduced to complement if not supersede the 'Greats' (Greek, Latin, Ancient History and Classical Philosophy). This programme was one of Oxford's most significant acts of modernization in the social and human sciences, though it would be after Gellner's time that political science and economics were professionalized to the standards of American universities. Philosophy was then widely regarded as the premier subject. As in other colleges, a measure of unofficial streaming took place in Balliol. Although philosophy was

---

71 Davis, 'An Interview with Ernest Gellner', p. 64. He seems to have lived in St Alban's, though not at the school, probably from 1940–41.
72 The point of the story was rather different, namely that close familiarity with the text did not lead to any clear understanding of the book's theses. Though the joke was a good one, Gellner had by this time been speaking French quite regularly in Morocco and became comfortable in his use of that language.
73 Davis, 'An Interview with Ernest Gellner', p. 64.

Gellner's great interest, he was initially judged to be slightly below par in that field and was accordingly pushed into a concentration in economics. He was tutored by Thomas Balogh, and rather disliked the subject.[74] His other tutors were for philosophy the Master, A. D. Lindsay, the liberal anti-fascist and expositor of Hegel; and for politics Frank Pakenham, the Catholic anti-fascist and historian of the Anglo-Irish Treaty (later to become Lord Longford).[75] Gellner was apparently a lively student, constantly in trouble with the authorities, mostly for coming home after curfew; but for the intervention of Lindsay, he would on one occasion have been expelled. He has been described as being incredibly handsome – lithe and athletic, 'Pan-like', brooding and Byronic, witty, intellectual, and very interested in going out with women.[76] He made friends with Paul Stirling, who was to introduce him to social anthropology at the London School of Economics; Donald MacRae, with whom he was to have considerable difficulty within the Sociology Department at the LSE; Michael McMullen, with whom he attended meetings of the Labour Club; Martin Milligan; and John Hajnal, later to become a distinguished demographer and colleague at the LSE. Hajnal's family was also Jewish in background, arriving in England from Hungary, through Holland, some years earlier. Gellner is said by Hajnal to have repeatedly insisted in their earliest conversations that 'it was a disaster to be a Jew in modern Europe'. In an immediate sense this is an all too comprehensible statement: the Final Solution had just begun. But Hajnal saw it then, and now, as a form of resentment at being Jewish.[77] The charge

---

74 T. Balogh would later author an astringent criticism of the UK's civil service, *The Apotheosis of the Dilettante,* and argue that the civil service required training in something like PPE (Philosophy, Politics, Economics). He was an advisor to Harold Wilson's first two Labour governments (1964–70).

75 A. D. Lindsay, later Lord Lindsay of Birker, political philosopher and academician, was the first socialist to head an Oxbridge college. As the Master of Balliol College Lindsay ran in a famous local by-election in 1938 against Quentin Hogg, a Conservative and Unionist, and later Lord Hailsham. Lindsay ran as a 'popular front' candidate of the broad centre-left on a ticket opposing appeasement. He lost. Frank Pakenham's *Peace by Ordeal: The Making of the Anglo-Irish Treaty,* London, 1935, is still regarded as definitive. Pakenham would later author a quasi-official biography of Eamon de Valera, but was best known in public life for his campaign to release the 'Moors murderer' Myra Hindley.

76 Interview with Michael McMullen, February 2003. Gellner took McMullen canoeing, and himself learnt to sail while at Oxford.

77 Interview with John Hajnal, June 1998 at LSE. In follow-up correspondence, 16 October 1998, Hajnal elaborated:

I had many conversations with Ernest in 1943–4 about his (and my) Jewish ancestry. It is not a matter of remembering a particular phrase he used. Ernest at that stage habitually expressed resentment about being Jewish. At any rate that is how I now remember it. I know my

of 'self-hatred' is commonly made against liberal, secular figures of Jewish origin, especially if they are not enthusiastic partisans of current Israeli governments. But this is a complicated matter, considered at length below.

Gellner seems to have been particularly prone to depression during and after the war years, and his mother would soon fear that he might allow himself to be killed in action.[78] After just a year at Oxford, Gellner was called up by the Czech authorities on 14 February 1944.[79] Deferment would have been possible, so it seems that he chose to join the 1st Czechoslovak Armoured Brigade, aged nineteen, on 2 August 1944.[80] The Brigade had been formed in September 1943 from remnants of the French Army's 1st Czechoslovak Division. The Brigade was apparently a rather inefficient unit, not least because it was comprised of very varied elements: Jewish refugees (Gellner among them, for his military identification was simply that of 'Jew'); former members of the International Brigades who had fought in Spain; and Czech Silesians who had been forced to fight first for Germany, then, when captured in North Africa, for the Foreign Legion, and finally transferred to the Brigade as the result of an arrangement between Beneš and De Gaulle.[81] On 21 August 1944 Beneš addressed the troops shortly before they left, outlining his hopes for a new Czechoslovak Republic to be built along the lines established by Masaryk – but noting that Germans and Hungarians would have a place in the new state only if they had fought alongside the Allies. Under the command of Major General Alois Liška, the Brigade of about 4,000 officers and men played the major role in besieging Dunkirk, alternately attacking and being attacked by the energetic German garrison. The Brigade's mission, to contain but not take Dunkirk, was achieved. The Allied Forces (for some French and Canadians were present) managed to keep the far larger enemy force of 15,500 bottled up, aided by

---

memory is fallible. Ernest's attitude was not uncommon among assimilated middle-class Jews of the capital cities of the Austro-Hungarian monarchy.

I do not dispute John Hajnal's memory, but no other interviewees reported, prompted or unprompted, similar assessments. This issue may have been a private one between the two young men.

78 Information provided by Susan Gellner, who was careful to say however that this is best interpreted in terms of the mother's feelings and attitudes, rather than as an accurate guide to the psychology of her son.

79 He wrote to his mother, addressing her as 'Dear Anny', on 26 November 1944, in a tone of some irritation: 'I don't see what "to have left Balliol was a mistake" means, as I had no choice being called up; whatever other reasons I might have had are no one's business'.

80 Apparently an alternative was to serve on the Arctic convoys taking war materiel to the Soviet Union.

81 Davis, 'An Interview with Ernest Gellner', p. 64.

a German shortage of supplies. The Germans only surrendered on 9 May 1945, by which time 167 members of the Brigade had been killed and 461 wounded. Gellner did not himself provide an assessment of the impact of his military service, but it clearly mattered to him: he returned with his wife to the scene of the siege at a later time, though he could not recognize the exact location of the lines. On 15 February 1945 he received the Military Memorial Medal from the Ministry of National Defence.

One memory Gellner retained from his service was the ability of Czech cooks, working from the same ingredients, to produce far better meals than their British counterparts. Another memory involved his political education. He recognized that a simple private, Drehulka, had great authority, and guessed that this reflected his political status, acquired as a member of the International Brigades that had fought in Spain. 'I remember arguing with him about the early *de jure* recognition by the USSR of Badoglio's government in Italy, which if I remember correctly preceded the similar recognition by the Western allies, and mocking him about the lack of fastidiousness on the part of the Kremlin concerning its allies – anyone would do'.[82] The considerable precociousness and self-confidence shown here can only have been massively enhanced by the experience of being continuously under fire. Crucially, his later habit of always speaking his own mind is likely tied to his escaping the possibility of an early death; he had joined up with two other men, one of whom died after being shot by a sniper's bullet.

Gellner later asked the Labour politician R. H. S. Crossman, who had served at Allied Headquarters during the war, why the Brigade was not placed under Patton's command since he was driving towards Bohemia. Apparently, the hatred between Montgomery and Patton was so intense that the British commander would not release any extra troops to his American rival.[83] Only when Prague was attacked by the Russians was the Brigade allowed to move, probably on 5 May 1945. This meant that the Brigade only reached Prague on 18 May 1945, eight days after the arrival of Soviet-sponsored Czechoslovak troops commanded by Ludvik Svoboda. Still, Gellner took part in victory parades in his native country, driving his half-track in Pilsen in May, where he was inspected as part of the guard of honour, and marching across Charles Bridge in Prague shortly afterwards.[84] As the Russians had occupied Prague, the Brigade was only allowed in the city between 28 and 31 May 1945, returning after that to their barracks in Silberberg.

---

82   'Return of a Native', *Political Quarterly*, vol. 67, 1996, p. 4.
83   Davis, 'An Interview with Ernest Gellner', p. 64.
84   'Foreword' to Schmidt-Hartmann, p. 7.

Gellner claimed to have carried four books with him in the toolbox of the half-track he drove to Prague for the victory parade in May: George Orwell's *Animal Farm*, Arthur Koestler's *Darkness at Noon*, James Burnham's *The Managerial Revolution*, and Cyril Connolly's *The Unquiet Grave*.[85] The first two were anti-Stalinist and indeed anti-Marxist novels, but their narratives were inspired by Marxism and treated it seriously. Burnham's work was described by Hans Gerth and C. Wright Mills as 'Marx for the Managers',[86] and is a founding (though often forgotten) text in the theory of industrial society – it argues that expertise rather than wealth is now the universal basis of authority. The authors of the first three books were disillusioned left-wingers, profoundly horrified at the consequences of Leninism: Burnham would end up as a right-wing Cold Warrior, while Koestler's evolution was more complex.[87] Connolly's book, as Gellner put it, was 'not formally counter-revolutionary but not a leftist edifying text'.[88] All four books would have reinforced the young Gellner's individualism and his opposition to communism. It is likely that they also contributed to his abiding intellectual interest in Marxism, and Marxist-influenced criticisms of 'actually existing socialism'. He never would embrace Marxism, observing that for a person of his age and background he belonged to 'what sometimes felt like a small minority . . . those who never passed through a Marxist phase'.[89] Three of the books in his toolbox must have whetted his later appetite for a sociology that would be influenced by historical materialism, that would take seriously stratification based on knowledge as well as on property, and that would reject Marx and Engels's utopian politics,

---

85   Gellner cites the books in 'Return of a Native', p. 4, noting proudly that the books were left behind, as pioneering pinpricks in the Iron Curtain. There is probably something wrong with Gellner's memory here. *Animal Farm* was only published on 17 August 1945, so it could not have been with him in May unless he had access to a manuscript copy, a possibility since Orwell took some time to find a publisher. He returned to England on short leaves in April and September 1945, the second time using a new Czechoslovak passport, and could also have brought the newly published *Animal Farm* back to Prague on the latter occasion.

86   H. Gerth and C. W. Mills, 'A Marx for the Managers', *Ethics*, vol. 52, 1942.

87   See J. Burnham, *The Machiavellians: Defenders of Freedom. A Defence of Political Truth against Wishful Thinking*, Washington, 1943; B. Crick, *George Orwell: A Life*, London, 1981; M. Scammell, *Koestler: The Literary and Political Odyssey of a Twentieth-Century Skeptic*, New York, 2009.

88   'Return of a Native', op. cit., p. 4. *The Unquiet Grave* is in fact a very personal, poetic and melancholic lament for Palinurus's (Connolly's) collapsed marriage. It is an affirmation of thinking for oneself, and promotes drawing upon the resources of past thinkers and poets to do so. Its confessional style and its aesthetic detachment from the war made it resonate with Connolly's contemporaries. See M. Shelden, *Friends of Promise: Cyril Connolly and the World of Horizon*, London, 1990, pp. 96–121.

89   Ibid., p. 4.

which in the hands of practical power-seekers had become a blueprint for totalitarian regimes.

His earliest philosophical enthusiasm was for Schopenhauer, a taste he shared with his great-grandmother, Friederike Lobl.[90] He also told of an early and avid interest, when a young soldier at St. Omer, in Sartre and Camus – indeed, if his later testimony is to be believed, he preferred literary magazines and these authors' books to the alternatives of the public baths or the local brothel.[91] This interest in existentialism partially explains his attendance at Charles University for a term.[92] He spent time at the lectures of Jan Patočka, later chosen as one of the spokesmen of Charter 77, a role which perhaps led to his death from a heart attack following prolonged interrogation at the hands of the police. Gellner claimed to have learned little from these lectures, finding them opaque, not least as the philosopher invented countless new words on the grounds that Czech was insufficiently flexible, 'but the intensity of his manner somehow kept me coming to the lectures'.[93]

But he did not stay in Prague for long. For one thing, the Jewish community in the Czech lands had been more or less wiped out: its numbers had fallen from perhaps a quarter of a million to less than ten thousand. For another, he was appalled by the expulsion of the Sudeten Germans, even though he fully understood the motives behind it.[94] His later conviction that the fate of national minorities was usually assimilation, expulsion or death had roots in the fates of both the Czech Jews and the Bohemian Germans. He was witness to moral devastation and to a new occupation – albeit a temporary one, as the Red Army troops soon left, only to return in 1968. In the fragments of a report, or draft short journal note, entitled 'No Winter's Tale' (and in another copy 'Bohemia Today'), he described seeing Red Army officers billeted in the family home, which must have been

---

90   J. Gellner, 'England Receives Me as a Human Being', p. 45.

91   'Period Piece', in his *Spectacles and Predicaments: Essays in Social Theory*, Cambridge, 1979, p. 102.

92   The German university closed at this time, its books left in the street for whomsoever wished to take them.

93   'Reborn from Below: The Forgotten Beginnings of the Czech National Revival' in *Encounters with Nationalism*. Patočka argued that the Czechs were the first nation to be successfully born from below, i.e. without ruling-class leadership, but because they had not liberated themselves they had the psychic pettiness of 'liberated servants'.

94   See the sympathetic treatment of the fate of the Sudeten Germans in A. M. De Zayas, *A Terrible Revenge: The Ethnic Cleansing of the East European Germans, 1944–50*, New York, 1994. Gellner's language was unambiguous: 'After the war, the Sudeten Germans were ruthlessly and brutally expelled in an act of collective and indiscriminate reprisal, though not without apprehension of an eventual German revenge' ('Munich in Prague', pp. 120–1).

traumatic, no matter how detachedly he presented it.[95] The text shows his partial contempt for the Czechs at that moment, noting the 'cheerful attempt by everyone to exculpate as many friends [from the charge of collaboration with the Nazis] as possible by any means at hand'.[96] He was irritated at how Czechs responded to those who had been forced to leave before 1940, deducing that 'there will always tend to be a psychological friction between the émigré and the home-stayer'.[97] He was also shocked at Jews' complicity in their own fate, trying 'to solve the enigma of the passivity with which people, knowing what was in store for them, went to death with no attempt at resistance or escape, even the young and the vigorous'.[98] He was struck by the explanations which insisted on the 'incredibly strong urge to obey whatever has the outward garb of rightful authority' and 'the human ability to bear the anticipation of anything provided there is a rut to get into'.[99] He also witnessed the incipient recovery of Czech nationalism, the Czech language and Czech literary life after six years of Germanification: 'The importance of such cultural issues can only be realized by someone acquainted with Irish, Welsh or Palestinian Jewish conditions, where a language and its literary tradition is being consciously built up or revived' – an important comment because it strikingly accentuates the extent of his own Czech identification.[100] In September 1945 he attended the trial of Josef Pfitzner, previously a professor at the German university in Prague who became mayor under the Nazis, and noted the failure of the trial to respect due process – somehow the time of his execution was known well before the jury went into session to pronounce the verdict. He observed the execution, and the novel torture of hanging the condemned by two ropes in order to prolong his consciousness. He carefully and anthropologi-cally noted the composition of the jeering and applauding crowd: 'in order of quantity: women, both proletarian and better dressed . . . , men, almost all working or lower middle-class, ... and Red Army men'.[101] The latter were the real power in the new Bohemia.

---

95   'No Winter's Tale', Gellner Archive. This must have been written in 1945–6. The title of the article plays on the fact that Shakespeare's *The Winter's Tale* makes reference to Bohemia, with one character speaking of a coastline that it does not of course possess.
96   Ibid., p. 4.
97   Ibid., p. 5.
98   Ibid.
99   Ibid.
100   Ibid., p. 9.
101   Ibid., p. 12. B. Frommer, *National Cleansing: Retribution Against Nazi Collaborators in Postwar Czechoslovakia*, Cambridge, 2005, pp. 97–9, describes the trial and execution in some detail, demonstrating the accuracy of Gellner's account.

He saw power change hands within his own Brigade as well as in the society at large. He remembered it vividly later:

> In the Brigade, the Communists had their own hierarchy and chain of command which, for them, overruled the formal command structure. To this day, I remember the name of a simple private soldier, Drehulka, who evidently had great authority over some fellow soldiers, irrespective of his rank in relation to theirs. Soon after we settled down in a country area he was suddenly promoted, or rather re-promoted, to the rank of lieutenant, which had been his grade in the International Brigade in Spain, thus confirming what I had guessed anyway about the basis of his otherwise mysterious influence . . . One of the most memorable recruiting posters of the Communist Party in Prague read: 'Anyone with a clean shield into the party!' Nominally, this meant that the Party welcomed those who had behaved well under the Occupation. The real meaning of the slogan was perfectly clear to all: if your shield is filthy, we in the Party will scrub it clean for you. We like people we can trust because we have something on them and because we know they are willing to do dirty work . . . [102]

He thought that Czechoslovakia was in for another three hundred years of oppression. There was significant and authentic local support for communism, and limited active opposition. The Czechs had no doubt that Germany would revive, and no faith that the West would protect them from that revival, quite naturally given their experience at Munich. They were therefore disposed to appease their own communists as the lesser evil, especially in light of the fact that they were expelling their own Germans. Gellner later placed part of the blame on the legacy of Masaryk, and in doing so he deployed Karl Popper's criticism of historicism. The Czechs had been taught to base their morals on historical evolution, and merely transferred their loyalties to communism once democracy failed: 'The truth is both ironic and bitter, but inescapable: Masaryk's philosophy of history did eventually lead to 1948'.[103] The failure of the Czechs to fight for them-selves and their consensual dispositions towards one another, in particular their failure to confront collaborators, be they Nazi or Communist, would always astonish him.[104]

---

102   'Return of the Native', pp. 4–5. Gellner's memory was consistent: he uses almost the same words in 'No Winter's Tale', p. 13.
103   'The Price of Velvet', p. 123.
104   He recommended reading V. Mastny's *The Czechs Under Nazi Rule: The Failure of*

In Prague he re-established contact with Eric Hošek, with whom he came to play table tennis – one special rule of which, established at Gellner's suggestion, was that the loser had to try to kiss the first girl who entered the room.[105] Hošek found him Anglicized and was not surprised that he eventually left, but Gellner's motivations were more complex than Hošek's implied thesis of de-Czechification.[106] The Red Army, the Holocaust, Czech collaboration with the Nazis, the great revenge expulsion of the Germans, and the coming victory of communism had thoroughly cured him of his schoolboy nostalgia for Prague. He returned to Oxford to complete his degree in 1946–7. He was never in fact formally demobilized. As he recalled forty-five years later, 'I was released on indefinite leave to complete my education . . . Technically I'm still on leave from No. 1 Company, Motorized Infantry Battalion, 1st Armoured Brigade . . . I spent about half a term at Prague University, and then I acquired the required papers and went back to England and Oxford'.[107] The decision was taken in a situation of fear and apprehension. He was an exile rather than an émigré.

Reprise

At the age of thirteen Gellner underwent the trauma of that dangerous journey across Europe, and lost his friends and his social moorings. In his teenage years he dreamed constantly of Prague, viscerally longing to go back.[108] The return to Prague led him to see this as an illusion, and he was forced to leave behind the feelings of belonging formed during his childhood. In this sense, the title of this chapter is entirely apt. But in another sense the title misleads. When parents speak to their children in moments

---

National Resistance 1939–1942, New York, 1971, alongside Gordon Skilling's *Czechoslovakia's Interrupted Revolution* as proof of this pattern of consensual collaboration amongst his co-nationals ('Gone and Gone Forever [Review of Gordon Skilling's *Czechoslovakia's Interrupted Revolution*]', *Government and Opposition*, vol. 12, 1977).

105   Gellner sent most of his books to Hošek. Many had inscriptions in Czech, which Hošek translated as '*Il n'y a que des bêtises dedans*'.

106   Hošek stayed for another decade before moving to France. Relations between the two friends were then restored. In 'No Winter's Tale', p. 5, Gellner wrote that 'the sense that the time between Munich and May '45 had not happened at all [for Czechs] was expressed to me by an old school friend who enviously remarked that I, abroad, had "lived" and experienced the six years, but to him they were a complete blank, remembered with no emotional colouring: he felt he was starting in '45 where he had left off in '39'. This old friend was certainly Hošek. Hošek did indeed live a life of internal exile during the war, spending the time learning Italian. The fact that he was not Jewish was of course key to this.

107   Davis, 'An Interview with Ernest Gellner', p. 64.

108   Ibid, p. 63

of trouble they reassure them, insisting that 'things will be all right'. This is not surprising since most parents – Gellner included – wish for their children to escape trauma. But a moment's thought makes one realize that trauma can enable just as it can crush. Certainly Gellner would not have been the person he became without experiencing his traumatic childhood.

One result of this background is that Gellner became deeply socially observant. In later years he noted that his first sociological observation, probably made in the 1930s, concerned the five ways in which young Jewish men lost their virginity. Three of these are clearly remembered: the son of the owner of a textile factory with a mill worker in Brno; a working-class boy with a prostitute; and the son of Prague intellectuals with someone from the same background while at summer camp – with a further observation probably describing the conditions of very traditional Jews, and another with a tourist in the spa town Karlovy Vary.[109] This is of course a trivial example, though the humour and the subject matter are characteristic of its author. But much more was involved here. Gellner was a natural anthropologist, an outsider constantly and with dry irony observing the customs of social and intellectual groups wherever he found himself. Many found him to be exceptionally stimulating company precisely because nothing was taken for granted. His mind was always at work.

The conclusion of Jiří Musil's account of Gellner's early years in Prague is on the mark. Gellner had seen the squalor and poverty as well as the prosperity engendered by capitalist modernization; but he had considerable appreciation for agrarian life, to some extent as it really existed, but mostly as it was envisaged by urban intellectuals. He was then transplanted against his will to England, then the most industrialized state in the world. He could, in short, understand the transition to modernity better than many of his future English contemporaries because he had witnessed and experienced it in a compressed form during his own abbreviated childhood.[110] He would become the philosopher of this transition. He had grown up, he would learn in retrospect, in the perfect laboratory for someone interested in nationalism. He had seen people 'metamorphose', not, Kafka-style, into insects, but into other identities. He could see within his own extended family the tensions between Zionism and acculturation, and he

---

109   I heard this story many years ago from Gellner himself. Without prompting, Eric Hobsbawm mentioned (in an interview in March 2008 which stressed how very witty and intelligent he had found Gellner) that he had been told much the same story, though he thought that four rather than five passages had been mentioned.

110   Musil, 'The Prague Roots', pp. 42–3. The relations between Musil and Gellner are described below.

was aware of Marxism, not least because of his father's background and the left's counter-assault on fascism. Gellner learnt early that authentic multi-culturalism, contrary to the sometimes naïve academic misrepresentations of recent years, could mean serious conflict, even extermination of some groups. It could compel a 'choice': assimilate or be expelled (or worse). His parents had had to choose an identity, and then were forced to leave and to 'choose' another. Bluntly, he had lived through a failed nation-building project.[111] As already noted, he argued in later years that there were but three ways in which national homogeneity could be achieved: through assimilation, genocide, or the creation of a new state of one's own.[112]

Finally, there was a visceral quality to his search for some sort of solid foundations by means of which to live his life. In later years, after admitting that he benefited from none of the solace that comes to believers, he noted certain consequent advantages:

> But, not having had a faith, I think I do understand – that's an arrogant claim, but I think I do understand – what Descartes and Hume and Kant were about, namely, the struggle to establish the foundations of knowledge. What those people tried to establish, I think I do understand. Never having been a member of a community but having been on the margins of a number gave me an understanding of what nineteenth-century romanticism is about, what the yearning for community is all about. Communal marginalism gives one that, and lack of faith gives one understanding of what the main thrust of thought is about.[113]

These matters will of course concern us later. What matters next, however, is something altogether more straightforward. The question which faced him upon his return to England was simple: what sort of identity would be provided by his adopted country?

---

111 Curiously, his theory of nationalism suggests that muti-national states are doomed because of the internal contradiction of inequality combined with ethnic difference. But Czechoslovakia more or less worked, as did Austro-Hungary, until war destroyed social relations. Czechoslovakia did not really fall apart: it was assassinated from the outside.

112 This view was sometimes expressed verbally. It appears in the preface to the Polish edition of *Nations and Nationalism*. The Poles initially objected to the preface, but less because of this comment than his quip that 'thanks to Hitler and Stalin' Polish life could now proceed more smoothly.

113 Davis, 'An Interview with Ernest Gellner', p. 71.

2

A New Start

Entering a new world as an immigrant is always hard. Gellner clearly had a burning ambition to succeed, but some of his character traits were bound to make this even more difficult than it had to be. There was the rebellious-ness that had always marked his personality. Then there was the fact that he had fought in the war, thereby gaining considerable self-confidence. Equally important was his Czech social-democratic background. All of this made it very unlikely that he would fit in easily in his new setting. British upper-class society, exemplified by Oxford and Cambridge Universities, was class-conscious in the immediate postwar years in a way that is not easy to convey, although the novels of Nancy Mitford, Evelyn Waugh and Barbara Pym set within this world can help provide some understanding. Snobbery was anathema to Gellner at all times in his life, and he had to contend with a great deal of it at Oxford. He made much of this a few years later when he was discussing with his friend Norman Birnbaum, the American sociologist, the advisability of the latter's planned move to Oxford. Gellner noted amongst other things the stupidity of class-based codes of behaviour which prevented the vast majority of Oxford's male students from taking out 'shop girls'.[1] This chapter records the difficulties he faced in the early 1950s, and describes the birth of a confidence suffi-cient to take on the idols of the age.

An Uneasy State of Mind

Gellner returned to Oxford in January 1946 just after his twenty-first birthday. Several witnesses attest to the impact that he made at the time. He was extremely handsome, at once lithe and tough, and took up sailing at this time in addition to his interest in canoeing. He rode a motorcycle.

---

1   The expression is that of Norman Birnbaum, interviewed in February 2008.

He was somewhat intense and enigmatic, at once attracted and attractive to women. He had a long-term girlfriend at this time, but he apparently had an affair at some point with the female undergraduate considered at the time to be the university's great beauty. He possessed a certain maturity resulting from the complexities of his background and his experience under fire. He was extremely serious, often locked up in his rooms working hard, especially on Kant's three great critiques – he took tutorials in that subject from Donald MacKinnon in Keble College, a brilliant and charismatic Kantian philosopher capable of giving tutorials from his bath, and probably Tom Stoppard's model for the character of George in *Jumpers*, his witty portrayal of Oxford philosophy.[2] He remained grateful all his life for this immersion into Kant; it formed a key part of his intellectual equipment thereafter. A certain exoticism was probably partly to blame for his engagement with existentialist thought, at once passionate and critical. Gellner knew Iris Murdoch during the 1950s, and it is possible that one of the characters of her first novel, *Under the Net*, is based upon him.[3] But what surely counted most was sheer brilliance. For one thing, he took an active part in a seminar run by Gilbert Ryle, one of the leading philosophers of the day and the editor of *Mind*, claiming later to have learnt more from him than from any other Oxford philosopher.[4] For another, there was his clear ability to think critically at the highest level, now made visible to us thanks to the preservation of an interesting intellectual exchange that took place during his first year back at Oxford.

Gellner was active in Oxford undergraduate philosophy circles, and sought out Karl Popper when Popper came to give a paper before Easter in 1946. He later recalled sitting and listening to the private discussion that took place after the lecture between Alfred Ayer, Isaiah Berlin and Popper, during the course of which Popper made much fun of the cloudiness of Hegelian language. At Popper's urging he read *The Open Society and Its Enemies*, the book which was to influence him more than any other.[5] His reactions were recorded in a long letter of 10 August 1946.

---

2 MacKinnon also played a particularly important role for Iris Murdoch (P. Conradi, *Iris Murdoch: A Life*, New York, 2001).

3 The novel was first published in 1954. When Murdoch wrote to Gellner on 26 November 1959 to apologize for a harsh review of *Words and Things*, she resisted Gellner's attribution to her of the views of Hugo Bounderby. She also asked if he was planning to go to one the meetings that led to the creation of the *New Left Review* in 1962.

4 Gellner to Ryle, 3 December 1959.

5 'The Rational Mystic: Review of Karl R. Popper, *In Search of a Better World*', *New Republic*, vol. 16, 1993.

As for your book – its problem, if I understand it, is to provide an answer to some widespread doubts of the 'rationalist' tradition which had led many of its adherents to desert it: this attempt at re-persuasion, I suppose, is what you meant by your claim that it is a 'fighting book'. The crisis arose as follows: the rationalists of the 18ᵗʰ century (largely) had two sets of value-beliefs, (1) what you call 'openness', the destruction of arbitrary and irrational authority, taboos, etc., and (2) amelioration of mankind's material state. They also believed, falsely, that the achievement of (2) would automatically follow the achievement of (1), i.e. they were 'liberals'. The first crisis arose when the 19ᵗʰ century showed the latter belief to be wrong; and this problem was overcome by the replacement of belief in (2) as an automatic consequence of (1), by the belief in (2) brought about by 'socialism' or 'planning'. (1) was still ardently believed in, but no longer as an agent for bringing about (2), but for its own sake only, and it was assumed, *usually tacitly*, that the process of material amelioration would not hinder (or would even aid!) the achievement of those factors of the Open Society other than material well-being (esp. intellectual freedom). The 20ᵗʰ century has on the whole shown the later rationalists' (socialists) belief in the absence of an incompatibility between (2) by 'planning' and (1) as false as the earlier rationalists' ('liberals') belief in (1) implying (2).

The manner in which the 20ᵗʰ century has shown this to be false is by the tendency of industrial masses to support totalitarianism, at any rate on the continent of Europe. Those of the rationalist tradition, the 'progressives' or what-will-you, now had a number of unpalatable alternatives: (a) abandon (1) for the sake of (2), the course of the communists, excused either by saying that (1) isn't really valuable, or that it will be re-established when (2) is achieved. Both excuses are invalid, though it is difficult to argue against the former; the latter at least is empirical, though it is true that there aren't enough facts available yet to make its disproof absolutely cogent. (b) To abandon (2) for (1), which on the Continent usually soon meant losing (1) as well, as the active movements opposed to socialism-become-totalitarian were themselves equally totalitarian. In Anglo-Saxon countries it may be possible to escape this dilemma. (c) Attempts to believe both in ameliorism and liberty, either by some neo-liberalism (which, even if it 'supplied the goods', doesn't stand a chance under contemporary economic conditions); or by just staying in the old planning-and-freedom against reason, by a plunge into mysticism like Arthur Koestler's Peter Slavek; one suspects that those Peter Slaveks who weren't forced into the 'mystic plunge of faith' by accidental circumstances, such as Jewish extraction, compelling them to take one side in the late struggle, usually took the course of passivity or even collaboration.

It was, I take it, to those wavering rationalists, that your book was addressed; your solution having two essential parts; firstly, the making explicit and independent of the liberty-element in the rationalist tradition, which had by socialists been so fatally left tacit and/or considered as having only derived value; and secondly the re-establishing of compatibility between planning and freedom through the distinction between Utopian and piecemeal social engineering.

Against the first point the following objections may be made: that the idea of the 'Open Society' is vague, and as such, on the one hand, inadequate in argument, on the other hand liable to abuse (like the pliable vagueness of ideas such as 'Fascism' or the equally convenient 'Anti-Fascism'.) You will no doubt reply that this (i.e. the Open Society), is precisely what cannot be defined, else it would not be Open. This seems, however, rather like Wittgenstein's paradoxical rule about permissible propositions which you yourself ridicule; for we must make assertions about what exactly the O.S. is if we are to avoid the Closed Society, and anyway you've made an assertion in forbidding all others. And moreover, 'Openness' (or 'liberty') must be more clearly formulated; for there are elements which though prima facie 'closed' (you mention friendship as an example), are desirable; and I think the desire for ordering facts in scientific systems has psychologically a similarity to the yearning for a 'closed' order. On the other hand, German Fascism, though amongst the masses it no doubt appealed to 'closed society yearning', surely has as a part of its philosophical inspiration, at any rate amongst some of its leaders, an intentional and systematic disregard for 'moral laws' which is, again, prima facie 'open'. I think this shows that the idea of liberty[6], apart from the problem arising from its relation to social engineering, needs re-formulating; the principle of 'freedom up to the limit of interfering with others' freedom' is perfectly useless, as the decision as to whether a murder interferes with the victim's freedom to live, or the victim with the murderer's freedom to murder, can be made only by appeal to norms which are arbitrary and varied from social group to social group; (in the case of murder most men are agreed; but on the important issues both sides can claim that the principle of 'freedom limited by others' freedom' is on their side.)

As for 'piecemeal engineering', I'm not clear whether it means engineering not too large-scale, or such s.e. as only removes suffering rather

---

6   Which I presume is synonymous with 'openness'.

than plans for others' happiness; or both. But surely the large-scale is inescapable for technical reasons; whilst alleviation of misery and planning for happiness are usually inseparable (rebuilding of slums and reduction of working-time involves also designs for the new houses and provisions for leisure). Some 'Utopian engineering' is inescapable.

Thus I don't think your attitude is a solution, but only a very much clearer re-statement of the problem. Also, surely it isn't admirable to translate the 'womb-yearning' into sociology under the name of 'yearning for the tribal society', as an explanatory theory; it is both unverifiable and, by being equally applicable to all striving for order, not useful.

Gellner later noted his naïvety in writing a negative critique, regretting that he had failed to mention how much he admired the book – with whose theses he continued to struggle, as we shall see, for much of his career. Popper's own notorious inability to accept criticism was, however, suspended on this occasion, for he replied warmly on 15 August 1946.[7]

I found your letter not only non-boring but really interesting. Your criticism is going to the roots of the matter, and largely valid, even though I think that there are a number of points – probably less fundamental points – in which I might successfully defend myself.

You have in your letter succeeded in looking at my book from an elevated point of view, as it were – looking at my position as a whole, rather than worrying about the details in my reasoning. (You have succeeded, but you should not think that this is the only or the right way of looking at it.) If I may try to do the same in regard to your letter, then I may perhaps say: the fundamental difference between your point of view and that of my book is that you think that I am too optimistic in my belief that we can have (1) 'Openness' or 'Freedom' and (2) Amelioration. I am just now in a less optimistic mood than when I wrote the book (even though I was not at all sure, when I wrote it, how the war would end), and therefore incline to sympathise with your point of view.

But you must not forget that the book is, and remains, anti-historicistic. My optimism was not the good news that rationalism will win in the end; it was, rather, a mixture of the following:
(1) We have no reason to be frightened out of our wits by the undoubtedly existing difficulties. Although we may never conquer them, this does not show that they are unconquerable.

---

7   Popper's reply first became generally known when it was published as an Appendix in I. Jarvie and S. Prolong (eds), *The Open Society after Fifty Years*, London, 1999.

(2) A statement of those values which, in my opinion, makes the conquest worth an effort: and those include 'openness' and rationalism.

(3) A reasoned argument against what I may loosely call competing solutions, by showing, in the main, that they are not worth while, because they sacrifice certain of these values, either because they are incompatible with others, or without even knowing what they are doing.

Surely, more can and should be said about the 'Open Society'. Why not? This is not the last word about it, rather the first (although it is not really the first, of course). I don't think, however, that this should take the form of a definition of the Open Society (see chapter 11, section II).[8]

I was grieved to read in your letter that you consider the principle of 'freedom up to the limit of interfering with others' freedom' as 'perfectly useless'. Although it is not enough, and although it must be supplemented by other moral ideas. I don't think you are right; and your arguments in this particular point are, I'm afraid, reminiscent of Hegel's (who contested the same point against Kant). This is why I am grieved!

You must not forget that, in these matters, as in all others, nothing can be said that is completely water-tight and/or completely precise. The art of talking about such matters is the art of talking with that degree of clarity or precision which is appropriate to the subject matter. Nobody who reads what I (or Kant) says on this subject can doubt that we do not consider the murderer's and the victim's freedom as equivalent. Therefore, we must have succeeded, somehow, it [sic] explaining our principle with sufficient precision. Don't forget that I at least (as against Kant) never try to prove such a principle, but that I am content with demanding that certain things should be done, and others not done.

No reply from Gellner to this letter has survived. But Popper continued to be a lodestone of Gellner's thought, with the idea that claims to knowledge should in principle be open to falsification – carefully reinterpreted by Gellner in later years – remaining a key and recurring element of open systems of thought.

Gellner was allowed to take a shortened degree because of his war service, and so took his finals in the summer of 1947 after only two and a half years at the university.[9] His final papers were in General Philosophy (from

---

8   Popper's reference is to his 'anti-essentialist' arguments against the hunt for definitional exactitude.

9   He had 'shortened' registration obligations 'owing to service with the armed forces of the Crown or to some other approved form of National Service', University Registry, Oxford, copy of Gellner's certificate, 13 December 1947.

Descartes), Logic, the Philosophy of Kant, Moral & Political Philosophy, and Principles of Economics. He received warm feedback from Lindsay on his excellent first-class degree.[10] In November of the same year he was *Proxime accessit* (runner-up) in the John Locke Scholarship in Mental Philosophy – a prize based upon extra exam papers. Ryle wrote warmly to Gellner at this time, admonishing him to watch his style and to treat Russell and Ayer as exemplars of lucid English, and ending by insisting that what was at issue was less the John Locke prize than Gellner's future contribution to philosophy.[11]

In those days a first-class degree from Oxford was a sufficient credential to start an academic career, and he had no difficulty in gaining employment. He led a summer seminar in Oxford on the 'Philosophy of History', and then in October went to Edinburgh for two years as assistant lecturer in Philosophy; Lindsay's networking and support were clearly helpful.[12] Lindsay also wrote to the Home Office on Gellner's behalf, helping him to get a work permit. Gellner gained naturalization, that is, became a British subject (rather than citizen), in October 1948, promising as part of the process not to seek to reclaim his Czechoslovak citizenship.[13] Edinburgh was a city he came to love, in part because of the resemblance it bears to Prague, but still more because he developed a new passion for mountaineering. Then there was some real intellectual engagement, albeit critical in character, with the philosopher John Macmurray, a profoundly Christian thinker of Calvinist hue.[14] Further, one imagines that Gellner's time in Scotland was responsible for adding to his understanding of Hume and his deeply felt admiration for the Scottish Enlightenment as a whole.[15] Beyond all this, however, is the fact that Edinburgh held a very different attraction: Scottish law made it possible to divorce more quickly and easily than was the case in England and Wales.

In his last year at Oxford he had married Lore Edith Herzstein. Her

---

10   Lindsay to Gellner, 25 July 1947.

11   Ryle to Gellner, 2 December 1947.

12   In his letter of congratulations on Gellner's First, Lindsay expressed the hope that he would get the job in Edinburgh, and mentioned that he had spoken to Professor Macmurray.

13   The Certificate of Naturalization, dated 21 October 1948, noted that his parents were already British.

14   Tom Nairn in personal correspondence notes that Macmurray 'believed that the Jewish story was essential to modern Western attitudes', suggesting further that he would surely have been deeply interested in Gellner.

15   In 1992 a small conference on the Czech-Slovak split was held in Edinburgh, co-organized by the Centre for the Study of Government in Scotland and the Centre for the Study of Nationalism. Tom Nairn recalls Gellner lecturing the Czech and Slovak participants at dinner on the importance of 'the Paris of the North'.

background was Jewish and German, but unlike Gellner she lost all her family in the camps. She was pretty and charming, possessed of a lovely laugh, but she suffered from her troubled background. Several sources suggest that the marriage was essentially quixotic: Lore had convinced him that the emotional stability of marriage would allow her to do well in her final exams.[16] This gamble did not pay off. The relationship may have faced practical limitations from the start: a shared home was never created, and Lore soon moved in with Gellner's parents in Makepeace Avenue while he was in Edinburgh arranging the divorce – they provided this service gladly in the hope that it would restore his chances of a successful career.[17] What is clear is that Lore became schizophrenic. Over time her situation deteriorated, so much so that one of her friends, the novelist Nina Bawden, was sufficiently worried for the safety of her own children during visits that she had a watch kept on Lore throughout the night.[18] Soon there were long periods of hospitalization, to which Gellner's parents made some financial contribution, before an early death. Some friends blamed Gellner to some extent, not for causing Lore's problems, for there was general understanding from the start that she was frail, but for making a romantic gesture that could not be fulfilled. Gellner himself later commented on the difficulty of marriage between two people from such troubled backgrounds, and one suspects that he determined to have a rather different sort of emotional life thereafter.

When this first job came to its natural end in 1949, he moved to the LSE as an Assistant Lecturer in Sociology with special reference to Ethics and Social Philosophy, with a starting salary of £450.[19] One reason for

---

16   Evidence on this point came from Gellner himself, from his sister Marianne Sigmon (interviewed February 2003) and from Michael McMullen (interviewed February 2003).
17   The divorce was finalized on 3 August 1949. Lore's address is cited as that of Gellner's parents. Gellner was the defendant – identified as 'Ernest (otherwise Arnošt) André Gellner'.
18   Interview with Nina Bawden, May 2003. Not surprisingly, these visits stopped, with Nina Bawden choosing instead to travel to visit Lore. Lore's character may be at work in Bawden's *Anna Apparent*, London, 1971. Bawden attended Oxford at the same time as Gellner, and they became friends. He provided ethnographic information about Morocco that features in one of her novels, *A Woman of My Age*, London, 1991.
19   There may have been some possibility of him continuing in Edinburgh. No confirmation on this point is available, but it may be that he somehow, undramatically, blotted his copybook. He admitted later to his son David that he had taught Mill's *Utilitarianism* without having read it. He was sure that he had not been a good teacher in this first job, and was surprised to receive a letter later from one Edinburgh student praising his teaching. He was promoted to a full Lectureship in 1951, with a salary of £600, to undergo review in five years, 'tenure-track' in today's language (Carr-Saunders to Gellner, 31 May 1951).

his getting the job was utterly accidental. The Director, Alexander Carr-Saunders, had two dominating passions: rock climbing and his belief that the university staff should be involved in extracurricular activities with the students. When Gellner responded to a question asking about his spare time in Edinburgh by saying that he had spent most of it climbing with students, the job was his. But the rather strange title Gellner held points to a second reason, namely the influence of Morris Ginsberg. Ginsberg had worked closely with L. T. Hobhouse and had followed him as the holder of the Martin White chair, the senior position in the department. Both Ginsberg and Hobhouse espoused what might be termed an ethical version of social evolution, purportedly showing that moral development was sufficiently advanced to place harsh and selfish Darwinian struggles to one side. Their position did a great deal to influence the areas in which Gellner had to teach. For a little more than a decade he gave twenty-five lectures a year to undergraduates on ethics, running parallel for many years to Ginsberg's own course on social philosophy. His lectures concentrated on the 'main contribution of Greek thought to ethical theory. The problem of modern ethics. Moral sense, conscience and rational intuitionism. The empirical school. Rationalism and ethics'. A further ten more advanced lectures on the same topic for graduates considered Sidgwick, Plato, Aristotle, Butler, Hume, Kant, Mill, Green, and Hobhouse – with C. D. Broad's *Five Types of Ethical Theory* serving as a piece of essential reading for the course.[20] The fact that he taught ethics should not for a moment lead to the conclusion that he was in agreement with Ginsberg. Uncritical evolutionary optimism of this sort could only deal with the horrors of the twentieth century by ignoring them; it reified its own values rather than investigating the world. 'The Notes' record some of Gellner's feelings:

> From the amount of arrogance, hierarchy and confidence about, one would think the most transcendent creativity, the most daring break-throughs, were taking place. On examination, it turns out the only available theory is the woolly evolutionism, mild and progressive semi-naturalism . . .

---

20 In later years R. Hare's *The Language of Morals* and C. H. Waddington's *Science and Ethics* were also listed as key reading matter. There were slight changes in the lectures offered, such as five offered in 1959–60 dealing with Concepts and Society: 'Alternative general views of society and man's place in it will be discussed, with special reference to their methodological and ethical implications'.

A new subject, like a revolution, must advance or collapse, but Morris Ginsberg managed to endow sociology with the sclerosis of an old subject.

Old philosophy (e.g. Morris Ginsberg) naïve taking of concepts for granted, naïve looking at world from outside with concepts drawn from within it. Linguistic philosophy is better than that.

Facts and values scratching each others' backs, culminating in ecstasy, of 'correlated growth'.

Underestimates sharpness of break between science and 'rationality' which preceded it, and likewise between industrialism and preceding progress.

The World Spirit at last revealed itself unto itself, and truth stood bare. And lo and behold, the mouthpiece of this truth is unhonoured, and people go talking quite different stuff, taking no heed. At one level he notices this, at another not.

Morris Ginsberg never sees he is only studying his own concepts.

Ginsberg: like a soundtrack half an hour later than the film. The Enlightenment (plus nineteenth century evolutionism) came to him late, and thus had a freshness and a closed-completeness for him. He was not anti-empiricist, but there was not much need for finding out because 1) the main things were known, and 2) his notion of the scholar did not require specific understanding or control (the rabbi neither knows nor cares how the Poles till their fields).

But weighing in against this were the personal and intellectual attractions of his return to London. For one thing, he returned to the family home. For another, London allowed him to develop his climbing career on the European continent. He joined the LSE's Mountaineering Club and made many trips, usually to the Alps, in order to climb. An account of a three-week trip around Zermatt in August 1952 is in the Gellner Archive, perhaps written by Denis Greenald, an undergraduate at the LSE and later an educational psychologist in London.[21] The account makes it clear that

---

21   Denis Greenald was to marry Gwen Guntrip, whose father was the well-known psychoanalyst Harold Guntrip. Gellner knew Guntrip and his work is dealt with harshly in *The Psychoanalytic Movement: The Cunning of Unreason*, second edition, Oxford, 1993, pp. 165–6.

Gellner knew the area well, and it gives the impression that he was exceptionally fit – racing ahead on at least one occasion with an ice piton.

There was also much that was attractive about the LSE. The School
was utterly different in character from Oxford. It had little of the feel of a
finishing school for the upper classes, which lasted for so long at Britain's
oldest universities. The fact that a significant number of colleagues came
from Central Europe, many of them with Jewish backgrounds, made things
simpler socially – and there was none of the anti-Semitism that was still
found within the British establishment. The presence of his intellectual
confessor, John Hajnal, certainly mattered. Then there was genuine intellectual exchange. The school was relatively small: meetings were frequent,
at tea and at lunch, and there was significant knowledge of work being done
in fields outside one's own. In those years the LSE genuinely was a school
for social science. There was one negative feature of the LSE in Gellner's
view, namely the presence of the political theorist Michael Oakeshott, the
exception to the rule as, according to Gellner, the theorist of the traditional
upper classes. But this negative was, so to speak, positive, in that it forced
Gellner to develop the powerful critique of Oakeshott that is considered in
the next chapter. In contrast, two other LSE influences were unambiguously positive.

Gellner very much enjoyed the seminars of Isaac Schapera and Raymond
Firth, which he attended as soon as he arrived at the school, and appreciated a measure of participation in a lively and genuinely intellectual
community.[22] His interest was perhaps initiated and certainly encouraged
by his friend Paul Stirling, who was then also at LSE. Gellner was a natural
anthropologist, as previously noted, an outsider looking in, always curious
about local customs and very often amused by the idiosyncrasies of social
behaviour. Anthropology, however, had a firm base in social reality, and
contrasted utterly, as we shall see, with the abstraction of the philosophy in
which he had been trained. He always made a great deal of the seemingly
minor matter that anthropology benefited from sustained immersion in the
field. Even a moderately gifted student would be able to say something
interesting after such immersion. Certainly good descriptive fieldwork was
better than bad theory. The contrast with philosophy was very great; so too
was the contrast with social science in general. He liked to repeat Poincaré's
joke that natural scientists gathering together discuss results, whereas social
scientists argue over methods. Crucially, anthropology provided an appropriate method for the study of social life – which is to say, of course, that
its method was powerful *because* it had a proper sense of the nature of social

22   J. Davis, 'An Interview with Ernest Gellner', *Current Anthropology*, vol. 32, 1991, p. 66.

life. This view is evident in the acknowledgements of the book that made Gellner famous, *Words and Things*:

> I should also express my thanks to the members of the Social Anthropology Department at the L.S.E., who taught me how, without prejudice to its validity, one should see a set of related ideas and practices as a system of mutually supporting, and sometimes conflicting parts, and interpret it in terms of the services it performs and the conditions it requires in the social context of which it is a part.[23]

Exactly the same point is made a quarter-century later in the acknowledgements to *The Psychoanalytic Movement*.[24] We can see here the impact of Bronisław Malinowski, who had been the leading figure at the LSE, and whose influence was pervasive. Gellner was to write a great deal about the revolution in anthropology pioneered by Malinowski, though he probably learnt quite as much from Radcliffe-Brown's cementing of that revolution – the latter's distinction between structure and culture pervades Gellner's work, most notably that on nationalism. Perhaps the key element of this new style of social anthropology was, so to speak, that social life was a serious business: food production and power relations dictated much of social organization, and ideas are often but a codification of the concrete ways in which a society works. This approach was utterly different from that of James Frazer, which had been dominant prior to that and which was so much concerned with ideas rather than institutions.

The presence of Popper, who had been appointed to the School in 1945 and who enthused to John Watkins at this time about Gellner's brilliance, was just as significant. Here was someone who took science seriously, and tried to explain how it worked. Equally important was Popper's attempt to rethink liberalism, and Gellner later regretted that Popper did not continue to work in this area in his later years.[25] Nonetheless, there was some distance between the two. Gellner attended Popper's seminar, but always took great care never to become a member of his inner circle, disliking Popper's hostility to criticism and noting with some delight the

---

23 *Words and Things: A Critical Account of Linguistic Philosophy and a Study in Ideology*, London, 1959. The same acknowledgements declared that his 'greatest individual debt' was to John Hajnal.

24 *The Psychoanalytic Movement*, p. xxxii.

25 This is made especially clear in a letter reprinted in Jarvie and Pralong, *The Open Society after Fifty Years*, addressed to participants at a conference on Popper's work that Gellner planned in 1995 but did not survive to attend.

continuing Oedipal revolts by members of Popper's clique.[26] This led to a characteristically sardonic joke, much repeated at the school and often attributed to Gellner, that Popper's great book should have been titled of *The Open Society by One of Its Enemies.*[27]

There was another rather different intellectual benefit to his return to London. He was clearly still close to the wider community of Oxford philosophers by whom he had been educated. He re-sat the papers for the John Locke Prize in Mental Philosophy in 1950, and this time succeeded – again receiving a warm note from Ryle, who continued trying to correct Gellner's writing style while allowing him to publish reviews and articles in *Mind.*[28] In the early 1950s Gellner regularly presented papers at Oxford, and their style is similar to that of the Oxford philosophy of the time.[29] He corresponded with the dominant figures in that scene, including not just Ryle and Murdoch but also David Pears, Elizabeth Anscombe, J. O. Urmson, Isaiah Berlin, and Stuart Hampshire.[30] The young Gellner's status within the world of Oxford philosophy is apparent in several letters from Richard Hare, addressed in a familiar manner to 'Ernest', and habitually signed 'Dick'. Hare arranged accommodations for Gellner when he came to speak at Oxford, and expressed gratitude for a paper Gellner wrote on ethics which distinguished between universalizable and particular doctrines.[31] Reading Gellner's work on Kant and Kierkegaard led Hare to scrap what he had written on the subject and start afresh.[32] This was a significant compliment, an important acknowledgement of Gellner's intellect given Hare's leading position as an ethical thinker.

Nonetheless, Gellner was far from an insider. Giving the eighth annual E. H. Carr Memorial Lecture at Aberystwyth in November 1991 he recalled:

---

26   He enjoyed telling stories about these mutinies, and kept an occasional file of squabbles amongst the core of Popperians, now in the Gellner Archive.

27   There is no evidence that Gellner claimed the joke as his own.

28   Ryle to Gellner, 9 February 1952. Ryle's injunctions contained some excellent editorial advice, against the use of parentheses and italicization, together with characteristic Oxford prejudices against the use of footnotes, colloquialisms and the citing of one's own work.

29   Something of the flavour of the Oxbridge philosophical milieu in the 1940s and 1950s is captured in D. Edmonds and J. Edinow, *Wittgenstein's Poker: The Story of a Ten-Minute Argument between Two Great Philosophers*, London, 2001.

30   He claimed to have kept clear of John Austin at all times, finding his intellectual technique intimidating and question-begging (see 'Poker Player' in *The Devil in Modern Philosophy*, London, 1974).

31   'Ethics and Logic', *Proceedings of the Aristotelian Society*, vol. 55, 1955, reprinted in *The Devil in Modern Philosophy*.

32   Hare to Gellner, 12 May 1955. Hare's reply, 'Universalisability', was read on 6 June 1955, and published in *Proceedings of the Aristotelian Society*, vol. 55, 1955.

I was not terribly impressed by the conventional wisdom which was then taught [in philosophy, politics and economics] and rather eagerly embraced by my contemporaries, but I lacked the confidence to repudiate and reject it with emphasis, at any rate at once. But the uneasy state of mind this engendered did at least make me receptive to someone who did not display the same faults as did advocates of the then current fashions . . . E. H. Carr's mind . . . clearly was not guilty of that near-total insensitivity to the diversity of historical situations and contexts which otherwise prevailed in the academic world.[33]

A certain independence of mind was apparent from the start, evidenced by two reviews on existentialist authors.[34] The predominant attitude of Oxford philosophers towards existentialism was highly critical, but Gellner expressed measured sympathy for a doctrine centrally concerned with the feelings provoked by the living of life. A central theme of his later thought, eventually used as the title of a collection of essays, that modern cognition undermines moral certainty is already present in the characterization of the French Catholic existentialist philosopher Gabriel Marcel's view of life as a predicament rather than a spectacle. But what really mattered was the appearance of a powerful and interrelated series of articles outlining Gellner's discontent with the philosophical milieu in which he had been educated. Later in life Gellner insisted that he had written the four articles in question merely to gain tenure, with the dearth of publication in the following years partly explainable by summers spent climbing in Europe. This may be so, but it understates the originality of the pieces, most of which were included in the first collection of his essays.

'Use and Meaning' attacked in the boldest terms the linguistic philosophy then acquiring hegemonic status at Oxford.[35] The insistence by the later Wittgenstein that one should not seek to establish abstract meaning but rather to understand usage was utterly misleading. Language does often function in contextual terms, but Gellner held it to be absurd to see it in those terms exclusively. Language equally serves as a sort of proto-science, providing descriptions which may or may not be correct, that is,

---

33 'Nationalism and the International Order', in *Encounters with Nationalism,* Oxford, 1994, p. 21. Carr's *Nationalism and After* was the sole book on nationalism on the reading list for Gellner's first course on Social Philosophy at the Extra-Mural Department of the University of London (c. 1949–50).

34 'Review of G. Marcel, *Being and Having'*, *Mind*, vol. 59, 1950; and 'Review of C. Astrada, K. Bauch, et. al., Martin Heidegger's *Einfluss auf die Wissenschaften'*, *Philosophical Quarterly*, vol. 1, 1951.

35 'Use and Meaning', *Cambridge Journal*, vol. 4, 1951.

which may be falsified by evidence or through the systematic application of consistent standards. This was further stressed in 'Knowing How and Validity', in which Gellner took aim at Stephen Toulmin and, to a lesser extent, at Ryle.[36] Great skill can be exhibited in learning and manipulating the 'know-how' operative at any particular time, but this practical expertise does not establish scientific validity. 'False or self-contradictory rules of deductive inference may be constructed and people may acquire the skill of operating them and manufacturing fallacies and contradictions'.[37] Gellner also emphasized the inherent impossibility of applying the doctrine that one should replace the search for abstract meaning with a careful appreciation of a culture's customs. A hidden presupposition of this view is that there is a single and consistent set of meanings to be found. But for every language there are people who wish to 'correct' and 'improve' usage, that is, those who wish language to be usage-independent. To search for some simple and consistent use is akin to seeking a noble savage: bluntly, states of innocence are projections rather than realities.[38] Further, many belief systems are riddled with internal contradictions, making nonsense of the view that clarification of use will somehow resolve moral or social conflict. French Jansenists argued that the Pope rather than the Gallican Church should be obeyed – only to be instructed by the Pope to subordinate themselves to

---

36 'Knowing How and Validity', *Analysis*, vol. 12, 1951, reprinted in *The Devil in Modern Philosophy*.

37 Ibid., p. 98. This general attitude also underscored 'Maxims', which appeared in *Mind* in 1951, reprinted in *The Devil in Modern Philosophy*. The formal purpose of this article was to show the compatibility of Kant with Gilbert Ryle's *The Concept of Mind*. Even if one accepted Ryle's critical attack on 'the ghost in the machine', that is, the view that mental states were occurrences which caused actions, there remained room for a Kantian-inspired concern with maxims or rules of action. At a purely phenomenological level Gellner noted a difference between 'he hit him because he was angry' and 'the glass broke because it was brittle':

You can alter a person's anger by conveying information to him; but *talking to glass notoriously makes no difference* . . . Though it may be true that ideas and states of mind are not occurrences, it is extremely important to note those of their features which differentiate them from things such as that of brittleness. These features are: the fact that some of them are true or false and dependent on evidence, and that all of them can be verbally quoted by the agent as justifications of his action, and that events, i.e. actions, can be influenced by the presentation of evidence or arguments relevant to the ideas involved in the rule . . . The causal connexion between the noticing of evidence and action is part of what we mean by such psychological terms as 'conversion' and 'conviction' (*The Devil in Modern Philosophy*, p. 71).

38 'Use and Meaning', p. 760.

the latter; American communists were at one time told by their leaders to embrace capitalism. Gellner is here introducing a rich line of argument, leading to an analysis of the ways in which absurdity and contradiction block social and intellectual development. This argument gained salience in his work thereafter.

'Analysis and Ontology' was a superb paper, suggesting that background presuppositions can be found in any philosophy, and that it is only within pre-established terms that philosophy makes sense.[39] He noted that Logical Positivism depended upon the assumptions of classical empiricism, whilst linguistic philosophy's concentration on usage would not have been possible if Logical Positivism had not made the analysis of language seem *de rigueur*. We are faced, he suggested, with different worlds of ideas, none of them securely grounded.

Gellner's intellectual interests in the early 1950s are clearly stated in a letter of 27 June 1952, addressed to Professor Frederic Lane of the Rockefeller Foundation, outlining the research that he wished to undertake during his upcoming fellowship in the United States. 'I wish to do work in logic and ethics, and in their relation, on what may be described as the logic of ethics. To do this I want to improve my command of modern symbolic logic. In this field Professor [Willard Van Orman] Quine is one of the greatest contemporary authorities (if not the greatest), which is the reason for my preference for Harvard.' It also indicated tastes which opposed the prevailing orthodoxies of his Oxford training. Logic should be broadly understood, Gellner suggested, as 'relevant to semantics, communication theory and the methodology of the social sciences'. He noted that he was working on three papers in this area, two already given to postgraduate seminars at the LSE, concerning the analysis and classification of 'philosophies of history'; a discussion of a 'causal' model of language as a signalling system; and a critical discussion of certain doctrines in the methodology of social sciences which had been elaborated by Popper and by some of his disciples. He felt that this project was relevant for social science because of the applicability and necessity of ethical theory, and because of the need to investigate the ethical presuppositions of the social sciences. Gellner's intention was to look as far into the past as the seventeenth century in order to examine utilitarianism and Kantianism, and to relate these to questions of propaganda and control. The relationship between ethics and logic would be discussed in connection with 'rationalism' and 'irrationalism' in ethical theory.

After visiting Harvard in 1954, Ryle wrote to Gellner to tell him that

---

39 'Analysis and Ontology', *Philosophical Quarterly*, vol. 1, 1951.

he was remembered there.[40] Gellner had attended lectures and seminars given by Quine, whose work he greatly admired and with which he would engage two decades later.[41] He also had meetings with the philosopher Morton White, with the Russian linguist Roman Jakobson, who had passed most of the interwar years in Prague, and with Noam Chomsky, then a junior fellow at Harvard. Gellner impressed Norman Birnbaum, who had been educated there, with the depth of his anthropological decoding of Harvard politics.[42] The period in America afforded some pleasure: he very much enjoyed New England, particularly the ease with which one could leave Cambridge to ski in New Hampshire. Nonetheless, he did not feel comfortable in the United States. He found most of American academia to be far removed from reality. In philosophy this had not always been the case; he viewed pragmatism as exemplifying American life and admired the thought of William James. But thereafter the subject had become too academic. Philosophy departments worked on a zoo-like principle, whereby each university had to employ one philosopher representing each school of thought. Interestingly, this did not lead to a world of Popperian contention. Gellner explained:

> [D]iversity is but skin deep. The cars, houses, wives, divorces, and psychi-
> atrists of a Utah personalist do not differ from those of a New Hampshire
> Heideggerian or a North Dakota neo-Kantian, or even a Louisiana
> Austinian. The ideological differentiation, in formal philosophy, seems
> to mean nothing in the souls or life-styles of the philosophers, or indeed
> in the society which harbours and sustains them.[43]

Gellner was a European through and through. His genuinely multicultural background, for all its problems, meant that he found the United States to be homogeneous. But this did not, as we shall see, translate into a crass anti-Americanism.

These feelings were minor compared to the personal crisis that engulfed him at this time. According to John Hajnal, Gellner told him that he had attempted suicide, and that Carr-Saunders knew about this. Both friends were

---

40   Ryle to Gellner, 1 December 1954.
41   The Gellner Archive contains a file of papers on Quine, clearly maintained for many years.
42   Birnbaum joined the Department of Sociology at LSE whilst Gellner was at Harvard; they became close after his return.
43   This passage is drawn from a 1973 essay ('Reflections on Philosophy, Especially in America', in *The Devil in Modern Philosophy*, p. 37), but 'The Notes', written from the late 1950s, already expressed similar sentiments.

prone to depression, though they could not agree as to whether its cause could be explained rationally or not. The attempted suicide has not been confirmed, and other friends from this period are divided – some think it possible, others that it was very unlikely. But Gellner was clearly deeply troubled. In America he would take long bus journeys and hope that they would never end, for this would mean that he need make no decisions. The fundamental cause of this crisis was intellectual. Gellner felt great self-doubt due to the fact that most clever people in his field were fully convinced by views which he found to be wrong-headed. Was there something that he was missing?

Added to this was surely the fact that his career ambitions, which might be threatened by his opposition to passionately held orthodoxies, were powerfully reinforced by his desire to find his place in a new society. And this was not all. Apparently, his difficulties were related both to a failed love affair and to his self-assessment that he lacked sufficient talent to become a mathematical logician.[44] There is clear independent confirmation of a personal crisis. The LSE had granted him leave without pay for a full year from October 1952. The Rockefeller fellowship was ended from June 1953. Carr-Saunders did the honourable thing by his young, pre-tenure member of staff: Gellner was reinstated with full pay from 1 July 1953, two months before the period of unpaid leave was scheduled to end.[45] Further, the Gellner Archive contains a 10 November 1953 letter from Gardner C. Quarton, MD, Department of Neuropathology and of Psychiatry, Massachusetts General Hospital and Harvard Medical School, apparently replying to a message from Gellner which had expressed doubts about the quality of his own work. Quarton noted that it had been hard for them to talk because of Gellner's own interest in the foundations of psychiatry, an interest which Quarton shared. One can imagine their difficulties, presumably based on infinite epistemological regresses, and only regret that Quarton, unlike Jacques Lacan, the famous French analyst, failed to have his sessions recorded and transcribed. It is worth noting in this connection that Gellner applied to the London Institute of Psycho-Analysis a few months later for library privileges, very probably to gain background for fieldwork on psychoanalysis – a project which Raymond Firth dissuaded him from pursuing. Still, Quarton retained an interest in practical therapy and suggested that Gellner undergo psychoanalysis now that he had recovered from his depression. Finally, Gellner himself wrote to the Rockefeller Foundation in 1954 noting that it had been difficult to write because of his deep depression at the time.

---

44   Interview with John Hajnal, June 1998.
45   Carr-Saunders to Gellner, 8 July 1953.

The correspondence with the Rockefeller Foundation is of further interest. In general, he was very critical of the way in which fellows were treated. The stipend had been acceptable to him, and he felt that it would be good to have stipends for more scholars. But he noted that the stipend provided less money than was attached to an average junior university position, and was a far lesser sum than that received by people in comparable positions at American universities. This would have been all right if other conditions had been acceptable. But herein lay the problem: he was very much opposed to the 'the closeness, pedantry and intellectual level of the supervision of a Fellow's work'.

> I would not wish to argue that people academically working in philosophy or some parts of the social sciences are kinds of poets, to be pampered and left alone in the hope that the wind of inspiration will blow their way sometime; but such a view would certainly be far nearer the truth than the conception of academic work underlying much of American academic practice and some of the procedure of the Rockefeller Foundation.[46]

This letter was written just a month after the death of his mother, and perhaps he was distracted by this. In any case, he wrote back in November apologizing for his lack of gratitude. 'I also feel that I should have expressed thanks for the patience shown towards me during the latter part of my illness when indecision may have made me very hard to deal with'.[47]

Family, Friends, Health

One indication of the difficulties that Gellner faced was the fact – extraordinary in light of the productivity of his later career – that he published virtually nothing for four years after the first flurry of articles in 1951. Things changed rapidly thereafter, for recovery proved to be swift and permanent. The full crystallization of Gellner's thought occurred in the second half of the 1950s, together with the establishment of a self-confidence that allowed him to express his views, which were often in opposition to allies as well as to enemies. At an intellectual level, the importance of the Harvard period was simply the lesson that the Oxford style of philosophy was only one option amongst others, and therefore it was as misguided as he had

---

46   Gellner's report on his fellowship, sent in a letter dated 26 October 1954.
47   Gellner to Miss Elderton, 22 November 1954.

suspected. Still, he could not have taken the path that he did without the stability of a healthy emotional life.

A fundamental factor in his recovery was simply being back in surround-ings that made him feel comfortable. His time in the United States had been marked by continual insomnia; apparently this ceased to be a problem the very first night he returned home. But another, even more impor-tant change was involved. His tutor, Tommy Balogh, apparently claimed that Gellner would never manage significant intellectual work until he was settled emotionally. He was lucky enough to find this peacefulness in the person of Susan Ryan. Her father came from a Protestant Scottish-Irish background, but culturally he was a perfect English gentleman, educated at King's School in Canterbury. He would tell his son-in-law that, as a foreigner, he might not realise that England was a 'snob country', and urged him to send his own son to a boarding school – advice which Gellner did not follow. Susan's mother was from an Anglicized Scottish family, the Impeys, with a tradition of service in India.[48] Susan herself clearly had a taste for intellectual life, knowing the LSE statisticians George Morton and Jim Durbin well enough to go on skiing holidays with them. Indeed, it was while skiing with them in the Silvretta mountains in 1952–3 that she first heard about their friend Ernest. The following year, Morton dropped out of a planned holiday and suggested that Gellner take his place. Gellner had been to the Alps with his sister in the winter holidays of 1953–4, supposedly in order to give her a rest – a notion provoking laughter amongst Gellner's friends given that at that time his company was potentially exhausting, not least due to his habit of walking very rapidly. An Easter trip to Zermatt was planned, and led to a meeting of Durbin, Morton, Gellner and Susan in a Lyons Tea House in London in late 1953. The ski trip took place as intended, with Susan then planning to teach English and work as an au pair for a family in Athens. Just as these arrangements fell through, she received a letter from Gellner asking her to join him in Morocco in the summer of 1954. He had taken a crucial decision. He had turned down the opportunity to go with the LSE Mountaineering club to the Himalayas in order to perform serious anthropological fieldwork in the Atlas mountains. Hence his first period of real fieldwork was undertaken that summer, supported financially in part by his father. On 30 July 1954 he wrote to his mother, announcing that he and Susan intended to get married when they returned, and possibly even sooner: 'main reason (only reason really) for this hurry being that it will be more convenient from the viewpoint of working at the Moroccan

---

48   Elijah Impey was impeached with Warren Hastings. The family still has an Indian photograph album.

material if we live together right away'. They wrote to her parents, but he asked his mother to telephone them as well, given that the post was unreliable. A further point was made:

> There is no particular secret about all this but there is one thing I don't want any misunderstanding about – though Susan is doing a lot of useful work here for me, she has come here at her own expense and I am NOT misappropriating research funds for her.

The letter continued by saying that they had walked through the whole region, sometimes sleeping in the tents of nomads – Gellner much disliking the way in which goats trampled on him in the night. They had eaten with a local notable, been entertained by dancing girls, and Gellner had forced himself into eating a little chicken after refusing mutton. He had decided to make Zawiya Ahansal the site for future fieldwork. A postscript requested a copy of his divorce certificate. Presumably this was forthcoming, because the marriage took place in Gibraltar on their way home.

The newly married couple soon made their home in the Ryan family house on Langside Avenue, near Putney in South London. Between 1954 and 1962 they had a separate apartment in the house, and Gellner retained a room in the attic for a further six years which he sometimes stayed in after they had moved away from the city. Susan's parents were welcoming, and perhaps relieved that the nuptials had already taken place since they had just hosted the large wedding of Susan's sister to William Trevor, the Anglo-Irish writer. Still, a large reception was held in a London hotel, and attended by several of Gellner's colleagues. Less happily, life in Makepeace Avenue changed dramatically in 1954, when Anna Gellner died of a heart attack – during perhaps the third visit between Susan and her new mother-in-law.

Anna had taught her daughter-in-law how to cook *wiener schnitzel* (one of the only forms of meat that Gellner would eat, precisely because it was so disguised), and Susan remembers her as a woman with an easy social manner and obvious natural intelligence, especially in her ability to pick up languages. But most of Susan's knowledge about Anna Gellner came from her husband. He told her that his mother once asked for 'pity' on account of her terrible son, something he much resented. Indeed, there was a good deal of bitterness within the family. Ernest had wanted a memorial for his mother, but one was arranged by his sister and father without his knowledge whilst he was in Morocco. Only recently did Susan Gellner discover that Anna's ashes were buried in the Liberal Jewish Synagogue in Dollis Hill. When Susan Gellner told George Morton, who had a Bohemian

Jewish background equivalent to Gellner's, that the family seemed to be riddled with tensions, he laughed and told her simply that it was a normal Jewish family.

Apparently when Ernest first met Susan – they were alone, in Great Portland Street, perhaps on the way to the Lyons' Tea House – he immediately thought that she would be a good wife. Certainly, this marriage was very different from his first, not least in allowing for a measure of entry into his adopted society. But the union was clearly based on love. This was particularly apparent to Youssef Hazmaoui, the Berber interpreter and guide who often worked with Gellner in Morocco.[49] On one occasion in the summer of 1954 or 1955 when the Gellners went to Morocco together, a trip was arranged to purchase supplies. On the way back Susan Gellner said she preferred to cross the river directly, rather than via the bridge. Gellner carried her, but dropped her halfway across, losing all their produce. They would climb and swim on the weekends, and explored a great deal. Gellner provided some characteristic details late in life when asked to provide information for a biography of the explorer Wilfred Thesiger, who had visited Gellner and Susan in Morocco in 1955. They went on several climbs, because the unstable political situation meant that travel was not possible. For some climbs the group consisted of Gellner, Thesiger and Thesiger's companion Colin Pennycuik; on others they were joined by Susan. One such climb, in which Hazmaoui also participated, took them up a gorge near Taria, a feat held by local belief to be impossible. In fact it was relatively easy, and at one wet spot everyone took off their clothes. Thesiger 'was too gentlemanly to take . . . a photograph of Susan, to the regret of his audience when he gave a slide show on his return'.[50] On this outing Thesiger probably saved their lives, correctly warning that a dangerous flash flood was imminent. They spent at least

---

49 Hazmaoui was interviewed by Brendan O'Leary in Marrakesh on 22 December 2005. He had started life as a shepherd, before becoming a guide and interpreter for a series of anthropologists of Morocco including Vincent Crapanzo, Ross Dunn and David Hart.One revelation, made without prompting and to O'Leary's surprise, was that Gellner became fluent in Berber. O'Leary queried this because he recalled another anthropologist's claim that Gellner could not speak the language and remembered Edward Said's assertion (discussed below, in chapter 11) that he could not speak any local language. Youssef firmly insisted that, as a Berber, he knew when someone could speak the language. David Gellner bears witness to his father's proficiency in Berber, having been present when his father had a conversation in the local tongue with a boy in Algeria (despite the difference in Berber dialects). Hazmaoui consistently stressed the intelligence of Gellner, and stated on several occasions that he missed him a great deal. Gellner was apparently appreciated during his visits to the Atlas mountains, always prepared to tell amusing stories.

50 Gellner to Asher, 9 January 1993. C. M. Asher, *Thesiger: A Biography*, London, 1994.

one night caught in a cave in such intense cold that Hazmaoui feared for their health. In general, Hazmaoui stressed how much fun the Gellners' visits were for him and other villagers in the High Atlas – the people of Zawiya Ahansal, for example, were amazed by Ernest's regular climbing exercises, namely abseiling from the window of the house in which he was staying.[51] When *Saints of the Atlas* appeared it was dedicated to Susan. The 'Acknowledgements' noted that 'during the crucial field trips which she joined, she did invaluable work as research assistant, secretary, nurse, cook, psychotherapist and PRO: in the words of my application for research funds, she performed services which, if purchased locally, might have been more expensive and less satisfactory'.[52]

The Gellner couple's sense of fun clearly carried over into a very active social life. In London they gave parties, and were friendly with Ralph Miliband, Raphael Samuel, Charles Taylor, Stuart Hall and Julius Gould, and rather more distantly with Anthony Crosland. Many dinners were held at Bertorelli's, an Italian restaurant in Soho. Several of these were centred on Claude Bourdet, a thinker of the non–Marxist left deeply opposed to French policy in Algeria, whom the Gellners would collect from Heathrow airport usingt the van they had acquired for fieldwork. Gellner himself contributed little to small talk, being both shy and occasionally so lost in his own thoughts as to be almost completely taciturn, but very much liked having friends and family around him. He noted to more than one person his dream of always being surrounded in this way, just as long as people did not talk to him too much. One way he had of dealing with this personality quirk, then and later, was to walk around a party endlessly topping up people's glasses. Socializing of all sorts continued throughout his life, not least in the two decades that he lived in Hampshire, in his own estimation the happiest years of his life.

The character of their life changed with the birth of their children, David, Sarah, Deborah and Benjamin, between 1957 and 1963. The Gellners purchased a house in the country, intending at first to go there for weekends and holidays. But the move became permanent from 1962 for many reasons, including the fear that drugs were entering London schools. So the children were raised in 'Old Litten Cottage' in Hampshire. It was

---

51   In 1956 Gellner was still climbing, in New Hampshire in the United States. His report to the Mountaineering Club made much of his limited capacities, but he was critical of the extensive American use of pegs and pitons ('The Brown Spot: A Letter from America, 1956', reprinted in the *LSE Fiftieth Anniversary Booklet*). But his climbing activities, which he loved so very much, would soon come to an end as a result of the drastic decline in his health that will be discussed below.

52   *Saints of the Atlas*, London, 1969, p. xiv.

here that some of his most substantial work was accomplished. Deborah has provided a nuanced sketch of how it seemed to his children:

There was no public transport, no shops, not even a village. An unlikely place, perhaps, for an urban central European Jew to put down roots. Yet he was proud of living there, and happy to be away from cultural and intellectual centres. After moving away, to Cambridge in 1984, he loved to reminisce about those 'twenty golden years' when he had everything – happily married, four children living in a beautiful place, and sons interested in football. The house itself, a small and somewhat cramped cottage onto which extensions were built, provoked deep and passionate feelings of loyalty in him . . . he enjoyed playing host in it, and showing it off . . . I recall my mother cooking, single-handed, lasagna or moussaka, for 12 or 15, the pre-lunch drinks and slightly awkward small talk, and the unlimited supply of red wine thereafter.

The true situation was, in fact, that we lived there, whilst he only did part-time. His work, which was his life, took him constantly to London and abroad. Consequently, I used to argue with him about his (as I saw it) self-indulgent and nostalgic picture, and his claim that those were the years of his greatest contentment. However, now I am not so sure. Possibly, the house where one's children grow up is, for many people, the most significant place one lives in. And probably all the more so if one's own childhood is, as his was, unhappy. He would say that he wanted to give us the happy childhood and stable upbringing that he never had. It's not realistic to expect children to be grateful. He certainly was not an involved, modern, nappy-changing father, and we were not slow to criticize. However, as the years have passed since those times, it has become impossible not to be aware of his commitment to us, his generosity, and the depth of his concern as to how we are doing in our lives. And that is probably why they *were* the twenty golden years for him; we were happy there, and therefore he was successful in his aim.

There is an interesting postscript to this description of his obsession with Old Litten Cottage . . . It was only years later when he was looking again at the work of the Czech artist Lada (whose illustrations in children's and other books had long been familiar to him) that he realized that idealized versions of Old Litten Cottage appeared in so many of Lada's sentimental paintings of Bohemian village life.'[53]

---

53   Deborah Gellner, 'Life at Old Litten Cottage', *Cambridge Anthropology*, vol. 19, 1996–7, pp. 100–1.

The family was particularly friendly with that of an attractive local doctor, Robin Ilbert, dubbed by Gellner the 'Kennedy' of the area. Ilbert's memoir also notes the passage just quoted, and confirms the picture of continual entertainment. Ilbert notes Gellner's complete freedom from the observance of social niceties. On one occasion, tired after a hot journey from London, Gellner left the dinner table with the water jug, went into the garden, poured it over his head, and returned refreshed. The memoir is as accurate on another facet of Gellner's personality, namely his extreme distaste for being worshipped or excessively admired. When one ponderous admirer asked him what the Berbers were *really* like he simply said, 'Hmph. Randy lot'.[54] One final point deserves underscoring. Gellner very much appreciated friends who were not academics, including several of his secretaries: Gaye Woolven (at the LSE and later in Prague), Mary McGinley (in Cambridge) and Vlasta Hirtová (in Prague). Further, his utter intellectuality was balanced by his physicality and appreciation of nature. He clearly felt that academics sometimes lacked much sense of reality, lost in theories that could only be sustained in the study.

But all was not perfect at the country home. The children did not always enjoy the steady stream of visitors, though they were more likely to accept them if they could be forced into playing soccer. The girls apparently felt sometimes that their father was particularly concerned with the careers of David and Ben, both exceptionally bright – David was able to beat his father at chess. What the girls perceived as favouritism was probably in fact his awkwardness with ordinary family affection, and a certain lack of interest in their world. Ironically, he felt himself to be excluded from their lives. Then there were tensions simply because Ernest, secure in his own powers of reasoning, did not always deign to argue – and was anyway rather good at winning arguments when they did take place, sometimes with a cutting phrase. His work clearly had primacy, with few holidays taken during their childhood – their summers were often spent at camps, as Ernest's were when he was a child.

We gain another insight by considering the dictum from Santayana that Gellner used as a legend to his own book on nationalism: 'Our nationality is like our relations to women: too implicated in our moral nature to be changed honourably, and too accidental to be worth changing'. This very accurately sums up a part of his emotional life. He seems to have been attracted to other women on more than one occasion. He delighted in flirting, and in making slightly outrageous comments to women he knew

---

54   R. Ilbert, *An Autobiography*, privately printed, pp. 274–77.

well.[55] He took considerable interest in, and was greatly amused by, other people's imbroglios, not least those that concerned his LSE colleague, the Hungarian philosopher Imre Lakatos. These attitudes clearly owed a good deal to his Jewish and Central European background. So too did his sense of irony. When someone made a comment about a gay couple, he casually remarked that sexual preferences mattered not at all for him as sex was ridiculous whichever way one did it. And sex was discussed relatively openly. He remarked to his son David that he had no trouble with sex itself, more with finding people to do it with. He went on to claim that he had never had his fair share, regretting this on the entirely unromantic grounds that only sex and chess could stop him from thinking about work. But there were strict limits to his behaviour. He understood fully that he needed the rock of personal stability, compounded by family and organizational backing, that allowed him to work. In the early 1980s his wife fainted at a theatre; he was visibly shaken by the thought that this might be serious – he had once said that he forbade her to die before him, as he would be helpless without her. The sentimental bond was reciprocal. When I visited Old Litten Cottage at about this time, I was shown a portrait of Gellner by John Bratby. It seemed marvellous to me, a whirling vortex around Gellner's face capturing some of the passion which clearly motivated him. Susan Gellner did not like it. It did not reflect his endless ability to make her laugh. Many of the people interviewed for this book, notably Steven Lukes, felt that the couple's relationship was particularly strong.[56]

This is the appropriate place to describe the health difficulties that plagued Gellner for much of his life. He never let his children know the agonies that he suffered. He never complained about it, and never used his chronic illness as an excuse. The seriousness of his problems can be observed simply by noting the change in his height: in the course of the late 1950s and 1960s he lost more than four inches from an original height of nearly five feet and ten inches. This was the result of osteoporosis, a lack of bone calcium that in his case caused a shrinking of the bones. It may well be that particular difficulty came from the fact that the bones did not all shrink at the same speed. The history of his illness can be briefly told. As early as the mid-1950s he suffered from periodic severe pain in his ankles, and this had meant missed days on the slopes during skiing holidays. Various remedies were tried, including massage, but no real diagnosis was made. The severity of the situation cannot be exaggerated. He travelled with his wife to Tunisia

---

55   Steven Lukes (interviewed by Brendan O'Leary, 27 February 2001) stressed the playful nature of this behaviour.
56   Ibid.

in 1962 only to discover that he was unable to walk once he was there. It
was at this time that he began to use a cane. He suffered broken bones with
some frequency, most notably a leg when skiing shortly after arriving in
the United States at the start of his 1968 sabbatical. Worse still were attacks
that left him paralysed in a chair, struggling hard to breathe. Obviously,
all this changed his life completely, though he never fully admitted it. He
continued to walk in the mountains when he could, purchased a house in
Italy that could only be accessed by a very strenuous walk, and for many
years replaced climbing with sailing, keeping a boat in Chichester Harbour
for many of the years that he lived in Hampshire.

He must have felt that an early death was possible, and said in later
years that he worked fast because his eye was on the clock. The move to
Hampshire brought a certain measure of salvation. Robin Ilbert took an
interest in Gellner's case and had him referred to various specialists. But it was
Ruth Glass, the wife of his senior colleague David Glass (celebrated for his
pioneering work in social mobility), whose help led to the breakthrough. She
encouraged him to go to University College Hospital to see a physiotherapist,
who rapidly realized the seriousness of the case and sent him to Professor
Charles Dent, the world expert in osteoporosis at that time. Gellner's condition was fully stabilized only in the late 1960s, after being hospitalized for
a month in London so that every trace of every substance and liquid that
entered and left his body could be examined. While in hospital he once read
through his medical notes with a student and was amused to discover the
facile way in which several previous consultants, unable to come up with a
diagnosis, had considered his pain to be merely psychosomatic. He would
spend the rest of his days living with pills, largely containing calcium that
arrested further bone loss. But the pain remained, although this too was partly
eased by a double hip replacement in the mid-1980s. Still, in the early 1990s,
when sharing a room with Jiří Musil, he paced all night because of the pain.

Saints of the Atlas

Gellner registered for doctoral work in anthropology under the supervision
of Raymond Firth shortly after his return from America.[57] The decision

---

57 Admission to the programme was given in 1954, but it was backdated to 1953.
Paul Stirling soon became a co-supervisor. Stirling was modest about his impact on a man
whom he admired and 'whom he may have slightly influenced in the 1950s'. His interest
in social anthropology long preceded Gellner's. As he put it: 'In the late summer of 1947, I
consciously decided not to try to become an academic philosopher, but instead to join social
anthropology. I never even dreamt, like Ernest, of doing both.' Paul Stirling, 'Ménage à
Trois on a Raft', *Cambridge Anthropology*, vol. 19, 1996–7, pp. 59–69.

to work in Morocco proved to be a turning point in his life. The choice of Morocco had a good deal to do with his love of mountains. But there were other reasons as well. A predecessor at the LSE, the Finnish anthropologist Edward Westermarck, had also worked there.[58] Further, he felt that the creation of Israel would set up 'a dramatic, tragic, perhaps insoluble confrontation with the Muslim world' that needed to be understood.[59] And he also insisted that the choice was altogether more personal:

> In the Prague of my youth, I was indeed aware of the difference between the people I knew best and could communicate with easily – urban, cerebral, mobile, rootless and uneasy intellectuals – and ideal man as conceived by the populist romanticism which was dominant in literature, art, even politics and philosophy. This confrontation was far stronger and sharper in the lands of Habsburg after-taste than it was in England, and it culminated in Nazism. But it stayed with me and played a major part in the decision to do field work, and the decision concerning where to do it. When I first saw Berber villages of the central Atlas, each building clinging to the next, the style wholly homogeneous, the totality crying out that this was a *Gemeinschaft*, I knew at once that I wanted desperately to know, as far as an outsider ever could, what it was like *inside*. I knew I had the motivation to undergo whatever hardships the inquiry would bring.[60]

There are very early descriptions of the work he wished to undertake, written even before his first visit. They describe his desire to work not just with the Berbers in the mountains but also with those who had become sedentarized in the plains, possibly by studying a small village community. This suggests that his initial desire was to contribute to the sociology of development in the broadest terms. The failure to do so probably reflects both his underestimation of the time commitment that such comparative work would have demanded, and the intensity of his fascination with the High Atlas. In any case, between 1953 and 1961 he made seven extended trips as part of his doctoral research (Christmas 1953–4, summer 1954,

---

58 Westermarck's key works are *Marriage Ceremonies in Morocco*, London, 1914; *Moorish Conceptions of Holiness, Baraka*, Helsinki, 1916; and *Ritual and Belief in Morocco*, London, 1926. Gellner's view of Westermarck's status is noted below, in chapter 11.

59 Davis, 'An Interview with Ernest Gellner', p. 66. John Hajnal suggested in an interview in June 1998 that this was a later rationalization. If this is so, the rationalization at least came many years before this interview.

60 'Reply to Critics', in J. A. Hall and I. C. Jarvie (eds), *The Social Philosophy of Ernest Gellner*, Amsterdam, 1996, pp. 679–80.

Easter–summer 1955, summer 1956, Christmas 1957–8, summer 1959 and Easter 1961).[61] The second and third trips seem to have been the most important: an untitled paper, probably given to the LSE Department of Anthropology seminar in the academic year 1956–7, contains many of the findings that would characterize *Saints of the Atlas* a dozen years later.[62] The fieldwork was extremely successful, leading first to a doctorate in 1961, and then to the publication of *Saints of the Atlas*, a classic of British social anthropology.[63] The boxes of field notes in the Gellner Archive at LSE attest to the depth and rigour of the research.[64] His understanding of Islam became a central pillar of his thought, and insights from the Muslim world affected his philosophy of social science as well as his views on nationalism and the pattern of the past. The immediate task here is to describe the fieldwork, leaving until later, in chapter nine, an assessment of both the fieldwork and the general sociology of Islam to which it so greatly contributed.

The baselines for Moroccan history can be identified in terms of the interplay between different ecological zones. The fundamental contrast is that between the *Bled al-makhzhen* and the *Bled al-siba*, that is, between the settled, governed city life of the plains and coast on the one hand, and the stateless situation of the tribes of the mountains on the other hand.[65] Gellner insisted against the obvious popular view, perpetuated by French

---

61   'Notes on Method', *Saints of the Atlas*, p. 303.

62   The paper was given as part of a series dealing with social control. It opens with interesting thoughts on informality and formality, suggesting counterintuitively that rule-bound organizations may be subject to informal control and informal organizations to formal controls.

63   'Organization and Role of a Berber Zawiya', PhD Thesis, London University, 1961. *Saints of the Atlas* appeared in French, Editions Bouchene, Paris, 2003, with a superb introduction by Gianni Albergoni.

64   The notebooks themselves are hard to read, but their subject matter can be spelled out. They concentrate on legal struggles, local legends, kinship, the precise wording of such rituals as the collective oath, visits to varied saintly centres and interviews with particular individuals. Some incidents in the notebooks were also recorded by his research assistant. Further, a large cache of letters in the Gellner Archive from the American anthropologist of Morocco David Hart give a vivid account of the general conditions of fieldwork in the late 1950s. Hart employed the same research assistant, Youssef Hazmaoui, and checked a very large number of ethnographic details for Gellner; the few surviving letters of Gellner to Hart show him both supplying detailed information and discussing rationales for specific theoretical positions.

65   Gellner notes (*Saints of the Atlas*, pp. 3–4) that a model stressing three circles – an inner core of the city guarded by watch dogs; a *contado* of sheep, that is, of sedentarized tribes subject to taxation; and a periphery of tribal wolves – is in fact more accurate. Nonetheless, emphasis is always on the basic opposition, on the grounds that the 'sheep' lack agency within the social formation as a whole.

colonial rule, that the tribes live in a condition of anarchy. To the contrary, a measure of order and trust prevails, the mechanics of which are at the centre of Gellner's study. Equally, there is no truth to the notion that these tribesmen are independent: they depend on cities, both to sell their produce and to purchase goods that their pastoral existence makes it impossible for them to produce for themselves. This last point is one of the central insights of *The Muqaddimah* of the late-fourteenth-century diplomat-scholar Ibn Khaldun. Gellner had discovered his work whilst working on his doctorate, and it became ever more important for him.[66] He pays immediate attention in *Saints of the Atlas* to the tragic contrast drawn by Ibn Khaldun between civilization and social cohesion, according to which the solidarity and trust created by the harsh conditions of pastoral life stand utterly opposed to the selfish asociality of urban life. This forms the basis of Ibn Khaldun's theory of the tribal circulation of elites, according to which a tribe can provide government representatives for the city for only the three genera-tions during which tribal solidarity endures in the face of urban influences.

Though Gellner was interested in the way that Morocco managed its government after independence in 1956, his own study concerned the anthropology of religion. The 'great tradition' of Muslim society was seen in the religious style of the city, represented by learned *ulama*, who stressed scripturalism (and so literacy), puritanism, strict monotheism, egalitarianism, and the absence of mediation through ritual in the relations between God and man. Gellner suggested a Weberian inner coherence to this social world. Townspeople are proto-puritan: they are literate, and prefer a religion of the book which underscores their natural identity. In contrast, the 'little' or 'folk' tradition of Muslims outside the cities depended much more upon the vagaries of nature. In this social world, rituals abound; monotheism is known but adulterated, not least by nature worship; and frequent recourse is shown to living saints possessed of holiness, making this form of Islam hierarchical rather than egalitarian. It was this latter world which Gellner

---

66   He was discouraged from making use of Ibn Khaldun when undertaking his doctoral research, on the ground that this was exactly the sort of speculation about origins that the Malinowskian revolution had attacked ('Origins of Society', in his *Anthropology and Politics: Revolutions in the Sacred Grove*, Oxford, 1995, p. 27). But the great Muslim scholar makes an early appearance in *Saints of the Atlas*, and later, when combined with the religious sociology of David Hume, stands at the centre of the general theory of Islam. Gellner reviewed a number of books about Ibn Khaldun, and made much of the publication of Ibn Khaldun's report of his encounter with Tamerlane in 1401 ('Talking with Tamerlane', *Times Literary Supplement*, 19 September 1980). He hoped that the report on North Africa that Ibn Khaldun wrote for Tamerlane might yet be found, and longed for a Shavian treatment of the meeting between conqueror and scholar.

chose to study. He felt that he was engaging in a situation utterly opposite to that of the European tradition. The puritans in Islam occupy centre stage, those, in Gellner's words, addicted to ritual occupied the margins; in contrast, the puritans of Europe objected to the hagiography and moral corruption enshrined at the heart of the main tradition. His focus on this contrast never led Gellner to ignore the obvious complexities. For one thing, he always paid attention to the mystical, intensely ritualistic tradition of urban sufism.[67] For another, Ibn Khaldun's views on the circulation of elites, which Gellner so emphatically endorsed, depended upon occasional bursts of puritanism among tribesmen.

The political and intellectual context within which Gellner undertook his study must be appreciated. The tribesmen of the Atlas are Berber, whilst the inhabitants of the plains are Arab. Berber was an oral rather than a written language when Gellner was in the field, lending the local social hierarchy a curious resemblance to that of early-nineteenth-century Austria: in both cases social mobility was associated with the adoption of the language and culture of the more advanced group. The Berbers, despite numbering perhaps five million, lacked a sense of national identity in the early 1950s, thereby demonstrating that not every ethnicity becomes a nation.[68] But nationalism was certainly present in the country. The French established a protectorate in 1912, and were finally able to subdue the tribes in 1933. They did so either by making use of local 'big men', or caïds, or by sending their own administrators into the mountains.[69] But the promulga-tion of the *Dahir Berbère* in 1930 meant that tribal custom was, with certain exceptions, to be respected.[70] This decree triggered Moroccan nationalism. It was interpreted as an attempt to divide and rule, and perhaps as a first move to convert the Berbers from Islam.[71] Furthermore, the support of the great *caïds* was seen as likely to ensure backwardness through the creation of a feudal class.[72] Nationalist indignation led to independence, with the

---

67   'Sanctity, Puritanism, Secularisation and Nationalism in North Africa', first published in 1965 and then reprinted in *Muslim Society*, Cambridge, 1981, and 'Flux and Reflux in the Faith of Men' (written some fifteen years later and the central essay of *Muslim Society*), pp. 48–51.

68   'Berbers of Morocco', *Quarterly Review*, vol. 294, 1956, p. 218.

69   Gellner spent a good deal of time in Marrakesh, and his review of G. Maxwell's *Lords of the Atlas*, London, 1966, in *Middle Eastern Studies*, vol. 6, 1970, reveals substantial knowledge of the Glawa of Marrakesh.

70   Blood feuds and slavery were exceptions (*Saints of the Atlas*, p. 14).

71   *Saints of the Atlas*, p. 19.

72   'Morocco', in C. Legum (ed.), *Africa*, London, 1961, p. 35. French Marxists also interpreted local big men in terms of feudalism. Gellner went to considerable lengths, largely through citing the research of Robert Montagne, to demonstrate that this appellation was

support of workers in the towns. Interestingly, the colonial power lost control of the areas that states had historically ruled successfully; in contrast, the tribes were at last manageable, and many supported the French until it was obvious that the Protectorate was coming to an end.

Gellner learnt a great deal from the local theorists of nationalism. 'The Struggle for Morocco's Past' presents two such theories. On the one hand, ben 'Abdallah's *Les Grands courants de la civilisation du Maghrib* was representative of the complex emotions felt by intellectuals in developing states as a result of contact with Western power. This led at once to an insistence on the achievements of local culture, together with an uneasy awareness that reforms were needed. In fact, ben 'Abdallah suggested that things were about to change during the constitutional crisis of 1908, implying that the seeds of progress were present locally. A somewhat similar point is made by Lahbabi's *Le Gouvernement marocain à l'aube du XXe siècle*, although here the analysis is markedly leftist in character. Tribal dissidence was interpreted as a form of proto-democracy by means of emphasizing the doctrine of consent. Once again the kernels of development were held to be present locally. Gellner noted that 'emergent countries have a particular need of guiding historical ideologies', but this did not for a moment mean that he felt that either of these views contained much good sociology.[73] Rather they were myths, charters for development. This was perhaps especially clear in the case of Mehdi Ben Barka, the leftist political leader whom he had met in Paris and who provided a preface for Lahbabi's volume. Ben Barka was a typical product of the city, who had accordingly been much offended by the scenes of rural 'licentiousness' he had observed when held as a prisoner of the French amongst the Ait Hdiddu.[74] Admiration for the theory of consent did not mean that tribes would have been left to themselves – if Ben Barka had come to power, that is, rather than being assassinated in Paris by the security services of independent Morocco.[75]

What mattered to Gellner much more for his actual fieldwork were the ideas of French scholars. The most prominent such scholars had occupied a role utterly different from that of their British counterparts, as active administrators for the French state. Gellner took care to obtain a report of a Capitaine Ithier on his own fieldwork site, and later visited this soldier when the captain had retired. But two other figures were of greater importance.

---

mistaken. On this see 'The Sociology of Robert Montagne 1893–1954', in *Muslim Society*, especially pp. 187–8.

73 'The Struggle for Morocco's Past', *Middle East Journal*, vol. 15, 1961, p. 89.

74 Gellner recounts this story in a review of Wolfgang Kraus's later study of this tribe (*Social Anthropology*, vol. 1, 1993, p. 163).

75 'Independence in the Central High Atlas', *Middle East Journal*, vol. 11, 1963, p. 249.

Robert Montagne knew Morocco as a naval intelligence officer, in which capacity he produced *Les Berbères et La Makhzen au Sud du Maroc: Essai sur la transformation politique des Berbères sédentaires (groupe Chleuh)*, a book Gellner considered a classic of social science.[76] Montagne argued that there was a pattern of oscillation between rule by great *caïds* and a balance of power system amongst egalitarian tribes – two poles which, not surprisingly, were mirrored in the two approaches of the French to the Berbers. Gellner accepted the theory of oscillation, and endorsed Montagne's view that the *caïds* were not feudal. He considered his own fieldwork to be the amplification of a casual observation by Montagne himself, namely that rule by saints created stability, thereby avoiding the oscillation to which tribes were otherwise doomed. Nonetheless, Montagne was mistaken in one crucial respect. Montagne had explained the relative stability at the tribal end of the spectrum in terms of what Gellner dubbed 'chequerboard' politics, that is, the balance that resulted from each tribe possessing a segment of land, a *leff* or moiety, in a series of valleys comprising a larger territorial unit. Gellner was so impressed that he went into the field in search of such moieties.[77] He rapidly changed his mind.[78] Gellner discovered that a respectable measure of order characterized social life within the squares on the chequerboard just as much as between them. He was able to explain this order once he had discovered the theory of segmentation present in the anthropological studies of Edward Evans-Pritchard, both amongst the Nuer of the upper Nile and the Sanusi of Cyrenaica.[79]

The second figure was Jacques Berque, whom Gellner came to know well, even though he was fifteen years older.[80] Berque had been born of

---

76   Paris, 1930. This book also introduced Gellner to Émile Masqueray's *Formation des cités chez les populations sédentaires de l'Algérie: Kabyles du djurjura, chaouïa de l'aouras, beni mezab*, Paris, 1886, but it was only later that Gellner worked out the intellectual provenance of French North African studies. Gellner began to correspond with Montagne, but the latter's death in 1954 meant that they never met.

77   'Reply to Critics', pp. 642, 645. One of his supervisors, Paul Stirling, informed Wolfgang Kraus in 1996 that Gellner initially had no idea of the relevance of Evans-Pritchard's work, as is noted in W. Kraus, 'Contestable Identities: Tribal Structures in the Moroccan High Atlas', *Journal of the Royal Anthropological Society*, vol. 4, 1998.

78   The initial statement of his criticism was made in a review of J. Berque, *Structures sociales du Haut-Atlas*, Paris, 1955 ('The Far West of Islam', *British Journal of Sociology*, vol. 9, 1958, pp. 76–7). The most complete statement of the disagreement, stressing empirical as well as theoretical matters, is in *Saints of the Atlas*, pp. 65–7. A distinction is drawn between two meanings of *leff* in his introduction to Gellner and C. Micaud (eds), *Arabs and Berbers*, London, 1973.

79   *The Nuer*, Oxford, 1940; and *The Sanusi of Cyrenaica*, Oxford, 1949.

80   Berque expressed reservations about Gellner's use of segmentary theory both in his

pied-noir parents in Algeria, then learnt Arabic and served as an agronomist in the western High Atlas before eventually becoming an academic in the Collège de France.[81] Gellner enthusiastically welcomed his study of the Seksawa tribe, *Structures sociales du Haut-Atlas*, which appeared in 1955.[82] Berque was far less interested – in Gellner's view, perversely disinterested – in the political sociology of the Berbers, but he was an absolute master of micro-sociology, in particular of the relation of land to clan, and the rituals of daily life. French intellectual life did not issue any edict against historical reconstruction – a view which Gellner found refreshing, as long as it was tied to clear appreciation of the importance of social structure.[83] As it happens, Berque's next book, *Al-Yousi: problèmes de la culture marocaine au XVIIème siècle*, was to furnish material for an alternative view of North African society which Gellner would thereafter dispute.[84]

With the exception of his critical commentary on the notion of *leff*, Gellner argued that the studies of Montagne and Berque were superb ethnographies whose conclusions he did not wish to contest. His own interest lay in a particular type of government, that of rule by saints. He wished to understand the role of living saints, that is, of *iggurame* – or *marabouts*, the French word following Arabic rather than Berber – held to possess *baraka* (charisma or holiness). Accordingly, his fieldwork concentrated on a centre of living saints, Zawiya Ahansal, and on surrounding saintly sites, all in the Central High Atlas. The saints were themselves members of a kin group, most of whose members were laicized, and so prone to indulge in characteristic tribal behaviour such as feuding. This was an area where pastoral tribes met; as the pastures of the lowlands dried up, transhumant pastoralists brought their sheep to the longer-lasting grazing lands of the mountains. *Saints of the Atlas* portrays the role of saints within a larger society of which they were a part. The fieldwork started a mere twenty-one years after the final pacification of the tribes, making it possible to reconstruct the workings of a social

---

L'Intérieur du Maghreb, Paris, 1978, and in the 1978 expanded edition of *Structures sociales du Haut-Atlas*; these reservations were repeated in his critical but appreciative review of *Muslim Society*, 'The Popular and the Purified', *Times Literary Supplement*, 11 December 1981. Gellner's obituary for Berque, 'A Fighter for Arab Culture' (*Guardian*, 11 July 1995), considered him a lesser figure than Masqueray and Montagne, but great appreciation was shown for the depth of his understanding of the encounter between the West and the Arabs.
81 Perhaps it was through Berque that Emmanuel Le Roy Ladurie – who made use of *Saints of the Atlas* in his famous *Montaillou* – became familiar with Gellner's work.
82 'The Far West of Islam'. Berque's material did not lend support to Montagne's oscillation theory, as is made especially clear in 'The Sociology of Robert Montagne', p. 190.
83 'The Far West of Islam', pp. 80–1.
84 Paris, 1958. This book is not cited in the bibliography of *Saints of the Atlas*. The dispute is discussed below, in chapter 9.

system not decisively influenced by a foreign presence.[85] Memories were strong, and the fact that the French had preserved local custom meant that the essential workings of the traditional order were still in place, although Gellner took care to note changed conditions when appropriate.

The absence of government in this area of the Atlas ought to have resulted in a Hobbesian situation of genuine anarchy. There were no local big men, let alone feudal lords, to provide order in the absence of the state, and relative egalitarianism characterized life amongst Berber pastoral nomads. Further, these tribesmen had a high 'military participation ratio': they were mobile, used to protecting their sheep and well trained in the use of firearms.[86] While order was neither complete nor always present, the fact of the matter was that relatively settled relations were maintained. Gellner explained this by the ability of different segments, defined through kinship terminology, to balance each other so that a measure of stability was created. Tribesmen are mobilized according to the level of threat that they face and by means of a tree of kinship relations. Thus all the descendants of a putative distant ancestor may mobilize when a serious common threat is faced, while at a lower level the descendants of two brothers may establish equilibrium.

Gellner suggests that four principles make a segmentary system work.[87] First, division and balance are the only organizational principles at work in society, suggesting that their presence must explain the maintenance of order. Second, in principle there can be no conflict of loyalty since the tree-like kinship system rules out crosscutting allegiances. Third, segmentation is most likely to rest on unilineal kinship. The crucial consideration here is that there must be one form of descent, for any more complex pattern might create conflicting loyalties. Fourth, every level of every group is 'monadic' – in the sense that its structural principle is the same as every other group. The introduction of this principle allowed, in his view, for key improvements on French ethnography: order could be explained within any particular *leff*; the search for the real group, to which French studies had been prone, could be abandoned; and the notion of *leff* could itself be seen as more flexible, occasionally referring to nothing more than mere political alliance.[88]

The practice of the collective oath neatly illustrated the way in which

---

85 'Reply to Critics', p. 656.
86 Levels of military participation had been theorized by S. Andrzejewski (later Andreski) in *Military Organisation and Society*, which Gellner enthusiastically reviewed in 'Reflections on Violence', *British Journal of Sociology*, vol. 5, 1954.
87 *Saints of the Atlas*, pp. 41–9.
88 Ibid., p. 88, footnote 3.

order was achieved.[89] When an accusation was made, the allegedly guilty party could clear his name if his kinsmen – defined in terms of inheritance rights, in numbers according to the seriousness of the offence – stepped forward to swear to his innocence at a holy site according to a prescribed ritual. If a co-juror failed to turn up, guilt was established, and fines were imposed on the absent kin member. On the face of it this practice might seem bound to increase conflict: the system seems to allow the defending kin groups to triumph in all situations, thereby surely leading to an ultimate escalation of conflict. In fact, co-jurors were prepared to let down a kin member whose behaviour was a continual nuisance, even if this meant that fines had to be borne. The absence of state authority means that the only way to maintain order within a group is by by the threat that the delinquent may not be able to rely on his kin on some other occasion. Care is taken to reintegrate the offender by making him pay the fine, thus maintaining the strength of the unit. One advantage of the system was that it allowed some room for justice. But Gellner suggests that there was another benefit. When very solid tribal cohesion is displayed, might does indeed triumph – but this is an advantage since it prevents the outbreak of asymmetrical conflicts, which the weaker party would be sure to lose.

These Berbers' segmentary system, based on patrilineal descent, was especially pure – so much so that in later years Gellner referred to it as a 'masterpiece' of this form of social organization.[90] Complex realities interfered with the perfection of the model, but most of the deviations did not undermine the workings of segmentation. A first deviation – that 'ancestors are not multiplied beyond necessity'[91] – is clearly more of an exemplification than a contradiction. The fact that genealogies are not accurate, rarely tracing back more than six generations, demonstrates the impact of segmentation – as well, perhaps, as showing realism on the part of the tribesmen themselves. Fusion does take place, for example, when someone leaves or is expelled by his kin. But this does not destroy the system. To the contrary, it is vital for someone without kin to join another group lest he be utterly defenceless. This could lead to the adoption of the kin terms of the new group, again a sign for Gellner of how realism is given priority over consistency. Quoting Gellner directly provides a clear sense of the view of human behaviour that he gained from fieldwork:

---

89   Gellner used this illustration himself on many occasions, including 'How to Live in Anarchy', *Listener*, vol. 59, 1958; 'Trust, Cohesion and the Social Order', in D. Gambetta (ed.), *Trust*, Oxford, 1988; and 'Tribal and International Law, Between Right and Might', in M. Heiberg (ed.), *Subduing Sovereignty*, London, 1994.

90   For example, 'Reply to Critics', p. 642.

91   *Saints of the Atlas*, p. 38.

We find that policy decisions do not necessarily follow the cleavages of the segmentary structure. Nothing would be more erroneous than to see the tribesmen enslaved in thought and deed to their clans, unable to weigh consequences or to act independently. But it would be equally wrong to disregard the ordered hierarchy of tribal groups as some kind of decorative elaboration, without weight when the moment of political decision comes. The segmentary organization displays a set of alignments, ratified not merely by custom, sentiment and ritual, but more weightily by shared interests which provide the baseline for alliances and enmities, for aid and hostility, when conflict arises. Calculation, feeling, new interests, diplomatic ingenuity, may at times cause the final alignments to depart at some points: but the initial and fairly strong presumption is that allegiances of tribe and clan will be honored, and that other inducements must have been operative if they were not honored.[92]

It was from fieldwork that he became convinced that the late Wittgenstein was wrong, that human beings are more than 'concept-fodder'.[93] A further example of the same point was provided when Gellner asked what would happen when twins were faced with filling the last position of a ten-man posse. The laughter of the tribesmen indicated a measure of infidelity to their rules and concepts, an ability to adapt them according to the necessities of their daily lives.[94] Nonetheless, the manipulative realism of human beings did not automatically allow a transition to a different social order. Humans could be discontented, but they were normally trapped within social structures from which they could not escape.

The living saints might seem to be a further deviation from the model of pure kinship. They were certainly a distinct oddity in being themselves pacific. Montagne saw that the oscillation between tribal republics and the rule of *caïds*, characteristic of the south of the Atlas, did not apply to

---

92   Ibid., p. 63.
93   Those British members of parliament who lack independence and influence are often referred to as 'lobby-fodder'. Gellner liked the term 'concept-fodder' as an accurate characterization of the view that humans are simply slaves to the norms of their culture.
94   *Saints of the Atlas*, p. 127. Gellner makes use of his ethnographic material to dig at his linguist philosophical enemies at a number of points. One further example is worth recalling:

A stereotype of the tribesman, popular among laymen, notably philosophers, is of a man totally enslaved to the rules within his in-group, and totally amoral outside it. This is doubly wrong. Segmentary societies are very common. Tribesmen within them cannot be enslaved to rules within them, for there is no absolute 'within': what is an in-group for one purpose, is an out-group for another. Secondly it is not the case that universal, open, impersonally formulated rules of morality are not present . . . (p. 45, footnote 1)

the saintly world of the Central High Atlas.[95] The stability of this more egalitarian system resulted from the presence of a hierarchical element; the presence of the saints weakened society's impulse towards the rise of the *caïds*. The division of labour in this society was remarkable, and something of a refutation of characteristic Weberian (and Marxist) expectations: the possessors of military might were dependent upon those who had renounced violence. How was this possible?

The saints performed a series of services for the tribesmen, enabling their society to work effectively.[96] The practice of trial by collective oath has already been mentioned, but not the fact that the oath-taking was arranged by and took place before a saint. Elections of *imgharen*, the tribal chiefs, depended still more on the saintly presence. The ideal-typical practice was, according to Gellner, that voting rights would be reserved for the segments of a tribe that the candidate did not belong to. Such a system was designed to rule out the possibility of permanent power: chiefs were instant lame ducks as they held power for only a year, and their status anyway depended upon the provision of hospitality that might well deplete their resources. Given these circumstances, together with the absence of a formal vote and the need for final decisions to be unanimous, saints played a crucial role in finding a hidden consensus amongst the assembled tribesmen. Just as important were the various ways – by serving as the court of final appeal, by offering mediation – in which the saints regulated disputes over pasture rights. This was really, in Gellner's eyes, the key to the whole situation. The main centre of the saint system was situated precisely where conflicts over summer pastures were most intense. Offshoots from this centre were found where new 'frontiers' had opened, that is, at new places where tribes came into contact in their searches for pasture.[97] Beyond these three crucial roles, saints also provided a series of smaller services, from the provision of sanctuary to the placement of those leaving a kin network, and from the provision of information to the protection of trade and travellers. The practical, even materialist quality of the functionalist explanations that Gellner offered did not mean for a moment that he denied the spiritual service provided by the saints, the linking of tribesmen to a large spiritual world. To the contrary, he concludes his treatment by stressing the enthusiastic

---

95   Montagne, *Les Berbères et le makhzen au sud du Maroc*, p. 411. Gellner notes how remarkable it was that Montagne saw the exception so clearly when no European had as yet visited the region (*Saints of the Atlas*, p. 65). He described his own study as filling in the details of Montagne's observation.

96   A full list of such services, only some of which are discussed here, is offered in *Saints of the Atlas*, p. 78.

97   Ibid., pp. 168–9, 230.

quality of their belief in Islam, referring to the role of the saints as 'spiritual lords of the marches'.[98] Still, Gellner came to be puzzled by the degree of tribesmen's allegiance to the norms of a civilization which regards their form of Islam as heretical, especially given the lack of any coercive apparatus available to the keepers of the great tradition.

The largest part of *Saints of the Atlas* is devoted to the lives of the saints. It is necessary to note the fundamental fact that saints, so to speak, multiply beyond necessity. The relatively fixed number of openings for the positions of saintly mediators means that some selection procedure is required, especially given that the saints themselves, in part because of their pacific nature, produce an excess of children. The local belief is that the possession of true *baraka* is the result of divine favour. Gellner felt certain that, in this case, *vox populi* was *vox dei*. This was not because of his own reluctance to admit the powers of any divinity; rather it was easy to identify the mundane mechanisms at work. A very subtle and continuous process of selection was applied to members of saintly lineages, the key principle of which was that success tended to breed still greater success. *Baraka* was recognizable, for example, in the ability to provide hospitality – but that ability in turn led to the very gifts which provided them with the resources to exhibit their status.

> But it would never do to have this overtly conceptualized: if baraka were merely the consequence of the decisions of the lay tribesmen, it could not claim authority over them. What is in reality a choice – albeit not one made by an individual and not on any one occasion, but by many and over a long time – appears not as a choice but as the recognition of an objective and indeed transcendental fact. This 'objectivity' of the allegedly recognized characteristic has the social consequence of absolving him who 'recognizes' it from the responsibility for it, which would attach to such an act if it were seen to be a choice.[99]

Social life depends, to adopt Sartrean terminology, upon bad faith. But Gellner's morality is not that of Sartre: one feels at all times in his account an admiration for the way in which truth is not sought at the expense of social efficacy.

The role of the saints was particularly evident when the French protectorate and the newly independent state increased and extended the power of government. For one thing, a dispute broke out – a War of the Dance

---

98   Ibid., pp. 297–301.
99   Ibid., p. 151.

– between the traditionalists of Zawiya Ahansal and rivals whose puritanism reflected the fact that they were on the very edge of the plain, and therefore were forced to deal with clients ever more aware of the heterodoxy of traditional Berber practice.[100] For another, the saints of Zawiya Ahansal played a complicated game during the period of French advance, keeping lines of communication open to both sides. What might seem at first to be craven behaviour was best understood, Gellner stressed, in entirely traditional terms: the saints were merely dealing with a new frontier, that between the French and the tribesmen as a whole. Despite all this, Gellner did recognize that the role of the saints was very definitely coming to an end. The key consideration was very basic. The ability of the state to finally provide order diminishes the attractiveness of pastoralism. In the absence of the state, kin were welcomed when they arrived to use summer pastures – for this would contribute to the tribal cohesion necessary for survival. When feuding is ruled out, handing over valued pastures to transient arrivals is far less appealing. Land deeds tended to be discovered and validated, allowing sedentarization to take place.[101] Gellner had few illusions in this matter. He recognized a beauty in both the elegant economy of the social system and in the vernacular architecture, yet realized that it could not be preserved. But the social scientist could preserve an accurate record of what would be lost.

Conclusion

It is worth underlining how much Gellner gained from his experience in North Africa. A leader such as Ben Barka wished to *build* a new society. Such social engineering would involve, Gellner argued, the creation of a schooling system which would allow a common culture, probably puritanical in character, on the basis of which modernization could take place.[102] This meant that Gellner had a real appreciation of the problems of development, and of their link to nationalism. Of course, this appreciation is scarcely surprising: he was open to this intellectual matter because

---

100 Ibid., pp. 246–50.
101 Ibid., pp. 171–2.
102 Gellner first identified the two tenets of what he termed in *Thought and Change* 'the modern social contract', that is, industrialism and nationalism, in 'From Ibn Khaldun to Karl Marx', *Political Quarterly*, vol. 32, 1961. In 'Independence in the Central High Atlas' he argued that the younger educated generation looked set to inherit the benefits of independence. His changing views on Moroccan development, the early expectation of radical change replaced by explanations for a remarkable degree of continuity, are noted in chapter 9.

his childhood experiences had made him aware of the move from country
to city, from agrarian to industrial conditions. He would soon teach, with
Tom Bottomore and Ron Dore, his colleagues in the sociology department at LSE, an exceptionally stimulating seminar on the Sociology of
Development.[103] This general interest led him to travel very widely
throughout the developing world in the 1960s, seeking to observe how
problems of development were playing out in the Islamic world. Crucially,
his own positive social philosophy would be constructed around the basic
fact of development. This was apparent in a comment Gellner made a few
years later, revealing critical distance from Popper. He could not accept
Popper's admiration for the Greeks, the turning of Periclean Athens into a
myth appropriate for the open society:

> [A]part from the slightly embarrassing matter of slavery, and the lower
> material standard of living (which one might accept), the Greek miracle
> was far too precarious to tempt emulation today. We might wish for the
> miracle, but not at the price of such precariousness. A modern society
> yearns for the security springing from the affluent contentment of its
> citizens. This is perhaps a weakness of a work such as Popper's *The Open
> Society and Its Enemies*, in as far as *its* image of 'the transition' is too much
> inspired by the Greek miracle. There may have been many breakdowns
> of tribal societies, most of them not very fertile, and all precarious. They
> can hardly now provide us with our crucial myth.[104]

Gellner wanted to do rather better in his search for the terms by which we
would live.

The late nineteenth century created the tension between ethnonationalism and cosmopolitanism which structured the ideas of a generation of
thinkers from Jewish backgrounds. One way to deal with the contradictions
between the Popperian closed and open societies was by moving to one
or the other polar position. Gellner did not take this route, insisting that
there were elements of both truth and error in these contrasting poles. The
tensions generated by history could only be amplified for Gellner by his
foundational intellectual allegiances. For there is a great deal of truth to

---

103   One participant was Robin Blackburn, who attests that he never again found such a
stimulating atmosphere.
104   *Thought and Change*, London, 1964, p. 159. Gellner's knowledge of tribal society also
led him to reject Popper's view of it as the exemplar of a closed society, of a world freed
from conflict over values: 'I have myself worked in a tribal society which is "structurally"
of a very simple kind, and moral dilemmas of this kind – choice between alternative sets of
values – not only occurred, but were for certain reasons an essential part of local life' (p. 84).

the somewhat stereotypical view that anthropology is necessarily relativist, valuing as it does the distinctive value systems of varied societies. In contrast, Popper's world was one which stressed concrete knowledge, the cognitive power of modern science – in Popper's case based on absolute admiration for the ideas and persona of Albert Einstein. One cannot know whether Gellner's choice of research area reflected an awareness of these tensions, or whether his decisions made it harder for him to imagine any easy escape from them. But his choices would certainly make his life more complicated, and much richer.

3

Moving Into Position

Mid-twentieth-century Central European intellectuals were often so grateful for their new British home that they became enthusiastic Anglophiles.[1] The title of the memoir by Gellner's uncle Julius, *England Receives Me as a Human Being*, is entirely typical in this regard. This love was sometimes reciprocated, as in the case of Isaiah Berlin – identified by Noel Annan and many others as the greatest intellectual of 'our age'.[2] Berlin's biographer nicely captures this trope:

> Isaiah more or less accepted everything the English liked to believe about themselves: that they were practical, untidy, eccentric, fair-minded, empirical, common-sensical and that ubiquitous word, decent. His was a version of Englishness frozen in the moment when he first encountered it in the 1920s: the England of Kipling, King George, the Gold Standard, empire and victory . . . Narrow-minded provincialism, philistinism and insularity played no part in his idea of England. If the English took to him it was because he offered them back their most self-approving myths.[3]

This sort of attitude was conservative, at least in the minimal sense of support for local customs.[4] Gellner's uniqueness lay in the fact that he did *not* give uncritical endorsement to the culture which he sought to join. His name was rather made by his attack on the dominant philosophy of the period, in his view part of a much more general complacency of the time. There

---

1 This particular burst of enthusiasm is part of a larger history well described by I. Buruma, *Voltaire's Coconuts or Anglomania in Europe*, London, 1999.
2 N. Annan, *Our Age*, London, 1990.
3 M. Ignatieff, *Isaiah Berlin: A Life*, London, 1998, p. 36.
4 P. Anderson, 'Components of the National Culture', *New Left Review*, no. 50, 1968. A brilliant contextualist meditation on Anderson's thesis has been provided by S. Collini, *Absent Minds: Intellectuals in Britain*, Oxford, 2006.

was a good deal of bravery involved. Gellner wished, at least sometimes and in a part of his character, to 'get in', to be accepted within British society, making traumatic his eventual break with the world of his Oxford teachers. This chapter describes the beginning of his attack on complacency, as seen in 'The Notes' and in an unpublished manuscript dealing with the work of his colleague Michael Oakeshott. A particularly striking contrast is with the ideas of, and still more with the role adopted by, Isaiah Berlin. The full-scale attack on Oxford linguistic philosophy follows from this, and it is dealt with in the next chapter. One final preliminary point needs to be made. A negative critique is always open to a simple line of attack: bluntly asking if the critic has anything better with which to replace that which he would destroy. This charge was levelled against Gellner, whose ambitions were wholly positive. So the attack on linguistic philosophy went hand in hand with the creation of a positive position, first in methodological and then in philosophical terms. The account of this concept's development begins in the next chapter and is continued in the one that succeeds it.

The Notes

Gellner had a talent for aphoristic writing, and for brilliant and caustic name-giving, as is obvious from his published work. This reflected his desire to refine general notions into concise, quotable nuggets. 'The Notes' contain a very great number of such pithy comments, often reworked to make them even more precise. They are Gellner's equivalent to Karl Marx's *Grundrisse*, revealing his sense of social realities, the steps that led him to his own position, his hatreds, and his view of our times. Several themes are identified, followed by some of Gellner's thoughts on them. It is impossible to date the material precisely, but one can see in it both crisis and its overcoming.

The first such theme concerns what he felt to be the complacency of intellectual life in 1950s Britain. This is scarcely surprising. Those years saw the emergence of 'The Angry Young Men', whose works Gellner read and occasionally cited; the dashing Byronic aspect of his character perhaps made him look as if he should be counted among them. Further, he held some left-wing views at the time, most obviously his disapproval of the intervention in Suez, and he published some of his earliest pieces in *Universities and Left Review* which became a component of *The New Left Review* in 1962.[5]

---

5   Though he was friendly with many members of the New Left in Britain, the 'Notes' demonstrate a good deal of critical distance, and critical acumen, as in this comment which perhaps concerned the Canadian Catholic political theorist Charles Taylor: 'Moral

The 1950s, era of complacency, in which social thought had postprandial role only. Essence of philosophy is conceptual hamletry, not the curing thereof.

To investigate 'concepts' is to put skids under oneself, to shake all coordinates, etc. Linguistic philosophy suggests the reverse, a recovery of firm ground. Balls: our concepts are generally shaky, and a little inspection upsets them.

If you wish to be sensible, why bother with philosophy in the first place. A philosophy of common sense, a contradiction in its own terms, according to which the philosophy could never give common sense more strength than it has independently. So why bore us?

The most terrible humanist culture, of people who got their affluence cheaply and without understanding.

A second theme is that of disorientation, together with comments on philosophers who fail to realize that we are, so to speak, lost, bereft of firm moorings.

How can one detachedly examine world when it is inside one?

'Know thyself' – an absurdity, presupposing a given determinate self.

Any general theory that makes too much sense of life cannot be true.

Life, between bumsucking and aggression.

Accidie – deep sense of impotence and unfittingness of one's concepts – and feelings.

Can one act in the dark? Can one act except in the dark? (Optimum is perhaps to be in the dark and think one is not)

Vertigo of heteronomous self-knowledge.

Puritanism and concern for level of culture – a strange dressing for extreme left, ally of the churches and the Arts Council. New Left: a new ancestry: not from Enlightenment, but (tacitly) from Christ via Young Hegel'.

World in ego, ego in world. Why identify with anything one does or is?

It is being subject to science, not being object to others (Sartre) which bothers.

Often we don't want to solve a problem, we want to know where we are. Talking of problems suggests that we already know general features of the world.[6]

Empiricist theory of knowledge: as though facts were flat, or lying down neatly in one plane on the desk, and all one had to do was to draw lines or curves which then would or would not extrapolate rightly. But facts do not lie down flat. They come not on a table like a jigsaw, but like a rubbish heap tipped out and so sprawly that it would never go back in the bin again, some bits are hard and angular and sharp and awkward shaped, bits of old bicycles, other bits are semi-smeary and semi-liquid, and so on.

Hume's howler: supposition that concepts were there, in sensations.

With depressions, the question really is why we sometimes do not have them (Cf. similar situations concerning military governments).

Oddest thing about Hamlet, that Shakespeare could describe him, and yet plainly in no way identifies himself with him, on the contrary. I am always tempted to suppose that anyone who saw the point – the dubiousness of the crucial and necessary premises of action – would also immediately become a Hamlet. But Shakespeare identifies rather with the final speech.

Perhaps the most striking feature of the material is the fact that it contains the hunches that informed virtually all of his later work. In this case it makes sense not just to cite the aphorisms, but to note where their ideas would re-emerge later on.

General prosperity is within reach; but liberty is precarious; and the connection between the two is not at all clear. This is the crucial fact for political thought.

---

6   This is directed at Popper.

Nationalism and Protestantism and industrialism: every man a clerk.

These two aphorisms contain the key insights of *Thought and Change* (1964).

Democracy presupposes not so much consensus – that is a misleading way of putting it – as a stable environment, structure. But no democracy when sitting on an avalanche.

This is the argument of 'Democracy and industrialization', in *Contemporary Thought and Politics* (1974).

Jealous god as ancestor of unifying non-eclectic theory: both non-arbitrariness and unwillingness to syncretise required.

This is the insight behind the most original part of *Plough, Sword, and Book* (1988).

'Trahison des clercs' begs question. They honestly see falsity of our own position, as messengers from the beyond.

The argument of '*la trahison de la trahison des clercs*', republished in *Encounters with Nationalism* (1994).

Nineteenth century: from the Cunning of reason to the Cunning of unreason.

Psychoanalysis between cause and meaning, facing both ways.

His analysis of the psychoanalytic movement, written two decades later, has as its subtitle 'The Cunning of Unreason'; within it the appeal of psychoanalysis is held to rest heavily on its ability to have it both ways, to hover between explanation at the level of cause and of meaning.

The humanity of man cannot be saved by fact or argument, etc. (as existence of deity cannot). A nonbehavourist or whatnot fact, an unreduced value, etc., . . . would still be one further fact . . . the tension must be there.

This argument (especially in a section dealing with Arthur Koestler) is used in *Legitimation of Belief* (1974, pp. 105–6).

Emile Durkheim's collective transcendental soul differs from Kant's. Kant's like a Balliol man, does its job effortlessly. Durkheim's has to be ever flexing its muscles. Hence ritual.

This line of argument appears more than once, becoming central in his last years at Cambridge, most notably in *Reason and Culture: The Historic Role of Rationality and Rationalism* (1992).

In the 'Notes', the reader can see Gellner's confidence regained in all sorts of different places, in comments about the world and in those about philosophy. All the same, the key aphorisms are the first ones. The relativity of beliefs, the fact that all sorts of ideas and values could be sustained in different social contexts, was something that Gellner felt deeply – exiled from one world and ill at ease in a new one, influenced by the cultural relativism that is nearly second nature to anthropologists. The oddity of his position was the insistence that there was no easy escape from this, much as he desired one. He would have no truck with irrationalist solutions. We are condemned to use reason to try to understand our situation. He liked to cite favourably Bertrand Russell's response to D. H. Lawrence's urgings to think with his blood: that he tried thinking with his guts but preferred in the end to use his head.[7] Still, Gellner's confidence rests on the fact that an escape *has been possible*, miraculously and against the characteristic pattern of human history. Here are some of the jottings that wholly foreshadow his general position.

We cannot jump out of our skins altogether, but we can do it more than suggested.

Moralising in philosophy is legitimate not because it is possible, but because it is inescapable.

Tolstoy wrong: science does, in one sense, tell us how to live (and anyway, nothing else tells us anything).

Traditional societies deserve nostalgia and detestation.

God wouldn't be so unsymmetrical and in bad taste as to allow e.g. Catholicism to be true.

---

7 B. Russell, *The Autobiography of Bertrand Russell. Volume Two: 1914–1944*, London, 1968, p. 204.

Science not capitalism ushered in modern world (contra Marx), though possibly individualism and wealth were required to overcome the home-ostasis and plain repressiveness of the traditional order.

During the last war, the West thought it was defined by 'democracy'. Balls. In fact by being affluent in a civilized way. Unless you are affluent you won't be civilized (few non-industrialized places look like Periclean Athens, anyway), and you may well be affluent without being civilized.

Of two evils: liberal societies seem to be far less precariously near a slump, etc., etc., than communist ones near tyranny (nor does the bourgeoisie need fascism when hire purchase will do).

Re Marx: truth not illusion is what alienates.

The absurd idea that the world is just so constituted that liberal values are somehow written into it.

Michael Oakeshott and Tradition

A more systematic way to understand Gellner's revolt against the local orthodoxies encountered in his adopted country is to look at his diag-noses of their exemplars, Michael Oakeshott and Isaiah Berlin. His most sustained statement is an unpublished manuscript of about 20,000 words entitled 'Conservatism and Ideology'. This manuscript seems to have held great importance for Gellner. When asked in 1961 and 1962 to provide a curriculum vitae to a promotions committee, he listed this manuscript and his work on the saints of the High Atlas as the two books on which he was working.[8] Further, in the mid-1960s he gave ten lectures on 'Conservatism and Ideology'. Nonetheless, the manuscript was never completed, though the ideas that it contained saw the light of day on more than one occasion.

The introductory passage of the manuscript makes clear that it is directed against both Oakeshott and Berlin, respectively regarded as the leading polit-ical thinkers in England on the right and the centre-left. Their predecessors in their chairs at the LSE and Oxford, Harold Laski and G. D. H. Cole,

---

8   'Conservatism and Ideology', n.d., Gellner Archive. Several versions of this manuscript exist, many corrected, further suggesting that he considered it important. It is extremely odd that the publication data that Gellner provided never mention that he was working on *Thought and Change*.

respectively, had taken for granted that it was possible both to understand and to improve society. Oakeshott and Berlin did not. This was particularly true of Oakeshott, who felt that only the preservation of long-standing tradition would guarantee civilized rule, and any attempt to impose rational standards was all too likely to lead to the dangers of schism and fanaticism.[9] But there was, in Gellner's eyes, a difference between the two: Oakeshott 'represents the dissenting sceptic or cynic at the time when the two assumptions still seemed to reign'; whereas Berlin offers 'a rather more complacent philosophy which ratifies a contentment rather than registers a protest'.[10] We will see in a moment that Gellner regarded Berlin as a less substantial and much less interesting figure than Oakeshott. After the introductory passage, he scarcely appears in the rest of the manuscript, which concentrates wholly on analysing the nature of Oakeshott's conservatism before subjecting it to withering attack.

There are many jottings in 'The Notes' about Oakeshott.[11] Some show respect and appreciation:

'[The] notion of 'intimation' contains a good epistemology. It is in this way, not Hume or Hegel, that we get our convictions.

But many more show what he found objectionable in Oakeshott, above all his avowed 'anti-rationalism', including the unbalanced attribution of all modern horrors to 'rationalists':

All evil [is] somehow credited to 'rationalism'; [it is] odd to find that Nazism is rationalism, not Irrationalism . . . Also: [this anti-rationalism] erodes moral indignation, allows every prejudice, fails to stimulate moral imagination and generosity.

Even those who reject his philosophy tend to talk of it amiably, as something terribly English and really innocuous, like afternoon tea. In fact, its one solitary idea is a spit image, if not a lineal descendant of, anti-Dreyfusard irrationalism, [the conviction] that too cold universal reason needed to be fought.

[There is a parallel] between linguistic philosophy and Oakeshott: both invert: the one treats thought as something to be cured, and confusion

---

9   M. Oakeshott, *Rationalism in Politics and Other Essays*, London, 1962, pp. 1–36.
10   'Conservatism and Ideology', introductory passage.
11   Gellner sent Oakeshott some of his early papers. One letter from Oakeshott to Gellner, 18 January 1952, defends the view that skills cannot be learned.

as paradigm of health; the other, real knowledge as disease, fumbling as health.

When all is said and done, the right is still short of thinkers (laudably and consistently), and it is easier to make a career being one. No leftist could make a reputation on anything so thin and abstract and inconsistent. Amongst us radicals, standards are a bit higher.[12]

'Conservatism and Ideology' begins by poking fun at conservatism in general. Most space is spent suggesting that the very idea of a conservative theory is self-contradictory. Either a social order works according to tradition, or we have to determine how to live our lives.[13] The idea that we might calculate in order to encourage the absence of thought is judged to be simply weird. The traditionalist cannot restore the world we have lost, the world before reason, before the Enlightenment. The heart of the argument, however, concerns Oakeshott's anti-Cartesian position. Gellner noted that no howl of protest met Oakeshott's stance, in comparison to that which had greeted the logical positivism articulated in Ayer's *Language, Truth and Logic*. 'Moral scepticism combined with Toryism clearly is not held to be so disruptive as moral scepticism alone – or perhaps people don't even notice that it *is* moral scepticism'.[14] Gellner observed that 'Conservatives from Plato onwards have invoked transcendental certainties to buttress up the social order. It is interesting to note that the denial of all transcendence, even in thought, and the denial of certainty, can be used for the same purpose!'[15]

Gellner's acceptance of moral diversity made him respect the insights behind Oakeshott's moral scepticism. But this did not lead him to endorse Oakeshott's attack on rationalism. To the contrary, the fact that it is hard to find objective standards does not mean that we can cease to search for them on the grounds that 'tradition' provides us with reliable knowledge. For one thing, not all power holders, whose intimations about tradition we are supposed to trust above the rationalist plans of intellectual outsiders, are modest and efficient – as the behaviour of the British political class over the

---

12   'Notes'.
13   The clarity of Gellner's formulation owed something to his knowledge of Islam. In later works he certainly made this point with reference to the medieval Muslim thinker Al Ghazzali who 'had noted that the genuine traditionalist does not know that he is one; he who proclaims himself to be one, no longer is one' (*Plough, Sword, and Book*, p. 208).
14   'Conservatism and Ideology', p. 10.
15   Ibid., p. 24. He noted that this position is far removed from the usual sources of modern irrationalism, which he characterized as a combination of Freud and Marx.

Suez crisis clearly indicated as far as Gellner was concerned. For another, the world has changed so much as to obviate any intellectual power that tradition once might have had. Cartesian rationalism and utilitarianism both drew their strength, in Gellner's view, precisely from the fact that the ancient received traditions of Europe, especially the religious and aristocratic, had in effect been cracked asunder. He cited a remark made to him by a Moroccan friend to the effect that '*nous sommes tous des orphelins*', bereft of our traditional moorings, obliged to think for ourselves.

Two further observations from 'Conservatism and Ideology' are revealing. On the one hand, Gellner draws on Malinowskian social anthropology to query the supposed autonomy of tradition: 'Traditions are manipulations of the past (not indeed generally actual fabrications) for the purposes of manipulating the present and propping up current arrangements'. On the other hand, he insists that although 'tradition may be elegance, competence, courage, modesty and realism . . . it is also bullshit, servility, vested interest, arbitrariness, empty ritual'. Underlying all this was surely the deep dislike of a doctrine which made it all but impossible for an outsider to gain social acceptance. He later quoted Oakeshott in this matter in order to make his point:

> Like a foreigner or a man out of his social class, he is bewildered by a tradition and a habit of behaviour of which he knows only the surface; a butler or an observant house-maid has the advantage of him . . . [16]

So despite his Czech experiences, which had made him hostile to organized communism, Gellner was never tempted by the conservative response to modernity. Its nostalgia, its romanticism, and its dishonesty were not for him. He was, like Russell, a monist and a rationalist. Further, as a social scientist of Malinowskian persuasion he could not accept a view that suggested that ideas – or, rather, bad ideas – determined what happened in society. In this he was opposed not just to Oakeshott, but quite as much, as we will later see, to the views of Elie Kedourie who wrote about nationalism somewhat under the spell of Oakeshott.[17] He had, however, found much that was stimulating and provocative in Oakeshott, despite

---

16 Oakeshott, *Rationalism in Politics*, p. 31, cited in *Legitimation of Belief*, p. 4.

17 'Reply to Critics', in J. A. Hall and I. C. Jarvie (eds), *The Social Philosophy of Ernest Gellner*, Amsterdam, 1995, pp. 635–6. This chapter contains crushing criticism of Oakeshott via a response to his Antipodean disciple, Kenneth Minogue, Emeritus Professor of Political Science at LSE, pp. 63–6. Gellner recorded the fact that Oakeshott listed his intellectual affiliation as that of his former Cambridge college when *Rationalism in Politics* was published in 1962 – that is, at a time when he had been based at the LSE for several years.

considering him a reactionary, and his posture bizarrely hypocritical. He later observed that the defender of so-called tradition came from a Fabian father and a 'progressive school, so non-U' that it played Gellner's 'incomparably more non-U' school at rugby.[18]

Isaiah Berlin and Jewish Identity

Gellner's dislike, even contempt, for the views and positions adopted by Berlin stands in contrast to the measure of respect he showed to Oakeshott. He regarded Berlin as a performer, rather than as a thinker, the 'CIA's J. S. Mill', and a 'Postprandial Hegelian', noting that 'after dinner, one does not wish to have one's mind strained'.[19] Perhaps this distaste explains why 'Conservatism and Ideology' does not discuss Berlin in detail. After all, 'why criticise a man of charm whose thought is almost wholly innocuous?' Gellner loathed Berlin's lazy criticisms of social science, his imposition of strictures so broad as to virtually rule out all possibility of social understanding.[20] He had little time for Berlin's defence of political theory in the face of T. D. Weldon's much discussed claim that the discipline was now defunct. In Gellner's view, Berlin's position remained formal, bereft of substantive results, at best a justification of the history of ideas. But 'there are times', Gellner would later publicly riposte, 'when it is not enough to preach the need to try to understand the world – when one must actually try substantively to understand it'.[21] Gellner disliked Berlin's forays into the history of ideas, finding, for instance, that the Montesquieu presented by Berlin was less the father of sociology than of its denial. He saw Berlin's work as 'always the same': the 'failures of past celebrities dragged together to justify not trying'. This rejection of Berlin's history of ideas did not mean that Gellner was uninterested in great thinkers past and present. He was irritated by Berlin's historical insensitivity, his conversion of past thinkers into versions of Isaiah. This co-optation, he maintained, could be deeply misleading: Berlin's John Stuart Mill, for example, was much too tolerant and relativist, a view which distorted Mill's search for general principles and his hard-headed willingness to endorse active social programmes of

---

18   'Reply to Critics', pp. 635–6.
19   Gellner's view of Berlin's social role informs his 1957 *British Journal of Sociology* review of the latter's celebrated lecture on 'Historical Inevitability'. The review ends by claiming that the brilliant painter of ideas can best be understood if one calls to mind Berlin's 'sonorous voice and accompanying manner'.
20   In a set of notes on Berlin, probably for a talk entitled 'The Entertainer', he wrote, 'questionnaires as likely as washing windows of college' . . . '"ideas", i.e., not facts'.
21   *Thought and Change*, p. 35, n. 1.

progressive transformation.[22] 'Isaiah Berlin on liberty, on Tolstoy, on sociology, [is] always the same, always polymorphism, nothing can be said
because too much has to be said, somehow liberty is made contingent on
absence of principles, normative or descriptive'. Such pluralism might seem
tolerant, but it was in fact dangerous.

Examining these views of Berlin enables us to consider carefully Gellner's
relationship to his own Jewish background. Gellner had no active religious
commitments, being in fact an active opponent of religious belief for the
duration of his public life. In his early years he wrote for *The Rationalist
Annual*, and was prepared to be cited as an Honorary Associate of the
Rationalist Press Association in the 1980s. He made endlessly crushing
and funny comments about the emptiness of modern theologians, and a
review of Leszek Kolakowski's *Religion* shows how seriously he took his
atheism.[23] But what matters more is the question of ethnic identification.
Let me redeem the promise made in the first chapter, namely to consider
John Hajnal's charge that Gellner suffered from Jewish self-hatred. This is a
very complex matter. But it cannot be avoided, not least because Gellner's
contempt for Berlin seems to have as its background the very different
ways in which these two thinkers reacted to British society in light of their
Jewish heritage.

Berlin made a striking contribution of his own to the notion of Jewish
self-hatred in an essay, directed at Arthur Koestler, on 'Jewish Slavery and
Emancipation'. The desire to get into a host society was often so great that
it led those from Jewish backgrounds to become theoretical experts in local
norms, thereby marking their very difference in a way that made assimilation more difficult. This vicious circle meant that it was all too possible to
come to hate those elements of one's background – above all, intellectuality, eagerness – which made it hard to fit in. A particular claim of Berlin's
was that the creation of the state of Israel changed everything for Jews,
whether religiously active or merely culturally loyal. On the one hand, it
made the decision to stay outside Israel a genuine choice; on the other, it
established a home in which all the unease and difficulties of living in a host
country disappeared, a situation in which life became simple. Surprisingly,
all this was a prelude to Berlin *rebutting* Koestler's claim that Jews now
faced a simple binary choice, between total assimilation and moving to

---

22   Similar points, and several others resonating with Gellner's views, have recently been
made, against the current of praise for Berlin, e.g. by P. Anderson, 'The Pluralism of Isaiah
Berlin', *London Review of Books*, vol. 12, 1990; C. Hitchens, 'Moderation or Death', *London
Review of Books*, vol. 20, 1998; and A. N. Wilson, 'The Dictaphone Don', *Times Literary
Supplement*, 17 July 2009.
23   'God, Man and Nature', *Sunday Times*, 28 February 1982.

Israel.[24] Berlin maintained that Koestler was blaming the victims, that Jews had the right to preserve their differences – that is, that integration rather than assimilation was a respectable ideal. At the end of their exchange he complained that:

> Arthur Koestler does not do justice to my argument. It is not, to use his words, that, 'unreason, however irritating or maddening, must be tolerated' or that Jews or anyone else 'have the right to be guided by irrational emotion'. My thesis was and is that to demand social and ideological homogeneity, to wish to get rid of minorities because they are tiresome or behave 'foolishly or inconsistently or vulgarly' (these are indeed my words), is illiberal and coercive and neither rational nor humane.[25]

Although Berlin did not directly accuse Koestler of Jewish self-hatred, this is precisely the charge levelled against Koestler by his biographer, David Cesarani. Koestler's homelessness led, in Cesarani's view, to a stridency and instability of views throughout his life: he swung from Zionism to communism, returned to Zionism after abandoning his communist beliefs, and ended with both an attempt to hide his Jewish background altogether and a strange denial of Jewish ethnicity in general – all of it linked to his callous behaviour toward women. This theme of homelessness is one that often arises, as noted, in discussions of thinkers and figures of Jewish background. The first generation of Bolshevik leaders was disproportionately non-Russian and Jewish, for the simplest of reasons: they had often

---

24   D. Cesarani, *Arthur Koestler: The Homeless Mind*, London, 1998, p. 429. Cesarani misdescribes Gellner as 'Viennese-born', p. 481, but records Gellner's attendance at Koestler's 1963 Christmas party, whose other guests included Cyril Connolly, Patrick Gordon Walker MP, the art historian Ernst Gombrich, Goronwy Rees and Andrew Shonfield. Koestler 'had first met Gellner in March and was discomfited to find that one so wise was so young' (p. 614, n. 37). The intellectual respect was mutual: long before they had met, three of Koestler's novels were prescribed reading for Gellner's first course in Social Philosophy at the Extra-Mural Department of the University of London (c. 1949–50) – *The Yogi and the Commissar, Darkness at Noon,* and *Spartacus.* T. Judt's interesting review of Cesarani's biography (reprinted as 'Arthur Koestler, the Exemplary Intellectual' in his *Reappraisals: Reflections on the Forgotten Twentieth Century,* New York, 2008) insists that the charge of Jewish self-hatred is overdone, a reflection of current concerns that distorts our understanding of Koestler – and to some extent of his entire generation of Jewish thinkers. The same argument is made by M. Scammell, *Koestler: The Literary and Political Odyssey of a Twentieth-Century Skeptic,* New York, 2009. A general point is worth making here. Koestler's scepticism followed the embrace of varied positions; Gellner's scepticism was altogether greater, ruling out allegiance to the main belief systems present during his life.
25   I. Berlin, in D. Villiers (ed.), *Next Year in Jerusalem: Jews in the Twentieth Century,* London, 1976, p. 106, cited in Cesarani, *Arthur Koestler,* pp. 529–30.

faced discrimination when attempting to join radical national movements, leading them to switch allegiances and become left-wing activists.[26] Malachi Hacohen makes a very similar argument in his brilliant work on Karl Popper, arguing that the open society is best understood as a cosmopolitan home ideally suited to figures of Jewish background, who in Popper's view were likely to suffer as a result of nationalism. Hacohen does not actually accuse Popper of Jewish self-hatred, but he does detect both anti-Zionism and anti-Semitism in the corpus of Popper's thought.[27]

A non-Jewish biographer can feel ill at ease here, as if peeking at an internal debate. This trepidation should not be necessary, given that feelings of self-hatred can apply just as easily in matters of religion and ethnicity and class, and therefore invite a more general understanding. More importantly, the charge at times moves quickly from description to prescription, as Gellner himself stressed when considering Sartre in 'The Notes'.[28]

> And authenticity – sociologically spurious concept (related to alienation) – all roles are contingent and are seen as necessary; also there is a regress – Jean-Paul Sartre ask[s] one to [be] an authentic Jew (for instance), but why not be authentically one not wishing oneself [to be such], etc., etc? Many roles incorporate their own rejection.

> All balls this existentialist talk of choice of self, then sticking to it, assuming responsibility, etc. In fact, most of us have numbers of cohabiting selves, in a way complementary even while logically opposed. (Like Czechs who in wartime always have a legitimate government with each side.) We could manage with one self about as well as with one suit.

But the question of self-hatred must be addressed. For Gellner did think about his Jewish background, which had been reinforced by historical events, as comments in 'The Notes' make abundantly clear.

> We mid European Jews – exactly like man according to existentialism – choosing attributes, being given none. Human situation, only somewhat more so. Unfortunately, it is of the essence of those attributes that they

---

26   L. Riga, 'Ethnonationalism, Assimilation, and the Social Worlds of the Jewish Bolsheviks in Fin de Siècle Tsarist Russia', *Comparative Studies in Society and History*, vol. 48, 2006.

27   M. Hacohen, 'Karl Popper in Exile: The Viennese Progressive Imagination and the Making of *The Open Society*', *Philosophy of the Social Sciences*, vol. 26, 1996.

28   This judgement also seems to apply to P. Birnbaum's remarkable *Geography of Hope: Exile, the Enlightenment, Disassimilation*, Stanford, 2008, which is discussed in the epilogue.

are not chosen but given. If chosen, are somehow false. Not surprisingly, a mainly descent-based society values givenness of attributes more than endeavour, contrary to Kant.

Being a Jew is also like human condition, in that there is no correct solution.[29]

Jewish disability: inability to act any role with conviction.

There will always be a false note, which ever you do ashamed of being ashamed, etc. *ad infinitum*, no equilibrium possible here; where would authenticity lie? Mate in three whatever you do. Sense of play acting, whatever one does. Impotence, ignorance, chaos, unreality.

We Jews are specifically like Sartre's picture of man in general – self-chosen and not liking it.

These crumpled private notes certainly demonstrate Gellner's awareness of the acute dilemmas of Jewish identity in the modern world, as does his later assessment of the cultural background to the work of Hannah Arendt.[30] Gellner was equally aware of the notion of self-hatred and would later level that charge against Wittgenstein, as we will see in the epilogue. And there are indeed similarities between Gellner and Koestler. When Jiří Musil was in temporary British exile after the Prague Spring of 1968, he visited the Gellners in Hampshire and was shown Prague memorabilia including tram tickets from before the war. This did not prevent Gellner from bluntly telling Musil during the visit that he felt 'nowhere at home'. Further, until his final years he tended to agree with Koestler in thinking, in light of the Holocaust, that the choice was between assimilation or establishing one's own state, if one wanted to survive.

With the current intellectual climate so favourable to diversity and multiculturalism, one might think that this last point would hand the game to Berlin, so to speak, and support the view that Gellner suffered from

---

29   Here again is evidence that Gellner worked out his views early on. When discussing the work of Hannah Arendt a quarter century later in 'Accounting for the Horror' (*Times Literary Supplement*, 6 August 1982), reprinted as 'From Königsberg to Manhattan (or Hannah, Rahel, Martin and Elfriede or Thy Neighbour's *Gemeinschaft*' (*Culture, Identity and Politics*, Cambridge, 1987, p. 84), he noted, 'Being a Jew is like awareness of sex or death; it is always present, there are no solutions for the problems it engenders, and one can only talk about it in aphorisms'.
30   Ibid.

Jewish self-hatred. But matters are not so simple. To say that Gellner felt ambivalence about these matters all his life is a far cry from saying that he suffered from self-*hatred*. There is no real evidence for this parlous state of mind, and such accusations should be firmly rejected.[31] He differed dramatically from some of the other figures mentioned. His profound devotion to rationalism did not translate into Popper's anti-national cosmopolitanism: to the contrary, he took nationalism seriously, understood its attractiveness, and felt that it was inevitable under the conditions of modernity. Gellner did not suffer from the enthusiasms, the endless search for and subsequent abandonment of varied causes that characterized Koestler's career. He was never a Marxist, and his attitude to Israel was consistent and moderate. He had been prepared to fight for it in 1948, visited it soon after, and was happy to visit again with his wife, at the invitation of the Jewish Agency, in the mid-1960s.[32] He also spent a term at Tel Aviv University's Centre for Advanced Study in 1981. But he was prone to saying that, whilst he was prepared to die for the country, he had no desire to live there – and offended Israelis in 1981 with comments made at a seminar on nationalism.[33]

Just as importantly, Gellner did not suffer from that extreme self-hatred which leads to hiding one's origins. He openly referred to his background, and addressed, as noted, the stakes that were involved in it, with force and clarity in his essay on Hannah Arendt – and was prepared on many occasions to offer analyses of the Jewish situation in general, and within the Islamic world in particular.[34] Crucially, his last book offers, as we shall see, an explanation of Wittgenstein's philosophy in terms of the situation

31   Gellner and his LSE colleague Peter Wiles attended a small conference in Venice in 1969 organized by Raymond Aron. The proceedings record Wiles saying at one point that Gellner seemed nowhere at home. Gellner remembered the comment many years later, referring to it as exceptionally rude. Herein lies the ambivalence, the problem facing someone who seeks acceptance: it is fine to say that one feels homeless, but an insult when others say it about you.

32   Some of the other participants in the trip were Steven Lukes, Eric Hobsbawm, Ilya Neustadt, Elie Kedourie and Leonard Schapiro. Lukes had just reviewed *Thought and Change* in a rather lukewarm manner, and remembers tension during the climb up Mount Sinai. The ice was broken when Gellner, who instantly liked Lukes's wife Jacqui, declared in a loud voice how wonderful it was to have met her. When asked why, he joked that without her presence he might have (or would have) pushed Steven off the mountain (Steven Lukes, interview with Brendan O'Leary, 27 February 2001).

33   I have not been able to discover the comments in question. *Nations and Nationalism*, published two years later, noted (p. 107) that the establishment of the state of Israel had 'solved a European problem by creating an Asian one, about which the Israelis have barely begun to think'.

34   'Prejudicial Encounters (a review of B. Lewis, *Semites and Anti-Semites*)', *Times Literary Supplement*, 22 August 1986.

facing Jews in early-twentieth-century Vienna. And a measure of cultural loyalty is perhaps present in occasional pieces written for the *Jewish Journal of Sociology* – and perhaps in a continuing interest in the circumstances of Jews in Morocco. His surname advertised his Jewish pedigree. His mother's Jewishness was transparent, and his first marriage was to a Jew. But his second was not. That he had some sentimental attachment to Jewish ethnicity cannot be in question. Consider the names of his children: David, Sarah, Deborah and Benjamin. Even though these choices were not the only ones considered and were shared by his wife, they suggest no desire on Gellner's part to hide his children's origins as a careful and vigorous assimilationist might have done. Both his parents and his grandparents had chosen non-Jewish, or not obviously Jewish, names for their children – Ernest André conveys no signals comparable to Benjamin or David – whereas he and his wife chose overtly Jewish names for theirs. This must count strongly against any thesis of Jewish 'self-hatred' on Gellner's part. But he also made no great show of his Jewish ethnicity, and was more likely to advertise his Czech rather than his Jewish roots, unsurprisingly given their greater role in his personal development. He wished to be accepted as 'normal', that is, without reference to a background which he did not deny but which he did not especially wish to be seen as relevant to his views or his opportunities in life. There were many facets to his identity, and he denied none – one consequence of which was his refusal to be caged within a Jewish identity.[35]

These are but general considerations. It is possible to go a good deal further in understanding the animosity between Gellner and Berlin and its

---

35 On 26 June 1989 he was interviewed by Guido Franzinetti, then working at the Central European University. Gellner explained why he had not chosen in 1939 to go to Israel or the United States:

> I've felt a kind of obligation to Israel. But, first of all, I'm totally secularized. My family had been secularized a generation earlier, without ever being converted or anything like that, they just kept the ethnic label, but not any religious practice. I've no religious feelings. I have a feeling of obligation to Auschwitz, not to Jerusalem. And this sense of obligation has led me to do what I have done, namely to try and understand Muslim societies, and that was always one of the motives why I always worked on that subject, and if I could use the knowledge to further a solution of that problem, then I would.
>
> Unlike my left-wing friends, who combine an ideological loathing for America with a great desire to go there, I've no ideological opposition to America, nor am I attracted by the Woody Allen world of the East Coast intelligentsia.

The full interview was published in Italian in *L'indice, Del Libri de Mese*, vol. 7, 1990. I am grateful to Guido Franzinetti for providing me with a copy of the original interview.

roots in Jewish dilemmas – and in a way which is at once interesting and, effectively, to Gellner's advantage.[36] To do so we must first spell out the elements of Gellner's critique of Berlin. The crux of their intellectual disagreement was Gellner's rejection of the idea that liberalism could or should be defended by stressing the 'incommensurability of values', Berlin's most prominent theme. 'If that is so, it is hard to see', Gellner wrote later, 'in what sense policy could ever be rational, any more than accountancy would be possible if it were to be carried out simultaneously in a set of mutually inconvertible currencies'.[37] Berlin's 'value-pluralism' was relativism, and in Gellner's view relativism opened the door to irrationalism. One could not tolerate everything, especially the counter-Enlightenment, if one wished to be a serious liberal. Gellner put the matter very clearly in the last year of his life, when reviewing John Gray's treatment of Berlin's thought.[38] Insisting that the incommensurability of values was relativism in all but name, he noted that this principle deprives us of 'the means, indeed of the right, for expressing deep revulsion. Given those incommensurates, how do you cope with societies which contain slavery, gulags, female circumcision, torture, or gas chambers, and whose apologists might well invoke that deep pluralism . . . '

---

36 Berlin did not openly attack Gellner, but interviews with Lukes and with Yael Tamir in 2000 revealed his position. His view of *Words and Things* is contained in a letter of 8 December 1959 to Norman Birnbaum:

What is true is that in the non-philosophical departments of Oxford the absence of ideas and fear of them is acute and dangerous. Among the philosophers the ideas may be inadequate or false but at least they are ideas. Hence again I think Gellner has shot at the wrong target; I think his own fate, if he goes on like this, will be very like that of Poujade – namely to be forgotten. He is an able man and in a way quite nice, but this was a very unworthy performance. Still he could, if he became serious, and got on with the positive side of his job, do a great deal of good. I wish this didn't sound so governessy, but I have a feeling about his book that it was a piece of private self-indulgence and a not a disinterested piece of rescue work (H. Hardy and J. Holmes (eds), *Enlightening: Letters 1946–60*, London, 2009, p. 712).

37 *Reason and Culture*, pp. 112–35.

38 Gellner wrote a long piece, excerpts of which appeared as 'The Prophet Isaiah' and 'The Savile Row Postmodernist' in the *Guardian* (7 February 1995) and the *Guardian Weekly* (19 February 1995) respectively. I quote from the unpublished review in the Gellner Archive entitled simply 'John Gray: Isaiah Berlin'. To cite a later piece of course disrupts the chronological treatment of Gellner's life. The justification for doing so is simple: his views were consistent across time, and the later piece contains some particularly lapidary formulations of those ideas. All unattributed quotations in the next two paragraphs come from this manuscript.

Like other relativists, Berlin grants himself a non-relativistic meta-theory: not merely so as to be able to articulate the theory at all, but because he allows himself a positive and general political theory, endowed with specific content. Just because values are plural and incommensurate, Berlin recommends politics of compromise and balance. A most commendable piece of advice, one I for one am happy to follow, but is it exempt from the pluralism of incommensurate (hence equal) values which is at the base of everything, which defines man? If it is not exempt, then who is to stop religious fundamentalists, for instance, from finding compromise on religious principles unacceptable? If it is exempt, what happens to the theory itself?

There was, however, a second intellectual criticism as well. Berlin never dealt with an obvious contradiction in his thought. In broad terms he favoured nationalism, not least in Israel itself, since communal feeling released the energies of a society. But what role was pluralism to play within national units?

'The Notes' contain, however, just as many comments about Berlin's social role as an interlocutor, as an organizer, as a grandee of the humanities in Britain. Several concentrate on Berlin's links to linguistic philosophy.

Why is he allowed to treat theories and outlooks *en gros*, impressionistically, etc., when other Oxford philosophers see that as supreme sin? (They cannot talk of determinism without distinguishing fifteen varieties, etc., etc.) Answer: because it is clearly understood that none of those theories is true, that this is only 'history of ideas', that nothing like this can be true, except when negative . . .

. . . Isaiah Berlin provided a flank cover for linguistic philosophy, . . . entertainment provided retreat for linguistic philosophy.

There are two points at issue here. The first concerns camouflage. Gellner found ludicrous the view that political theory was dead, not least because he could not imagine for a moment that revolutions, riots and wars would have been prevented by clearer linguistic usage. But even those without much interest in history were troubled by the idea of the death of political theory.

It was Berlin who found a much more acceptable way out of this little difficulty. Political theorizing was rendered *salonfaehig* after all. Political philosophy was not to be exactly dead, but not too embarrassingly alive either.

The history of ideas became something of a game, in which thinkers were damned as dangerous because anti-pluralist or praised for endorsing the incommensurability of values. 'Either way, everything will "remain as it was", which is what the fashionable philosophy of the time required'. The second point concerns the retreat. Oxford philosophers gradually abandoned their initial claim that solutions to key philosophical problems – or rather dissolutions – could be expected imminently. Berlin distracted students' attention from the failure to fulfill this promise.

Gellner was angered that a fellow intellectual of Jewish origin, a fellow exile from the disaster zones of Europe, could be, in his eyes, so infuriatingly complacent – and that he could transmit that complacency to others. He also disliked Berlin's invocation of his Jewish origins, and his implied comfortable integration. He told his friend Anatoly Khazanov that he considered Berlin to be a 'Court Jew'.[39] Berlin, prematurely, made British society seem more tolerant, integrationist and welcoming to Jews than it actually was before the 1960s. Berlin was tolerated because of his academic skill and visibility, and because he was prepared, in Gellner's view as 'a success-worshipper underneath', to accept a set of complacent intellectual assumptions. There is a sense in which Gellner is reversing the charge of self-hatred that has been discussed. Berlin was so anxious to be accepted, in Gellner's view, that he compromised his integrity.

Some final comments are in order. It may well be that visceral Jewish self-hatred was in part a generational affair. Kafka's generation seems prone to this feeling because their situation was so stark, blaming their fathers for making them either too Jewish or too cosmopolitan. Such feelings should be distinguished from the resentment that was symptomatic of later generations, for example Gellner's. To find that life is made especially complicated because of one's background can be deeply irritating. But in Gellner's case resentment did not lead to a desire to escape or deny his identity, but rather to a sense of resignation. In the last analysis, what is noticeable is that his identity was stable. There was no personal crisis caused by his Jewish background. Insofar as a Jewish identity was present, it was imposed from outside. There was no need for any personal struggle, no need to break with the ideals of his childhood. There was the continuing self-confidence of the ex-soldier, the climber, and the witty iconoclast. All in all, Gellner seems wise enough not to have chased after any singular form of authenticity,

---

39   Interview with Anatoly Khazanov, January 1999. Court Jews were financiers affiliated to the courts of rulers and nobles in pre-emancipation Europe. They were given special privileges, typically being allowed to live outside ghettos. Their social climbing encouraged obsequiousness.

accepting instead the ambiguities of life. With reference to Berlin, what is striking is that Gellner was content with his lack of roots. He dipped into various social worlds, and was marvellously adept at characterizing them, but did not choose to completely immerse himself in any. His absolute insistence on rigorous intellectual honesty follows directly from this. No comfort could be found in social life, only in unvarnished allegiance to the truth. Perhaps this last stance does reflect his Jewish background, in a way – and a particularly honest and striking approach to it.

Gellner's Problem, His Personal Response

By his early thirties Gellner was clearly his own man, prepared to attack the sacred cows of his era and to choose a unique path, diverging intellectually even from those to whom he was close personally. For example, several essays written in the late 1950s show him distancing himself from Popperian concerns. 'On Being Wrong' deals amusingly with a series of philosophies, notably Popperianism and existentialism, which try to make a virtue out of contingency. Gellner's critique is similar to that later elaborated by Thomas Kuhn, the American philosopher of science, in his celebrated *The Structure of Scientific Revolutions*. Scientists are not as pure as Popper imagined, and tend to abandon positions for pragmatic rather than logical or empirical reasons. Behind this lies a larger truth: that we fear certainty as much as we desire it. Even more important was 'Explanation in History', which critically assessed the doctrine of methodological individualism championed by Popper, that is, the insistence that social science accounts can never be considered to be complete, especially given the falsity of the assumption that social 'wholes' existed, until the dispositions of individuals had been laid bare. Gellner's attitude to this claim was ambivalent. On the one hand, he felt that social holism could not be dismissed as a basis for analysis. Sometimes brute events, from earthquakes to wars, structured social life, even if reactions might be best understood by reference to individuals. Just as importantly, the lives of individuals are shaped by institutions, especially in the pre-modern conditions studied by social anthropologists. Accordingly, the behaviour of individual tribesmen may illustrate the workings of a segmentary system, but any personal views that they have might do little to explain how that system functions.[40] On the other hand, this questioning of methodological individualism does not mean that Gellner saw human beings as mere homunculi, trapped within systems of thought and ideas without wills of their own. Rather, social behaviour often involves

---

40 'Explanation in History', in *Cause and Meaning in the Social Sciences*, London, 1973, p. 14.

resistance to institutional pressures, though this resistance is largely inef-
fectual in pre-modern societies due to the constraints of power and belief.
Gellner would later claim that it was only in the rarest of circumstances
that rational criticism would contribute to progressive ends. There are also
some interesting relevant comments from 'The Notes', including those for
the 'Popper paper':

> One doesn't believe a thing because it is testable but because one thinks
> it is true.

> Criticism unacceptable because a) upsets too much b) who is to assess it?
> That would only be possible if truth were manifest.

> 'Irrationalist' is cheap gibe. Does he want a society ruled by arguers? And
> who is to tell which arguments are to be listened to?

> Too quick on the draw – but error, confusion, unhomogeneous language
> is the safety margin, the protective belt of the open society, or should be
> (must not the open society have a certain lukewarmness about the truth?)

> Prophet not even in alien land.

The Gellner Archive contains some pages, from a long manuscript,
dealing extensively with Popper's view of the nature of a closed society.[41]
Tribal societies did not lack a variety of options in Gellner's view, and
their members faced contested ancestry, status ambiguity and generalized
anxiety. These societies were not closed, nor were they driven by a desire to
return to some uncomplicated womb-like existence; the tribes that Gellner
knew embraced the notably universalistic values of Islam. Bluntly, Popper
was guilty of the same disease – psychologism – that he had diagnosed in
thinkers whom he disliked.

In general, Gellner was instinctively opposed to all lazy thinking, clichés,
and conventions, whether of the right or the left. His intellectual integrity
needs to be approached now from a different angle: that of the philosophical problem that distinguishes him from his contemporaries and lends his
thought its particular character. To some extent the problem derives from
Gellner's background, but it could also be argued conversely that his understanding of the problem helped to consolidate his feelings about his roots.

41　It seems that the pages are from a manuscript that would become *Thought and Change.*
It may be significant that these pages were kept.

Gellner was well aware, as anthropologist and as exile, of the diversity of morals. The intellectual world in which he had been educated was not, in his view, deeply troubled by such diversity. Berlin tried to make a virtue of pluralism. Oakeshott denounced rationalist attempts to establish universal standards. The later Wittgenstein and his followers at Oxford, as we shall see in a moment, went one step further, insisting that it was impossible to escape the set of concepts within which we think – and that it was better to simply bow to reality, to accept that one had to live within these bounds. Gellner could not accept this. He knew viscerally that certain values were repulsive and dangerous: they had, after all, played a part in killing many of his relations.[42] He felt that this made him deeply sympathetic to much of classical European philosophy.[43] Social life is filled with error and absurdity, making the desire of a Descartes to find secure footing absolutely comprehensible. In responding to this problem, Gellner's thinking becomes idiosyncratic and highly original.

Consider his early views on two main streams of ethics, Kantianism and existentialism. The former seeks to reliably universalize values, to insist that anything contingent cannot be of use. Gellner's enormous admiration for Kant does not, however, go so far as uncritical acceptance. To the contrary, he says bluntly that Kant's system cannot work. Such a formal position cannot accommodate a unique set of circumstances, despite its efficacy in providing a set of abstract rules. If more data is given by specifying the details of a situation, then universalism ceases to apply. It is this failing of Kantianism that gives life to existentialism, seen here in terms of Kierkegaard, whose work privileges choice based on some ungrounded leap of faith. Gellner has no doubt but that this is so, but argues that this existentialist position (termed type E) is quite as weak as is Kantianism.

> It is equally responsible for the failure of the doctrine in its imperative formulation: for to the extent of possessing *an* arbitrary element all valuations are of type E, and consequently *that* cannot be made into a principle of selection; and as for the recommendation to make our valuation as much of type E as possible (the cult of the *acte gratuit* aspect of existentialism) *that* second order recommendation can neither be justified nor

---

42   This is a good point at which to note a criticism that Gellner directed at some of Oakeshott's followers. He enjoyed the company of Ken Minogue, but often remarked (for example in his 'Reply to Critics', pp. 633–4) on the particular blindness that derived from his background in New Zealand and Australia. European settler communities had been born modern; intellectuals from that world were too nice to realize that the traditions they admired were often brutal and vicious.

43   J. Davis, 'An Interview with Ernest Gellner', *Current Anthropology*, vol. 32, 1991, p. 71.

is it itself, with its great generality and abstractness, particularly of type E. On the contrary, it paradoxically provides a general open premiss for E-type maxims, thus in a way undermining their E status.[44]

The paper ends by saying that both views are operative, and that he has no sense of how one could choose between them. Richard Hare replied to the essay, arguing that morality was nothing but the universalizable.[45] Gellner could not accept this, arguing in another paper a year later that preferences were often supported by '*je ne sais quoi*' concepts, ineffable pseudo-notions exemplified by fascism's stress on the solidarity of blood. The fact that such concepts were even mentioned supported Hare's view that universalizability is desirable, but the existence of the concepts Gellner identified effectively preserved particularity.[46] The diversity of morals, differently put, was very great indeed – and not subject to any easy philosophical solution. Gellner's early love for existentialist hunches could not be sustained. Much more importantly, there were question-begging elements – which he would return to for the rest of his career – in the work of thinkers such as Descartes, Hume and Kant, on which his mature thought rested.

This was not merely an intellectual question, as is clearly revealed by a comment made to Gellner's friend and colleague Ron Dore during a visit to Old Litten Cottage soon after its purchase. The two men went for a walk into the woods to deliver a weekly tobacco consignment to a homeless hermit who had built a hut. 'Shyness on both sides made the conversation far from easy. But as we came away, Ernest began speculating on the real advantages of shedding all responsibilities, and speaking of it as a choice which any human being might equally make. There was no gush of pity; nor joking about the matter'.[47] Gellner's great interest in people from very diverse backgrounds rests on this, the insistence that universality was hard to find, thereby making all sorts of choices seem attractive and rational. 'The Notes' make especially clear his awareness of the arbitrariness of all social arrangements:

An argument: All society is iniquitous, because under any arrangement, alternative arrangements are conceivable and indeed plausible under

---

44   'Ethics and Logic', *Proceedings of the Aristotelian Society*, vol. 55, 1955, here in *The Devil in Modern Philosophy*, p. 90.

45   R. Hare, 'Universalizability', *Proceedings of the Aristotelian Society*, vol. 55, 1955.

46   'Morality and "*Je ne sais quoi*" Concepts', in *The Devil in Modern Philosophy*.

47   This passage forms part of Dore's address at the Memorial Service for Gellner in King's College Chapel on 24 February 1996. Another colleague in the sociology department, David Martin, remembered the same hermit, to whom the Gellner family frequently gave food.

which some groups would be better off, ergo, all societies also have
phoney ideologies, for those groups cannot be persuaded rationally not
to rebel, hence all societies are based on a lie, which explains universality
of (some kind of) faith. The idea of a rational open society, or of rule of
law, is absurd: it presupposes that a society could have really rational rules
which rational citizens could perceive, but on the contrary society needs
to be protected against the rationality of some of its citizens, ergo all
power must be arbitrary, so as to be able to check those whose deviance
cannot be checked rationally. In societies where there is rule of law technically, the arbitrariness is in the informal realm.

One consequence of these feelings was that Gellner became a brilliant sociologist of belief, deeply interested in and sensitive to the mechanisms that
allow for the maintenance of faith, precisely because he felt that none were
properly philosophically 'grounded'. Consider this comment:

> [B]eliefs must be difficult to be satisfying. Thus it is a travesty to say
> that martyrs die for Truth. Real truths seldom require such dramatic
> testimony, nor is one either asked or tempted to give it. Martyrs have
> in general defended in the face of death beliefs which they would have
> found somewhat harder to defend in the face of logic.[48]

This returns us to the world of relative standards, a world utterly unacceptable to Gellner. His thought aims to discover what is seemingly impossible:
how to ground thought when grounding is impossible. The beginnings
of an answer lay in the fundamental changes that he saw around him, that
is, the impact of science. Some grounding might be possible, after all, if
one could describe the nature of one particular social formation which
had transformed the world – and in what Gellner would seek to justify
as a progressive direction.[49] However, that sort of sociological grounding
would likely have to consider institutions just as much as ideas, given that
ideas alone cannot ensure that social benefits will result. But before he
could embark on positive explanations it was first necessary to undertake a
negative critique, to show, once and for all, that the complacent philosophy
in which he had been trained was misguided and dangerous nonsense.

---

48   'Is Belief Really Necessary?', in *The Devil in Modern Philosophy*, p. 55.
49   Of course, this characterization of higher standards of living as 'progressive' is open
to challenge from romantic thinkers who prefer simplicity and poverty – often, it should be
noted, for other people – to the affluence brought about by the division of labour. It is this
that makes Gellner's grounding, for all its power and plausibility, merely partial.

As an aside, a good deal can be said about the character traits that this research encouraged. Most obvious was irony, a mood which infuses all of Gellner's work. The anthropologist Eric Wolf recognized this, and suggested that irony is a form of frustrated idealism, turned back in toward the would-be idealist.[50] Gellner's irony was directed foremost at those who thought they knew it all, who were complacent and self-satisfied. His wit here was sly, malicious and marvellously amusing. One can see two rather different elements at work. The first element, to be discussed at greater length later, is that of irritation, envy, and even anger. In this mood Gellner could be powerfully wounding, his name-calling exceptionally effective. But the other element was a delicious sense of fun, a teasing capacity to puncture all balloons, in recognition that life is so very absurd. This is the realm of Czech low humour, reinforced by a disdain for pomposity. It is hard to recreate this: the quips and jokes were of a high standard and often almost instantaneous. Still, some examples are in order. He found a biography of Hannah Arendt, in its excessive and disappointing piety regarding her love affair with Martin Heidegger, characteristic of contemporary trends:

> The author treats [the affair] with hushed reverence. One had hoped for something like this: 'Martin's left hand was still firmly grasping *Die Phänomenologies des Geistes*, whilst his right hand began gently to unbutton Hannah's blouse . . .'[51]

Equally typical were funny and neat encapsulations of more serious intent. Brendan O'Leary was with Gellner on the last evening of his life, and remembers being confronted with a deadpan expression that foretold a dictum of some kind. Gellner announced that he could explain the history of the Czech lands in a single sentence – and did so, telling the Irish scholar simply that the other side had won the Battle of the Boyne.[52] No one was spared, even those he admired the most. Perry Anderson's insistence that the failure of bourgeois revolutionary forces in England led to later social distortions prompted Gellner simply to say: 'It really is most naughty of

---

50   Wolf to Gellner, 15 April 1967. The letter was prompted by a second reading of *Thought and Change*. Wolf also remarked on that Gellner had an intelligence which tried to keep cool, but had an undercurrent of hot lava within it.
51   'From Königsberg to Manhattan', p. 81.
52   This quip was good enough to have been used on more than one occasion. It is present in 'Reborn from Below: The Forgotten Beginnings of the Czech National Revival', in *Encounters with Nationalism*, p. 138.

history'.[53] Further, he loved to collect and to retell jokes. Many of these were personal, as in the story of two planes crashing over Tel Aviv airport, both of them containing Shmuel Eisenstadt, one of the world's most avid conference attendees.[54] Still more were from the socialist bloc, as in the Czech joke about the astronaut, which showed that the Party was held in contemptuous derision rather than fear. The space traveller was told that he would be accompanied in the spaceship by a monkey, and that he should only read his orders after take-off. The orders were simple: 'Feed the monkey'.[55]

But it is important not to overstate this. Just as important was a deep seriousness, based on high principle, and always apparent. The world needed to be understood, and our available options within it made plain, in order to allow the best chances for human decency to prevail. The lack of this commitment in others could make him very irritable. He told David Martin how disappointed he was after listening to Maurice Freedman's inaugural lecture at the LSE: it had been too soft, too cultural – too weak to suggest that anthropology could become a cognitively powerful subject, and certainly not strong enough to disrupt the complacent assumption of the school's economists that they were the leaders of social science. He similarly disapproved of the spread of phenomenology, complaining to the same colleague that they taught in the London School of Economics, not the London School of Phenomenology.[56] And he disliked the work, but not the person, of Anthony Giddens, on the grounds that he offered verbal rather than substantive solutions to problems. This seriousness was often linked to a sense of gallantry. The attack on Edward Said that will be discussed below originated in part because Gellner felt that younger scholars like Michael Cook and Patricia Crone, for whose work he had unstinting admiration, were in effect being slandered by Said; a dismissive sneer seemed to be an acceptable substitute for reading their work. And his

---

53 'A Social Contract in Search of an Idiom: The Demise of the Danegeld State', in *Spectacles and Predicaments: Essays in Social Theory*, Cambridge, 1979, p. 287.

54 The joke was often changed by his friends so as to apply to Gellner himself, who must have attended quite as many conferences, especially as an expert on nationalism in the last decade of his life. A further joke, equally applicable to both men, concerned arrival at the airport without a ticket. Known to the staff, problems would have been smoothed out – but for the fact that the hyperactive traveller is unable to remember his destination.

55 'Getting Along in Czechoslovakia', *New York Review of Books*, vol. 25, 1978. The joke was apparently also told of Polish policemen, in which version it appears in S. Lukes and I. Galnoor, *No Laughing Matter: Collection of Political Jokes*, London, 1985 – a volume whose richness owes a good deal to Gellner's input.

56 Interview with David Martin, March 2008.

late attack on postmodernism had a similar origin, in his distress that jobs were being refused to those who did not bow before the current intellectual fashion.

Of course, Gellner positively enjoyed contention, and amused himself by wondering who amongst his targets – Needham, Taylor, Said, Quine, Winch, Feyerabend, and eventually Chomsky – would wish to contribute to an anti-*Festschrift*. But underlying the pleasure he derived from independent thought, and from winning arguments, was real courage. Saying exactly what he wished to say meant that he made enemies, most obviously within the philosophical establishment. And his bravery was physical as well as intellectual. After a mugging outside a London tube station, he chased after the thief without regard for his own physical limitations. He astonished many with his determination to walk – over endless bridges at a conference in Venice, time and again up the difficult path to his summer house in Italy, through snow and rain in Prague and Budapest – without complaint, and without regard to the pain that he must have suffered. His friend, the Soviet anthropologist Vladimir Kabo, noted that walking was particularly difficult for him in Petersburg, 'but he overcame his ailment by force of will and once even toured the rivers and canals . . . alone in a rowing boat'.[57]

---

57   V. Kabo, *The Road to Australia: Memoirs*, Canberra, 1998.

4

Concepts and Society

By the late 1950s Gellner was publishing a steady stream of papers, attacking various arguments of linguistic philosophy and their proponents.[1] Most important, however, were two talks given on the BBC's Third Programme in 1957, later published in *The Listener* as 'Reflections on Linguistic Philosophy'.[2] Gellner was clearly out to wound his enemies, claiming that genuine philosophical inquiry had been replaced by mere analysis of linguistic usage, which was best pursued by studying the Oxford English Dictionary. One person who heard the 1957 radio talks was Victor Gollancz, the publisher of leftist books for many years and a publicist of genius. He asked Gellner to adapt his views into a book. In the period before publication, further publicity was assured by a debate on the radio pitting Gellner and John Watkins against David Pears and Geoffrey Warnock. The debate was heated, and Gellner was accused of inventing a straw man – a charge that seemed to stick as he had mentioned no specific names, while Warnock and Pears insisted that they were not a part of the movement that Gellner had purportedly conjured up. The debate seemed to make Gellner more determined, not least to cite the names of guilty parties when he was on the attack.[3] He received much encouragement at this time. H. B. Acton and

---

1   'Determinism and Validity', *Rationalist Annual*, 1957, was directed at Anthony Flew, and to a lesser extent at Ryle; 'Logical positivism and after or: the spurious fox', published first in *Universities Quarterly*, vol. 11, 1957, and a year later in *Universities and Left Review*, led to exchanges with both Stephen Toulmin and Alasdair MacIntyre.

2   *Listener*, vol. 58, August 1957.

3   After the publication of the book this issue of naming led to an exchange of letters with H. L. A. Hart, who was often cited to suggest that linguistic philosophy was not as far removed from real political concerns as Gellner argued. Gellner argued that a single exception did not invalidate the general rule, especially since there was something of a split between practical activities and philosophical viewpoints. Gellner also noted that listening to a paper by Hart was one episode that had formed his image of linguistic philosophy

Bryce Gallie wrote in support, and John Hajnal was a constant sounding board.[4] But what perhaps mattered most to him was the encouragement of Bertrand Russell. Gollancz had sent the radio talks to Russell, who then invited Gellner to tea. When a draft of the book was available Gollancz asked Charles Taylor to assess it. Taylor accurately predicted that it would raise a big stink: 'violent exception will be taken to it by most professional philosophers, and indignant letters will be written in all directions'.[5] This was exactly what Gollancz had hoped for, and he took the trouble to have Russell write an elegant and incendiary preface to the book. It must have delighted Gellner, not only due to the attention that Russell's status would certainly bring. Gellner and Taylor discussed the proper direction for philosophy when Taylor came for dinner after Gellner had received his comments on the manuscript. Taylor's admiration for continental theorists, above all for Maurice Merleau-Ponty, was completely opposed to Gellner's pronounced enthusiasm for Russell, apparently on the grounds that Russell took science seriously.[6] Gellner's second book, *Thought and Change*, would be dedicated to him.

Anthropology of Philosophy

Sociologists make use of the notion, derived from Max Weber, of ideal types: the practice of highlighting and drawing together elements of reality into a model, the coherence of which is designed to assist theoretical thought. *Words and Things: A Critical Account of Linguistic Philosophy and a Study in Ideology* posits an ideal type in exactly this way, seeking to describe the character of a belief system, its compulsions, defences and significance.[7]

(Gellner to Hart, 1 February 1960). Hart's demand for a statement that would clear him of membership in the movement led Gellner to a sharp response:

> Unkindly, I might add that if my book were as inaccurate about the movement as a whole as is now claimed by some, granting you special exemption would be something hardly worth having. If on the other hand it is worth having, this seems to imply that the general charges are not wholly off the mark.

An excellent discussion of the Oxford philosophical scene of the 1950s (and one that implicitly supports Gellner's sociological charges) is available in N. Lacey, *A Life of H. L. A. Hart, The Nightmare and the Noble Dream*, Oxford, 2004, especially chapter 6.

4 W. B. Gallie to Gellner, 10 October 1957.
5 Gellner kept a copy of the unsigned review; Taylor later confirmed that he was its author.
6 Interview with Charles Taylor, 2000.
7 London, 1959.

If the basic arguments in Gellner's book were derived from his previous papers, there were several changes as well. First, Gellner responded to the charge of abstraction by citing particular works, and dealing with particular thinkers. We have already seen that he was in close contact with most of the leading figures at Oxford, only omitting – as far as is known – correspondence with J. L. Austin, the dominant single figure of the movement.[8] The book's argument was enriched by setting it within a general overview of philosophy. There are also many foreshadowings of Gellner's future work, both as anthropologist and philosopher. Gellner's book and its reception concern us here, leaving a discussion of its arguments' validity for our conclusion (after an analysis of the methodological benefits that Gellner gained from his encounter with linguistic philosophy). It presents an account of a particular social world which he was able to write, as the acknowledgements made clear, because anthropological method had taught him to look at a system of ideas without prejudice as to its truth or falsity. Gellner was an outsider looking in on a world made strange to him by his background and experience, and sought to understand its social roots and emotional appeal. The acerbic nature of his portrait seems to have caused more offence than his purely philosophical assertions.

For Gellner, the central notion of linguistic philosophy was the insistence that the world is what it is. This was no trivial tautology when joined with a theory of language which asserts that we are, so to speak, concept-bound, that our reality consists of the meanings that set the terms by which we live. The immediate professional consequence of this view was to turn philosophy into the practice of unpacking various confusing conceptual puzzles. Gellner distinguished between different periods of this movement, noting that the initial, almost revolutionary insistence that the classical philosophical problems could be definitively solved within a generation had given way to a more technical, purportedly neutral set of analytic practices suited, in his view, to well-established humanist intellectuals out of touch with social reality.[9] Let us flesh out this general view by specifying what

---

8   The account of the debate about *Words and Things* written by the Indian journalist Ved Mehta, *The Fly and the Fly Bottle*, London, 1965, is multiply inaccurate. Mehta claimed, for instance, that Gellner said that Russell was now 'gaga' – something he would never have thought. This allegation was deeply hurtful to Gellner, and he considered suing Mehta. Gellner is, however, also cited by Mehta as having deliberately distanced himself from Austin, certain that the latter would eventually attack him. This has the ring of truth to it, and is confirmed by 'Poker Player', in *The Devil in Modern Philosophy*, London, 1974.

9   An unsigned article in the *Times Literary Supplement* on 9 September 1960 (written by Peter Strawson), entitled 'The Post-Linguist Thaw: Getting Logical Conclusions out of the System', described the method of linguistic analysis as awe-inspiring in its potential, and

Gellner had to say about the recent history of philosophy, the views of 'the movement' on language, and on knowledge and the world, before turning to the passages on the nature of ideology and sociology which caused the gravest indignation.

Gellner distinguished four eras in British philosophy in the first sixty or so years of the twentieth century. The Hegelian idealism and holism exemplified by F. H. Bradley had been subject to withering critique by Bertrand Russell, who shaped what would become 'logical atomism' by his effort to purify language so that individual words reflected or captured elements of external reality. There was a subtle difference between the constructive purposes of this logicism and the third movement, that of logical positivism. This Viennese-inspired approach had a brilliant local representative in the person of A. J. Ayer, whose *Language, Truth and Logic* posited a verification principle – this principle determined that statements which could not be verified, or which were not logical truths, were meaningless, and so should be consigned to the flames as David Hume had recommended.[10] Gellner kept a close eye on Ayer's work, admiring his refusal to join the Wittgensteinians and appreciating his clarity of expression. He seems to have done his 'fieldwork' here as well, attending Ayer's Saturday morning seminar at University College in the 1950s for at least two years. Gellner later recorded Ayer's refusal to believe that the Viennese logical positivists once had sympathy for Freudianism.[11] The judgement that he came to in 'The Notes' was, however, damning. Ayer had become so comfortable in the British establishment that the critical potential of his outlook was sadly dimmed.

> Ayer. Sorcerer's apprentice who worked out well. Used an enormously powerful device – for one little task – polishing off a few academic idealists – and then managed to stop it doing all the other things it can do . . .

---

asserted that the imminent 'finishing off' of traditional philosophical problems was realistic. Gellner kept a copy of this article – presumably as evidence that such hopes were expressed in the face of later denials that this had been the case.

10   D. Hume, *An Inquiry Concerning Human Understanding* [1748], New York, 1955, p. 173.

11   Gellner very much enjoyed Tom Stoppard's BBC television play *Professional Foul*, in which an Ayer-like figure faces the complexities of the erstwhile socialist bloc while travelling to a philosophy conference as an excuse for seeing a soccer match. He showed a video of this play to his students in Prague in his later years. Gellner was far from wrong about Ayer's status within the establishment, as is made clear in B. Rogers's excellent *A. J. Ayer: A Life*, London, 1999.

This view lies behind a sustained set of articles and reviews dealing with Ayer's work. 'Ayer's Epistle to the Russians' argued firmly in 1963 against Ayer's view that philosophy does not make predictions, claiming that such formalism falsely suggested that philosophy could be insulated from scientific advance.[12] Gellner again made the same point against Ayer two decades later in an essay reviewing the latter's *Philosophy in the Twentieth Century*.[13] More generally, he felt that Ayer's strength as an analyst made him a rather poor guide to the work of Moore and Russell, and to that of Wittgenstein. Imaginative sympathy was needed to really understand the appeal of philosophical systems.[14] This criticism was particularly true in the case of Ayer's book on Wittgenstein. 'You must be able to feel romanticism in your heart, before you can struggle with it effectively, rather than merely wrestling with its peripheral, often accidentally selected arguments'.[15]

Gellner considered linguistic philosophy, centred above all in Oxford, to be the fourth and final stage. It had little time for logical atomism, because its intellectual equipment derived from the later work of Ludwig Wittgenstein who had repudiated his previous commitment to atomism. Gellner made much, then and later, of the way in which Wittgenstein's *Philosophical Investigations* characterized his early work, *Tractatus Logico-Philosophicus*, as a prime example of nothing less than *the* basic error of philosophy. The first book had taught that the world and language could be lined up in a neat one-to-one manner, allowing for a scientific language able to distinguish between the meaningful and the meaningless. In contrast, *Philosophical Investigations* insisted that language was messier; it only had meaning within particular social contexts on which it was wholly dependent. In consequence the book sought to end the vain Promethean ambition of establishing any sort of universal language.[16] A similar attitude endeared G. E. Moore to the linguistic philosophers. His pedantic concern with common sense seemed to exemplify the way in which philosophy ought to be done. The attitude among linguistic philosophers toward logical positivism was far more pragmatic: if it was called upon occasionally to deflate opposing views,

---

12 'Ayer's Epistle to the Russians', in *The Devil in Modern Philosophy*.

13 'Verbal Euthanasia', *The American Scholar*, vol. 52, 1983. Gellner considered this review essay to be of some importance, considering it at one time for inclusion in *Spectacles and Predicaments: Essays in Social Theory*, Cambridge, 1978.

14 'Ayer on Moore and Russell', in *The Devil in Modern Philosophy*.

15 'Positively a Romanticist', *Guardian*, 13 June 1985.

16 The details of Gellner's analysis show great insight into Wittgenstein's ideas, particularly in the suggestion that there were notable continuities between the two periods of his thought, both in the belief that one could 'see the world rightly' and in the curious mixtures of realism and idealism.

its admiration for natural science and its concern with 'facts' were seen as errors that had been overcome.

Gellner argued that four interrelated claims make up linguistic philosophy, each of which he criticized. The 'Argument from Paradigm Case' suggests that words mean what they normally mean, and that their meaning is their use. This encouraged the facile resolution of classic philosophical problems. Free will could be established by observing a smiling bridegroom marrying a girl of his choice. As the concepts made sense of this situation, free will was vindicated.[17] Such argumentation seemed to Gellner to be merely silly. What mattered was to distinguish connotation from denotation.

> The fact that there are standard cases for the application of a term such as 'miracle' in a given society in no way proves that such terms have a *legitimate* use. They do certainly 'have a use' but this in no way proves that the terms are justified. The term may in fact have no empirical application though members of a society think it has, or alternatively the term may even be incapable of having application, being internally inconsistent. The fact that a term has a use, a range of uses, or a paradigm use only shows that the users, apart from attributing to it some sense, also suppose that this sense so to speak finds the object to which it refers, in other words its denotation. *It in no way establishes that they are right in this supposition.*[18]

'The Generalised Naturalistic Fallacy' was a second pillar. The intuitive idea was simple: 'How could we challenge the norms implicit in a language we speak, without in fact merely introducing another language?'[19] But the criticism directed at it was the same, namely that philosophy ought not to deal with questions inside a category but rather should question the category itself, examine the viability and validity of a particular way of thinking. The third pillar, the 'Contrast Theory of Meaning', was more technical, insisting that any term must have not just a use but also a contrast. This was but the inverse of the 'Argument from Paradigm Case', but it led, in Gellner's view, to a neat paradox, namely that 'a language should sometimes be usable without contrast, so that "contrast" may have a contrast'.[20] But the more important criticism levelled against this pillar was that languages are not neat and fully determinate systems.

---

17 *Words and Things*, p. 53.
18 Ibid., p. 56.
19 Ibid., p. 60.
20 Ibid., p. 63.

[C]ontrasts often overlay presuppositions which are worth bringing out, and sometimes worth denying: the contrast between good and bad witches is worth ignoring for the sake of denying that either kind exists. Far from thought generally moving within a tacitly determinate system of contrasts, it often happens that by refining a concept which at the time is contrast-less, a new contrast, a new concept is brought into being.[21]

The last pillar of linguistic analysis was that of 'polymorphism'. Gellner admitted that any language is likely to be complex, but refused on this ground to accept that that the work of philosophers was merely to explicate the complexities involved. He opposed 'multiplication beyond necessity'.[22] This sort of practice in effect prejudged matters, ruling out the possibility of clarifying usage by such means as the pointing out of contradictions. And the practice of linguistic philosophy was open, in Gellner's view, to a brutally direct challenge: if normal usage was correct, why philosophize?

Gellner regarded linguistic philosophy as a form of naturalism, that is, a theory insisting that the world was essentially unmysterious and easily understood. This notion was conveyed in various aphorisms endorsed by linguistic philosophy: 'Philosophy only states what everyone admits'; 'Philosophy begins and ends in platitude'; and 'Everything is what it is and not another thing'.[23] In the most important passages of the book dealing with knowledge, Gellner would have none of this.

[E]pistemology, the theory of knowledge, has always succeeded in presenting powerful objections to a naturalistic world view. Roughly and briefly, it has always been able to point out that nature, in terms of which everything was to be explained, had after all to be *known* before things could be explained in terms of it, and hence knowledge was prior . . . Naturalism was a kind of Third Person outlook on the world . . . Epistemology was always able to point out that before there could be a Third Person view of the world, there had to be a First Person view of the world. By making the Third Person view derivative, the First Person view primary, it made nature derivative of knowledge and placed knowledge outside it.[24]

---

21 Ibid., p. 65.
22 Ibid., p. 147.
23 These *obiter dicta* are those of Wittgenstein, John Wisdom, and Bishop Butler, respectively – the last phrase used by G. E. Moore as the motto of his *Principia Ethica*, and one of Isaiah Berlin's many tropes.
24 *Words and Things*, p. 130.

In consequence Gellner suggested that respect be shown to various strategies, most obviously the privileging of sensory data, that sought to stand outside established conventions. That such strategies were impure and hard to achieve in no way undermined their necessity. Two additional weaknesses cited by Gellner should also be noted. Most noticeable was the internal contradiction he found in Wittgenstein's position:

> [S]omething outside any and all languages had to be said, or at least conveyed, in order to explain the point and purpose of the exploration of the limits of individual, actual language. The truth that we cannot say how things are outside of all saying, cannot be a truth inside some particular language, but is outside and about all of them. So, at least one language-transcending truth remained (albeit a sadly negative one), and Wittgenstein was conveying it, *and* yet also saying that it was unsayable in virtue of being outside any given language game.[25]

But, for Gellner, quite as important was the bizarre justification for religious belief that could and sometimes did follow from the assumptions of linguistic philosophy. Religion could not be justified simply because people used religious terminology, in large part because most religions make transcendental claims themselves. Differently put, religions often gain adherents precisely because they make empirical claims about the world.[26]

There is a sense in which these arguments were simply amplifications – only the most basic of which have been discussed here – of Gellner's 1951 paper on 'Use and Meaning'. But there was great novelty in the bite of the attack, highlighted in the subtitle of the book (*A Critical Account of Linguistic Philosophy and a Study in Ideology*). First, there was sheer mockery. A diagram was presented, to be used as a parlour game, showing how linguistic philosophy worked – or, more precisely, how many of its seemingly trite observations could be backed up, especially by appeals to common sense. Second, Gellner considered linguistic philosophy to be inherently evasive. He chronicled and attacked most of all the sliding scale of claims: if one asked exactly which philosophical problems had been resolved, one was met, in his view, with a retreat to modesty – that it was too soon for results, or that all that was offered was a method of sharpening thought. Ryle's thought was seen as an honourable and brave exception to this pattern, Warnock's as its very exemplar.[27] Third, Gellner further developed

---

25 Ibid., p. 153.
26 Ibid., p. 179.
27 Ibid., pp. 47 and 249. There was in fact considerable distance between Austin and Ryle.

an earlier line of argument about the nature of belief systems in order to understand the appeal of linguistic philosophy.[28] An ideology became powerful when, at one and the same time, it seemed to explain and to threaten, to appeal and to offend. In this case, the emphasis on language and on common sense appealed, especially when set against the high-handed abstractions of some philosophical systems, whilst offence lay in the claim that well-known philosophical problems were not in fact troublesome in any way. Suppressing knowledge of such problems 'without real conviction is the acceptance of an absurdity which binds the adherent to the movement. (This is also what is liable to produce such anger in him when he encounters a doubter of the movement.)'[29] Fourth, Gellner made much of the fact – developed at greater length in his next book with reference to C. P. Snow's claim of an opposition between two cultures, those of science and humanities – that linguistic philosophy simply ignored modern science. The movement had no sense of genuine knowledge, or of real intellectual puzzlement, and as such tended to be dangerously conservative, effectively irrational and dreadfully trivial.

These points were, however, mere nit-picking compared to his provocative sociology. He charged that linguistic philosophy was a kind of populism, its purveyors the Narodniks of North Oxford.

> Linguistic Philosophy, at long last, provided a philosophic form eminently suitable for gentlemen. Nothing is justified. It is merely explained that justification is redundant, that the need for it is pathological. The philosophy is simultaneously esoteric – it is so refined and subtle in its effects that a prolonged habituation to its practices, and hence leisure, is necessary before one sees the point – and yet its message is that everything remains as it is, and no technicality is required. No vulgar new revelation about the world, no guttersnipe demands for reform, no technical specialisms are encouraged.[30]

A second charge was that perhaps the key institution of Oxford life, the one-to-one tutorial, was very far removed from its justification as an open, egalitarian and Socratic affair. To the contrary, the situation was highly unequal, with an older tutor all too able to establish a particular set of rules which a young student would find nearly impossible to challenge.

---

28 The argument in fact derives from the Danish philosopher Søren Kierkegaard's *Sickness Unto Death*, as Gellner made particularly clear in 'Notes Towards a Theory of Ideology', in *Spectacles and Predicaments*. Particular use of Kierkegaard's concepts is also made in *The Psychoanalytic Movement* (2nd Edition), Oxford, 1993, chapter 2.

29 *Words and Things*, p. 255.

30 Ibid., p. 260.

This was a no-holds-barred assault on a philosophical movement, but *Words and Things* became a sensation for an entirely different reason. If one truly wishes to bury a book, it is best to ignore it totally. Gilbert Ryle, in his capacity as editor of *Mind*, flagrantly broke this rule by returning the review copy to Gollancz on the grounds that the level of 'abuse' in the book disqualified it from treatment as a serious contribution to academic life.[31] Gollancz immediately forwarded the message to Bertrand Russell, who then wrote a letter of protest to *The Times* on 3 November 1959. His second paragraph ensured that public controversy would follow:

> Such a partisan view of the duties of an editor is deeply shocking. The merit of a work of philosophy is always a matter of opinion and I am not surprised that Professor Ryle disagrees with my estimate of the work, but *Mind* has hitherto, ever since its foundation, offered a forum for the discussion of all serious and competent philosophical work. Mr Gellner's book is not 'abusive' except in the sense of not agreeing with the opinions which he discusses. If all books that do not endorse Professor Ryle's opinions are to be boycotted in the pages of *Mind*, that hitherto respected journal will sink to the level of the mutual-admiration organ of a coterie. All who care for the repute of British philosophy will regret this.

A series of letters followed. Ryle asserted on 6 November that *Words and Things* made approximately a hundred charges of disingenuousness against identifiable teachers of philosophy; Gellner himself denied this accusation on 9 November, making clear that his charge was rather that there was an inherent evasiveness within linguistic philosophy. A majority of letters printed held that the refusal to review the book was unconscionable, many pointing out that it would have enabled a refutation of Gellner's arguments. Russell had the last word in the correspondence columns to deal with comments made against him *en passant*. But the matter came to a close with an editorial, which came down very firmly on Gellner's side. After even-handedly chastising Gellner for excessive polemical zeal and Ryle for being ridiculously thin-skinned, it addressed the heart of the matter in these terms:

> The school has had . . . some of the outward marks of an esoteric cult, the initiates of which cultivate amongst themselves a highly specialised form of intellectual activity. Again, the school, though far from homogeneous, has a considerable vogue and possesses enviable academic patronage.

31   Ryle to Gollancz, 28 October, 1959. Gellner kept a copy of this letter in his files.

Further, it is, or it used to be, the habit of these philosophers to regard philosophical problems as a sort of cerebral neurosis which it is their job to alleviate. The fact that they practised the therapy chiefly on themselves did not reconcile those of different views to the bland and seemingly patronising attitude inherent in this doctor-patient relationship . . . [32]

Gellner could have asked for no more. But more was yet to come. The book was very widely reviewed, and the scandal much commented on – and not just in Britain. Sales were impressive. The reviews were of course divided, but most of them chastised Ryle for his decision not to review the book, often stating firmly that it should be read. The historian Hugh Trevor-Roper praised the book in *The Sunday Times*.[33] Further praise came from the political theorists Bernard Crick and Maurice Cranston, and from Arnold Kaufman in the United States.[34] But the most important review supporting his key contentions was by the Oxford logician William Kneale, who declared that if members of the general public 'ask for an opinion about the correctness of Mr Gellner's story, it must be admitted that there are individuals and coteries who hold the views he describes and behave in a way that justifies his irritation'.[35] There were of course many negative reviews from Oxford philosophers. Geoffrey Warnock reviewed the book in *The Cambridge Review* on 7 November 1959, denying the existence of a school of thought, insisting that simple work was being done on simple problems, and suggesting that the approach should stand unless and until there was a more rewarding task presented for philosophers to undertake. Very similar points were made by Michael Dummett a year later, in an abusive review.[36] Iris Murdoch in the *Observer* also denied that there was any single school, but suggested that the approach of the later Wittgenstein might still solve various philosophical problems.[37] She wrote to Gellner before the piece was published, regretting that she would review it negatively, calling the book brave, but noting that this was probably not an issue

---

32   *The Times*, 24 November 1959.

33   H. Trevor-Roper, 'Time for a New Game', *Sunday Times*, 11 October 1959. Gellner and Trevor-Roper corresponded for some years, sending each other offprints on a regular basis.

34   B. Crick, *Political Quarterly*, vol. 31, 1960; M. Cranston, 'Polite Philosophy', *Guardian*, 16 October 1959; A. Kaufman, 'The Gellner Affair', *Socialist Commentary*, January 1960.

35   W. Kneale, *Hibbert Journal*, vol. 58, 1960, p. 197. Kneale was cited by Gellner in 'The Saltmines of Salzburg, or, Wittgensteinianism Reconsidered in Historical Context', his introduction to the reissue of *Words and Things*, London, 1979 – this edition had a new subtitle, namely *An Examination of, and an Attack on, Linguistic Philosophy*.

36   M. Dummett, 'Oxford Philosophy', reprinted in his *Truth and Other Enigmas*, London, 1978.

37   Iris Murdoch, 'Mr Gellner's Game', *Observer*, 29 November 1959.

for him since he did not care for the persons he offended.[38] Finally, Bernard Williams debated the book with Gellner on the radio on 24 November 1959, claiming that there was no united school of linguistic philosophy, thereby invalidating the book. And negative reviews came from other quarters as well. Alasdair MacIntyre, writing for the *New Statesman*, clearly enjoyed the polemic but felt that Gellner had failed to prove his points.[39]

There are footnotes to the scandal that should not be forgotten. Gellner wrote to Ryle on 3 December 'to express my regrets at any embarrassment that may have been caused you by recent events'. This was not because he had changed his views in any way, but rather because 'I feel extremely indebted to you and your admirable seminars, having learned from you more than from any other Oxford teacher'.[40] There was also further correspondence with Russell. Gellner was outraged by Ved Mehta's treatment of the controversy. It had cited without comment various snooty remarks by Oxford philosophers suggesting that Gellner was good on Moroccan tribesmen but not really the stuff of which philosophers were made.[41] This was obvious nonsense, not least as he was immersing himself in both linguistics and psychoanalysis at this time.[42] Mehta systematically misquoted sources, and Gellner wrote to Russell about this with the possibility of legal action at the back of his mind.[43] Russell said that he and Ayer had indeed been misquoted, but showed no interest in legal action, noting that misrepresentation was something that he had come to expect when saying something important, and that he wore it as a badge of pride. Gellner dropped the matter.[44]

---

38   Murdoch to Gellner, 26 November 1959.

39   A. MacIntyre, 'The Hunt Is Up!', *New Statesman*, 31 October 1959.

40   Ryle replied the next day thanking him for the letter, which he felt pleased to receive. Both letters are in the Gellner Archive. Gellner returned to Ryle's *The Concept of Mind* in *Legitimation of Belief*, discussed below in chapter 7.

41   Mehta, *The Fly and the Fly Bottle*.

42   On 9 February 1961, Dr G. Herdan of the Department of Philosophy at the University of Bristol wrote to Gellner. After thanking him for his letter, he noted with delight that Gellner was serious about studying linguistics, and sent a copy of his own book on that subject to help his efforts; he also noted that Gellner's style, above all in its joke-making, was highly reminiscent of Karl Kraus. As to psychoanalysis, there is an outline for a long article or book in the Gellner Archive dated January 1961.

43   Gellner to Russell, 16 December 1961. The Gellner Archive amply demonstrates the total falsity of Mehta's claim that Gellner had told him that *Words and Things* had been dictated: there are many drafts of key passages, just as there are drafts of whole chapters of his next book, *Thought and Change*. When word processing became available, he would take away complete drafts of books and rework them considerably.

44   Gellner to Russell, 5 February 1962.

Gellner's position in intellectual circles changed hereafter. On the one hand, he gained new allies, particularly on the left. He commenced a friendly correspondence with C. Wright Mills.[45] The latter wrote to the editor of Oxford University Press in America, hoping that they would bring out an American edition on the grounds that *Words and Things* did for British philosophy what he had attempted for American sociology in his *The Sociological Imagination*.[46] He followed this up with a letter to 'Dear Comrade Gellner' full of admiration for his style, and urging him to abandon North Africa and move to the United States where his talents could be fully exercised.[47] Noam Chomsky wrote admiringly of the book, wishing only that more space had been given to demonstrating the practical workings of the four pillars that Gellner had identified.[48] The book also made its mark on the generation of scholars who would soon take over *New Left Review*, most notably Perry Anderson. As a student at Oxford, Anderson's championing of the book led to considerable troubles with his college.[49] Thereafter, Anderson kept a close eye on Gellner's work, citing *Words and Things* favourably in his celebrated 1968 assault on the complacency of British culture.[50] On the other hand, Gellner was more or less excluded from the mainstream philosophical community. He rarely attended philosophical conferences during this period, which is remarkable considering the huge number that he would attend later, especially in the last two decades of his life.

There was one further exchange between Russell and Gellner. In October 1961 Russell asked Gellner to join 'The Committee of 100' of the Campaign for Nuclear Disarmament, whose members would engage in civil disobedience in order to draw attention to the need for nuclear

---

45   Mills had written to the *New York Times* asking if he could review Gellner's book for their Sunday edition, and on 25 June 1960 Mills wrote to the Soviet Friendship Society, perhaps at the prompting of Gellner, to suggest that Gellner be invited to the Soviet Union. On 17 September 1960 Gellner wrote to Mills 'just to say how much I liked your "Letter to the New Left"'. Mills replied on 25 September 1960, shortly before his death, asking whether Gellner would like to spend a year teaching in Cuba, where he had recently been himself.

46   Mills to Elizabeth Cameron, Oxford University Press, undated, probably June 1960. An American edition of the book did appear, but from Beacon Press.

47   Mills to Gellner, 16 June 1960.

48   Chomsky to Gellner, 5 November 1960.

49   I attended Oxford at the end of the 1960s. Some colleges even then had refused to buy the book, while several contemporaries studying PPE were told not to read it. Needless to say, this made it quite fashionable for students to be seen carrying copies.

50   P. Anderson, 'Components of the National Culture', *New Left Review*, no. 50, 1968.

disarmament.[51] Gellner replied that he was sorry not to be with Russell in CND: 'In part, my foreign origin would make me reluctant to be active: if the English prefer to be dead rather than red, it seems wrong for one who has voluntarily chosen to live in their country, just because of its liberal institutions, to urge them to change their mind'.[52] However much Gellner disliked the complacency of linguistic philosophy, he retained fundamental gratitude towards the country that had received him. He had the warmest appreciation for British social democratic achievements, in fighting against Hitler, and in pioneering the welfare state and allowing decolonization – though he argued later that this very success was perhaps a precondition of political complacency on the part of the ruling elite.[53]

Philosophy of Anthropology

Gellner claimed that if 90 per cent of linguistic philosophy was trivial nonsense, the remaining 10 per cent was of the greatest interest. More particularly, Oxford philosophy in fact offered a view of the world, even though its formal concentration was on language.[54] What mattered was the notion that a society was held together by its concepts, a view which had profound implications for social-scientific methods. The seriousness with which Gellner took this view is demonstrated by his Wittgensteinian questions to the tribesmen of the High Atlas. His fieldwork greatly rein-forced his sense that the late Wittgenstein was wrong. Human beings are more than concept-fodder. But for Gellner, questions for anthropology then expanded in a wholly fruitful manner. A letter came from Raymond Firth in 1956, aiming to discourage him from doing a similar study on psychoanalysts on the grounds that he needed to concentrate on his Moroccan venture, noted in passing that he understood Gellner's primary motivation for undertaking a doctorate in anthropology to be the study of methodological matters.[55] In one sense, this proved to be inaccurate, in that Gellner's thesis, published as *Saints of the Atlas*, is a wholly substantive work.

---

51 Russell to Gellner, 2 October 1961.
52 Gellner to Russell, 5 February 1962.
53 'Contribution to a discussion on "The Future of Britain's Vitality"', in A. Clesse and C. Coker (eds), *The Vitality of Britain*, Luxembourg, 1997, pp. 306–9.
54 *Words and Things*, p. 218.
55 Firth to Gellner, 21 December 1956. The Gellner Archive contains what is very probably the earliest idea for the thesis. It is entirely philosophical, suggesting a study of the different types of explanation found in anthropology. Six types – causal, functional, teleological or purposive, and explanations in terms, respectively, of desires, needs and wants – were noted, as was the need to find criteria by which to assess these different types.

Nonetheless, Gellner did produce a series of papers on anthropological – or rather social scientific – method that have an exceptional inner coherence. The volume in which they were collected, *Cause and Meaning in the Social Sciences*, is impressive and successful – perhaps, indeed, the most important intellectually of all his works.[56] Its key statements deserve consideration.

Gellner's first intervention in this area – 'Time and Theory in Social Anthropology', published in *Mind* in 1958 – was a precocious piece seeking to do nothing less than amend a central element of social anthropological practice then current.[57] His starting point was the parallel between functionalism in anthropology and linguistic philosophy's emphasis on finding the meaning of words in usage. Gellner's admiration for functionalism as a method was virtually unbounded, but the paper argued that it could be dissociated from its refusal to consider historical material. Malinowski insisted that a society's view of its own history reflects current interests, but this is no reason to ignore available archives and records. Crucially, no credence should be given to the notion that a society actually functions as a smooth, self-maintaining system. To the contrary, a society can be made up of competing interests, with contest between them leading to social change. This point was well made by Edmund Leach in his *Political Systems of Highland Burma*. In his attempt to explain social change, Leach was driven to propose that there were two ideological systems at work within the same society. Gellner had two objections to this view, both of which he developed in subsequent years. First, societies were comprised of more than beliefs; the functionalist method should not be interpreted in the idealist terms favoured by Leach. Second, there was no logical need to suggest that there were two opposing systems of thought, each as clearly delineated as

---

56   This is of course a personal opinion. Others favour different books: Perry Anderson *The Psychoanalytic Movement*, Brendan O'Leary *Nations and Nationalism*, and Lilli Riga *Language and Solitude*. Still, it was not surprising that *Cause and Meaning* (published in London in 1973) enjoyed a second life when reissued in 1987, on the initiative of John Davey, by Blackwell as *The Concept of Kinship and Other Essays* – following Gellner's election to the William Wyse Professorship of Social Anthropology at Cambridge. His essay collections were often very well received, e.g., E. Leach, 'General, Applied and Theoretical', *American Anthropologist*, vol. 77, 1975; and 'Field-work in Philosophy', *Times Literary Supplement*, 21 September 1973 (reviews of *Cause and Meaning in the Social Sciences*); G. Steiner, 'States of Mind', *Sunday Times*, 24 November 1974; and B. Crick, 'The Devil Rides Out', *Observer*, 9 February 1975 (reviews of *The Devil in Modern Philosophy* [and *Legitimation of Belief*]; B. Crick, 'A Devil of a Philosopher', *Times Educational Supplement*, 2 February 1980 (review of *Spectacles and Predicaments*); and R. Shweder, *Man*, vol. 22, 1987 (review of *Relativism and the Social Sciences*).

57   The essay is reprinted in *Cause and Meaning in the Social Sciences*. It had its origin in the fact that he took the book with him on one of his fieldwork trips to Morocco.

the other. To the contrary, a single system might well have inconsistencies within it, available for exploitation by reformers or radicals.

Gellner would return to this theme – the usefulness of Malinowski for exposing the genetic fallacy, so much practiced by his great predecessor James Frazer, together with his insistence that this revolution did not necessitate a sense of absolute timelessness – in later years. Indeed, he would become something of the theorist of the 'historical turn' that was already taking place in the work of such anthropologists as Jack Goody and Alan Macfarlane. But if this line of argument set out to correct and amend the practice of social anthropology, most of Gellner's other papers sought to explain the actual workings of anthropological method, to explain how it was able to produce such powerful knowledge. He made his case largely through negative critiques of Wittgensteinian approaches to social science, based upon preconceptions about the nature of social reality. He was deeply opposed to the 'entry of the philosophers', that is, to the use made by Wittgensteinian philosophers of anthropological examples when seeking to establish rules for social-scientific method. But there was a minor target as well, namely the infatuation of anthropologists – such as Leach – with philosophical ideas that Gellner considered to be meretricious. This secondary critique became more important in later years, as the 'plague' of Wittgensteinian ideas moved into anthropology.[58]

A very striking preface can be presented here before the details of Gellner's position are further described. Gellner was close at this time to the social anthropologist most often cited by the philosophers he criticized. Edward Evans-Pritchard liked to have him to dinner at All Souls College in Oxford, and wrote to him regularly – approving of his 'Concepts and Society', and appalled at the decision to name Leach the Provost of King's College, comparing the appointment to Caligula's decision to make his horse a consul.[59] Perhaps it was because of this connection that Steven Lukes informed Gellner of a debate held in Oxford between Winch and MacIntyre, in which both made much use of Evans-Pritchard's famous work on the Azande – paying particular attention to the importance of cattle in Zande society. Towards the end of the debate Evans-Pritchard, present in the audience, stood up, and noted simply that the Azande did

---

58 J. Davis, 'An Interview with Ernest Gellner', *Current Anthropology*, vol. 32, 1991, p. 66.

59 Evans-Pritchard to Gellner, 30 August 1962; and 3 January 1967. Gellner was apparently surprised to be the audience for these views. But there can be no doubt of the admiration in which he held Evans-Pritchard. He felt that Mary Douglas's treatment of Evans-Pritchard (*Evans-Pritchard*, London, 1980) was shoddy, and took obvious care himself when writing a long introduction to Evans-Pritchard's *A History of Anthropological Thought*, London, 1981.

not possess cattle. This allowed Gellner to write a withering attack on the manner in which philosophers engaged with the anthropological world, keen to instruct even when they knew very little about the societies in question.[60] Gellner was then accused of citing unpublished work, without reference to changes that had been made to the published versions of the papers in question that later appeared. This allowed Gellner to make his point still more forcefully. After defending his use of the early versions, on the ground that they had been widely circulated and had all the appearance of being finished, he turned to the published versions. Noting the correction from Evans-Pritchard (which had affected the published versions of the papers), he asked whether the philosophers had chosen to reconsider their interpretation of the symbolism surrounding the fictitious cattle.

> Not a bit of it. Winch mechanically substitutes *crops* and *harvest* for *cattle*. MacIntyre, more cautious but less grammatical, uses various substitutions including the simple device of replacing cattle by the pronoun *they* . . . Do the two authors really suppose that ecology makes no difference to the symbolic life of a people, that one can give a 'deep' account of the people's concepts on totally mistaken background assumptions, and then leave everything unchanged, except for a mechanical substitution of one environment by another?[61]

The amusement to be had from the debate should not for a moment hide the seriousness with which Gellner spelled out and articulated a systematic position of his own.[62]

---

60   'The Entry of the Philosophers', *Times Literary Supplement*, 4 April 1968. The section of this text concerned with 'the great Meaning of Cattle debate' was omitted from the version later collected in *Cause and Meaning in the Social Sciences*, for reasons noted in this paragraph. The explanation for the mistake of the philosophers is easy to make. Evans-Pritchard was the author of two classic studies, of the Azande and of the Nuer – who most certainly did have cattle. The philosophers mixed up the two books.

61   'Letter to the Editor', *Times Literary Supplement*, 18 April 1968.

62   Gellner seems to have maintained cordial relations with Winch, and was prepared to debate with him on more than one occasion. Relations with MacIntyre, already troubled as the result of an exchange over linguistic philosophy ('Reply to Mr MacIntyre', *Universities and Left Review*, Summer 1958), did not improve. MacIntyre had already reviewed *Thought and Change* negatively, and he would later treat Gellner's *Legitimation of Belief* more extensively and still more harshly. Gellner's particular charge in the debate is that MacIntyre's view that causation in social events could be seen as a matter of logic, that is, as the coming to fruition of the essence of a particular idea, was far too idealist, not least as it suggested ignoring material pressures and historical contingencies. But his main attack on MacIntyre came in 1971 when reviewing *Against the Self-Images of the Age: Essays on Ideology and Philosophy*.

'Concepts and Society' stands closest to the critique of Oxford philosophy, and to the analysis of Leach's monograph on Burma. At its heart is a philosophically adept demonstration that our theories can dictate what we perceive in external reality. An initial reaction to oddity and difference (Gellner cites as an example Evans-Pritchard's account of the Nuer calling a twin a bird) is to see illogicality, even the workings of a primitive mentality. But anthropologists of functionalist persuasion dealing with belief are likely to be much more charitable. A key purpose of Gellner's analysis was to highlight the resemblance between Wittgensteinianism and such functionalists: both see links between use and meaning. It is at this point that Gellner makes his own point, insisting that interpretative charity, the presupposition that an ideology provides a suitable and effective conceptual foundation, can be overdone. A series of diagrams demonstrates that *a priori* belief in the ability of a set of concepts to make sense, to provide sufficient meaning for use, can lead an investigator to so curtail fieldwork as to fail to understand what is really going on. Differently put, too much benevolence or charity in interpretation may lead to insufficient attention paid to context – and to the way in which ideologies may actually work. Gellner draws examples from both Evans-Pritchard and Leach of anthropologists bending over backwards to make sense of seemingly absurd statements by means of specious arguments asserting that such statements were not sincere or were merely symbolic. Gellner wishes to say, in effect, that this is reverse conceptual discrimination. For the point about some concepts is precisely that, when studied in proper context, they do *not* make sense. He makes this point to begin with by means of a seemingly fanciful example. 'Bobility' can refer either to someone who possesses certain characteristics of bravery and virtue, or to the holder of a particular office. These are of course very different things, but Gellner argues that many societies do not in fact distinguish between them. The relative incoherence of such a concept is, however, of the utmost social importance:

> Bobility is a conceptual device by which the privileged class of the society in question acquires some of the prestige of certain virtues respected in that society, without the inconvenience of needing to practice it, thanks to the fact that the same word is applied either to the practitioners of those virtues or to occupiers of favoured positions.[63]

After noting MacIntyre's serial enthusiasm for most of the self-images of the age, including Freudianism and Marxism, he concluded presciently: 'A heart so avid will not be denied, and though prediction is normally perilous, we can feel absolute confidence that, in the end, we shall see the reunion of Father MacIntyre and Mother Church' ('The Belief Machine', in his *The Devil in Modern Philosophy*, p. 197).

63 'Concepts and Society', in *Cause and Meaning in the Social Sciences*, p. 39.

The point is that the very incoherence of concepts can lend them social functions. 'To make sense of the concept is to make nonsense of the society'. On the basis of these points Gellner moves to a summary of his case.

> Excessive indulgence in contextual charity blinds us to what is best and what is worst in the life of societies. It blinds us to the possibility that social change may occur through the replacement of an inconsistent doctrine or ethic by a better one, or through a more consistent application of either. It equally blinds us to the possibility of, for instance, social control through the employment of absurd, ambiguous, inconsistent or unintelligible doctrines. I should not accept for one moment the contention that neither of these things ever occurs; but even if they never occurred it would be wrong to employ a method which excludes their possibility a priori.[64]

This point is accentuated by a comment on Durkheim. Gellner remarked that the great French theorist had tried to find a sociological solution to Kant's problem about the compulsiveness of our concepts – and interestingly so, stressing that ritual was required to maintain the sense of compulsion. But he also noted a similarity to Wittgenstein, bluntly asserting the superiority of Durkheim for having at least been concerned with the need to explain social change. The solution at which Durkheim hinted – that of the presence of two conflicting sets of belief – had been fully developed by Leach, as noted above. Gellner continued to resist this approach. Social change may result simply because a subgroup in society 'has chosen to exploit the imperfect application of those ideas, and to iron out the inconsistencies and incoherencies'.[65]

An altogether more radical challenge to the hegemony of conceptualist analysis was developed in a set of papers concerning kinship, published in *Philosophy of Science*. The first of these was Gellner's own 1957 paper on 'Ideal Language and Kinship Structures'. This rather formal piece of philosophy – surely based, however, on awareness of the theory of segmentary societies – challenged the tenets of linguistic philosophy by suggesting that an ideal language could be constructed for kinship, and that it could be anchored in physical reality. This latter assertion, that an understanding of the biological or physical aspect of kinship could make a contribution to social analysis, proved to be something of a red flag to those anthropologists convinced that the social is all that matters. The case against Gellner was

---

64   Ibid., pp. 39–40.
65   Ibid., p. 44.

made first by Rodney Needham, the Oxford anthropologist. Needham did not propose, as we will see Winch doing somewhat later, a relativist position claiming that the standards of knowledge referred to by Gellner are 'Western' rather than universal. Rather, Needham insisted that anthropology is concerned with social understandings rather than physical realities. What matters about paternity, for example, is the social determination of the father. This view allowed respect for the concept of adoption; as a consequence, Needham claimed that biological facts are irrelevant to anthropological study.[66]

Gellner disputed this in a fabulously rude paper on the grounds that 'the possibility of classifying offspring as adoptive, depends on the observer's knowledge of the disparity between the social and the physical relationship, and it is this disparity which gives the term its meaning'.[67] John Barnes joined the debate at this point.[68] He made two points against Gellner. On the one hand, he sought to socialize the notion of physical kinship, to say that what is physical is itself socially constructed. This was to make Needham's point again, albeit at a much deeper level. On the other hand, he added an epistemological injunction, namely that we cannot ever know about such a private thing as reproductive practices. Gellner argued against both these points. To begin with, anthropologists are not without resources when it comes to examining putatively private life. They can observe, listen to gossip, and check as best they may. There may be difficulties in saying much about such private acts as copulation or murder, but difficulties are not impossibilities. More important is the distinction that can be drawn between the socially-physical and physical-physical father, that is, between the socially attributed genitor and the actual biological genitor. Gellner's point remains here the same as it had been when answering Needham, namely that one only knows that someone is socially determined to be the father if one possesses secure and universal knowledge that this is not in fact the case biologically.

It is important to see how Gellner supports his position. He insists that it would be a strange anthropologist who returns from fieldwork in a society

66   R. Needham, 'Descent Systems and Ideal Language', *Philosophy of Science*, vol. 27, 1960.
67   'The Concept of Kinship, with special reference to Mr Needham's "Descent Systems and Ideal Language"', *Philosophy of Science*, vol. 27, 1960. This paper was carefully amended by Gellner when it was included in *Cause and Meaning in the Social Sciences* (where this quote appears on p. 165). Gellner wrote to Ian Jarvie to explain: 'Denunciation of this kind, when its object is not present, to present his own case, and is not famous enough for his case to be well known, makes a bad impression' (Gellner to Jarvie, 14 February 1973).
68   J. A. Barnes, 'Physical and Social Kinship', *Philosophy of Science'*, vol. 28, 1961.

which said that a child had more than one genitor – or indeed that all
children were sired by a single male – and reports that this was indeed the
case. This sort of explanation is ruled out by the characteristic practice
of anthropology. This matters enormously because it brings to the fore a
crucial part of what anthropologists actually do in their fieldwork. Given
their refusal to accept the local beliefs as true on the basis of their universal
acceptance, satisfactory explanations will offer an account of how beliefs
are sustained, what social effects they have, and how they are squared
with counter-examples.[69] The same general point can in effect be made
negatively.

> The anthropologist's account, far from being committed to respect the
> truth, in its context, of the belief . . . is in fact based on a recognition of
> its falsehood. Anthropologists do not generally give complex accounts of
> how a tribe manages to sustain the faith in fire burning, wood floating,
> etc.: indeed, it would require an anthropological account if the tribe
> managed to sustain a *denial* of these.[70]

Although the idea in this passage is present in the debate with Needham
and Barnes, the quotation is taken from Gellner's main discussion of the
work of Peter Winch, 'The New Idealism – Cause and Meaning in the
Social Sciences'. Gellner had immediately welcomed the appearance of
Winch's *The Idea of a Social Science* in 1958 on the grounds that it bravely
spelled out the full social implications of the later Wittgenstein. This was
desirable, even necessary, given the notion that the authority of forms of
life had to be accepted. Wittgenstein and his followers were blind to social
consequences in all their forms, and Gellner felt that it was entirely to
Winch's merit that in effect he did for Wittgenstein what behaviourism had
done for empiricism – namely, describe with sufficient clarity a model for
the better exercise of judgement. The extremity of Winch's position – the
insistence that we live in worlds of concepts, and that every such world is
different, and none better than any other – allowed Gellner to state his own
position with absolute precision.

Were Winch's injunctions followed, anthropology as hitherto understood would be impossible, and the knowledge gained through encounters
with others would simply amount to an insistence that they do things

---

69 'Nature and Society in Social Anthropology', in *Cause and Meaning in the Social
Sciences*, p. 199.
70 'The New Idealism', p. 70.

differently elsewhere.[71] Gellner insisted that rational scientific knowledge made it possible to ask all sorts of questions, notably about belief and especially about the way in which belief was maintained in the face of apparently disconfirming evidence. But Gellner's attack went much further.

One set of arguments concerns the nature of belief systems, and more particularly the idealist insistence that social understanding can only give us an account of beliefs because we live within the terms that they set.[72] Gellner argued that belief systems are not as coherent as Winch presupposed. Many belief systems contain within themselves histories of change. It makes little sense, for example, to write of Western history without paying attention to the Reformation and the Enlightenment. Moreover, the attempts at self-improvement involved in these movements were not, as Winch occasionally seemed to suggest, somehow mistaken, nor were they anything but central to the civilizations involved. At this point Gellner's argument about excessive contextual charity comes in. Interpretations which presume that concepts make sense are inherently misleading due to the presence of various options within belief systems. Winch and many other idealist philosophers of social science offer a 'seamless wonder' view of the role of concepts in society. Gellner made use of George Orwell's *1984* to accentuate why this is very wrong.[73] In that novel, great efforts are made to purify the dictionary so that certain thoughts will become unthinkable, making their enactment impossible. To control the commanding conceptual heights of society is everything. But ideologies are not at all like this. They tend rather to be loose and shapeless monsters, permitting escape clauses and alternative options. Christianity was interpreted quite differently by peasants than it was by the upper orders, that is, by those who either prayed or

---

71   Of course, it is more than likely that such encounters would lead, especially given different levels of development, to the argument that things were done *badly* elsewhere. This is what happened when Europeans first encountered much of the rest of the world, leading to those theories of the savage mind discussed above. Differently put, Winch smuggles in as a presupposition the notion that all cultures are equal.

72   Concentration here is on his principal confrontation with Winch. But he also engaged with A. R. Louch's *Explanation and Human Action*, Oxford, 1966. He gave a paper on this book in 1968, reviewed it in 1969 (*Sociology*, vol. 3, 1969), but only found time to revise his argument in 1975 as 'A Wittgensteinian philosophy for (or against) the social sciences', in *Spectacles and Predicaments*. The principal charge here was that Louch made an illicit slide from the sensible assertion that concepts constrain, to the false notion that *only* concepts constrain. Nonetheless, Gellner much admired the logical rigour of the book, its ability to spell out a position fully.

73   He did this when presenting the argument of what would become *Legitimation of Belief* in lectures at the London School of Economics on 'Modern Ideologies' in 1972–3.

fought.[74] Likewise, as soon as Marxism became an official ideology it made sense for opponents of the regime to justify their actions in terms of the humanist writings of the young Marx. These examples might not convince because they derive from complex societies, but Gellner later made the point most forcefully with reference to the Azande, whose culture was endlessly cited by Winch and his colleagues. Evans-Pritchard had warned that Zande culture was 'a thing of shreds and patches', incorporating at least twenty different cultural groups and speaking seven or eight different languages within a part of the territory it inhabits.[75] This ethnographic fact matters enormously. If ideologies are not elegant and tight but confused and slack, the social scientist must start to ask which group emphasizes which set of beliefs in order to advance its interests. To enter into this line of questioning takes us away from the search for meaning and returns us to causal analysis, to the evaluation of interests, to groups and the nature of social structure. And there is a corollary. As a practising anthropologist, Gellner sees man as more than concept fodder for positive as well as nega-tive reasons. It is more than just that people's lives are not totally bound by a set of concepts, but also rather that they take their beliefs with a pinch of salt, conducting themselves with a measure of humour and irony. This is not to presume an easy escape from the ideological and practical constraints on life: the ability to manipulate does not necessarily lead to the emergence of more rational styles of thought.

Other arguments are directed against Winch's relativism, against the notion that rationality can only be seen within the terms of a particular culture – making Western science merely one cognitive approach amongst others. This is held to be wrong on four accounts. First, self-contradiction stands at the heart of relativism as a philosophical position. Why should we accept the view that truth is different, as Pascal had it, on the other side of the Pyrenees unless this very statement has universal status? In Winch's case, there is something decidedly odd in his insistence that cultures are, so to speak, separate and equal. If one is genuinely caged by a single culture, the standard reaction to another is that difference is error. The fact that Winch stresses that all cultures are equal suggests that he possesses, *pace lui*, at least some universal standards. Second, relativism seems attractive because it makes much of avoiding the imposition of one set of standards upon other people. Gellner takes care to highlight Winch's position at

74   E. Le Roy Ladurie, *Montaillou, village occitan de 1294 à 1324*, Paris, 1975.
75   E. Evans-Pritchard, *The Position of Women in Primitive Society and Other Essays in Social Anthropology*, London, 1965, somewhere between pp. 106 and 110, cited in *Legitimation of Belief*, Cambridge, 1974, p. 143.

this point by quoting a comment made by the latter to the effect that missionary activities were reprehensible. This line of argument – stressing the dominating qualities of Occidental reason – was to become much more prevalent in the 1970s and 1980s.[76] But relativist tolerance is potentially phoney. It allows those ruling the commanding heights of a society's conceptual apparatus to rule out of court, as a heretic, someone who wishes to challenge local practice. Differently put, relativism can indeed be repressive, can itself generate conformity.[77] Third, Gellner admits that Winch's picture of social life might have been largely veridical in some early stage of history, before the emergence of world religions keen to proselytize, and in the absence of much intercultural contact. But he insists that most of the historical record is utterly unlike this, as everyone – including the members of the few tribal societies remaining in the developing world – now knows. One thing that follows from this is that relativism's injunction to 'do in Rome as the Romans do' becomes completely vacuous:

> What is 'Rome'? The upper class of the contemporary municipality of that name? Central Italy? The Common Market? Catholic Europe? Countless boundaries, geographic and social, vertical and horizontal, criss-cross each other in a rapidly changing world. Relativism is not so much a doctrine as an affectation.[78]

Finally, Gellner argued that it is a mere conceit, sustainable only within the study, to imagine that magic is the cognitive equivalent of modern science. Relevant here is his earlier argument about social science's dependence upon the understanding of the natural world that was brought about by Western science. But the point that he stresses more is that the problem of relativism has been solved asymmetrically. The power of scientific-industrial civilization is so obvious that any theory which cannot cope with this fact has to be rejected. Powerful cognitive equipment does not guarantee social progress, but it does at least make possible – and, by and large, for the first time – human decency.[79] It is a view that underlies his general philosophical position, to which we turn in the next chapter.

---

76 Behind this charge lay the epistemological adventures of such French theorists as Michel Foucault and Jacques Derrida, with whose works Gellner, perhaps curiously, never seriously engaged – although he hinted at his views toward the end of his life, as will be seen below in chapter 11.

77 This point very nicely made in *Legitimation of Belief*, p. 48.

78 Ibid., p. 49.

79 'The New Idealism', pp. 70–1.

Assessment

If Gellner's reputation was made by the scandal surrounding *Words and Things*, there were costs attached. He resigned from the Mind Association, and was effectively expelled from Britain's philosophical community. It is hard to tell whether this episode had a formative impact by shattering any illusions that he might be capable of uncritical assimilation – or whether any desire to 'fit in' had long been eclipsed by stronger aspects of his personality. Whatever the case, there can be no doubt that his determination to spell out his own views was undiminished – indeed, it was perhaps encouraged. On the one hand, he reasserted his views on linguistic philosophy on numerous occasions, and he complemented them, as we shall see, with a penetrating interpretation of the social background of Wittgenstein's ideas. On the other hand, he sought to move from a negative critique to a positive understanding of the nature of the modern world, and of our options within it. Before turning to his positive philosophy, it makes sense to assess the extent to which his early work retains its power.

The most sustained attempt to revisit the debate occasioned by *Words and Things* is Jonathan Rée's essay 'English Philosophy in the Fifties'.[80] Interestingly, the analysis broadly parallels that of Gellner, but it adds interesting sociological details. For one thing, Gellner was surely right to concentrate on Oxford given the sheer numbers – more than fifty philosophers, compared to a mere six in Cambridge.[81] For another, Gellner was correct when identifying the privileged class background of Oxford philosophers, as the detailed list Rée provides makes clear.[82] Going beyond this is to encounter one of the saddest discoveries to be made about the academy, namely that all too much is driven by pure fashion. Approaches die out less because of intellectual defeat than from simple boredom; moves towards new approaches are often driven largely by novelty. This consideration makes it hard to judge the impact of *Words and Things* on the linguistic philosophers. One suspects that Gellner's book did have some effect; but quite as important was the fact, which he himself often emphasized, that the approach itself was dull – and in part sustained by the charisma of Austin, who died in 1960.[83] In Oxford there was certainly great interest

---

80   *Radical Philosophy*, vol. 65, 1993. Cf. Lacey, *A Life of H. L. A. Hart*, chapter 6.
81   Rée, 'English Philosophy', p. 6.
82   Ibid., p. 20.
83   There is another consideration of the debates surrounding *Words and Things*, T. P. Uschanov's 'Ernest Gellner's Criticisms of Wittgenstein and Ordinary Language Philosophy', in G. Kitching and N. Pleasants (eds), *Marx and Wittgenstein: Knowledge, Morality and Politics*,

in the work of Chomsky by the late 1960s, although this led to no new movement, rather to a situation in which pluralism replaced a dominant paradigm. In any case, there is no doubt but that the approach is now dead, with some members of the movement publicly and somewhat wryly admitting as much. A particularly important witness in this regard was Bernard Williams, admitting at last that a 'revolutionary' movement had existed and that he had been a part of it.[84] In response to a question, which recalled an Oxford philosopher of the time saying that one did not need to know anything to do philosophy, cleverness and interest being enough, Williams replied:

> I think a lot of people thought that but would not have had the cheek to say it. It is quite an interesting historical reflection that that remark would certainly have sounded a great deal less quaint when it was uttered than I think it does now.
>
> The revolutionary feeling about philosophy made people overly self-conscious about what philosophy was and encouraged the feeling that it was frightfully different from anything else. That, in turn, made everybody think that the sciences, for instance, were not philosophical . . . I think now that people would once more be very conscious that there are parts of science which are [philosophical].[85]

More was conceded. Austin's declaration that the identification of multiple meanings for words was as justified as noting the existence of 10,000 types of beetle was rejected by Williams, more or less in the spirit of Gellner's acidic remark about multiplication beyond necessity. Theory was necessary, for Williams, so as to locate the problems which mattered.[86] This had been precisely Gellner's point.

Attention also needs to be paid to the way that the privileging of culture and concepts, of meanings rather than causes, became so very marked in

---

London, 2002. Uschanov regrets the passing of linguistic philosophy, considering Gellner's attack to be unjustified. Uschanov may be right at some points of detail, but he wholly fails to grasp the social atmosphere of Oxford in those days.

84 'Bernard Williams on the Precise Meaning of Linguistic Philosophy', *The Listener*, 9 March 1978. A slightly more limited autocritique, admitting the presence of an orthodoxy, but still insisting on diversity within it, came still earlier, in a special issue of *Mind* dealing with its own history: G. Warnock, 'Gilbert Ryle's Editorship', *Mind*, vol. 85, 1976. It is worth noting that both Strawson and Warnock themselves turned to metaphysics in the 1960s and 1970s.

85 'Bernard Williams on the Precise Meaning of Linguistic Philosophy'.

86 Ibid.

much of social science from the 1960s. One source of this tendency was the influence of Wittgenstein. For academic life is not marked only by fashion but also by its uneven diffusion, and approaches abandoned in one area gain sudden appeal elsewhere. Gellner certainly felt this to be the case within the social sciences during his lifetime. We shall have occasion to note some of his later arguments against the privileging of meaning above cause, particularly as it affected social anthropology, and to analyse his later, ever more sophisticated accounts of the workings of traditional and scientific modes of thought. But we can conclude here by noting the most sophisticated critique of his position from within social anthropology, and tying it to his most general statement of anthropological method.

Talal Asad's critique of 'The New Idealism' – a key essay in a self-consciously iconoclastic volume attacking the sacred cows of the anthropology of the time – associates the very notion of translating the terms of one culture into those of another with the arrogance of Western imperialism. He goes so far at one point as to say that anthropology itself may play some part in establishing unequal power relations in the world. If a good deal of scepticism should surely be directed at the latter claim, serious attention needs to be given to a different argument.

> If Benjamin was right in proposing that translation may require not a mechanical reproduction of the original but a harmonization with its intention, it follows that there is no reason why this should be done only in the same mode. Indeed, it could be argued that translating an alien form of life, another culture, is not always best done through the representational discourse of ethnography – that under certain conditions a dramatic performance, the execution of a dance, or the playing of a piece of music might be more apt. These would all be productions of the original and not mere interpretations . . . .[87]

The element of truth here resides in the indisputable fact that significant areas of social life are best seen in relativist terms. Who indeed is to say that one form of dance is better than another? Nonetheless, there remains a great deal to be said for the continuing importance of Gellner's arguments. For one thing, social-scientific method does and should draw on modern science when addressing matters that go beyond symbol and expression. It is the very falsity of certain beliefs, as Gellner stressed, that makes possible

---

87   T. Asad, 'The Concept of Cultural Translation in British Social Anthropology', in J. Clifford and G. E. Marcus (eds), *Writing Culture: The Poetics and Politics of Ethnography*, Berkeley, 1986, reprinted in his *Genealogies of Religion*, Baltimore, 1990, p. 193.

an investigation into the ways in which they are sustained. It was this insight that allowed him to become a brilliant sociologist of belief. For another, there is great value in a method which does not automatically presume that belief is all, that meaning makes the world go round – not least because most societies in history have faced severe material constraints. Accordingly Gellner suggests that the more open method of classical British social anthropology, concerned with power accounting, is likely to do most to advance social understanding.

> This consists of showing how the persistence of a given political or economic, etc., system is the result of the interplay of given forces in the given environment . . . without placing too much explanatory strain on the assumption of an automatic persistence of strange beliefs, etc. The assumption is that people are very roughly similar all over the place, and are not perfectly socialized, i.e., are not total slaves of either the overt or the tacit norms of their society. Men will go off any kind of social rails. A Power Balance-Sheet shows how the system maintains itself even on the assumption of a reasonable amount of disturbance (and, incidentally, a reasonable amount of external disturbance as well).[88]

There is nothing here to rule out the recognition of those historic moments when ideological innovation is autonomous. But there is also acknowledgement that power and wealth can matter just as much, and can have their own moments of autonomy as well.

If these are general points, something more specific needs to be said about Gellner's attitude towards functionalism. He was certainly no naïve functionalist, citing Lévi-Strauss's quip that to say a society functions is a truism, and to say that it works perfectly an absurdity.[89] Nonetheless, in critical comments on an early version of Ian Jarvie's doctoral thesis, he insisted that functionalism could simply be a causal account written in reverse.[90] This is as problematic as the view that social systems automatically maintain themselves. Durkheim rightly distinguished the causal origins of an institution from the role that it might then play in society, thereby escaping from the danger of presuming that a functional need of

---

88   'Sociology and Social Anthropology', pp. 125–6.
89   'Concepts and Society', p. 20.
90   In the early 1960s Gellner offered comments on Ian Jarvie's attempt (later published as *Revolution in Anthropology*, London, 1964) to assess anthropology in light of Popper's view of science. Dictated notes, probably from 1961, seek to defend functionalism from the charge of teleology on the grounds that functionalism is really only causal theories written in reverse.

society will automatically create the necessary institution. Functionalism is illegitimate when it is teleological in this way, but vital when it seeks to understand the role of ideas and institutions after they are established within a social order. We will need to ask, time and again, whether Gellner's method led him to a teleological rather than causal analysis, as many have claimed about his theory of nationalism.

But it is clear that he benefited enormously from non-teleological functionalism, that is, from a concern with and ability to trace the social roots of ideas and institutions. In the ideological sphere, for example, he continually stressed that many systems of thought are created, but only those which fit with contemporary social circumstances thrive. This other functionalist method is perfectly respectable, an account of the spread and maintenance of an ideology. The key ideas behind psychoanalysis were more or less created by Schopenhauer and Nietzsche, but they only spread widely once society was sufficiently mobile and open for a form of pastoral care based on this approach to become an attractive and pressing necessity.[91] Similarly, many bursts of egalitarian rhetoric are present in the historical record, but that ideology came to dominate only when modernity brought sufficient social mobility to make the viewpoint more a description of reality rather than a mere prescriptive position.[92] One can go further and say that Gellner's account of all modern ideologies, from psychoanalysis to Marxism and from nationalism to Islam, is based on a single perception, namely that of a fundamental breakdown of social structures such that human beings lack social moorings. And a final consideration must be borne in mind. Loose, licit functionalism of the sort just described is only powerful if its account of a society's functional characteristics is realistic and convincing. The extent to which this is true of Gellner's own account of modern society's workings will be at the centre of much that follows.

---

91   This is perhaps the central argument in his account of psychoanalysis, discussed at length below in chapter 7.
92   'The Social Roots of Egalitarianism', in *Culture, Identity and Politics*, Cambridge, 1987.

5

Gellner's Philosophy

Thought and Change is an extremely ambitious book, aiming at nothing less than to provide a social philosophy for modern times. The treatise sought to find a middle way between two dangerous positions. On the one hand, Gellner accepted the need to avoid millenarian views, that is, those promising to provide absolute truths along with plans for human perfectibility. He was at one in this regard with Berlin and Oakeshott. On the other hand, he insisted that meaningful thought was still needed, that one could not react to the recent history of total ideologies, of Bolshevism and fascism, by presuming, as had Oakeshott and Berlin, that all was well, that local traditions were acceptable and in fine order. Monistic standards were needed, but they needed to be held in a critical spirit.

'The Notes' had made it quite clear that for Gellner the grounding of thought was a personal necessity, the attempt to find some mooring for someone whose identity, never fully formed, had fallen further into question as a result of historical events. But the claim of the book, in effect, is that his personal experience was representative of something much larger. The world as a whole is being transformed by the possibility of development. Gellner illustrated what he felt was involved with reference to Kafka's *Metamorphosis*, in which a man wakes to find himself turned into a beetle.

> [The loss of] fixed identity . . . constitutes the very paradigm of a moral problem. Interesting moral crises are not those in which the question is simply whether individual or group will or will not succeed in maintaining or attaining some given and assumed standard – a kind of moral weight-lifting – but those in which the aims or criteria, the identity of the solution, are themselves in serious doubt.[1]

---

1   *Thought and Change*, London, 1964, p. 52.

The approach of the late Wittgenstein suggested that it was impossible to find general criteria. Gellner admitted the difficulty, but insisted that the situation of being lost, of being thrown into the sea and needing somehow to swim, meant that 'must implies can', especially since linguistic philosophy in any case had a wholly implausible implicit sociology.[2] Gellner's strategy – or, rather, the only strategy he claimed to be available – was to specify the values that followed from or were allowed by the sociology of the modern world, properly understood. If pure and absolute truths could not be found, values could nonetheless be found 'as fellow-travellers, second-class, of new ways of conceiving the world, new ways which impose themselves by their superior truth, accuracy, and controlling and predictive power'.[3] The claim that grounding was possible, even if in this backhanded manner, made this an optimistic book. 'The book is meant to be a continuation of *The Open Society*', he noted, 'but related to the post-war world, and more sociological'.[4] This is an accurate description, not least in seeing the book as part of a post-war world. He was to become anxious as that context changed.

A few observations about *Thought and Change* can usefully be made before turning to Gellner's justification for his historicist take on industrialism. An arresting stylistic feature of the book was the presence of striking aphorisms – 'Philosophy is about industrialization', 'Or, if you like: philosophy is about the failure of 1789' – culled from 'The Notes'.[5] At a substantive level, the most impressive element of the book, welcomed by many, was its discussion of nationalism, so powerful that it eventually set a new agenda for this important topic. Then there was the blunt and basic claim of the book, that two phenomena – industrialism and nationalism – must be present if a polity is to gain legitimacy in contemporary circumstances. This might suggest a sort of brute simplicity to the book. Nothing could be further from the truth. For one thing, systematic attention was given to the philosophy of science. Industry depends upon science, and its character affects our ethics and our identity. For another, Gellner had a great deal to say about political liberty, consciously excluded from his definition of the modern social contract. All of this can be put in a nutshell: we were offered a general view of the world. By the time he was forty he knew where he stood; the book foreshadows nearly all his later work.

---

2   Ibid., p. 77.

3   Ibid., p. 78.

4   Gellner to I. C. Jarvie, 28 January 1965.

5   A charming essay by Roman Szporluk ('Thoughts about Change: Ernest Gellner and the History of Nationalism', in J. A. Hall [ed.], *The State of the Nation: Ernest Gellner and the Theory of Nationalism*, Cambridge, 1998) describes the impact of the aphorisms, and his attempt to link them together in his own career.

The Episode of Progress

Gellner took particular care in the opening of the book to specify the way in which validity could be based upon an interpretation of time. The account was initially negative. The first general notion attacked was that concentration on a fundamental episode, often that of a social contract, held to mark off a prior condition of backwardness from our modern and superior condition. There was a logical problem with this position: a contract changing everything would only be attractive to and adopted by people already possessing advanced normative standards.[6] Gellner argued that such episodic theories tend to be sociologically thin. Most episodic theories have been concerned with the questions that obsess political theory, namely, those that deal with political obligation and the conditions of liberty. The drama of our age, in Gellner's eyes, concerned development.

In contrast, he showed much greater sympathy to theories of social evolution. One great attraction of this view was its habitual use of a much more plausible sociology. We do not suddenly, by an act of will, become modern: to the contrary, this is a long and specifiable process. A second benefit was the fact that this perspective assumed the unity of mankind: differences between human beings were merely the result of societies being at different stages of development. There was no need within this paradigm to talk of 'the savage mind': to the contrary, many primitive thought-styles were 'proto-rational'. Still more important, thirdly, was the philosophical coherence of this approach. The idea that one can somehow step outside of society so as to judge it *is* somewhat comical. Evolutionists were logically consistent because they did not try to escape the naturalism they preach.[7] Despite all this, Gellner firmly rejected grand evolutionist theory. On the one hand, there was a further sociological problem, though of a different kind. Those at the bottom of the evolutionary ladder were in effect being told to suffer through a series of stages in order to reach the favoured end point. Such a view suggested that change is inevitably gradual. But this was emphatically not the way people in the developing world experienced social change in the twentieth century. Stages were skipped because there were models to copy – and, very often, external forces which dictated national

---

6   This consideration made him utterly opposed to the revival of contract theory pioneered by and exemplified by John Rawls. He had only derision for 'Mayflower' philosophy.

7   *Thought and Change*, pp. 24–5.

patterns of development.[8] On the other hand, Gellner saw evolutionary theories, at least in their pure form, as empty.[9] The central problem was that mere serialism, that is, the identification of the requisite stages of development, told us nothing about the motor of social change. Ironically, once a particular mechanism was posited or established, then the stages themselves lost much significance.

Another criticism has often been levelled against evolutionist theories, namely that they are morally craven in encouraging us to jump on the bandwagon of projects aiming to promote historical progress. To imagine that morals can be justified in this way, rather than in their own terms, was to commit the naturalistic fallacy – or, to use the equivalent Popperian term, to be historicist. This criticism gained power and plausibility when the two great bandwagons of twentieth-century Europe ended in the horrors of Nazism and Marxism-Leninism. Nonetheless, Gellner admitted to being historicist.[10] At a purely philosophical level he suggested that cravenness was more or less unavoidable, for morals were always likely to be influenced by any social formation that seems viable.[11] But Gellner's historicism was particular and limited. The sociological and ethical claim he wished to put forward was neo-episodic.[12] The transcendence he sought was not universal, but referred to specific features of social life – poverty, disease, short life expectancies – that were everywhere in the historical record but were now made avoidable by modern industrial society. Very simply, this involved the privileging of industrial society, of a social formation allowing affluence and longer life, yet free from any promise – or, rather constitutionally unable – to create heaven on earth. Gellner claimed that it was possible to choose a reliable bandwagon, that of the industrial mode of production.

He was deeply influenced by Raymond Aron. The great French social scientist's principal use of the term 'industrial society' would help to detect similarities and differences between liberal capitalism and state socialism, a choice of subject matter that naturally appealed to Gellner given his own background. But Aron had a sense of our place in history, and *Thought and Change* noted one 'admirable' essay that applied the term to the developing

---

8   Ibid., pp. 27–9.

9   Ibid., pp. 15–20.

10   Ibid., p. 69.

11   Gellner will later argue that criticism – revered by Popper as the alternative to historicism – is insufficient as a means to ground our knowledge and activities. See below, chapter 7.

12   *Thought and Change*, chapter 2.

world.[13] This intellectual appreciation for Aron was certainly enhanced
by Gellner's belief that the Frenchman had shown great bravery in his
career. Aron's famous attack on Marxism as the 'opium of the intellectuals'
impressed him, and the book of that title was often on his reading lists. He
claimed that Aron uniquely combined a sense of reality with an ability to
understand left-wing French thought from the inside. But if Gellner was
wont to refer to him as the greatest living sociologist, he had little time
for Aron's own attempt, deriving in part from phenomenology, to create
a formal language dealing with the nature of historical experience.[14] Still,
he remained on the six-person editorial board of the *European Journal of
Sociology*, which he had joined at its inception in 1960, until shortly after
Aron's death – and often told stories of Aron's views on the papers that
were submitted for publication.[15] But underlying this intellectual influence
was surely Gellner's lived experience, the witnessing of mass migration
from country to city both in Czechoslovakia and in North Africa. One
detects too the legacy of *the* theorist of industrial society, Saint-Simon,
though there is no indication that Gellner read his work at any stage of his
career. But Masaryk had read Saint-Simon, and this certainly influenced
the worldview he sought to foster in Czechoslovakia – aiming at general
depoliticization in order to create a space in which 'experts' could flourish.

The Modern Social Contract

Gellner's claims about the modern social contract – seen less as a contract
and more as a sociological condition – were both more precise and more
extensive than has been noted thus far. His contention was not just that a
contemporary social order will be accepted if it provides a decent standard
of living and allows for rule by those sharing a culture with other members
of the society, but that this ought to be so. It is worth underscoring the
fact that these claims were at once sociological and moral. Certain social
processes were identified, but we did not know enough, in Gellner's view,
about the variations in form that they allow. And equally, these developments were to be endorsed on moral grounds. Differently put, we should

---

13   R. Aron, 'The Theory of Development and the Historical Interpretation of the
Contemporary Era', UNESCO, 1960, cited in *Thought and Change*, p. 144.
14   'Time Machines', *Time and Tide*, vol. 42, 1961. This is a review of Aron's *Introduction
to the Philosophy of History*, the translation of his 1938 doctoral thesis. Aron noted later that
Gellner was astonished by the attention he gave to Sartre's Marxism (R. Aron, *Mémoires*,
Julliard, Paris, 1983, p. 592).
15   The next chapter records an exchange of views between them. Aron admired Gellner,
but noted on more than one occasion that he found his views 'a little severe'.

quite self-consciously commit the naturalistic fallacy. The real and the rational did, in this one case, converge.

1. Industrialism

Gellner was not only making the sociological claim that an industrialized society would be stable because it would be legitimate. A secondary socio-logical claim was that the transition of industrial society was taking place.

> The mechanics which ensures the necessity of the transition seems to me quite simple. Its crucial premiss is simply that men in general will not tolerate a life of poverty, disease, precariousness, hard work, tedium and oppression, when they recognize that at least most of these features can be either obviated or greatly mitigated.[16]

Gellner noted explicitly that this was a brutally simple argument, empha-sizing at its core a matter of general psychology rather than a feature of social organization. This was sociologically sound, though he glossed his position in an interesting way. While the mechanisms involved were varied, the imitation by states of new techniques might play an important role; such imitation could destabilize existing social conditions, releasing forces for change. But this scarcely mattered, for 'the secret is out' that affluence was possible.[17] This was not the case with the earliest industrialization in Britain, nor indeed with its initial European emulators. But the name of the game since 1945 has been that of development. Any regime which failed to achieve development was likely, in Gellner's view, to be short-lived, either because it would be overthrown from within or because it would be destroyed by external forces.[18]

The moral claim was equally straightforward. It was entirely proper to commit the naturalistic fallacy, since we must prefer a mode of social life that brings comfort, health, long life and the possibility of decency, when scarcity had previously ensured that social advance was almost necessarily at the expense of one's fellow human beings.[19] This was a powerful if banal point, stated more clearly in *Thought and Change* than anywhere else in his work, and Gellner clearly felt that it barely needed justification. A striking passage, much mulled over in 'The Notes', made the point by ridiculing

---

16   *Thought and Change*, p. 70.
17   Ibid., pp. 70–71.
18   Ibid., p. 70.
19   Ibid., pp. 145–6.

Pascal's view that the human condition is exemplified by a condemned man in a prison cell – on the grounds that life does not have a predetermined end, and is not necessarily lived out in a situation of relative comfort.

> So if we must have a comparison, it cannot be the condemned cell . . . but something like Auschwitz: you can live a little longer, and a little better, provided you are very lucky and are willing to participate in the degradation and extinction of your fellows . . . The moral significance of *the* transition is of course that soon, human nastiness will become a matter of choice rather than necessity. We do not know what *other* factors – inherent in the social organization of industrial society, or, perhaps, in the human psyche – may operate in that regrettable direction nonetheless: we ought to find out. But we do at least know that the dire material imperative of nastiness is on the way out. Nastiness, hitherto necessary, will henceforth be contingent.[20]

Further, Gellner aligned himself with John Stuart Mill's response to those who claimed that utilitarianism – with its insistence on such 'philistine' concerns as decent sewage, health and food production – was a philosophy fit for pigs: the critics were the real exemplars of a callous and piggish mentality.[21] Their arguments had been inherited by 'cultural entertainers' afraid of modern science. A 'fairly modest annual rate of growth, sustained over time, can do more to alleviate human misery than all the compassion and abnegation that past ages could muster'.[22]

Gellner's privileging of industrial society was not complacent:

> To say this is not to say that existing liberal affluent societies are things of great beauty and warrant complacency. They aren't and they don't. The surviving areas of poverty and underprivilege are obscene precisely because they are now totally unnecessary.[23]

Joined to this were several passages in which he had a great deal of fun attacking the unrealistic presuppositions of neo-classical economic theory.[24] The idea that everything could be left to the market made no sense when the infrastructure of industrial society required state provision of standardized

---

20 Ibid., pp. 144–5.
21 Ibid., p. 73.
22 Ibid., p. 219.
23 Ibid., pp. 118–9.
24 Ibid., pp. 117–8.

education for all.[25] We hear in these passages the imprint of Gellner's back-ground, of Czechoslovak social democracy, concerned with creating a soft and inclusive managed capitalism. Still more important was the way in which these concerns point to, and underlie, his view of the age of nationalism.

11. Nationalism

The two leading social theories of the modern world, Marxism and liber-alism, had both held that nationalism would disappear with time, doomed either by the spread of international trade or by the emergence of a working class which owed no loyalty to the nation.[26] While history had judged the falsity of this prediction, a general enlightenment about the character of nationalism did not then result. Very much to the contrary, nationalism came to be seen as a deeply irrational force, such that men were subject to 'Dark Gods', prone to act in accord with their sense of blood and belonging. It was this view that was questioned in the famous opening sentence of a book by Gellner's LSE colleague Elie Kedourie – 'Nationalism is a doctrine invented in Europe at the beginning of the nineteenth century'[27] – by suggesting that nationalism was contingent rather than necessary and universal. Gellner claimed to have been 'woken from his dogmatic slum-bers', as Kant had been when he read Hume, by Kedourie's demonstration that nationalism was not a universal feature of the human soul.[28]

Several interrelated and powerful factors were adduced by Gellner to support the notion that nationalism was contingent. Most immediately, rule by co-culturals, that is, obeisance to the notion that state and culture should coincide, was conspicuously absent for most of the historical record. The identity of most human beings was given to smaller units – tribes, cities and peasant communities – none of which had much awareness of the wider, external world.[29] This sociological consideration was scarcely contradicted by the presence of empires, for these rarely had the inclination or the means to interfere with local loyalties within their conquered terri-tories. To the contrary, empires often encouraged self-rule by different cultural groups in the interests of peace and good order. The classic instance was the millet system of the Ottomans, which tolerated Christian entities

---

25 Ibid., chapter 7.
26 Ibid., pp. 147-8.
27 E. Kedourie, *Nationalism*, London, Hutchinson, 1960, p. 1.
28 Gellner, *Nationalism*, London, 1997, p. 10.
29 *Thought and Change*, p. 152.

within a nominally Muslim empire on the condition that taxes and slave soldiers were delivered on a regular basis. Still, such large imperial entities did exist, and for good reason. Many ruling regimes are of foreign origin. Especially when rival internal groups compete, it makes sense to have a ruler that is indebted to neither side, and preferably one with inherited skills in administration. Thus the Mamluks provided rulers throughout the Mediterranean during the classical period of Islam. In a similar spirit, universities bring in external chairs when rivalry between factions makes life dysfunctional. External rule has often been welcomed.

It is scarcely surprising to discover that Gellner was unwilling to accept Kedourie's explanation for the emergence of nationalism, namely that it had been invented by a handful of German intellectuals at the turn of the eighteenth and nineteenth centuries. This was simply too idealist, especially as an alternative explanation was available. This explanation had two parts to it, each of whose character can usefully be highlighted. On the one hand, Gellner sought to demonstrate that the characteristic cultural units of the past — tribes, city-states and peasant communities — were simply too small to support the workings of modern society. Differently put, what was offered here was an account of the functional requirements of modernity. On the other hand, Gellner described the causes of nationalism. If most units are too small, why is it that development cannot take place under imperial aegis? In linguistic terms, if standardized languages are needed for the functioning of modern societies, why would those languages not be those of the great nineteenth-century European empires? Why are such units too large? Let us consider the two sides of Gellner's explanation in turn.

The character of modern social life is approached through negative and positive considerations. What mattered negatively, Gellner maintained, was a change from structure to culture.[30] In ideal-typical pre-industrial circumstances, the fact that life was, so to speak, obviously structured — that is, that for virtually everyone it involved manual labour of the most difficult sort — meant that communication between groups did not really matter. Gellner cited Claude Lévi-Strauss's account of a band in which the necessary tasks of daily life were so obvious that cooperation between the band's two sections was possible even though they spoke different languages.[31] The rigidity of this world, in which roles are ascriptive cages, was contrasted with that in which we live.

---

30   Ibid., pp. 153–7.
31   Ibid., p. 154.

[A] very large proportion of one's relationships and encounters . . .
are ephemeral, non-repetitive, and optional. This has an important
consequence: communication, the symbols, language (in the literal or
in the extended sense) that is employed become crucial. The burden
of comprehension is shifted from the context, to the communication
itself . . . If a man is not firmly set in a social niche, whose relationship as
it were endows him with his identity, he is obliged to carry his identity
with him . . . his culture becomes his identity. And the classification of
men by 'culture' is of course the classification by 'nationality'.[32]

If one side of the coin is the collapse of structure's tight constraints, the other
side was positive, namely the acquisition of identity through membership
in a large and impersonal community thanks to the educational system
supported by a state.[33] To swim in modern society, basic literacy was
required; everybody needed to be a clerk in order to have basic life chances.
Such a high level of generic education is likely to be provided using a single
language. A contrast was drawn between the situation of most European
countries in which vernacular languages become state-regulated, and that
faced outside Europe, notably in Africa, where languages and dialects are
so varied and diffuse that the language of the state (whether one such local
language, a borrowed non-European language or even that of the former
colonial power) is imposed upon the peasantry. In the former case, the
mother tongue comes to predominate in the school, whereas the latter
condition sometimes sees the language of the school being adopted at the
family level. In any case what was involved was extreme social engineering,
as in the decision to make all Algerians Arabic-speaking or in the Kemalist
diktat that changed the alphabet of modern Turkey. This led to a firm
conclusion. Nationalists in power are, so to speak, hypocritical: they
pretend to protect folk culture but in fact create new and uniform social
worlds, distinctly opposed to most customary practices. The end result of
their actions is cultural homogeneity.

Limits on the size of modern states are derived from the impact of nationalist movements. Gellner's argument was simple. Industrialization created a
suffering class, thereby causing social tension. In many European societies
the privileged and the suffering masses shared much in common, notably
a pre-existing language, allowing for citizenship to be extended after the
period of dreadful pain accompanying industrialization. The contrasting
situation saw the disadvantaged masses share almost nothing with those

---

32   Ibid., pp, 155, 157.
33   Ibid., pp. 157–64.

in power. In these circumstances, secession could seem very attractive. It was at this point that the North African context of Gellner's initial theory became important. For he stressed that nationalism tended to have two sources of support. One was the native intelligentsia, often trained in the metropole but, on returning to the homeland, having its social mobility restricted on account of colour or religion. The second was the urban proletariat. There was an interesting addition to the theory. In Algeria mass support came from the Aurès mountains.[34] This demonstrated, in Gellner's eyes, that the disruption brought by industrialization could be anticipatory; the wave of modernization might be felt before it actually broke, though this was certainly not true of the Moroccan situation in which crucial support came from the *bidonvilles*. But in either case, disillusion was likely to surface amongst the nationalist masses. Gellner very firmly stressed a contrast between the two groups, namely that the intelligentsia clearly benefited from secession (or decolonization), not least by gaining employment of real importance, whilst the hardships of proletarians might well increase given 'the drive for rapid development and the fact that national government can sometimes afford to be harsher than a foreign one'.[35] This fact was the result of a contention absolutely central to Gellner's vision. Nationalists in power were often social revolutionaries, creating a nation where none had really existed before. Traditional groupings which had resisted imperial pretensions – notably the tribes of the Atlas Mountains which had switched allegiance to the cause of independence shortly before its triumph – were doomed to still greater disappointment at the hands of the new, modernizing elite. The language of a new nationalism stressed folk traditions, invented or not; but what mattered was the social transformation that made such customs irrelevant.

A particularly striking element of Gellner's initial sustained attempt to explain nationalism was its open-mindedness. Complexities could result from the tidal wave of modernization hitting groups within a single territory at different times.[36] Equally, a group might wish to secede not because it had trouble adapting to modern conditions, but rather because it was in fact more suited to them.[37] Any minority group with a cultural advantage of this sort was in a dangerous position: its abilities might incite covetousness, turning it into a scapegoat – and hence pushing it towards secession more

34   Ibid., p. 168.
35   Ibid., p. 169.
36   Ibid., p. 171.
37   Ibid., p. 169.

out of fear than desire.[38] Care was taken to mention cases which might
seem to contradict the argument. He noted that some pre-modern loyalty-
invoking political units, particularly those of Europe's Atlantic seaboard,
were maintained in the age of nationalism. These seemed to be examples
of nationalism and nation-states before industrialization.

He offered three potential ways of dealing with these anomalies.[39] First,
it might be that nation-building activities had been underway since the
Reformation. Second, these cases might be excluded altogether from
the theory of nationalism, on the grounds that they represented different
social processes. Third, a dynastic state might develop alongside, or coincide with, a culture and language, allowing for continuity in territory over
time. Finally, weaknesses of nationalism were noted. 'The world is richer
in cultural differentiations, *and* in systematic injustices, than it has room for
"nations"', making it rather hard to predict exactly which national claims
would result in the successful establishment of a state.[40] Nonetheless, Gellner
made some attempts in this direction. Once a high level of education had
been achieved, the need for a single shared language might diminish, as
in the Swiss case, precisely because levels of understanding are so high –
though Gellner noted that both Canada and Belgium had not reached any
such state of ease.[41] Equally, some cultural groups can decide not to press
claims, either doing well inside a larger society or fearing destruction by a
brutal state (which might at the same time be confident enough to hold out
prospects of genuine autonomy).[42] Finally, Gellner noted that the success of
certain claims could be much aided by geopolitical events, as was clearly the
case with the establishment of Czechoslovakia in 1918.[43]

Gellner finished his account with a set of reflections on the character of
the world polity, that is, of a system in which new nations co-existed with
older powers, mostly of course now bereft of their erstwhile empires.[44] This
division within the global system was judged to be advantageous. Gellner
suggested that some new nations had benefited from the construction of infrastructure during colonialism, but he insisted nonetheless that independence
was fundamentally progressive – releasing energies, generating enthusiasm,
and allowing for development to suit genuine domestic needs rather than

38   Ibid.
39   Ibid., p. 173.
40   Ibid., p. 174.
41   Ibid.
42   Ibid., pp. 174–5.
43   Ibid., p. 175.
44   Ibid., pp. 175–8.

those of the metropole.[45] In this connection, he noted that a genuine struggle for independence might help a new nation establish both loyalty and organization. But for Gellner the most important advantage of the world's power structure was political, namely that it allowed political liberalism to survive. Had there been a single unified world polity, it would be tempted to act repressively, to create an apartheid-like world polity.

> A consequence of the political world system generated by nationalism has been that the convulsions and inescapably centralized efforts to lift oneself by one's own shoelaces, economically, do not need to be re-imported into the developed, previous imperial, territories . . . This is a boon: and so is, in the long run, the cultural diversification of the world . . . pluralism is some kind of insurance against both tyranny and political folly.[46]

Consequences

The two principles, industrial affluence and nationalism, comprising the modern social contract did not close off sociological understanding. Very much to the contrary, the exceptional clarity of the argument brought to the fore two further issues, at once sociological and philosophical. Let us consider in turn the consequences of this vision both for the way in which the world is experienced and for the chances that political liberty might spread within it.

1. Being and Knowing

The rationale for endorsing the capacities of industrial society was far from Gellner's only statement on our moral situation. His original post at the LSE had been, as noted, to teach ethics to sociologists, and this surely influenced the amusing mapping of ethical theories which stands at the heart of *Thought and Change*. Since much of what Gellner had to say was negative, it should be noted that he viewed certain thinkers positively. Both Dostoyevsky and Nietzsche were praised for powerfully conveying the sense of disorientation – of beetle-hood, to recall Kafka – with which Gellner had begun. In contrast, most philosophies prejudged matters, by using language which incorporates a solution derived from the very terms

---

45   Ibid., p. 176.
46   Ibid., p. 178.

that are used. Before turning to his suggestive map of moral theory, something of its tone can be seen immediately in his comments on Kierkegaard
and Hume. The Danish philosopher had assailed the facility of Hegel's
world growth story, yet replaced it not with a continuing sense of difficulty
but rather with still greater facility—that is, the notion that one could make
some sort of leap of commitment. Epistemological considerations – the
inability to ground causation, the lack of guarantee for the continuity of
nature – famously led Hume to despair, but also to a surprising means of
escape from that condition.

> The *intense* view of these manifold contradictions and imperfections in
> human reason has so wrought upon me, and heated my brain, that I am
> ready to reject all belief and reasoning, and can look upon no opinion
> even as more probable or likely than another. Where am I, or what?
> From what causes do I derive my existence, and to what condition shall
> I return? Whose favour shall I court, and whose anger must I dread?
> What beings surround me? And on whom have I any influence, or who
> have any influence upon me? I am confounded with all these questions,
> and begin to fancy myself in the most deplorable condition imaginable,
> inviron'd with the deepest darkness, and utterly deprived of the use of
> every member and faculty.
>
> Most fortunately it happens, that since reason is incapable of dispelling
> these clouds, nature herself suffices to that purpose, and cures me of this
> philosophical melancholy and delirium, either by relaxing this bent of
> mind, or by some avocation, and lively impression of my senses, which
> obliterate all these chimeras. I dine, I play a game of backgammon, I
> converse, and am merry with my friends; and when after three or four
> hours' amusement, I would return to these speculations, they appear so
> cold, and strain'd and ridiculous, that I cannot find in my heart to enter
> into them any further.[47]

Gellner felt that it was difficult 'to read this part of his work without
embarrassment'. Hume commends his own moral convictions 'with the
tone of a man whose vantage point is fixed and secure. In the theory of
knowledge, he is not like this . . . Had Hume shown the same honesty and
self-knowledge in ethics, which he had shown in logic, he would have
been that much more lovable'.[48]

Gellner divided ethical theories into six types, noting that particular

---

47   D. Hume, *A Treatise of Human Nature* [1739], London, 1985, p. 316.
48   *Thought and Change*, p. 58.

thinkers occasionally tried to combine the insights of more than one type.[49] First, he held Platonism, then and later, to be a superb description of the ideological apparatus of a settled agrarian society; it underwrote the values of such a society by the moral flavours attached to the concepts which make social life possible. But excellent sociology made for poor philosophy; moral problems arise when codes conflict, typically because of social change. Secondly, theories which suggested that we should 'be true to our inner self' took several forms, with many suggesting that the true self could be found once a sense of harmony was achieved. But harmony was 'far from being some kind of independent standard for sorting out values, [it] only receives any concrete content as a consequence of some determinate specific set of chosen values'. The many theories of this sort that expressed themselves in psychological terms tended to assume the existence of a true self, waiting to be awakened like Sleeping Beauty. The insistence that we follow a rule, the third type of theory, could be quite as question-begging. It appealed to cultures which favoured religions of the book and bureaucracies, and was therefore open to the romantic objection that what really matters is free expression, the breaking of conventions. Fourth, and still more question-begging, was 'the way of residue', that is, theories – Marxism, Wittgensteinianism, psychoanalysis – that suggested that truth will simply be present, ready to give herself up, the moment that egregious error has been removed. Fifth, most space was devoted to the ethical strand inaugurated by Aristotle which encouraged us to aim at a particular target. The supreme example of this position was held to be utilitarianism. Gellner did not for a moment think that the way in which human beings were portrayed in this approach, as a sort of blend of gourmet and accountant, was at all powerful, nor did he think that any formal proof was available that happiness is our ultimate target. But he defended the approach because of its empiricism.

> Utilitarianism, on the other hand, commends constant reassessment, a constant shaking-up of the tie-ups between characteristics and evaluations in the light of fact – without respect for existing associations. Of course (and contrary to the mistaken psychology of the utilitarians) neither pleasure nor happiness are some kind of inner sensation-accompaniment, the readings of an inner thermometer: these words are just ways of conveying that we like something, and add nothing to that liking. The utilitarian commendation to re-assess everything in terms of happiness – which as it stands may be a tautologous, vacuous recommendation,

---

49   Ibid., chapter 4.

amounting to no more than: choose what you like by what you like –
amounts however in practice to a most non-vacuous recommendation of
revaluations-without-prejudice, a transvaluation of values in the light of
what contributes to general contentment.[50]

Nonetheless, Gellner offered two withering criticisms of utilitarianism.
First, our aims were not as rigid and constant as the theory imagined.
Roughly speaking, aims were likely to have that character under condi-
tions of scarcity. But affluence allowed aims to become varied, and open
to manipulation – making them unavailable as a court of ultimate appeal.
Second, utilitarianism was of little use when it was needed most:

> [I]n traditional society, habitual associations are more or less sacrosanct and
> the experiential reassessments are forbidden or discouraged. Transitional
> contexts, on the other hand, do have an overwhelming aim – 'develop-
> ment', 'industrialization' – but this aim in the transitional period notoriously
> involves such massive suffering that Utilitarianism must, in effect, be sinned
> against rather than observed.[51]

Gellner will have a good deal more to say about the claim that a vale
of tears must be crossed in order to reach affluence. He termed the final
ethical approach the 'rail' – in effect, the recognition of an obvious necessity, or, differently put, the decision to jump on the bandwagon of history.

The central point made by this typology of ethical theories was negative,
namely that the ground on which we stand is none too firm. That said,
some positive notes were struck. Theories which concentrate on both target
and rail had something to offer, though only when properly interpreted.
Admiration was shown *en passant* for Kant's attempt to join a concern with
the inner self to the notion of following a rule. The insistence that nothing
can be based on the contingent produces a philosophy of such minimalism
that Gellner felt it did possess a real sense of the transition, of trying to
locate order amidst chaos. Of course, Kant was as much concerned with
knowledge as with ethics, allowing us to make a transition from traditional
ethical theories to what concerned Gellner most, namely the nature and
consequences of modern science. His interest was in nothing less than a
complete change in the relation between being and knowing.

But before considering this, it is important to note that the initial description of the new social contract suffered from a particular confusion. What

---

50   Ibid., pp. 97–8.
51   Ibid., p. 100.

was the place of knowledge? Was it somehow a third, autonomous force? This was suggested when he spoke of knowledge as 'the principal agent' of the transition to modernity.[52] His later work became much clearer on this point. *Plough, Sword, and Book* and *Reason and Culture* claim that science played a creative and autonomous role in the emergence of modern society. But something much more important needs to be stressed, namely the importance of science − wherever it came from − as 'the form of cognition of industrial society'.[53] Human beings may have invented, luckily, this particular way of gaining knowledge; but the knowledge is real, able to change the world, and so able to change us. Accordingly, industrial society distinctively exhibits an active and autonomous style of thought as much as a new form of social organization. *The particular culture of modern rational science can change societal structure.*[54] Finally, we should recognize that *Thought and Change* says little about the actual mechanics of scientific knowledge; *Legitimation of Belief* was to fill that gap, offering a survey of modern epistemological practices.

The technical strategy at work in modern science was the effort to establish a small redoubt of certainty within the self upon which knowledge and morality could be established. Approaches of this sort resembled the practices of Robinson Crusoe, forced as a castaway to think without the benefit of social support. An alternative name for the same method, that of 'cosmic exile', was coined by Quine − who ridiculed the notion, unfairly as far as Gellner was concerned. In general, Gellner preferred to speak of the Pure Visitor. The tradition can usefully be seen as commencing with Descartes, but the sensationalism of Hume and the minimal assumptions of Kant about our cognitive equipment make them quite as central to its development. Gellner admitted that there was no clear and obvious rationale for this view; rather, it is slightly ridiculous given that we must think through, or by means of, the cognitive equipment that we inherit. Still, the attempt to bracket assumptions remains vital. His later work went to great lengths to show that ridiculing attempts to step out of one's skin should be very firmly rejected.

A second strand to modern theories of cognition was identified, and termed 'sour grapes'. The central idea here was simply that no one can be quite sure of truth, thereby encouraging toleration of different opinions. Gellner had noted earlier that such toleration was only desirable once

---

52   Ibid., p. 72. A slightly different formulation is on p. 65.

53   Ibid., p. 72.

54   R. Schroeder, *Rethinking Science, Technology and Social Change*, Stanford, 2007, draws on Gellner, and underlines this part of his work.

argument had led to the dismissal of implausible views, an opinion he
repeated later in a powerful essay on 'The Dangers of Tolerance'. So there
was no sudden slide here into relativism.[55] The particular justification given
derives from Popper's falsifiability criterion, that is, the view that science is
the practice of offering explanations that can be refuted, thereby increasing
human knowledge. This view was held to represent an advance upon the
ideas of J. S. Mill because it allowed for continual correction, rather than
imagining that a pure nugget of selfhood could be found once all carapaces
have been removed. But Gellner refused to make things easy for himself,
noting that cast-iron grounding for this viewpoint is not really available.

> But these arguments, valid though they are in a sense, will only have
> cogency for those who have previously espoused as their prime value a
> respect for a certain kind of truth – for not treating as certain that which
> is not, for not endowing with objective and given status that which prop-
> erly lacks it. We have no way of compelling people to subscribe to such
> values. Indeed historically and sociologically, such values are minoritarian,
> and probably have to be. Most societies have overrated the certainty of
> their own beliefs . . . [56]

Gellner later explained why this vision became so powerful, and he would
offer a fuller exposition of the workings of modern cognition. But he
insisted here, and in the essays on anthropological method that have been
discussed, that science does provide powerful knowledge, that is, it works
even though formal grounds for some of its practices are not available.

Two arguments follow from this.

If Ved Mehta is to be believed, Gellner regretted his inability to use the
analytic tools of Sir Charles Snow's 'The Two Cultures and the Scientific
Revolution' in *Words and Things*.[57] Certainly, part one of the final chapter
of *Thought and Change*, on 'Knowledge and Society', claimed – in a way
that must have immensely irritated the philosophical establishment – that
Snow's essay was 'one of the most important philosophical essays to have
appeared since the war'.[58] A contrast was drawn between humanist intellectuals and modern scientific experts, wholly to the disadvantage of the
former. At this point, Gellner devoted considerable space to a reformu-
lation of his attack on the complacency of the Wittgensteinian position

---

55   'The Dangers of Tolerance', in *Contemporary Thought and Politics*, London, 1974.
56   *Thought and Change*, p. 113.
57   V. Mehta, *The Fly and the Fly Bottle*, London, 1962.
58   *Thought and Change*, p. 209.

that had so influenced Oxford philosophy. The monopoly on literacy had once given intellectuals real power, and thereby the ability to devise moral systems in which they had expertise, but this had been undermined by the spread of mass education systems. What mattered more was the creation of much more powerful knowledge, and a consequent dependence on scientific experts in certain situations – undermining assumptions that were hitherto taken for granted.

The second set of considerations was more important still. Gellner suggested that there were three stages in the history of cognition. If the first was concerned with how we can know anything at all, the second was far more confident, seeking to understand how it was that we had come to know so much – roughly speaking, the former is exemplified by Descartes and the latter by Kant.[59] The third stage was that in which we started to fear science, on the grounds that it might devour us. Two elements are at work here: firstly, we turn to experts for real knowledge, thereby diminishing the importance of received opinions; secondly, the inability of science, based as it is on continuous change, to provide much moral certainty. All this was summed up in the notion that epistemology had replaced metaphysics – or, rather, that epistemology is our metaphysics. These factors change the balance between being and knowing, with such morals as we have limping behind science, put aside and treated with irony and scepticism. But there was a further consideration: 'the more we understand and control, the more we also see how we ourselves can be understood and controlled. The achievement of power is also the discovery of impotence'.[60]

The self was that which was not explained, thereby being considered unique and idiosyncratic; the possibility that our behaviour, intimate or otherwise, might be understood was a challenge to the notion of individuality. Gellner admitted that there was a necessary limit to this, for any theory about human beings must be held by someone – just as any book describing determinants of behaviour can only make sense to a reasoning being. Nonetheless, what impressed him in general was the diminution of space for humanity. The cost of modern science was clear: technical power diminished moral warmth and certainty.

11. Democracy, Industrialization, Liberty

Gellner often argued that theories gain their power from what they exclude as much as from what they include. Utilitarianism's insistence on pleasure and pain would matter little without the rider that *nothing*

---

59   Ibid., p. 205.
60   Ibid., p. 213.

else existed. *Thought and Change* has this same character because liberty is deliberately excluded from the modern social contract. Nonetheless, Gellner held liberty to be desirable in itself, and a great deal of his later work concerned itself with the possibility of producing liberty within societies deprived of it, so to speak, by historical necessity. Let me fill out this picture.

Industrialization established unavoidable parameters of social life, but it did not thereby rule out all options. Gellner warmly endorsed the value of political openness, but systematically demonstrated the relative feebleness of arguments for political liberty.[61]

1. A first argument was the Popperian view that science is based on refuting conjectures, rather than on establishing universal and unchanging knowledge. Nonetheless, uncertainty is, so to speak, reliable. Unfortunately, this view of science is most likely to appeal to those already living inside a liberal society.

2. It may be that political liberty is necessary for the knowledge upon which modern science depends. However, while this might have been true of the initial breakthrough to a new cognitive style, it is not at all certain that it applies to later imitative development.

3. Liberal societies have a greater capacity for change than illiberal and rigid regimes. Gellner made the honest observation that the second and third argument do not fit with the first – for they offer the very certainty that had initially been ruled out.

4. The argument that clearly appealed to Gellner himself was Kantian in spirit. The fact of openness, of being free from any established state of affairs, whether institutional or intellectual, is attractive to those who wish to be masters of their own fate. 'Liberty and equality but not fraternity', seems to be the message as to what should be valued.

5. In the long run, affluence will be generalized, thereby suggesting that concentration on other political objectives – above all, the establishment of safeguards against tyranny – was more important. This argument was likely to have significant appeal only for those who are convinced that universal affluence really is inevitable.

---

61 Ibid., pp. 115–9.

His own wry comment on these five points must be recorded.

> This set of arguments, not fully consistent with each other, and at widely divergent levels of abstraction, does not, alas, amount to a rousing manifesto for liberty. The very disparateness of the arguments may worry one: any one of them alone might have sounded more convincing than their conjunction. One must heed Kant's warning against supporting one's values by a mishmash of arguments, which weaken rather than reinforce each other. But if the arguments one can muster do not match up to the degree of one's conviction, it is perhaps as well to confess it.[62]

This was, however, only one way of looking at the fate of liberty in the modern era. Gellner drew an interesting distinction between different routes to modernity. The original European routes were largely unplanned and accidental, the product of long and complex historical processes. But the situation for each state thereafter was completely different. Planning becomes possible because of the general realization that a new social order exists. It is this consideration that underlay nearly everything that he had to say about liberty in modern social conditions. Roughly speaking, liberty was a fortunate accident for the countries making the original transition; thereafter, the centralization of power for developmental purposes almost necessarily places softer political rule at a discount.

Gellner's position on the centralizing impact of development is best reconstructed by considering his important 1967 essay 'Democracy and Industrialization' in tandem with various staccato comments in *Thought and Change*.[63]

In the essay, he argued that democracy is best understood as having two meanings. On the one hand, it can mean the rule of the people; on the other, it can mean softer political rule, constitutionalism and liberty. Gellner argued that the former is neither logically nor sociologically bound to produce the latter.[64] It is very, very difficult to disagree peacefully at any time, and almost impossible when immense issues are involved. Democracy works best, Gellner insisted, in societies where much is shared, limiting disagreement, and accordingly keeping resentment and irritation

---

62   Ibid., pp. 119–20.

63   'Democracy and Industrialization', in *Contemporary Thought and Politics*.

64   An implicit assumption in this formulation is revealing. Much of what is being said concerns the way in which a majority can 'tyrannize' a minority, a worry that perhaps reflects his Jewish background. More positive views of democracy come from within majorities that have been controlled by dominant minorities.

to bearable levels. He pointed out that Tocqueville's argument that shared
religion strengthened democracy in the United States rested on precisely
this consideration. He further related it to the modern, realistic theory
of democracy – that is, to the Schumpeterian theory which states that
democracy is merely a means of changing leaders within a particular social
structure, rather than a genuine 'rule of the people' that would allow fundamental changes to the social structure itself. This distinction is arguably a
useful one, and the seemingly dull and limited realistic theory often seems
convincing. In contemporary Iraq, the potential democratic tyranny of
the majority Shi'ites is limited by entrenched clauses – established without
much consultation by the Americans, albeit later passed by a national refer-
endum – which give complex veto powers to national minorities, thereby
creating a constitutionally limited democracy.

'Democracy and Industrialization' turns to transitional societies to make
these arguments about the nature of democracy. But the implications for
the polities of developing countries were clear, and stark. The absence of
consensus caused by the lack of a settled social structure – or, rather, the
fact that it is being created *ab novo* – means that democracy in transitional
societies was very unlikely to create regimes which favour limited rule.
Utilitarian choice makes sense within a stable context, but this philosophy,
as Gellner had argued, was useless as a guide to the transition because
'during something inherently so painful, what hope is there for government
by consent? It seems almost a contradiction'.[65] He underlined a particular
irony: real choice is impossible at the moment when crucial choices are
inevitably being made.

More elaborate arguments explained why industrialization is likely to
rule liberal politics completely out of court. For one thing, the unsettling of
traditional societies – by increased hopes, by old regimes seeking to catch up
– created discontent that fuelled revolutions. Once in power, revolutionary
regimes were likely to create a new industrial order. Industrial economies
do not have large rural workforces, thus it seems rational to encourage
urbanization. Creation *ab novo* applies still more to nation-building. In
the Algerian case, national homogeneity was to be increased by declaring
Arabic the official language of the state. This required force, both to make
the Arabic-speaking peasants send their children to school and to prevent
the use of Berber and French as alternative *linguae francae*. Gellner summed
up his position by insisting that it is the logic of the situation rather than the
actions of bad politicians which creates unfavourable results.

---

65   *Thought and Change*, p. 141.

In stable contexts, one can play for marginal advantages, and accept defeat, tolerate opposition, and refrain from pushing every advantage to the utmost, in the knowledge that tomorrow is another day. In transition, tomorrow is not *another* day: it is an *other* day, altogether. He who is in control now will mould that tomorrow, and hence control now is incomparably more valuable than the quite spurious hope of a later 'turn'. Rival politicians in transitional societies like to think of each other as the local Kerensky. The knowledge of this inevitably 'escalates' the stakes of politics, and brings it close to a kind of total politics in which nothing is barred.[66]

The implication is that we must recognize the necessities involved in seeking to transform and to improve societies. In this matter Gellner called for support from a distinguished English thinker:

The early difficulties in the way of spontaneous progress are so great, that . . . a ruler full of the spirit of improvement is warranted in the use of any expedients.[67]

This is John Stuart Mill, the paragon of liberalism, writing about the conditions necessary for liberty. This, too, is a matter on which Gellner did not change his mind, quoting the passage from memory at a small conference in Prague in 1993.

It is in this context that Gellner offered his interpretation of Marxism.[68] Great admiration was expressed for 'its stress on social structure, on conflict between the component parts of it, and on the influence of ecology and the division of labour on that structure'. Further, Marxism avoided the characteristic serialist weakness of evolutionary theories because it possessed, in class conflict, a concept that sought to explain the transition from one stage to another. Nonetheless, Marxism was judged to be poor at prediction. 'The historic role of Marxism seems to be not to lead societies out of the crises of industrial society, but to help them to pass over the big hump of industrialization'. There were other ironies:

---

66 Ibid., p. 67.

67 J. S. Mill, *On Liberty* [1859], in J. S. Mill, *Three Essays*, Oxford, 1975, p. 18, cited in *Thought and Change*, p. vi.

68 *Thought and Change*, pp. 131-6, from which the quotations in this paragraph are drawn. It may be useful to point to the four stages of Gellner's relationship with Marxism: admiration for Marx himself, great distaste for modern Western Marxism, deep interest in and fascination with Soviet Marxism followed by an attempt to explain why Marxism failed so badly as a moral creed.

The correct political behaviour of the revolutionary is to wait for the ripe moment in advanced societies? On the contrary, Marxism is embraced by the impatient, in backward societies, in order to break out of vicious circles of stagnation which otherwise grip such societies. It leads them to behave in a markedly Utopian manner. Are advanced societies driven to economic imperialism? There are constant complaints that they do not export enough capital to the underdeveloped world. Capitalist countries without empires prosper, and those which cling to them are the poor-white nations like Portugal, themselves underdeveloped . . . . Workers have nothing to lose but . . . the T.V. set, etc.? Capitalism contains the seed of its own destruction? It seems, on the contrary, to lead to a social structure which dampens all revolutionary ardour. Proletarians have no country? It is nationalists above all who flirt with Marxism . . . As for the state withering away: Leninism appears, on the contrary, to provide a regrettably well-adapted rationale for the concentration of power . . .

All of this was summarized in the notion that Marxism was best understood in Weberian terms, as a modern protestant ethic. Gellner made his position crystal-clear in a debate on socialism in Africa, arguing that moralistic concerns had been replaced by economic considerations.[69]

This analysis signalled a key part of Gellner's intellectual agenda, to which he would devote enormous energies for the rest of his life. He had no doubt but that Marxism was a danger to liberty, above all because its very plausibility led people to treat it with the kind of seriousness which leads to persecution. But he had powerful hopes to set against this. The very fact that Marxism was adopted for partly pragmatic reasons, as a development strategy, might allow for some freedom of manoeuvre. Then there was the hope that the ideology itself was sufficiently flexible that it could continue to serve as official ideology without demanding strict obeisance. His view here resembled that of David Hume's sociology of religion: fanaticism can be diminished by custom, with intolerance undermined by the hollowing out of belief systems. But the absolutely crucial question, given that the centralization of power for development purposes is well-nigh inevitable, was whether softer political rule could be established once an industrial mode of production was in place. He was very hopeful in this regard, believing that the unfolding logic of the industrial mode of production – that of an ever greater increase in specialization, itself based on scientific knowledge – might allow softer forms of political rule to emerge.

---

69 M. Roberts, E. A. Gellner, A. Crosland, R. Serumaga and P. Mbayi, 'Talking Aloud on African Socialism', *Transition*, no. 24, 1966, p. 45.

'Democracy and Industrialization' insisted that it is pluralism which, so to speak, makes democracy attractive, or liberal. Softer political rule may well have the best chance of enduring when plural elements manage to survive the process of transition.[70] Moreover, there may be something to the older view that pluralism in the advanced world depends upon some economic power being kept out of the hands of the state.[71] Insofar as this is a defence of capitalism, it is a very mild one, for Gellner had no time at all for the view that a modern society can be run according to laissez-faire principles.

Assessment: Liberalism and the Limits of Necessity

There are intimations of all Gellner's later work in *Thought and Change*. A six-fold agenda was established. First, one can see a fascination with closed worlds, self-reinforcing ideologically and thereby hard to escape. This stands as the background to a second area of interest, namely the need to explain how a move from closed worlds to something more open becomes possible. A third part of his agenda is related, but slightly different: whatever the cause of the transition to an open society, description is called for in order to understand how it functions. Gellner is aware that initial transitions are odd, and that later ones, able to imitate earlier examples, are likely to be wholly different. So a fourth element of his agenda was to concentrate on the likely character of other transitions, notably those under the aegis of Marxism and Islam. As imitative development is likely to take place by the use of centralized coercive power, the fifth part of Gellner's agenda concerned the possibility of liberalizing regimes once they had passed through the trauma of development. The final matter, always at the centre of his mind, is examining the character of our lives within an industrialized and rationalized world. No modern thinker has stood so close to Weber in insisting that our times must be disenchanted – an insistence which did not prevent Gellner from paying great attention to attempts to create closed ideological worlds within modernity. These themes structure the chapters which follow.

If this agenda was proof of great intellectual ambition, the book was not well received, at times not properly understood. Though there were letters of appreciation from David Riesman, Claude Lévi-Strauss and Eric Wolf,

---

70   'Democracy and Industrialization', p. 37.
71   Ibid., p. 40. There is a marked resemblance here to Weber's endorsement of capitalism in his lecture on socialism. (M. Weber, 'Socialism', in W. G. Runciman [ed.], *Max Weber: Selections*, Cambridge, 1978).

the reviews often wished for a clearer, more sustained and less polemical treatise.[72] Alasdair MacIntyre's review was typical in describing an 'exceptionally fertile thinker' who had produced a thin book in which there were 'twenty-five fat ones screaming to be let out'.[73] It should be acknowledged that there is an obvious truth here. Two central arguments of the book seem to be in contradiction. On the one hand stands the structural argument stressing the need for a shared and common national culture, in order to socially integrate dislocated masses and to help with the functioning of industrial society. A more intellectualist concern, on the other hand, insists that modern scientific knowledge is so much based on openness and so characterized by perpetual change as to rule out depth or fixity to any modern culture. One sees here the tension at work in Gellner's general position, caused by the desire to respect both the national principle and the open, cosmopolitan world of rational science. The tension was resolved, at least in some of his later work, in an interesting manner. Nationalism will cease to be threatening once affluence has been achieved, for a diminution in the stakes involved will lessen overt and violent conflict. More generally, the desire for riches will lead to a measure of respect for openness, less because of any general intellectual maturity than because of changes in the unfolding logic of industrial society. The final result is clear: all that is available is 'ironic cultural nationalism', a limited cultural identity within a world of high living standards.[74]

An interesting review by George Lichtheim characterized the book as 'the liberalism of the technocratic age. This kind of liberalism is no longer tied to the bourgeois institutions of private property and the market, though it remains indifferent to socialist considerations . . . The tone is optimistic, and the stress is on the bright new vistas opened up by technology'. The book, Lichtheim concluded, 'lacks the tragic sense'.[75] A long and affectionate letter from Ron Dore also noted the book's fundamental optimism, but went a little further by regretting that it had little to say about the management of conflicts that were likely to occur within advanced liberal societies.[76]

---

72   Lévi-Strauss to Gellner, 19 January 1965; Riesman to Gellner, 15 March 1965; Wolf to Gellner, 15 April 1967.

73   A. MacIntyre, 'Thoughts about Change'. Similar views were expressed by A. Arblaster ('Industrial Society', *Tribune,* 15 January 1965), A. Ayer ('The Real and the Rational' *Sunday Times,* 17 January 1965), S. Lukes ('Punting Names About', *New Society,* 21 January 1965) and W. G. Runciman ('Doubts and Redoubts', *The Observer* 31 January 1965).

74   *Legitimation of Belief,* Cambridge, 1974, chapter 9, especially pp. 191–5.

75   G. Lichtheim, 'Neo-Liberalism', *New Statesman,* 15 January 1965, p. 81.

76   Dore to Gellner, 10 January 1964.

Gellner's optimism did not last, at least regarding two of what were then considered to be the three worlds of modernity.

'A Social Contract in Search of an Idiom: The Demise of the Danegeld State' argued in 1974 that the First World's combination of liberalism and capitalism had become unstable.[77] The political economy had deprived itself of the stick of coercion and was now, given the oil crisis, without the carrot of Danegeld. The actions of a half-integrated working class accordingly did much to create stagflation. Gellner vigorously attacked the two theories trying to make sense of this situation. Economic theory arguing that a solution could be found in a return to market forces was useless. The infrastructure of modern industrial society was so huge, and so much provided by the state, that the notion that individual effort lay behind these achievements no longer made much sense. In general, there was simply too much awareness that politics set the terms by which the market worked, making any notion of a market-derived just price merely risible. This was not to say that the free market had never had any force. To the contrary, the short period in which economic forces were not politicized, when producers had been small enough to introduce a new mode of production, had played a vital role in the development of a liberal system, in which power was not in a single set of hands.

It was this that led to Gellner's criticism of leftist theory. It was a dreadful mistake to imagine that everything was amiss, to condemn without reservation. Liberal institutions needed to be maintained, and this was no easy task. In these circumstances, Gellner argued firmly for a social contract based on corporatist institutions, adding to this the idea, derived both from an analysis of Czech stratification under socialism (discussed below) and from Fred Hirsch's *The Social Limits to Growth*, that social peace might be enhanced if rewards take the form of status as well as money. In particular, he suggested that those performing the objectively worst and least interesting jobs might be given higher rewards, in large part because jobs of intrinsic interest and satisfaction would in any case be filled, even with lower levels of remuneration. These views, of course, reflected more immediate practical concerns. His quip at the time was that British politics needed 'Maggie [Thatcher] to be followed by Roy [Jenkins]' – that is, a measure of social discipline restored, before a return to a more realistic social democratic position. Such views were not uncommon at the time, and he did nothing to hide his own position, notably writing a piece entitled 'Ostrichism', not accepted for publication, in which he argued that the Labour Party – post-Callaghan and pre-Blair – was so far removed from

77 'A Social Contract in Search of an Idiom: the Demise of the Danegeld State', in *Spectacles and Predicaments*.

reality as not to deserve election.[78] Visceral feelings were often involved. When Ken Livingstone took over the Labour Party leadership of the Greater London Council immediately after their victory in the May 1981 election under a different leader, Gellner felt that a coup had been carried out. He had genuine fears of a Labour Party under the leadership of Tony Benn. His fears were vastly exaggerated at this point, the uncritical transposition of his Central European experience to a wholly different political culture. Altogether more balanced was his view that the provincialism of British politics might be alleviated by a firm commitment to Europe. 'Better the Bundesbank than the Bank of England' was another quip of his during this period, reflecting his view that the solidity of social peace in Britain was not matched by an equivalent interest in economic efficiency – the situation in France was held to be the complete inverse. On multiple occasions, Gellner made clear his endorsement of British cooperation in the European Union and its predecessors, though there are no signs that he favoured the creation of a European super-state.

His worry about the Third World was rather different. The patronizing, *de haut en bas* tone of books about development such as his own, he noted in 'Recollection in Anxiety: *Thought and Change* Revisited', made little sense given that the politics of late-developing societies were gaining force.[79] These reflections were written at the time of the second oil shock. But what impressed him more than changes in the economic realm was the emergence of powerful ideologies within the developing world. He suggested that there was a move away from figures such as Lenin to alternatives symbolized by the Ayatollah Khomeini.

There was one final set of criticisms offered by Karl Popper.[80] After acknowledging the importance and ambition of the book, and noting that his criticisms were 'less good' than those which Gellner had earlier made of his own *Open Society*, he offered several comments. He began by complaining that Gellner could not, so to speak, let go of the Wittgensteinians. 'My point is that you fall in with those in my opinion quite incompetent philosophers who take Wittgenstein [plus his followers] seriously, as representing something characteristic or at least intellectually important: and that you, indirectly, strengthen this view'. He also thought that Gellner took Snow too seriously, arguing that he was 'linked with very

---

78   Ian Jarvie kindly supplied me with a copy of this text, which is not in the Gellner Archive.

79   'Recollection in Anxiety: *Thought and Change* Revisited', in *Culture, Identity, and Politics*, Cambridge, 1987.

80   Popper to Gellner, 15 January 1965.

local English phenomena and social fashions', thereby being 'quite unlikely to have that kind of universal significance in our present society which, so it seems to me, you attribute to [him]. (For example, in Vienna there were never two cultures. Freud is in this respect only typical)'. But the central charge that Popper made was that Gellner's allegiance to historicism led him into basic error.

> Although you would of course agree that there is *interaction* between Thought and Change, it *seems* to me that you say 'thought must not be blind to social change' – which is true enough as a criticism of Wittgenstein [and his followers]. But apart from the fact that historicists and followers of sociologism have been saying so for a long time, the main function of thought is to influence change; and I do not see that, or why, philosophy cannot, or should not, do this; simply by searching like science for the truth, in connection with problems of its own; of course, changing problems. It is the search for truth which has, in fact, brought about the greatest changes – very often, more often than not, by missing the truth by a wide margin.

One does not have to accept Popper's intellectualism to recognize that any evaluation of the nature of Gellner's liberalism must concern itself with his historicism.

Gellner's grounding of liberalism is at once partial and powerful. The limits of this grounding were stressed by Gellner himself. On the one hand, science does more to undermine belief than to create it. On the other hand, there is an even more obvious difficulty: Gellner's insistence that different worlds are imaginable imposes necessary limits on his position. It is possible to argue that a life marked by poverty and disease is ultimately better than one blessed by the comforts of science. Gellner's position derives from the fact that very few are prepared to make this ascetic case, fewer still to actually live it – though he wrote before the greening of the left wing of European democratic systems. There is everything to be said, at least in my view, for his concern with the welfare of normal people, the belief that a society with increased life expectancies and a diminution of human suffering is morally desirable. He replied to a note from Perry Anderson (occasioned by the 'anxious' reflections that have just been noted) in a way that highlights his beliefs:

> As for myself, I am deeply Philistine, and that aspect does not bother me too much. Some bits of it do – I really can't stand the sack of Bath and of Edinburgh, and the beginnings of the same in Leningrad. In fact

I wrote a letter to *The Times* protesting against that atrocious hotel next to the Finland Station, urging that the guns of the Aurora be turned against it and put to good use, and that the architectural department of the Leningrad Soviet be promptly sent to the Okhotsk Canal, but they never published it. But otherwise, all in all, I am prepared to pay the price of vulgarity for peace, reasonable diffused prosperity and equality. If God obliged me to choose for mankind, giving the option of living in a universalized Vienna of 1975 or 1905, I think I would, albeit with some private bitterness, be obliged to opt for 1975.[81]

Behind this conviction lay his admirable range of interests, notably his appreciation of modern science and concern for the developing world – and of course the roles of nationalism and Marxism within it. His deep concern with social improvement makes his liberalism all the more impressive. How wonderful to have a liberal thinker sceptically undermining the narrow little orthodoxies of the age, all so keen to wrap us in swaddling clothes! He even embraces a measure of emptiness as a value in itself, a sign of mankind's maturity, rather than seeing it as a loss. To these moral considerations should be added a sociological fact: the retreat to simplicity is simply not possible.

This discussion of Gellner's grounding of liberal values brings us to his practice as a liberal. Gellner systematically engaged in audience-hopping. Everything that follows derives from the paradox, so central to his work, involved in stressing the presence of different, utterly viable worlds whilst insisting at the same time that modern science possesses world-historical and utterly transformative cognitive power. Accordingly, one audience to whom he speaks is 'us', the advanced world which pays allegiance to rational science. He was arguably seeking to help us understand ourselves better, not least so that we might be up to defending our world if the need arose, as it did in the face of fascism and Bolshevism. But when he tries to explain the workings of this world amongst other worlds, he becomes a universalizing liberal searching for a way to speak to people within those different worlds. There is thus a constant oscillation. An ironic but important contrast can be drawn between Gellner's audience-hopping and the position of other contemporary social philosophers. A broad tendency suggested that inter-faith dialogue can manage diversity – the work of the Canadian philosopher Charles Taylor is its exemplar. My own experience suggests that, at the deepest level, this approach does not recognize diversity at all, presuming rather that discussion will bring agreement because

---

81 Gellner to Anderson, 16 January 1981.

humans share so very much in common.[82] Gellner was rather different in his views, a Weberian aware of genuine difference, of allegiances to different Gods, and an anthropologist who had lived through the different worlds of modern Europe, both pre-war and postwar. There is a sense in which he sought to respect such difference, while suggesting only the likelihood of a shared interest across cultures in technical power.[83] In this his approach was, so to speak, sly and Machiavellian: adopt the technical means, and the bastions of closed belief systems would eventually fall. But this is an area in which he wobbled, as we will see in chapter nine, later slightly shocking some of his colleagues in refusing to 'preach' to the Muslim world in the wake of the Rushdie affair – though this did not for a moment, he stressed, make him a relativist.[84] It is worth underlining his irritation at the political conflicts within liberal societies in the 1970s. Talking to people in different worlds was less effective than the power of example. Worryingly, the self-indulgent failures of liberal society would increase the coherence of anti-Western ideologies, above all Islam.

What of Popper's rejection of the historicist base of Gellner's position? Popper's insistence that thought should determine rather than reflect reality was unlikely to appeal to Gellner. Societies had structures: only when we understand them do we know our real options. At the back of Gellner's position was the view just discussed, namely his insistence that different worlds have their own standards. It was hard to escape closed worlds. It was this that led him to criticize the work of one of his closest friends, Ian Jarvie, judging as far too cheerful his Popperian belief that refutation led to improvements in knowledge even in pre-industrial societies, a view that Gellner felt lacked awareness of primitive thought systems' capacity to evade falsification.[85] The transition from one world to another was often by an existential leap rather than as a gradual progression by means of rational trial and error, the abrupt replacement of one set of standards by an alternative system. Chapter seven will consider the varied works in which he offers a full and considered assessment of Popper's philosophy of science.

---

82   Exactly the same point can be made about Jürgen Habermas's 'ideal speech' situation and John Rawls's 'original position'.

83   A comment on Ayer's philosophy, in the context of a discussion of the importance of Snow's two cultures thesis, implies in my view that brute scientific progress is likely to be much more comprehensible to members of developing societies than more abstract philosophical considerations. See *Thought and Change*, p. 208.

84   *Conditions of Liberty: Civil Society and Its Rivals*, London, 1994, chapter 29. A. Macfarlane was one of those shocked.

85   'A Cheerful Philosopher of Social Science', *Times Literary Supplement*, 1 September 1972.

But the distance from Popper can be seen at this time in a passage implicitly aimed at Popper's admiration for the Periclean dictum that everyone can judge a policy, even if only some propose it.

> *Can* they? I certainly cannot. Any issue in the modern world, for instance, has repercussions in a number of fields, each one of which requires a high-powered expertise for its comprehension. The experts whom one knows generally impress one by their lack of expertise in fields other than their own, notwithstanding the crucial importance of cross-implications. Naïvely one may suppose that those at the Top who take decisions are polymathic supermen, somehow qualified to assess the many-sided implications of their decisions. Acquaintance with any of them dispels such illusions . . . In the modern world it is truer to say that almost anyone can initiate a policy, but no one can judge it.[86]

Gellner maintained this view throughout his career, even applying it to high-stakes issues within liberal societies.[87] Nonetheless Gellner *did* have a good deal of respect for expertise. The passage following this quotation continues with a series of assertions about the importance of scientific knowledge, not least in providing the material comfort which matters so much for the modern social contract. He would not change his mind on this matter. A decade later, in *Legitimation of Belief*, he argued that people turned from traditional 'knowledge' to genuine science whenever the stakes were high.[88] And the argument of his social philosophy as a whole is that we do indeed know certain things. Social science is not an abject failure. We know that mass education and nation-building – the two being, of course, intimately related – are necessary preconditions for the modern social contract. If we know these things, they can be and should be acted upon, as Mill suggested – and as they will be by elites all over the world, whether Marxist, Comtean or Islamic in character. Failure to do so is to let poverty continue. The process involves enormous pain, but it is sensible to recognize necessity.[89] There is an air here of a wise elite, dictating changes to those who do not understand. Politics understood as voice, compromise or as blocking capacity is thereby ruled out. Equally, there is no sense that

---

86 *Thought and Change*, pp. 64–5.
87 *Plough, Sword, and Book: The Structure of Human History*, London, 1988, pp. 209–10.
88 *Legitimation of Belief*, p. 196 and passim.
89 S. Avineri objected to a talk that Gellner gave in Amsterdam in 1992, suggesting that the proper policy – in connection with nationalism, as I recall – was always to support the weaker party. Gellner vehemently disagreed. Some changes had to be accepted: to block them might even put minorities at risk.

social movements gain their character from their treatment by the state more than from social structures. This is a crucial matter, as it affects the odds of successful liberal constitutional change, and is a factor in the assessments offered below of his work on Islam and on nationalism.

Recent scholarship has supported many of Gellner's claims about the ways that forced industrialization is likely to diminish political liberty. Atul Kohli's exceptionally powerful work is relevant here.[90] The economic success of South Korea rests upon a coercive-capitalist route, in which the state works with leading capitalists, accumulates capital for infrastructural and industrial development by repressing wages, and establishes from above clear developmental strategies.[91] In contrast, development has been in part stymied, in part merely slowed, in both India and Brazil because democratic pressures prevented either the adoption or the maintenance of developmental strategies which involved short-term social costs.[92] Kohli further analyses the case of Nigeria, wholly bereft of an effective state and accordingly having the gloomiest prospects for political and economic development. Interestingly, Kohli concludes with moral qualms similar to Gellner's, noting that development may come at the expense of liberal democracy. It may be that the fifth and last of Gellner's arguments noted in the previous section apply to Brazil and India. But moral complexity is added by the recent history of South Korea. Its developmental regime certainly provided improvements in living standards. Yet this does seem in turn to have contributed to a social base for political liberalization. The chances for consolidated democracy now look greater in South Korea than in Brazil, perhaps greater even than those of India. So here is a case in which great social pain may be followed by successful political decompression.

Rather similar concerns can be raised about Gellner's view of nationalism. Of course, it can be said bluntly that his characterization of nationalism as homogenization is powerful. The Czech case supports Gellner's position. The tricultural world did collapse in the Second World War, with

---

90 A. Kohli, *State-Directed Development: Political Power and Industrialization in the Global Periphery*, Cambridge, 2004. Similar points are made in Matthew Lange's equally impressive *Lineages of Despotism and Development: British Colonialism and State Power*, Chicago, 2009, which draws a striking contrast between levels of state power resulting from direct and indirect rule within the erstwhile British Empire. Direct rule that changed social structures is shown to have beneficial consequences for later economic development.

91 Of course, this strategy follows on from the land reform and the bureaucratic innovations imposed by the Japanese.

92 There are complexities at work here, requiring more research. Failure might have been caused by appalling policies, it therefore being a nice point as to whether such policies were mandated by democracy.

further simplification – the secession of the rich Czechs from the poor Slovaks, discrimination against gypsies – taking place in the years after 1989. Crucially, Czechia is representative of twentieth-century Europe. To be clear, this is not to say that Gellner's sociology captures the social forces that brought about this state of affairs, on which much more will be said later. What matters is the Gellnerian premise, the future-oriented claim, so to speak, that national homogeneity is necessary for societal success. There is a good deal to be said for Gellner's position. Economic flexibility is often aided by the ability of a homogeneous national community to act together, not least because external threats are seen as a common problem.[93] These generalizations hold true, for instance, for Denmark, whose success owes much to the way that it divested itself of territories and peoples because of its remarkable ability to lose wars. This point is made clear by an extremely powerful and highly technical paper explaining how the Danes took over the English butter market from the Irish in the nineteenth century. Homogeneity allowed the Danes to set up cooperatives and to improve the quality of their butter, for this was where profits lay. In contrast, the main avenue to advancement in Ireland lay in the courts – that is, in claiming land from the English.[94] Might it be that a background element to recent Irish success – the emergence of the 'Celtic Tiger' – is the creation of a homogeneous community in the Republic? One may further add that national homogeneity – as in South Korea in contrast to Nigeria – can help economic development, a factor omitted by Kohli.[95] Further, welfare spending is certainly related to homogeneity, for the simple reason that people are more prepared to be taxed at high rates when the monies are spent on people like themselves. And liberal democratic politics do indeed become easier in circumstances of homogeneity. For one thing, an end to stalemate between competing groups allows decisions to be made; for another, the regulation of differences at the heart of democratic politics is much easier when the differences in question are bounded by shared identity.

The most obvious thing about the views expressed in *Thought and Change* is, as Lichtheim and Dore noted, their essential optimism. The book

---

93   J. L. Campbell and J. A. Hall, 'Defending the Gellnerian Premise: Denmark in Historical and Comparative Context', *Nations and Nationalism*, vol. 16, 2010.

94   K. O'Rourke, 'Late Nineteenth-Century Denmark in an Irish Mirror: Land Tenure, Homogeneity and the Roots of Irish Success', in J. Campbell, J. A. Hall and O. Pedersen, (eds), *National Diversity and the Varieties of Capitalism: The Danish Experience*, Montreal and Kingston, McGill/Queens, 2006.

95   The omission is curious for Kohli writes well elsewhere – 'Can Democracies Accommodate Ethnic Nationalism? Rise and Decline of Self-Determination Movements in India', *The Journal of Asian Studies*, vol. 56, 1997 – on this very matter.

was written in an era of national reconstruction, soon after the horrors of Nazism had been brought to an end. It reflects the sense that development is possible.[96] National cultures can be created which will allow people to be included – with national identities likely, as noted, to lose intensity as affluence advances.[97] Finally, there is the hope that liberalization might follow from forced industrialization. All of this suggests that the pain of transition, of getting over the big hump, is worth it. This is a powerful case, to which something can be added, namely that there are dangers to outright democratization, understood simply as majority rule. It behooves us to realize that the outcome of democratization in the absence of institutional guidelines and constraints can indeed be repulsive.[98] For Gellner, good things do not always go together; the hard-headed realism of his work is classical in nature.

But one can and should remain uneasy. To begin with, there appears to be a contradiction in his work. Gellner's appreciation of the distinctiveness and viability of different social worlds is undercut by his insistence that there is a generalized awareness that affluence is possible. If this is so, development per se may have democratic elements after all. Secondly, there is something to be said for the view that political liberty is more widely recognizable than Gellner admitted. One component of modernity seems to be anti-imperialism, whether in communist Poland or in contemporary Iraq. It would be madness to presume that anti-imperial sentiment automatically translates into the consolidation of democratic regimes. Nonetheless, there is here, so to speak, a moral base for liberty to which Gellner gave little attention.

There are still more important considerations. Bluntly, not every centralization of power, even when justified as a means to development, has resulted in human progress. The 'authoritarian high modernism' identified by James Scott gave us the disasters of agricultural collectivization in

---

96 Gellner reaffirmed his views about the universalizability of industrial society late in life, having little truck with the idea that a 'fourth world' might never develop. In contrast, his views on nationalism became more troubled in the last decade of his life, leading, as will be seen in chapter 10, to a significant change in his general position.

97 Optimism at this point applied to the situation of Jews, and those of Jewish background: Gellner considered the general situation after 1945 to be not too bad. This irritated his student Anthony Smith, who disliked still more the claim that the Holocaust was simply a mistake of industrial society (Interview with Anthony Smith, September 2008).

98 This realization stands at the heart of J. Snyder, *From Voting to Violence: Democratization and Nationalist Conflict*, New York, 2000, and M. Mann, *The Dark Side of Democracy: Explaining Ethnic Cleansing*, Cambridge, 2005.

the Soviet Union and compulsory villagization in Tanzania.[99] Dore was equally sceptical about the functional benefits of higher-level credentials within developing societies.[100] Such criticisms cannot be ignored. Perhaps there is something to be said for the rise in educational standards in erstwhile socialist countries, since this might help economic development now that the Cold War has ended. But against that must be weighed the record of genuine economic disaster. Russia was one of the world's great grain exporters in 1914: collectivization so ruined agriculture that the country is now dependent on the outside world for its food supply. More generally, it seems certain that socialist planning from above, bereft of any market mechanisms, is a dead end for technical progress.

His views about nationalism, summarized here and at greater length below in chapter ten, deserve a similar critique. That pre-existing cultural homogeneity might have benefits may well be true, but this is not to say that forcible homogenization should be or need be encouraged. Many attempts at forcible homogenization, especially in Africa, have been dismal failures, bringing misery to millions without corresponding benefits.[101] Equally, the history of territorial partitions has been wholly dreadful.[102] Then one wonders if there are elements of false necessity in Gellner's praise for Kemalism. The consequences of the Turkish route have often been far from benign: given the enormous authority of the elite resulting from its success in war, was it really necessary to impose a form of official nationalism that so disadvantaged the Kurds?[103] It is just as important to remember that federal and consociational schemes have sometimes worked, even though many have failed.[104] This is to question an implicit assumption in the Gellnerian premise of homogeneity, namely that a modern state must have *complete* cultural unity in order to succeed. His understanding of the necessary functions of modern society can be challenged at this point. India works as a state-nation rather than as a nation-state, and its example

---

99   J. C. Scott, *Seeing Like a State: How Certain Schemes to Improve the Human Condition Have Failed*, New Haven, 1998.
100   R. Dore, *The Diploma Disease: Education, Qualification and Development*, London, 1976.
101   D. D. Laitin, *Language Repertoires and State Construction in Africa*, Cambridge, 1992, chapters 3 and 8.
102   B. O'Leary, 'Analyzing Partition: Definition, Classification and Explanation', *Political Geography*, vol. 8, 2007.
103   G. Lewis, *The Turkish Language Reform: A Catastrophic Success*, Oxford, 2002; P. Anderson, 'Kemalism' and 'After Kemal', *London Review of Books*, 11 and 25 September 2008.
104   Excellent reviews of the mechanisms in question are contained in the papers in S. Noel (ed.), *From Power Sharing to Democracy: Post-Conflict Institutions in Ethnically Divided Societies*, Kingston and Montreal, 2005.

suggests a better way forward for many countries of the world than does the European experience. It may be that a *limited* measure of unity sufficient for the workings of a modern economy can be gained by the recognition of diversity.[105] Gellner would move toward this position in his final years.

This brings us to the question of democracy as a restraint on the exercise of power. Absolute catastrophe – notably the great famines caused by collectivization and the Chinese Great Leap Forward – results from the absence of any internal check on a core executive. Despite the difficulties of development in India, the ability to curtail disastrous policies has meant, as Amartya Sen famously argued, that this huge South Asian country has never experienced a truly catastrophic famine.[106] Liberty may not be in the cards, easily, generally and automatically, but one can reasonably give it a more central place in the scheme of things than that allowed by Gellner. The importance of public discussion can be exaggerated, but one should be wary of discarding it altogether. This is a prescriptive point, but it has some descriptive aspects that make it reasonable. All in all, the world's emergent political shape presents a more varied picture than that depicted in Gellner's work. There are cases which support him, and cases which distinctly contradict him. It is reasonable therefore to seek liberal limits to the recognition of necessity.

---

105   D. D. Laitin, *Nations, States and Violence*, Oxford, 2007, chapters 4 and 5.
106   A. Sen, *Poverty and Famine*, Oxford, 1978.

6

Components of a Career

In the two decades following the publication of *Thought and Change*, Gellner ranged far and wide intellectually, spelling out various implications of his basic world-view. He was extraordinarily productive in these years, generating four collections of essays, three edited volumes, and five monographs. His continued attention was directed toward such diverse subjects as nationalism, Soviet Marxism, Islam, historical development, the nature of modern rationality compared to relativism, linguistics, Islamic fundamentalism, psychoanalysis, and Czechoslovakia, and he made important comments on thinkers as diverse as Arendt, Quine, Popper, Winch, Taylor and Feyerabend.[1] Systematic attention to some of the main pillars of his thought – to science and its emergence, and to nationalism and Islam – is offered in the next chapters. This one, however, describes the main trajectories of his career during his forties and fifties. It begins by considering the academy in the strictest sense, that is, his involvement with the LSE until 1984 – the final years of his career in Cambridge University and in Prague are left for later consideration. It then turns to some of his intellectual engagements, leaving mostly to one side his striking critiques of particular

---

1 Ian Jarvie and Joseph Agassi first had the idea of collecting the essays, which they co-edited on five occasions. Jarvie helped with the remaining collections, and he continued work on the complete Gellner bibliography even after Gellner's death. Some points of editorial etiquette can be found in Gellner's correspondence with Jarvie. Gellner occasionally revised the essays, over whose production and selection he in fact retained complete control, not least in writing his own introductions to all but the first three volumes. Also see chapter 4, note 67 for Gellner's explanation of the softening of his attack on Needham in a collection versus the original version of the essay. To be set against this, however, was an occasion when Jarvie suggested toning down an essay written for *Philosophy of Social Sciences*, which he co-edited. 'Normally when editors ask for permission to exclude offensive remarks', Gellner wrote, 'I make one further offensive remark to the editor in question' (Gellner to Jarvie, 2 May 1975).

thinkers, since these are best considered within their own particular intellectual contexts – as was the case when dealing with his critique of Peter Winch. Finally, our attention turns to his more directly political engagements. There is of course a fine line between the intellectual and the political, perhaps especially so in Gellner's case. In general, he was prone to say that intellectuals should contribute specialized knowledge when they possessed it, but was somewhat sceptical of reformist activism – fearing, one suspects, that hope would replace analysis.[2] Certainly, his most important political involvement – the concern with liberalization – contained a great deal of intellectual content. The case that came to matter most to him was that of the Soviet Union, and this necessarily required a major confrontation with Soviet Marxism.[3]

Academic Politics

Gellner spent thirty-five years at the LSE, and came to be seen as one of its luminaries. Indeed, to a considerable extent he identified himself with the school, noting shortly after he left that he had not really cut the umbilical cord that bound him to it. He was made an Honorary Fellow in 1986, and continued to return to speak on nationalism, often at the invitation of Anthony Smith.[4] Further, some of the issues that he raised in his later career – notably those concerning the nature of civil society – were debated most fully at that institution. Finally, he came to admire the professionalism of the school's bureaucracy, preferring it, as we will see, to the situation in Cambridge. There was a touch here of an attitude identified by Kierkegaard, that we live our lives forward and understand

---

2   Ron Dore wrote Gellner a note in response to his review of Dahrendorf's history of the LSE, discussed below, suggesting that he was too optimistic about the rationality of politics – evidenced by his surprise that the neo-liberals and Oakeshottian conservatives failed to recognize their fundamental differences. A reply came quickly with the retort that Dore was far more subject to naïve rationalism, writing letters to the newspapers and believing that intellectual ideas could change the world. The story is contained in Dore's 'Address' at the King's College Memorial Service, 24 February 1996.

3   His interest in Soviet Marxism, treated in its entirety here, began in this period, but extended into his first years at Cambridge. In contrast, his thoughts on the failure of Marxism belong wholly to the Cambridge and Prague years, and so are discussed later.

4   His offhand comments started at least one significant career. Bill Kissane, now of the Government Department at LSE, began his long-term comparison of Finland and Ireland as the result of Gellner noting in 1994 that, in the twentieth century, Ireland was the only partitioned state in Western Europe, Finland the only non-partitioned state in Central Europe (B. Kissane, 'Nineteenth-century Nationalism in Finland and Ireland: A Comparative Analysis', *Nationalism and Ethnic Politics*, vol. 6, 2000).

them backwards. But the touch was probably a small one, for the time that Gellner spent at the LSE, despite its great intellectual benefits, was also marked by a fair amount of struggle and dispute. This story can be dealt with first, before turning to his role within the school and then to his own analysis of the school's contribution to intellectual life.

There was early recognition at the LSE of Gellner's intellectual power. There had been no difficulty – for a committee comprised of the Director (Carr-Saunders), Karl Popper, Tom Marshall and David Glass – in appointing him to a lectureship in 1951 for a period of five years, with a starting salary of £600. Gellner always claimed that his first articles had been written to gain the tenure associated with this position. The fact that he had won the John Locke prize in 1950 was noted by the committee. Two years later Carr-Saunders wrote on his behalf to the Rockefeller Foundation, making it clear that he was regarded as 'a coming man'; as noted, he also helped Gellner with his return to the LSE after the difficulties in Harvard, writing to him personally to wish a speedy return to good health. In the same year, Morris Ginsberg asked the Director to help Gellner gain recognition from the University of London for his teaching prowess; this effort succeeded in July 1954. And there was a further sign of support. In 1956 a casual comment at a committee meeting, reluctantly supported by Popper, had led to criticism of the clarity of Gellner's teaching style, and in particular to his occasional stuttering. The Director wrote to Ginsberg asking if he would like to intervene. My later exposure to his lecturing style suggests an explanation: Gellner spoke almost without notes, preferring to take listeners along with him as he laid out an argument. Ron Dore captures this style nicely:

> [H]is presence in the lecture room was something more. That staccato delivery, the insistence on not using a script, nor, for the most part, notes, so that one could experience the argument being worked out, or rather reworked out, as an act of creation, in which one was invited to share, enjoying, as his flickering grin showed that Ernest was also enjoying, the irony of the paradoxes and the craftsmanship of the occasional elegant *bon mot*.[5]

It is very probable that this searching for a particular phrase, often polished previously in private notes, irritated some listeners. But, for others, there was an immediacy that was exceptionally gripping, with key points being memorably encapsulated in striking aphorisms. Ginsberg seems to have

---

5 Dore, 'Address'.

shared this view to some extent, for he wrote to the Director refusing to criticize Gellner, suggesting rather that he be taken on his own terms.

In 1956, when Gellner's lectureship was up for renewal, David Glass as Convenor of the Sociology Department pressed the Director to confer a readership on Gellner.[6] The request, considered by Sidney Caine (the new Director), Raymond Firth, Michael Oakeshott and by Glass himself, failed. But Glass persisted at the end of the same calendar year, writing at length to Richard Titmuss, who replaced Oakeshott on the committee that considered promotions, with the result that Gellner was appointed Reader in Sociology in 1957, with an initial salary of £1,475. The Director was entirely aware that Gellner's presence lent real distinction to the school, and noted that his students had performed particularly well in exams. Despite all this, there were problems – possibly indicated by the fact that he very nearly accepted an offer at this time to leave the LSE for a professorship in Malaya.[7] Even more dramatic was the drafting of a letter offering his resignation.

Julius Gould had been elevated to a readership ahead of Tom Bottomore. Many of the younger staff were opposed to this, both because of Bottomore's greater intellectual distinction and because of a feeling that his chances had been ruined by an unfair 'whispering campaign'. Perhaps as important was the fact that Gould stood to the right politically, Bottomore to the left. The younger staff members were dissuaded from sending a letter of protest to the Director, but the subsequent resignation of Bottomore led Gellner – and his friend Norman Birnbaum – to submit their own letters of resignation.[8] Gellner's letter began by stating the matter in these terms:

> What I am suggesting is that events preceding the election have created an impression of injustice, the effect of which on the junior staff of the department makes it hard to conceive of the department functioning

---

6   Glass admired Gellner, his wife Ruth still more so, but he seems to have found Gellner somewhat difficult to deal with, not least because of his utter independence of mind – remarking on one occasion that he did not know if the next revolution would come from the right or the left, but that Gellner would be the first to be shot in either case (J. Davis, 'An Interview with Ernest Gellner', *Current Anthropology*, vol. 32, 1991, p. 68).

7   Several potential moves will be noted in the next paragraphs. Some were for limited terms, and were very much an expression of his desire to see further societies within the developing world. But others were for permanent positions. Interest was almost certainly evidence of his unhappiness at LSE.

8   The Gellner Archive contains several letters from Birnbaum written at this time. Many are about tactics, giving the impression of an *éminence grise* at work in the affair. As the Archive contains little personal material, the saving of documents in this instance suggests that the affair was serious and disturbing.

satisfactorily, unless this disquiet and its grounds are recognized more formally than they have been, and more convincing steps are taken to restore confidence.[9]

Gellner enclosed a statement, undated and previously submitted to Richard Titmuss, specifying details of the whispering campaign and laying bare the real worry of the younger staff – namely, that favouritism rather than merit might affect their own careers. He was clearly sticking his neck out to protect the junior members of the department, most of whom however would have been his age. He did not find his action to be easy:

> I should like to say that I write this with misgivings verging on a depression, in view of the probable impact of this on my personal relations with some of my colleagues. (It has been a great source of pleasure to me that my relations to my colleagues have been without hostility – I think – in the past, and my enjoyment of my work in part depends on this being so. Moreover my eight years in the department leave me so profoundly indebted to it and various members of it that I cannot do this without a feeling of guilt.)[10]

Discussions were undertaken with David Glass, and with the Director, and somehow or other matters were papered over, the Director writing to Gellner on 18 September that he would take no further action in regard to the letter of resignation. Gellner himself wrote to Gould realizing that harm had been done, expressing agnosticism on his ultimate intellectual merit and thanking him for never having 'cut him' for his actions.[11]

A somewhat similar conflict occurred in 1961/2. David Glass moved from a mainstream sociology chair to the senior named chair in sociology, the Martin White chair – held previously only by L. T. Hobhouse and his intellectual descendant Ginsberg. The chair that Glass had left vacant was taken by Donald MacRae. It may be significant that MacRae had not been part of the protest in the Bottomore case, although this may be explained by the fact that he was acting as Convenor at the time because Glass was in India. But there can be no doubt that hostility between Gellner and MacRae was becoming intense in this period, and that it would mark the next fifteen years of Gellner's stay at the LSE. More must be said about this relationship.

---

9 Gellner to Caine, 1 July 1957.
10 Gellner to Titmuss, undated.
11 Gellner to Gould, 1 July 1957.

Gellner told his wife Susan when he met her that MacRae was the only person in the department who could have given everyone's lectures. This was recognition of a great promise of brilliance, perhaps also of an early friendship – MacRae had been a friend of the family, and continued to see them even when Gellner's own links with his family were strained. MacRae was a consummate insider, purportedly about to write a major work in sociological theory – the book's failure to appear led to ever greater expectations, making it, one imagines, harder and harder to write.[12] 'The Notes' give some sense of Gellner's view of MacRae, as did acidic asides to colleagues about 'MacRae's mythical manuscript': 'DGM: Morally incapable of egalitarian relationship, and intellectually incapable of leadership. So . . . ' What is clear is that MacRae never delivered on his promise. By the end of his career at LSE he was a very sad figure indeed, prone to drink so much at lunch that he would snore through Academic Board meetings when they were held in the afternoons.

Gellner was considered for a professorship in 1961, but reservations about his relative youth meant that the promotion was not granted. But there was pressure for him to climb the professional ladder. One reason for this is that Gellner had itchy feet: he was tempted in 1960 by a temporary position as a UNESCO representative at the University of Dhaka in East Pakistan (now Bangladesh), where he would have served under Tom Marshall, and in 1961 by a Chair in Philosophy at the University of Witwatersrand in Johannesburg. Another reason seems to have been disquiet resulting from the fact that MacRae had received a professorship before Gellner. Glass wrote to the Director saying that he would call a meeting with the two of them, being confident that he could smooth things out. In any case, a committee of the Director, Glass, Popper and Firth assessed Gellner's work in 1962, and recommended his promotion.[13] Popper's support was very enthusiastic, fully endorsing the ideas of *Words and Things*, albeit regretting its polemical formulation (which he nonetheless noted as likely to have

---

12 Gellner reviewed MacRae's *Ideology and Society: Papers in Sociology and Politics* (London, 1961): 'Inquiring into Society', *Times Literary Supplement*, 18 August 1961. He noted thereafter that one essay – 'The Bolshevik Ideology' – had particular merit, not least as a piece of autobiography. He was referring in particular to a passage (p. 191) in which MacRae claimed that the true believer 'accepts contradictions and denies facts in a way disconcerting to the non-Bolshevik, and frequently he does this in good faith'.

13 Deliberate care was taken when listing external referees to avoid scholars linked to linguistic philosophy. Here is the list of names put forward to London University: K. Britton (Newcastle), P. Corbett (Brighton), W. B. Gallie (Belfast), C. Grant (Durham), W. Kneale (Oxford), S. Korner (Bristol), D. Mackinnon (Cambridge), G. Mure (Oxford), D. O'Connor (Exeter), H. J. Paton (Oxford) and W. J. Sprott (Nottingham).

more effect than a quieter tone) and calling him perhaps the most independent critical thinker of his generation. Firth endorsed his fieldwork,
and was also clearly stimulated by his work on the philosophy of anthropological method. The Director had some reservations, expressing worry
that his only published book to that point had caused so much controversy.
But the greatest concern came from a different quarter. Ginsberg had finally
realized that Gellner did not share his benign conception of social evolution
as an inevitable growth in rationality. Ginsberg's considerable influence
within the LSE led to Gellner gaining a very peculiar title, 'Professor of
Philosophy with special reference to Sociology', with an initial salary of
£2,650, though the post was held within the Department of Sociology.

The struggles with MacRae did not end there. Difficulties arose in 1967
when they both asked for leave, with the Convenor and Director worried
that they might have to choose between them. As it happens, the dilemma
was avoided when MacRae chose not to go on leave, allowing Gellner
to spend a year at Berkeley from 5 February 1968. That particular year
was filled with drama in the United States: the student movement, protest
against the war in Vietnam, the continuing struggle for civil rights, the
assassinations of Martin Luther King and Robert Kennedy and the election of Richard Nixon. Further drama awaited him on his return. 'The
troubles' at the LSE culminated in 1969 with the destruction of the gates
in Houghton Street and the sacking of Robin Blackburn of the Sociology
Department for allegedly encouraging violence. Gellner was supportive
of Blackburn, and continued to see him thereafter. Furthermore, in
a 1969 *Times Educational Supplement* review of an account of the events
by a senior LSE administrator, Harry Kidd, he took the opportunity to
offer Blackburn further support. He drew attention to the obscurity of
the school's governing structure, and suggested that its actions had been
exceptionally heavy-handed. A school of social science was bound to have
some radical staff, and dismissal on those grounds – unless there was indisputable evidence of a commitment to fomenting violence – would result
in an institution that failed to reflect reality. What mattered was whether a
radical staff member was driven ultimately by academic rather than political
values, and 'our far-away politbureau clearly did not possess such intimate
knowledge' in Blackburn's case.[14]

This certainly did not mean that he shared Blackburn's views. To the
contrary, he published two essays in 1969 – 'Myth, ideology and revolution' and 'The panther and the dove' (the latter written for *Anarchy and
Culture*, a volume critical of the students, edited by David Martin of the

---

14 'Behind the barricades at LSE', in *Contemporary Thought and Politics*, London, 1974.

Sociology Department) – which sought both to criticize and explain.[15] Gellner's central point was that the protest movement was bereft of serious ideas – with the absence of serious thought seen, interestingly, as an all-too-faithful mirroring of the ideological situation to which they were opposed. Gellner excoriated the 'end of ideology' school for complacency, for sugar-coating liberalism rather than seriously examining the conditions necessary for liberty. The consensus favoured by this school was seen as self-justifying, rather than based on reason; a similarly flaccid and vague air hung around the ideas of the protest movement. An amusing distinction was drawn between the styles of American and European movements, the former marked by a painfully halting sincerity, the latter by stricter stand-ards of theoretical practice. But the assessment offered of both was similar: neither would have any real impact on the workings of their societies. Nor was it the case that the radicals really wanted fundamental change. The sharpest expression of this view came a few years later in *Legitimation of Belief*, the book that he had begun in California:

> The new pseudo-cultures continue to rely on this [advanced] technology for a standard of living to which its members are accustomed and which they are most certainly not seriously prepared to forego. These monks go out to an air-conditioned wilderness. It is all rather like Tolstoy re-enacting peasant life in one part of his house and maintaining his habitual standards in another. So many Tolstoys these days . . . [16]

Gellner found it hard to make up his mind as to whether this situation was healthy or dangerous. If triviality was no threat, sloppiness in thought might yet undermine 'respect for truth and sap the vigour of the drive toward it. If everything is true in its own fashion, truth cannot matter very much'.[17]

To some extent Gellner withdrew from the LSE after returning from his sabbatical, not least so as to lessen conflicts within the department. He gave up his attic room in Langside Avenue, and thereafter stayed in London on a more occasional basis – sometimes in his room at the university, sometimes taking a room in the Reform Club. Nonetheless, troubles with MacRae became more serious over the next years, under a new Director. Ralf Dahrendorf was well acquainted with Gellner as one of the fellow founders of the *European Journal of Sociology*, and he had played an active role in Gellner's recruitment – on one occasion fighting to keep him on the short list

---

15 Both essays were collected in *Contemporary Thought and Politics*.
16 *Legitimation of Belief*, Cambridge, 1974, pp. 192–3.
17 'Myth, Ideology and Revolution', in *Contemporary Thought and Politics*, p. 16.

in the face of opposition.[18] Dahrendorf's support seemed to matter: he did not take up a position at the University of Singapore in 1974, and he also withdrew his application for a chair in philosophy at University College, even though he had been invited to apply. Still, LSE records show that by 1976 he wished to leave the sociology department. He met Dahrendorf at the end of that year to discuss different ways in which he might contribute more to the school – noting that in departmental matters he had 'become somewhat converted to procedural pedantry and a Weberian vision'.[19] MacRae was Convenor at this time, and certainly seemed to be making life difficult for Gellner when it came to his applications for short-term leave.[20] Gellner had complained to Dahrendorf that MacRae had spoken to him on the telephone 'in a tense, impatient and dismissive manner, which verges on the discourteous', but would not then come to see him on the grounds that 'psycho-therapy for furious professors is not normally a part at least of the manifest definition of your job'.[21] Conversations about his position seem to have continued, and Dahrendorf apparently offered him 'a quasi-research' chair. Gellner was not very keen on the idea, noting that students would suffer and colleagues might be prone to resentment.[22] In 1977 he applied, unsuccessfully, to become warden of Nuffield College.[23]

------

18   Lionel Robbins wrote to Gellner (5 September 1973) saying that he had been convinced by Gellner that Dahrendorf was the right choice, and that the school would accordingly owe Gellner a great deal if the appointment went through. At this time Gellner believed that Dahrendorf might well become the first president of a united Europe – an unlikely eventuality given Dahrendorf's tendency to align himself with small centrist parties, the FDP in Germany and the SDP in Britain, that went nowhere. He was close to Dahrendorf in another way in the coming years. The *Times* keeps obituaries in reserve, so to speak, and asked Gellner to prepare Dahrendorf's. To that end he interviewed Dahrendorf in 1977, and wrote an elegant obituary in 1980. It was not used when Dahrendorf died in 2009.

19   Gellner to Dahrendorf, 12 November 1976.

20   For example, MacRae wrote to the Director (18 February 1977), without sending a copy to Gellner, about an application by Gellner for a week's leave to visit Tunisia, noting that he himself had turned down such invitations during term time. Gellner's application to MacRae in this instance – 4 February 1977 – noted that he had not solicited the invitation which was, however, directly relevant to his research. In reply on 18 February (this time copied to the Director, as was much of this correspondence) MacRae snidely remarked that few people solicited invitations, and suggested that he apply directly to the Director as he felt the matter to be beyond his control. Gellner was still seeking permission from the Director on 2 March. He was, ultimately, able to accept the invitation and travel to Tunisia.

21   Gellner to Dahrendorf, 4 October 1976.

22   Gellner to Dahrendorf, 21 February 1978.

23   A letter from A. H. Halsey to Gellner, 9 June 1977, suggests that the winning candidate – Brock, a historian of the United States – gained the position in part because the vote had been split between Gellner and Halsey, who had also allowed his name to go

He applied a year later for the politics chair in Cambridge previously held by Bryce Gallie, with a generous reference provided by Dahrendorf. The application was rejected.

If Dahrendorf tried to accommodate Gellner in small matters, he was nevertheless particularly craven in his lack of support regarding a more serious issue. The Martin White Chair of Sociology was vacant at this time. Gellner spent the year in Aix-en-Provence because French colonial archives are held there, writing *Muslim Society* at the Centre de Recherche et d'Études sur les Sociétés Méditerréenes. MacRae campaigned actively within the LSE for the position, an outrageous breach of academic etiquette. Dahrendorf admitted that it was hard to resist someone with such significant local power, sitting on all the key committees.[24] But the committee in charge of the chair also discussed Gellner's position and suggested that he keep his title whilst moving elsewhere. Anthropology apparently responded coldly to the idea, perhaps because Ioan Lewis was intimidated by Gellner's reputation, but the philosopher John Watkins had no such qualms and Gellner moved into Popper's old department on his return from France. Gellner thanked Dahrendorf for the transfer, noting that it would make little substantive difference to his teaching. Dahrendorf replied assuring him that he was one of the great assets of the school, and that there was general awareness of this fact.[25] Dahrendorf wrote to him frequently in the following years, often thanking him for offprints of articles, sometimes discussing matters to do with the *European Journal of Sociology*; he also helped arrange for a German translation of Gellner's *Muslim Society*.

The years with the philosophers were very happy ones in personal terms. A change in his living situation, made possible thanks to the great and continuing administrative efforts of his wife, made a big difference. Commuting to and from Hampshire was tiring, so they acquired a house in Kennington, South London: this made things much easier, and led to greater participation in London social life. But a more fundamental change

---

forward. Steven Lukes has suggested (in an interview with Brendan O'Leary, 27 February 2001) that Gellner would have hated the job in any case, since it involved a great deal of administration.

24　Interview with Dahrendorf, May 2002. The desire to leave well alone was also felt by newly appointed, younger members of staff. They treated MacRae 'as unreliable, dishonest, a man of no substance whatever. But given his power locally, it was considered better to have nothing to do with him rather than provoke him . . . I thought he was a bit sad – a man of great learning but no achievement. But my sympathy was undercut by his being a congenital liar'. (Personal communication from Michael Mann, November 2007. Mann was a Reader in Sociology at LSE in the late 1970s and early 1980s.)

25　Gellner to Dahrendorf, 13 February 1979; Dahrendorf to Gellner, 20 February 1979.

was the purchase of a house in a small Italian village in the hills of Liguria. During his stay in Aix, Gellner had gone driving throughout Provence and in Northern Italy, often with one of his daughters, seeking a summer home of some sort. They eventually found one in a small peasant village, occupied at the time only by one elderly couple. The village was at the top of a valley, and it had been settled in a time of demographic expansion – chestnuts provided a large part of the staple diet, supplemented by hunting and the produce grown on small terraces built at the sides of the valley. Gellner adored being there, and spent quite considerable portions of his remaining summers in Italy. He described part of the attraction in these terms:

> Italy was marvellous. It was all the pleasure of fieldwork without the pain. I like living in simple circumstances, but I hate bothering people with questions. Fieldwork obliges one to do both, but living here only contains one of the two elements.[26]

Invitations to visit him in Italy went out to a large number of friends, many of whom braved the Spartan atmosphere of the early years – including the walk of a mile or so up a steep and narrow path to reach the village in the years before a road was built. Further, he persuaded his old friend Eric Hošek to buy a house in the same valley, though Hošek would not visit quite as often. Gellner wrote several books there, most notably perhaps his volume on psychoanalysis. While he was writing it the family car was loaded with tomes on Freud and psychoanalysis, some of them collected from below each time a trip was made for food or to the restaurant lower in the valley. Gellner made an impression on the local inhabitants, partly by means of a certain ploy. In 1987 he gave a paper at Pope John Paul's summer seminar at Castel Gandolfo, and much enjoyed being told by the Pope that Polish communist leader Wojciech Jaruselski did not understand intellectual matters at all. He took care to bring along a camera so that he could be photographed with the Pope. The picture was hung in the local restaurant, thereby establishing his status among the villagers.

Just as important were his excellent personal relations within his new departmental home, with younger colleagues like Elie Zahar as much as with John Watkins, and most certainly with Gaye Woolven, the head secretary who would eventually follow him to Prague. The MacRae problem was put aside, and he took pleasure in returning to Popperian concerns. Life became somewhat easier because Dahrendorf allowed

---

26   Gellner to I. C. Jarvie, 13 October 1981.

him some research funds – meaning that the seminars accompanying his lectures could be given by an assistant. He played a key role in pioneering a new M.Sc. in Social Philosophy, and had an amusing impact on the department. In due course he became the convenor, undertaking the task seriously but with obvious boredom – in large part because these were exceptionally productive years intellectually. His younger colleagues tried to free him from his administrative burdens, but in the process seemed to gain a sense that writing was crucial, for the output of the department increased dramatically. Finally, the department became rather socially active, with a large number of parties, held either at the LSE or at Gellner's London house.

Nonetheless, he found the concerns of these late Popperians somewhat technical, less interested in the social side of Popper's thought than in abstruse details of the philosophy of science. He longed for something less abstract, not least because a good part of his work at this time focused on Russia and Eastern Europe – and scholars from within that world were often invited to spend time at the LSE. In early 1984 he asked the pension office how much he would receive should he retire early. Monies might have been sufficient to allow this, but it proved unnecessary when he was elected to the William Wyse Professorship of Social Anthropology in Cambridge in 1984. He left feeling somewhat saddened: he had been tolerated, but his concern with the social underpinnings of philosophy left no marked impact on the department, and the LSE as a whole had not offered much recognition of his stature as a thinker.

Two sets of comments should be made about Gellner's role as a teacher at the LSE. The first set concerns the subjects on which he taught. The impact of Ginsberg was great and long-lasting. As noted, Gellner taught a compulsory course in ethics throughout the 1950s, only dealing with his own more central concerns within his department after he gained a chair. In the early 1960s he lectured on 'Concepts of Society' ('Alternative general views of society and man's place in it will be discussed, with special reference to their methodological and ethical implications') and on 'Modern Social Philosophies'. These slowly evolved into a course of twenty lectures on 'Values and Society', offered from 1972, and then into a similar course on 'Ideologies: the Sociology of Belief Systems'.

> The problems of relativism and rationality. Devices used by belief systems to overcome relativism and vindicate their own authority. Theories about the place of values within belief systems, and various types of validation of values. Philosophical theories as social commentary and as legitimation of social orders. Interaction of intellectual and social

factors in belief systems. One pre-industrial and several contemporary ideologies will be examined as specimens. Some pervasive ideological traits of industrial society.

He taught this course for most of his last decade at the school.[27] In addition to these main commitments were lecture series for undergraduates on Islam (sometimes considered as part of courses dealing with ideologies) and an inter-university graduate seminar on Islam, jointly chaired with Ioan Lewis.

Interdisciplinarity most certainly had a place at the LSE, and Gellner was able to run a seminar in the 1950s with Isaac Schapera and MacRae on 'Comparative Social Institutions'. More importantly, his lectures were attended by students from most departments. A similar point can be made about the second element of his teaching practice, namely the very large number of doctoral students he supervised during his career. He was held by his colleague David Martin to be a very reliable supervisor within sociology, on very varied topics indeed, albeit with a concentration on nationalism.[28] But his role as supervisor went far beyond this, notably in looking after a very large number of anthropology students concerned with tribal societies of the Islamic world.[29] Many doctoral students found him very intimidating, often speaking little, but habitually returning draft chapters with detailed comments very quickly indeed. He made a point of socializing with many students, meeting them to see foreign films, and often eating with them in cheap Indian or Greek restaurants. He clearly delighted in the anthropology students, visiting several of them in the field, and keeping in touch with them after their graduation. He was exception-ally generous with his time with regard to PhD students, and with many young scholars in diverse fields, consistently acting as a reliable and trust-worthy referee. He offered continuing support to students who took a long time to complete their degrees, either because they were studying part-time or because their material demanded it. Further, he took considerable care

---

27   The following books were recommended as background reading: R. Aron, *Opium of Intellectuals*; I. Berlin, *Four Essays on Liberty*; C. D. Broad, *Five Types of Ethical Theory*; N. Chomsky, *Language and Mind*; R. G. Collingwood, *Autobiography*; M. J. Cowling, *Mill and Liberalism*; D. Emmett and A. MacIntyre (eds), *Sociological Theory and Philosophical Analysis*.
28   His students in this area included Anthony Smith and Marianne Heiberg. He was extremely proud of them. He disagreed with Anthony Smith, as we shall see, but admired his intellectual development. He expressed satisfaction that the Oslo Accords were made in Marianne Heiberg's kitchen (her husband was the Norwegian Foreign Minister).
29   His students in this area (most at the LSE, but some at Cambridge) included Shelagh Weir, Katie Platt, David Seddon, Cynthia Myntti, Bryan Turner, David Shankland, Donal Cruise O'Brien, Gabriele vom Bruck, Madawi Al-Rasheed and Helen Watson.

Gellner's parents, Rudolf and Anna.

Gellner as a schoolboy (probably in his last year in the Prague English Grammar School).

Autumn 1944, aged nineteen, 1st Czechoslovak Armoured Brigade.

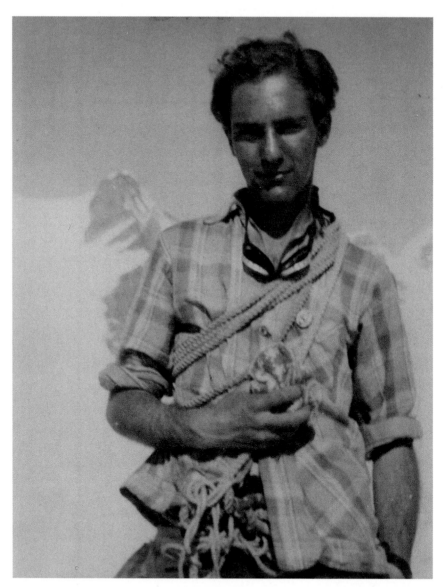

The young climber, late 1940s.

Summer 1952, Gellner in the Valais Alps, Switzerland.

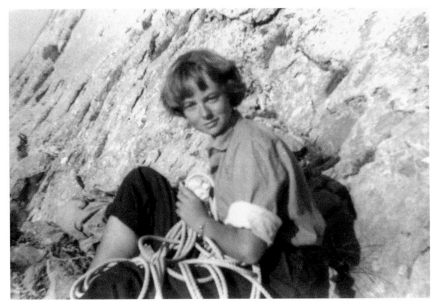

Susan Gellner, Morocco, 1955.

Ernest Gellner with mule: Christmas holiday in the Atlas Mountains, 1957–8.

Gellner in his office at the LSE, early 1980s.

Southern Bohemia, 1995.

to involve students in the academic worlds to which they aspired, inviting them to lunch or dinner, in London or in Hampshire, with famous visiting academics. He certainly enjoyed being a part of students' social circles, and was notably at ease with their children. When asked by a niece of Shelagh Weir if one had to be clever to be a professor, he scarcely paused before replying firmly in the negative. Finally, he spent much time trying to get his students' work published, and could be relied upon at all times to help them find employment.[30]

His own views about the school were made public when he reviewed Dahrendorf's 1995 centenary history of the LSE.[31] There was nothing romantic or uncritical about Gellner's long attachment to the institution. Somewhat to the contrary, he had little time for that 'English style of unity and practice', exemplified by Sidney Webb and William Beveridge, on which Dahrendorf waxed eloquent. The pathetically naïve positivism of the Webbs had led to unvarnished praise for Stalinism at its darkest moment, whilst Gellner himself underlined the scandal of the institution being run by Beveridge while under the thumb of the school's administrator, Mrs Mair, who may or may not have been his mistress. More significantly, he argued that the tradition as a whole lacked theoretical power and importance. Despite his admiration and respect for the welfare state, Gellner considered Richard Titmuss's Department of Social Administration to exemplify this

---

30 There are several sources for these general comments, including written and oral communication with Cynthia Myntti (July 2008), Shelagh Weir (July 2008), Anthony Smith (September 2008) and Marianne Heiberg (1999).

31 These views overlapped those expressed in an earlier piece, 'The LSE – A Contested Academy', *Times Higher Education Supplement*, 7 November 1980. Some observations made in the earlier article but not repeated later are worth noting. First, he regretted the increase in the school's size since it allowed a degree of specialization that made multidisciplinary approaches more difficult. Equally important in this connection was that the hiring of several professors in each department made intellectual renewal less likely than when a single great figure, unable to influence the choice of his successor, dominated a department. Second, he considered the figure closest to the Founders' position to have been Richard Titmuss, and he recorded his experience of teaching Titmuss's students. He set a question on the Marxist doctrine that the state would wither away in communist society. His expectation, that this view would be dismissed as silly, was far from met. He received essays about the immorality of such a view, bothering less to dispute the prediction than to denounce the aspiration. But he also gave considerable space to the Hobhouse and Ginsberg tradition, stressing its progressivist evolutionism, its sense that the world was moving to a collective sense of rationality and harmony. He noted an exam question that Ginsberg was wont to ask – '"Individualism has been definitely overcome in English political thought". Discuss' – to which a positive answer was expected. Nonetheless, he claimed that their views, combined with the panache of Harold Laski, gave the Labour Party much of its intellectual muscle in 1945.

theoretical weakness. The spirit of that department was characterized by Gellner as:

> [A] kind of embourgeoisement of noblesse oblige – a mildly paternalistic egalitarianism concerned with the eradication of poverty by research and administrative action, a little insular (hostility to the Common Market was shared by Titmuss and Oakeshott), though keen on retaining Commonwealth links, not for power-political reasons, let alone to exploit the backward, but to *aid* them.[32]

Gellner found that the LSE as a whole was suffused with a rather dreadful atheoretical atmosphere. In particular, the political right – a force as influential on the Conservative Party, Gellner rightly noted, as the reformist tradition was on the Labour Party – had two contradictory tendencies within it that never, to Gellner's bemusement, came to blows, intellectual or otherwise. Oakeshott's romantic traditionalism, adopted by William Letwin, Kenneth Minogue, Maurice Cranston and Robert Orr, stands in stark contrast to the asocial, calculative rationalism of such economists as Peter Bauer and Lionel Robbins. Gellner felt that one could not endorse both positions simultaneously. In this he was slightly mistaken, since such a coalition was achieved, albeit with obvious stress, during the first administration of Margaret Thatcher.

In contrast, he naturally made much of Popper's importance, but also noted that his department was not an easy place to be during the period of his pre-eminence.[33] The very opposite was true of his view of social anthropology. The department had Isaac Schapera, Raymond Firth, Ioan Lewis, Julian Pitt-Rivers, Maurice Freedman and Lucy Mair, as well as his friend Paul Stirling, among its established members; younger colleagues included Maurice Bloch, Peter Loizos and Johnny Parry. Gellner insisted that the Malinowskian revolution was a great intellectual contribution. Importantly, as will be noted again later, Gellner eventually came to see much more in Malinowski than just a method.

Individuals in the sociology department were of considerable intellectual importance. A seminar in the sociology of development was a third source of stimulation, particularly thanks to Ronald Dore and Tom Bottomore. This certainly gave Gellner occasion to search for the specificities of modern society, and the social routes by which this condition

---

32   Ibid.
33   'How much passion there is in the Popperite world! In our department, we just hate each other without any doctrinal or intellectual accompaniment' (Gellner to I. C. Jarvie, 27 November 1970).

is achieved.[34] Tom Marshall was an important presence, and David Glass a senior member with an outstanding reputation for his studies of social mobility. Alongside these figures, the department also included Robert McKenzie and David Lockwood, together with younger scholars such as John Peel, Keith Hopkins, Colin Crouch and Michael Mann. He socialized with many members of the department, and was much admired by the younger members (toward whom, in David Martin's view, he behaved 'like a Jewish mother'). For instance, on at least one occasion he was the only professor to invite a new staff member to his home.[35] Nonetheless, he regarded the department as a whole as a terrible intellectual failure.[36] One reason for this was the influence of Morris Ginsberg, perpetuating the uncritical evolutionism of Hobhouse for far too long. Still, there were many able members of the department; but many of them had left.[37] Gellner's general view of the matter is contained in comments cut from his final assessment of the school. He first noted a simple statistic: those who were pushed out accounted for half of the fellows of the sociology section of the British Academy, the proportion even higher if one included those who refused to join in the first place. He laid the blame squarely on MacRae

---

34   This was an influential seminar, not least for its discussions of subjects such as nationalism and slavery, as the later work of scholars such as Orlando Patterson and Robin Blackburn demonstrates.

35   Interview with David Martin (March 2008) and personal communication from Nicos Mouzelis (February 2008). Martin also noted that Gellner was fascinated by the opacity of English culture, and stressed that he was not good at winning verbal arguments with MacRae in departmental meetings, and often would leave them very upset. Mouzelis expressed gratitude for the very detailed attention that Gellner gave to one of his earliest, and most important, articles. A further detail is provided by Ron Dore. He was very nervous on arrival at the LSE, not sure if he could live up to his new label as a sociologist. 'It was from Ernest that I learned not to give a damn about disciplinary tribes. He was a *franc tireur* of the disciplines, a zestful poacher who cocked a snook at all fences and all gamekeepers' (Dore, 'Address').

36   A. H. Halsey, the historian of British sociology, does not put the matter this strongly, but there is considerable overlap between his account and Gellner's views – not least in regard to the deleterious influences of Hobhouse and Ginsberg, and of MacRae (*A History of Sociology in Britain*, Oxford, 2004. See also *British Sociology: Seen from Without and Within* (Halsey and W. G. Runciman [eds] Oxford, 2005), which usefully distinguishes the evolutionism of Hobhouse and Ginsberg from that of Runciman. Halsey was trained at LSE and attended some of Gellner's first lectures there; he later recalled their brilliance in conversation. Halsey quotes approvingly a comment from the Canadian sociologist Rosaire Langlois that Gellner's 'mischievous wit may be the closest thing to a naughty pleasure that sociology affords'.

37   Gellner's calculation is slightly unfair. Some who left the LSE simply wanted their own professorships.

(with something of a dig at Dahrendorf perhaps), then the manager of the LSE 'team':

> It had signed up what looked like a promising young striker, but he never manages to score, yet would seem to be extremely skilful at easing out players who might show him up by doing better. He only allows players who pass to him, but proves quite incapable of converting the chances so created into something that would appear on the score sheet. In football, the new manager would know that he has to get rid of this player, or he will lose his job himself. Academe is different, we have tenure. (I am in favour of this principle, but there is a price.)[38]

Intellectual Engagements

The Gellner Archive has no set of diaries that would allow a careful chronicling of his activities. But he was clearly a fount of energy. His passports permit some of his major engagements to be outlined, whilst such correspondence and documentation as does remain at least hints at some of his services to the larger academic community. Let us take each in turn.

Gellner was an inveterate traveller. For one thing, he constantly visited British universities, giving talks on widely varied subjects, often at the request of former students and colleagues who now worked in provincial academies. For another, he was very frequently out of the country. In the late 1940s and early 1950s he went mostly to Switzerland, but sometimes to Italy, in order to climb. Thereafter, even after osteoporosis set in, there were numerous trips to Europe, and many more to most of the world's other regions, usually to attend conferences – with the apparent exceptions of Australia and China. He gave extended series of lectures in Brazil in the late 1970s, thanks to his friendship with the scholar-diplomat José Merquior, and in India in 1986.[39] He spent the Michaelmas term of 1982 at the Mortimer and Raymond Sackler Institute of Advanced Studies

---

38   Manuscript version of 'No School for Scandal', Gellner Archive.
39   Merquior wrote one of the first (and still one of the most accurate) appreciations of Gellner's work, 'The Politics of Transition: On the Work of Ernest Gellner', *Government and Opposition*, vol. 16, 1981. Merquior was an exceptionally interesting figure with doctoral degrees from Brazil, Paris and London – the latter, published as *Rousseau and Weber: Two Studies in the Theory of Legitimacy*, London, 1980, completed under Gellner's supervision. Gellner wrote a preface to one collection of Merquior's essays, *The Veil and the Mask*, London, 1981, and wrote affectionately about him in an obituary when he died at a tragically young age.

in Tel Aviv. Some of these travels were systematic and multiple. Some destinations are predictable, particularly those in North Africa and the Islamic world, and those in the socialist bloc, and their intellectual import, is discussed below. There were, however, four other locations which received his sustained attention.

The first is France. Gellner's initial contact with the country was via his research in Morocco. He had great admiration for French scholarship on North Africa, from Masqueray in the late nineteenth century to Robert Montagne and Jacques Berque in the mid-twentieth century. Then there were frequent trips from the early 1960s in connection with his involvement in the *European Journal of Sociology*. The six board members routinely had at least one of their twice-yearly meetings in Paris. This allowed Gellner to establish contacts with a large number of French intellectuals, from Aron, Jean Baechler and Éric de Dampierre (all members of the board), to such figures as Jean-François Revel, as well as many scholars of Islam including Fanny Colonna, Magali Morsy, Lucette Valensi, and eventually Gilles Kepel (whose *doctorat d'état* he examined, with admiration for its arguments about Egypt). He read quite widely in French in the early part of his career, and was clearly influenced by a powerful French school of the philosophy of science whose key members included Georges Canguilhem and Gaston Bachelard. His own comments on French life are sophisticated. In an unpublished review for the *Independent* of B.-H. Lévy's *Adventures on the Freedom Road: French Intellectuals in the 20th Century*, left on his computer at the time of his death, Gellner disputed Lévy's view that Malraux would have enjoyed Sartre's status as symbol of the age if he had not turned Gaullist.

> The anguished Sartre really did express the spirit of the period in a way in which the poseur Malraux did not. Malraux's great PR talent, employed on his own behalf, enabled him to present himself as the writer-of-action, whereas Sartre expressed the more characteristic state of mind of those honestly haunted by the sense of having failed to act. Malraux articulated the fantasies of the period, Sartre recorded its realities.[40]

---

40   The review, retained in the Gellner Archive, was hostile, seeing the book as far too lightweight for such an important subject. Gellner's distaste for snobbery came out strongly in some personal comments.

> On the one occasion on which I met the author, I was immediately struck by the thought that here there was a very poor man's Albert Camus: he is ever such a pretty boy, acutely conscious of this fact, with exceedingly expensive clothes deployed with an infinitely careful casualness. My intuition proved correct, in as far as there is a long passage conveying an

All the same, over time the pleasures of going to Paris dimmed somewhat. His interests lay outside Europe.

A second region to which he devoted sustained attention was Africa. He visited Ghana in 1961, and returned between April and July as a visiting professor at the Institute of African Studies at the University of Ghana. Conor Cruise O'Brien was Vice-Chancellor while Thomas Hodgkin headed the institute. At this time O'Brien received significant funding from Ghanaian President Kwame Nkrumah, who was following British precedent in establishing professorships akin to Britain's 'regius chairs', that is professorships which could be given – expatriates having been dismissed – to scholars of the favoured ideological tendency.[41] In those years he travelled widely in West Africa, to Senegal, Mali, the Republic of Niger, the Ivory Coast, Chad and Nigeria.[42] Obviously a good deal of this had to do with his interest in Islam, more particularly his desire to see whether it would maintain the same features once bereft of the pastoralist base which he believed did much to sustain it in its classical heartland. These trips surely did a great deal to highlight for him the importance of economic development, thereby reinforcing his general intellectual framework.

A third important destination was Turkey. He later recounted that his first trip in the 1960s was to attend a conference organized by Şerif Mardin, with whom he maintained contact thereafter. While the subject of the conference was rather general, concerning the socio-political role of religion, Gellner learnt something very specific from it. He felt that he was in the midst of modernizers, determined to develop Turkey. This meant that democracy was endorsed, as long as it led to economic development. If, at any moment, that economic development looked likely to be challenged by popular will, above all by peasants from Anatolia loyal to Islam rather than to secularism, it was understood that the army would step in – less as a

---

eager identification with Camus and the conviction that if only Camus had lived, they would have been chums, liking the same kind of women, loving to live it up, and so on. Now sartorial affectations are his own business, but the corresponding conscious-casual style of writing affects the quality of what he has to say. A random casualness is presented as being, really, an elegant form of profundity. In fact, it is simply random casualness.

41   Perhaps Gellner's appointment was made more likely by his background. Certainly many of those appointed came from Eastern Europe. It is here that Gellner first met the Slovak anthropologist, Petr Skalnik.
42   He went to Nigeria on two occasions, largely to help decide whether the University of Ibadan should have a philosophy department. He lectured on the first occasion on 'The Philosophy of Modernization', and referred to his lecture when writing his final report endorsing the establishment of a new department.

reactionary force than as the guarantor of social progress.[43] He continued to travel to Turkey whenever possible, attending another conference in 1975 that compared North Africa with the Middle East, held on the Princes Islands in the Marmara Sea just outside of Istanbul.

There he met a young graduate student, Huri Inan, the daughter of a political figure who had spent five years in jail in the 1960s. Gellner was fascinated by the choices he made throughout his political career, and very much enjoyed talking to him. Typical too was Gellner's request for a boat with which to visit a smaller island, to swim and rest. The boatman was dismissed, and Gellner took Inan and Shmuel Eisenstadt away for a day. The relationship with Inan continued in London, where he would tease her about her admiration for Louis Althusser, whom he had met and characterized as resembling a provincial French lawyer. In 1980 Inan invited him to give lectures at the Middle East Technical University, at that time something of a centre for Turkish Marxists. The British Council paid for his trip, but was worried that his lecture topics – Islam, Marxism and nationalism – all looked capable of causing trouble. Gellner was delighted to be considered dangerous, and asked an official to give him a signal (a tug on the tie) if he went too far out of line. These lectures – apparently repeated at the University of the Bosphorus – caused quite a stir, being in large part an assault on the thinking of the Turkish left. And he showed considerable bravery during this visit. On one occasion Inan was trapped in a university hallway, with fascist forces outside threatening to shoot if the programme went ahead. In the midst of the stalemate Gellner raced up the stairs, within range of the fascists, to extract her.[44]

The final destination that we will consider was Nepal. In the early 1970s, the British Council considered funding a research institute at Tribhuvan University in Kirtipur, just outside Kathmandu, and asked Gellner to write

---

43   'Kemalism', in *Encounters with Nationalism*, Oxford, 1992, p. 83–4.

44   These details come from a personal communication with Huri Inan, February 2008. Professor Inan made two further points. In 1981 Gellner visited Inan and her family in Berkeley, where she was then living in exile. She remembers them listening to Hamid Algar, a Cambridge don who had converted to Shi'ite Islam in the 1960s. Algar was a considerable scholar, but at this time he was also the 'ambassador-at-large' for the revolution in Iran headed by Ayatollah Khomeini. 'During Hamid's lecture, Ernest, in an entirely non-sceptical tone, bent over to me and said, "This is a dangerous man"'. Gellner went to Ankara in 1990, and partly to help Huri Inan deal with the depressing situation caused by years of military rule, asked her to organize (with David Shankland, a former doctoral student working in Ankara) a conference on post-socialist societies. The conference was held in 1993, and much of the discussion concerned ways to keep the former Soviet Union together in the absence of socialism. Gellner arrived late for the conference, and chose to sleep in the local mosque on his first night rather than to find a hotel.

a report. He went there, and immediately fell in love with the mountains and the elegant Newar towns of the Kathmandu Valley. He said that they reminded him of Goethe's response to Italy, namely that it was only after visiting that he felt fully alive.[45] He wrote the report, which has since been lost, and which had a good deal to do with the appointment of Sandy Macdonald as the first director of the Institute of Nepal and Asian Studies. Gellner argued that it was irrelevant that Macdonald was an expatriate because the Nepalis wanted him, and pointed out that he himself was only a naturalized Briton. He returned in 1975 and became very familiar with anthropologists working there, not least Alan Macfarlane, who would eventually become a Cambridge colleague.

This experience resulted in a series of book reviews and an article on 'The Kathmandu Option', outlining the basic contours of Nepali society.[46] There were four main elements at work – Hindu invaders, hill tribesmen, the Hindu-Buddhist Newaris of the towns, and the ecologically distinct rich sub-tropical lowlands of the *terai* – held together by an authoritarian oligarchy backed by the British and by independent India, which desired peace on its northeastern frontier. Gellner's particular interest was in the way in which this arrangement was coming undone. He sent graduate students there, and visited again in 1983 when asked to review the progress of what had become the Centre for Nepal and Asian Studies – on that occasion travelling overland by bus and second-class train from Delhi via Agra, Fatehpur Sikri, Khajuraho, Allahabad, Benares, Pokhara, and Gorka to Kathmandu. This interest in Nepal would make a significant impact within Gellner's own family: his eldest son David became a Nepalologist. David's earliest work was very erudite, seeking to interpret Newar Buddhism from within, though his more general interest was in the question of whether Nepalese society could provide information about the nature of early Hindu society and Buddhism's relation to it.[47] David now holds Evans-Pritchard's chair in social anthropology at Oxford University, and his interests in ethnicity and conflict in Nepal have come to resemble closely those of his father – perhaps an inevitable development given the changes that have taken place in Nepal itself.[48]

----

45 'The Kathmandu Option', in *Spectacles and Predicaments: Essays in Social Theory*, Cambridge, 1979, p. 358.
46 Ibid.
47 D. N. Gellner, *Monk, Householder, and Tantric Priest: Newar Buddhism and its Hierarchy of Ritual*, Cambridge, 1992.
48 D. N. Gellner, J. Pfaff-Czarnecka and J. Whelpton (eds), *Nationalism and Ethnicity in a Hindu Kingdom*, Amsterdam, 1997; and D. N. Gellner (ed.), *Ethnic Activism and Civil Society in South Asia*, Delhi, 2009. Both are powerful collections, deserving of general attention.

Ernest Gellner's belief that the royal family might play a key role has been proven wrong; rather, expressions of ethnic identity have broken out all over the place, making Nepalese society something of a laboratory for the variables that concerned him. But Gellner did not write about these developments, on one occasion stating that he did not wish to embarrass his son by interfering in an area in which his lack of expertise was obvious.[49] This may well be a rationalization, at least in the eyes of the son ('in the end one has only one body, and there are only twenty-four hours in a day'), and it was simply impossible to undertake further fieldwork in Nepal given Gellner's own physical limitations and his intense interest in developments in Russia.[50]

David's comment also makes sense given the bewilderingly large number of Ernest's other professional commitments. He did a great deal to support various academic journals. The prominent role he played on the board of the *European Journal of Sociology* was matched by his work with *Government and Opposition* and the *Maghreb Review*. His general involvement with academic journals was much wider, not least as a very prolific reviewer. There is a good deal of evidence that he sent papers written by his research students, along with his recommendation that they be published, to a broad range of journals, including the *British Journal of Sociology* which was housed in the LSE itself. He played a particularly active role as the editor of 'The Nature of Human Society' book series, published by Weidenfeld and Nicolson. His great coups were acquiring the rights to Raymond Aron's classic two-volume survey of *Main Currents in Sociological Thought* and Claude Lévi-Strauss's *The Savage Mind*, both of which sold well. His own *Thought and Change* and *Saints of the Atlas* appeared in this series, as did further works by Aron, Eisenstadt, Bernard Crick, Ali Mazrui, Lucy Mair, Paul Stirling and Melvin Richter. He was an active editor, and there is evidence that he tried to recruit Frederik Barth to write for the series.

Some of the research money he received from Dahrendorf when leaving the sociology department went towards a seminar on the philosophy of history, held during his last four years at the LSE. 'Patterns of History', eventually co-chaired with Michael Mann and the present author, had a paradoxical character. Gellner drew on his full range of acquaintances, inviting specialists on every period of all major world civilizations, and archaeologists and anthropologists as well – participants included figures such as Colin Renfrew, Edmund Leach, Raymond Aron, Patricia Crone,

---

49 J. Davis, 'An Interview with Ernest Gellner', *Current Anthropology*, vol. 32, 1991, p. 68.
50 D. N. Gellner, Personal Communication, October 2008.

Peter Wiles, Lew Binford, Garry Runciman, Anthony Smith, John Hajnal, Peter Burke, Michael Cook, Richard Gombrich and Quentin Skinner. Though attendance was very low, the discussion was at the highest level, and Gellner added quite as much as he gained from the papers that were presented.

He was elected to the British Academy in 1972 – a status marker which had real significance for him, at least if we are to judge by the way that he described himself on his book jackets at the time. This led him to play an active role in that organization, helping to gain admission for Alan Macfarlane despite initial resistance to the latter's intellectual innovation in bringing together history and anthropology. He also organized, or helped to organize, a very large number of conferences. He published seven edited collections of papers on Muslim societies, most of them deriving from conference proceedings. But he also stepped outside his specialist areas with other projects. A volume on populism was particularly striking because it dealt with both the movement of intellectuals towards the people in Eastern Europe, and the wholly different phenomenon of anti-trust agrarianism (and of the political culture that it both represented and reinforced) within the United States.[51] *Patrons and Clients* was equally useful in contrasting the political cultures of northern and southern Europe, and it remains a standard reference in its field.[52]

It would be wrong to end this discussion of his career with a mere listing of professional activities, for doing so would neglect the spirit in which they were conducted. Gellner clearly loved controversy, and adored making forceful arguments. This was particularly true of his conference appearances, where he spoke in the most direct and challenging way – sometimes causing a furore, occasionally dominating the proceedings, always providing a talking point. One example will suffice. British archaeology became notably theoretically sophisticated in the 1970s, in part because of the dynamic leadership of Colin Renfrew. Gellner was accordingly asked in the early 1980s – without much sense, one suspects, of what he might say – to one of the yearly conferences of the Theoretical Archaeology Group. He had twenty minutes to speak, and used just fifteen of them to suggest that the interest then shown by British archaeologists in French structuralism was overdone. His full argument was later published, in a highly developed form, usefully placing the structuralism exemplified by Lévi-Strauss within the context of Western philosophy.[53] Most memorable

---

51   E. A. Gellner and G. Ionescu (eds), *Populism: Its Meanings and National Characteristics*, London, 1969.
52   E. A. Gellner and J. Waterbury (eds), *Patrons and Clients*, London, 1977.
53   'What is Structuralisme?', in *Relativism and the Social Sciences*, Cambridge, 1985.

about the conference was the way in which he chose to illustrate his main point – that social structure constrained behaviour far more effectively than did culture – by pretending to fine himself fifty pence each time he used some particular combination of words or grammar. Something of this remains in the published version: he contrasts social structural analyses' emphasis on scarcity with the fact that cultural symbols are so flexible as to constrain little. It was the acting out of this contrast which produced a riveting performance.

The Logic of Liberalization

In the late 1970s Gellner was troubled by the stagnant state of First World liberal capitalism, and by developments within the Third World of late-developing societies. In contrast, he was essentially optimistic about the Second World, effectively understood by Gellner to include not just the realm of state socialism but also that of authoritarian developmental capitalism. For the remainder of his life, much of his energy was devoted to exploring various facets of the latter, and this naturally calls for attention.

Gellner's many journeys to the Second World are prefaced by 'A blobologist in Vodkobuzia', a meditation on the morality of visiting authoritarian countries.[54] Two poles are drawn, those of wholly authoritarian and securely liberalizing states. If it was easy to refuse an invitation in the former situation and just as easy to accept in the latter, endless ambiguities emerged when trying to judge societies, and types of behaviour characteristic to them, which struggled between these poles. He clearly found this tension fascinating, and moreover felt that 'he fitted in' within these in-between worlds. His kind of 'squashed–dago looks' were quite common, and his clothes so poor that he was not usually taken to be an outsider. It was difficult to tell when one was being told the truth, but he clearly was deeply impressed by the calculations of those trying to transform these societies from within – pressing for change but trying not to provoke a repressive response from the powerful. He heard about the leader of an institute who was apparently orthodox but who had hired innovating, even dissenting scholars – and had perhaps protected them using a front of political correctness – and was led to Yulian Bromley in Moscow. The idea of an intellectual who had never soiled his hands acting out a sort of inner emigration was perhaps sparked by Gellner's friendship with the Soviet anthropologist V. R. Kabo, but it was just as applicable to the country house of Jiří Musil in

---

54 This first appeared in the *Times Literary Supplement* (23 November 1979), and was then reprinted in *Culture, Politics and Identity*, Cambridge, 1987.

Southern Bohemia – its internal courtyard powerfully impressed Gellner as a symbol of society's turning away from the state. Musil certainly claimed to recognize himself in Gellner's article, but so, to Gellner's amusement, did many others.

Gellner had first met Musil while visiting Czechoslovakia for the first time since the start of his second period of exile, probably in 1967.[55] After lecturing at the Institute of Sociology, and meeting his few relations remaining in Prague, Gellner visited the Musils at home. They had a good deal in common. Musil had a Jewish background, though his childhood was spent in Slovakia.[56] Musil had become a distinguished urban sociologist – choosing to work in an area sufficiently apolitical that he could avoid joining the Party. At this time, Gellner's insistence that certain freedoms had already been established in the socialist bloc slightly irritated Musil, who felt that Gellner was not sufficiently aware of the subtle, informal pressures that made life difficult. This is an interesting comment, suggesting that Gellner was imagining the signs of liberalization that he so wanted to see. He had arrived at a moment when the seeds of change, some coming from within society but quite as many from within the party itself, were beginning to bear fruit. The Prague Spring was underway, and the closing of that chapter with the Russian invasion affected Gellner profoundly. At a personal level, he did a great deal to help Musil, who had been listed in the 'White Book' as an enemy of the state. After a short period at the University of Kent, Musil came to the LSE as a reader following a personal interview with the Director. He taught for a short period in the Sociology of Development course, specializing in state socialist societies. The times were difficult, and the departmental seminar once saw a blazing row between Musil and Blackburn over the nature of socialism. Gellner encouraged Musil to write a book on sociology after revolution. Though the book was written, it was never published because Musil returned to Prague. 'Czechs are most reluctant to leave their country, and sometimes speak of emigration as a form of moral turpitude', Gellner noted later when remembering the torments of Musil and his wife in 1969. 'The supposition that whatever life has to offer, it may be found in its most

---

55 Musil remembers the meeting as taking place in 1965, but there is no stamp in the relevant passport for any visit made in that year.

56 Musil was sent to the camps at the very end of the war. On his return to Prague he went to see the home of the woman with whom he had been in love, certain that she was dead, as she was also Jewish and had been sent to Terezín. She had survived, and suddenly opened the window at which he was staring. They married, and she became a distinguished French translator.

agreeable form in Bohemia is not totally absurd'.[57] Still, the return was very much against the advice of Gellner, who insisted that it would be terrible to lack the freedom to publish one's ideas.

Gellner was also involved in Czech politics in less personal ways. He had become familiar with the work of Pavel Machonin, a Czech expert on social stratification, and introduced him at a 1969 conference in Ditchley House – one year before the publication of Machonin's major research, part of a very large volume on *Czechoslovak Society* – as 'the best Czech sociologist'. Gellner spelled out the nature of that research in an article on 'The pluralist anti-levellers of Prague'. He took care to have this analysis circulate by producing two further versions of the same argument. He began by making clear the repression that character-ized the years following the invasion. But he then turned his attention to the substantive arguments of *Czechoslovak Society*. Machonin argued that the Czechoslovak political economy was being deformed by two forces: excessive egalitarianism and bureaucratic interference. What was necessary, and what was in fact happily emerging, was the presence of meritocratic stratification, relatively mild and perhaps temporary, to help the growth of the economy. The idea that an industrial society had certain functional needs appealed to Gellner. But what interested him even more was the idea, more or less consciously held by the Prague reformers, that curtailing egalitarianism might permit the emergence of pluralism – which might then form the base for a more liberal society. Gellner was amused by the response of a Czech economist to a Western colleague who had suggested that decentralization of the economy would not create efficiency. In the end this did not matter, the Czech insisted, inefficiency being a price worth paying for liberalization. There were plans to have the volume translated, a venture supported by Karl Deutsch.[58] Objections were raised that doing so might endanger some of the authors. Gellner's view was that publication should go ahead anyway, but this did not in fact take place. When Steven Lukes told this story to one of the book's

57 'An Exile and His Leftovers', *Times Literary Supplement*, 8 March 1985, p. 256. This is a particularly insightful review of Josef Škvorecký's *The Engineer of Human Souls*. He contrasted Koestler with Škvorecký, arguing that the former gives the flavour of passionate involvement with Marxism as a creed, the latter with the dull world that it created. He showed himself to be familiar with Škvorecký's work as a whole, insisting that *Tank Battalion* and *Miracle*, neither of them translated into English, were masterpieces, continuing to develop the world created by Hašek in *The Good Soldier Švejk*.

58 The findings of the earlier volume, together with an update after the collapse of communism, can now be found in J. Krejci and P. Machonin, *Czechoslovakia, 1918–92*, Basingstoke, 1996.

contributors, by then employed in menial work, he was told simply that 'he understands us very well'.[59]

Gellner found it difficult to return to a Czechoslovakia under communist rule, but did manage at least two more trips in 1978 and 1980 – on the latter occasion acquiring the visa, which had been denied him in London, whilst attending a conference in Istanbul. The first of these visits led to 'Getting along in Czechoslovakia', which appeared anonymously.[60] He continued to insist in this article that the period of Stalinism was over, that a measure of liberalization had already been achieved, and drew upon his vast store of Eastern European jokes to show that the police had come to be seen for the most part to be as stupid as they were threatening. But his account of daily life stressed the seediness and grubbiness involved in making endless compromises to ensure one's children's education. He described a new text by Patočka which argued that Nietzsche's philosophy had proved to be a better guide to twentieth-century Bohemia than had the democratic optimism of Masaryk. This viewpoint seemed to touch a nerve. Gellner became, as we shall see later, ever more critical of what he saw as the Czech tendency to compromise – suggesting informally that 'Czech military victories' would be an appropriate entry in a competition held by the *Spectator* to name the shortest books imaginable.[61] He returned again to speak to the seminar of Julius Tomin, the dissident philosopher whose network in the West, based at Oxford University, was supported by George Soros. On this occasion he was chased around town by the police, an unpleasant experience that would prevent him from being issued a visa thereafter. On each occasion he left books behind, including those of Miroslav Hroch, Michael Hollis, Alan Macfarlane, Steven Lukes and Geoffrey Hawthorn. Books were indeed necessary. The very fact that Czechoslovakia had been so advanced, and so close to a striking softening of communist rule, made 'normalization' all the harsher. But he retained his interest in the country, constantly writing reviews about its history and progress, and placing it within a larger context.

---

59 Lukes interviewed by O'Leary, 27 February 2001. The publisher approached, Oxford University Press, got cold feet given that copyright issues could not be resolved. The dissident in question was a close friend of both Lukes and Gellner, whom she much admired. Lukes notes that Gellner had several Czech friends, and served as something of a permanent adviser to the members of the philosophy seminar in Prague organized by Julius Tomin, which Western philosophers would attend (as did Gellner on one occasion), often supported by funds from the Soros Foundation.

60 'Getting Along in Czechoslovakia', *New York Review of Books*, 9 November 1978.

61 He later added to this 'Russia's Road to Democracy'.

Gellner's continuing investigations into the possible liberalizing of communist society brought him repeatedly to the socialist bloc. In 1983 he spent time with the Hungarian social anthropologists Michály Sarkhany and Michály Hoppal, and was deeply impressed by the irony a postcard from Moscow that he received from the latter at the time of the invasion of Afghanistan, which showed the Red Army as protectors and liberators. His engagement with Poland was still greater. He had visited in 1979, and returned in 1984 to attend the centenary celebrations of the birth of Malinowski – an event which, as we shall see, led him to amend his own views. He stayed on after the conference, and offered general reflections about Poland in an article initially designed for *Government and Opposition* but eventually published elsewhere under a pseudonym.[62] The most interesting part of the piece emphasized diversity within East Central Europe, a subject which he liked to discuss with both Chris Hann and Teodor Shanin given their expertise on the varieties of collectivization under communism. The broken civil society of Czechoslovakia was contrasted with the smoother cooperation seen in Hungary. In Poland, state and civil society were seen as wholly in opposition. He noted the marked freedom of expression in that country, and adapted the old joke to highlight the difference between Russia and Poland: 'Answer: in Russia no one can speak his mind except for Chernenko, and in Poland everyone can speak his mind except Jaruselski'. All the same, four days spent walking in the Carpathians led him to believe that the state retained sufficient control to limit expressions of opposition.[63] He returned in 1985 to a meeting of anthropologists, bringing whisky, which he sipped whilst listening to his Polish colleagues. As these visits took place during martial law they were much appreciated, as were the links established with British academic life – Grażyna Kubica, notably, was able to spend a term at Cambridge. Furthermore, from the 1980s he was very interested in Estonia, and he developed close friendships with Andrus Park in

---

62 'The State of Poland', *Times Literary Supplement*, 17 August 1984. The article ends with a discussion of Calderón's play *Life is a Dream*. Gellner adored the play, as we shall see, and was very irritated that *Government and Opposition* wished to cut this part of the article.

63 Ibid. Gellner noted the absence of mountaineering groups, and used it to argue that civil society had been suppressed. His colleague Chris Hann objected to such impressionistic methods in 'Philosophers' Models on the Carpathian Lowlands', in J. A. Hall (ed.), *Civil Society: Theory, History, Comparison*, Oxford, 1995. Gellner did not give in on this point in his 'Reply to Critics', in J. A. Hall and I. C. Jarvie (eds), *The Social Philosophy of Ernest Gellner*, Amsterdam, 1996, p. 678. Grzegorz Ekiert, then a student in Krakow, suggested in a personal communication that the state of mountaineering at that time might simply have reflected the fact of martial law.

Tallinn and Eero Loone in Tartu. He would also travel occasionally to East Germany and Bulgaria.

This account of his engagement with East Central Europe has run slightly ahead of his major theoretical statement about liberalization, expressed in 1976 in 'From *the* Revolution to Liberalisation'.[64] The argument was that the myth of *the* revolution, so central, for example, to the thought of Jean-Paul Sartre, was losing its force; what mattered instead was the question of liberalization. The social basis for revolutionary fervour had been the total illegitimacy of *ancien régimes*, resulting from the awareness of industrialization, in combination with the messianic belief that a new order could be as total as that which had preceded it. Traditional *ancien régimes* were now in short supply, and messianism somewhat curtailed by failed expectations. In contrast, there were many regimes which had some meritorious elements, notably the achievement of some level of development, but which were nevertheless morally unattractive. Gellner made it quite clear that his concept was meant to be generic, that is, he held it to be as valid for authoritarian capitalism as it was for state socialism – and accordingly he had visited Greece shortly after the Colonels came to power, Spain during the transition to democracy, and Brazil during one of its attempts at democratic restoration. The concept of liberalization was meant to refer to a process that had already begun, for dissidents were already disciplined more by the law book than by a fear of the gulags. Such persecution gave intellectuals a sharp awareness of their conditions, making liberalization something of a carnival for intellectuals. The danger existed that a lack of self-discipline among intellectuals might lead them to make demands which could be seen by the regime as a real threat, and have the unintended effect of intensifying repression. The other extreme was an equally unattractive option, namely demanding so little that the old regime persisted unchanged. What was needed was the ability to dribble like the great footballer George Best, to sell dummies right and left and swerve past defenders with ease. This emphasis on skills was complemented by a series of questions about the structural conditions – ranging from regionalism, nationalism, and the state of the economy, to the presence of a set ideology, the difference between left and right attempts, and the occupational structure of the society – within which the game as a whole was to be played.

Gellner's position gained the attention of Raymond Aron.[65] Gellner's concern had really been with softer political rule rather than with democracy

---

64   'From *the* Revolution to Liberalisation', in *Spectacles and Predicaments*.
65   R. Aron, 'On Liberalisation', *Government and Opposition*, vol. 14, 1979. Aron had made much the same case earlier in *Plaidoyer pour l'Europe décadente*, Paris, 1977.

per se. A presupposition of Aron's article was the need to distinguish between the two, and he wrote with great subtlety about the relationship between them, with detailed reference to historical and contemporary events in Europe. Aron's main argument was Tocquevillian. England had benefited from liberalization early on, later allowing the extension of the franchise to proceed with relative ease. In contrast, the failed liberalization of France allowed a revolutionary elite to come to power praising democracy while effectively controlling popular sentiment. This led Aron to distinguish between the liberalizations under way at that time in southern Europe and the concurrent attempts to reform communism. The former were somewhat akin to the English model: some liberties were already in place, making it at least possible that liberal democracy would be established.[66] The revolutionary centralization of power in the socialist bloc left much less room for manoeuvre. The Party might allow intellectuals a little more say, but it was likely to place very strict limits on any process of decompression for fear that its hold on power would wither away.

Gellner replied, giving reasons for greater optimism. He was not opposed to Aron's desire to distinguish different factors at work, even different routes to softer political rule. Nonetheless, he felt that there was an overwhelming logic to the development of late industrial society that favoured change.

[A]n advanced industrial society requires a large scientific, technical, administrative, educational stratum, with genuine competence based on prolonged training. In other words, it cannot rely on rigid ideologues and servile classes alone. It is reasonable to assume that this kind of educated middle class, owing its position to technical competence rather than to subservience, and inherently, so to speak professionally, capable of distinguishing reality and thought from verbiage and incantation, will develop or has developed the kind of tastes we associate with its life-style – a need for security, a recognition of competence rather than subservience, a regard for efficiency and integrity rather than patronage and loyalty in professional life, a recognition of the fact that errors in good faith are not morally culpable but part of the normal healthy working of institutions and call for no witch-hunts, a measure of freedom in leisure activities. At the same time, this class is large enough and indispensable enough not to be lightly or pointlessly thwarted. It can exercise a sustained, quiet, pervasive pressure. It may infiltrate high places. Overt

---

66 Aron remained cautious, fearing that the extreme left might be so disgusted at the retention of power and privilege by members of the *ancien régime* that it would cling to revolutionary hopes and practices.

dissidents are its minuscule, heroic, probably indispensable, yet expend-
able advance guards: but the real battle may be won by the incomparably
larger, cautious, compromising but pervasive and persistent main body,
which advances like an insidious sand dune, rather than by dramatic self-
immolation. This class is large, and it cannot be penalised effectively
without a cost to the economy which may no longer be acceptable.[67]

At all times, Gellner stressed the difficulties of liberalization. By the early
1980s, he had come to believe that the Czech attempt to liberalize had been
particularly clumsy, both because it was too threatening and because the
intellectuals' demands ran completely out of control.[68] His great admiration
for Calderón's 1636 play *Life is a Dream* suggested pessimism as well – for
here the crudity of the old regime's attempt to restore order led to complete
revolt, although in this case the leftist leader, perhaps implausibly, concludes
the play by disavowing his radical supporters in order to embrace elements
of the previous regime. Gellner's hopes for controlled decompression within
the socialist bloc were to be disappointed by the collapse of communism and
then of the Soviet Union in the years after 1989, leading him to move closer
to Aron's position. Decompression in socialist societies was very unlikely
to be liberal because privileges were prebendal, and giving up a position of
power meant losing everything; in contrast, authoritarian capitalist societies
might become liberal because the privileged classes could at least hang on
to their wealth.[69] But throughout the 1970s and 1980s, he remained fundamentally optimistic as to the possibility of liberalization. This is explained by
his deep involvement with the Soviet Union.

Fascination with Russia came naturally to a thinker with Czech roots.
Geopolitical alliance with Russia had sometimes been seen by Czechs as
a means of counteracting German power. Masaryk and Gellner's own
father had been deeply interested and immersed in Russian culture. When
Gellner first met his future wife Susan, he insisted on taking her to Covent

---

67   '*Plaidoyer pour une libéralisation manquée*', in *Spectacles and Predicaments*, p. 339.
68   'The Captive Hamlet of Europe', in *Culture, Identity and Politics*. This is an analysis of
Milan Šimečka, *Obnovení Pořádky* (*The Restoration of Order*) and J. Slàdaček *Osmašedesátý-
Pokus o Kritické Porozum ní Historickým Souvislostem* (*1968: An Essay at a Critical Understanding
of Historical Connections*), the work of dissidents who remained in Czechoslovakia after 1968.
Gellner had evident distaste for thinkers such as Šimečka who had been true believers in
the 1950s, at the time of the Slánský trials, but he praised the absolute lucidity of the
analysis, accepting its pessimistic conclusion that normalization looked set to work, perhaps
especially because of the Czech refusal to resist.
69   With hindsight, we can see that Gellner was not quite right. Some cadres morphed
into oligarchs through the privatization/piratization of public property.

Garden to hear Mussorgsky's opera *Boris Godunov*, which centres on the late-sixteenth-century Russian Regent – a significant decision given his dislike of opera and the sheer length of this particular work. The intensity of this interest, then and even more so after the suppression of Solidarity in Poland, derived however from the belief that developments within the metropolis would determine what was possible in the satellite countries. By the early 1970s he was making sustained efforts to visit, wishing to spend his 1972 sabbatical in that way. Difficulties with the Soviet authorities made it impossible for him to do so, but these difficulties were suddenly resolved, allowing him to make the first of many trips in the winter of 1972. The six weeks he spent in Moscow were later recalled as among the loneliest of his life, despite the pleasures of attending the city's theatres.[70] But his ties with the country increased rapidly, and his first important article on his Soviet experience was published in 1974, providing some of the empirical data for the theoretical article just discussed. The Soviet Union gained ever greater importance for him. He fell in love with the Russian language, and he very much admired the sheer cognitive power of leading Russian intellectuals, feeling very comfortable during his 1989–90 sabbatical in Moscow – in part perhaps because he was welcomed so eagerly.

He made his first and most important contacts by situating himself at the Institute of Ethnography of the Soviet Academy of Sciences. He was fascinated by its director, Yulian Bromley, who, as already noted, gave the impression of orthodoxy but seemed to protect those with more dissident views. But Bromley was important for another reason. He had placed the study of ethnicity at the centre of the institute's agenda, and this naturally had immediate appeal for Gellner – theoretically, substantively, and in terms of the limits to Marxist theory. Equally, his own expertise on nationalism must have made him very interesting to his Soviet colleagues. But there were other intellectual strands present within the institute. One concerned 'primitive society', meaning, in Marxist terms, pre-class societies; another of still greater interest for him was purely ideological, the specification and elaboration of Marxist theory itself. Beyond these considerations lay personal relationships. The figure who mattered most was Anatoly Khazanov, the historian of the Scythians and author of *Nomads and the Outside World*, a genuine masterpiece of modern social science, which Gellner successfully pressed Cambridge University Press to publish.

Khazanov's Jewish background led to his becoming a *refusenik*. Gellner would make a point of visiting Khazanov to provide him with some protection – Khazanov always knew when Gellner was about to come because

---

70 *State and Society in Soviet Thought*, Oxford, 1988, p. viii.

the elevator in his building would be disabled in an attempt to discourage Gellner, given his health, from visiting the fifth-floor apartment. On one of his visits, the guide who met Gellner at the airport told him that he would not be permitted to meet Khazanov. After a pause Gellner made it clear that he respected local views but had his own principles, and asked to be taken immediately back to the airport. His status was sufficient by that time to ensure that, after a series of frantic phone calls, the visit was approved, and the bar would not be reimposed.[71] Khazanov was eventually allowed to emigrate to Israel, and Gellner perhaps played some part in the decision – he told Khazanov's immediate authorities that they would have fewer problems releasing than imprisoning him. But it is important to remember that Gellner, for all his support for dissidence, harboured deep admiration for those who bent rather than flouted the rules, on the grounds that they might be better agents of liberalization. His views on this matter were articulated with exceptional clarity as part of a prolonged but private disagreement with Noam Chomsky in 1986:

> The Soviet Union today is a society incomparably different from what it was under Stalin. Dissidents are harassed more or less according to the law book, as opposed to simply disappearing. The number of political prisoners, according to those who make it their business to collect the data, are measured in thousands, when in earlier conditions, they were counted in millions. All this must in part be due to the fact that at the top, there are people who, whilst quite determined to hang on to power and not to hand it over, nevertheless wish to do it with the minimum amount of oppression. It seems to me well worthwhile trying to understand the mechanics which help them to do so, or which push them in that direction, and also to understand the limits which are possibly set by those endeavours. For that reason, such spare time as I have had in recent years has been directed to studying these problems, and I go there when I have the opportunity. They have no illusions about my views (privately many of them share them in various degrees), and I have been helpful to people in trouble whenever I came across it. I think I am less of an embarrassment to the authorities, because of what they consider my 'reactionary' views, than a leftist who is liable to suffer disillusionment and get very excited about it.[72]

---

71   A. Khazanov, 'Gellner and the Soviets', *Cambridge Anthropology*, vol. 19, 1996/7.
72   Gellner to Chomsky, 27 October 1986. We will see that his favourable attitude towards the Soviet Union led to a later disagreement with Khazanov.

Certainly, he admired and became close to a whole series of Soviet anthropologists. Ties were formed with the Leningrad anthropologist V. R. Kabo, an expert on primitive society whose Jewish background eventually led him to move to Australia, and with the great Africanist Dimitri Ol'derogge, about whom he later wrote an admiring obituary.[73] But the connections abounded in many directions. V. N. Basilov visited the LSE for extended periods, whilst Rashid Kaplanov, Victor Shirnelman and Khazanov came to Prague, the last two for extended periods. Further connections beyond the world of the social anthropologists were made in his sabbatical year, particularly with Lena and Yuri Senokosov, and these were maintained for the rest of his life.

He persuaded the Wenner-Gren Foundation to fund a conference in 1976 which would allow Western and Soviet anthropologists to meet and discuss their rather different ways of looking at the world. The proceedings, published as *Soviet and Western Anthropology* in 1980, contain his programmatic statement explaining the inherent interest of Soviet anthropology, to which his own contributions, over several years, would respond. The essays in question – but not an extensive set of reviews – were collected in 1988 as *State and Society in Soviet Thought*. The essays are remarkable, the record of a genuine engagement with a different world, whose contours are delineated with sympathy and care. They were written over a fifteen-year period, from his early fifties onwards, and show his mind at full stretch. They amount to a second sustained piece of fieldwork. But the research was terminated by the tectonic shift of power in the world polity. Gellner went to the Soviet Union for the academic year 1989–90 expecting to continue this line of research, and hoping as well to do additional fieldwork outside Moscow.[74] But it seemed ridiculous to continue working on this subject and he chose instead, as we will see below, to observe every aspect of the great transformation that was taking place.

When he collected his essays in 1988, one remained unchanged – 'The Soviet and the Savage', first published in 1974 – on the grounds that it served as a record of his first impressions. Two particular elements are striking, and are present in later essays as well. The first is his sheer

---

73   V. Kabo, *The Road to Australia: Memoirs*, Canberra, 1998; 'Academician Ol'derogge', *Africa*, vol. 58, 1988.

74   He had planned to continue writing essays on key pieces of Soviet anthropological research. Early versions of his discussion of M. V. Kriukov's *Sistema Rodstva Kitaitsev* (*The Chinese Kinship System*), Moscow, 1972, are lodged in the Gellner Archive. Particular fascination on this occasion seems to have been with the differential speed with which kinship patterns changed in different civilizations – a topic bound to have an impact on Marxist views of the essential unity of humankind.

admiration for Soviet scholarship. Intellectual power was the least of it: more important was a firm sense of reality, the fact, as he put it, that Soviet Marxism was short- rather than long-haired. Life was serious in this world, given the horrors of history and the difficulties of finding space for free thought, and little time was wasted, in his opinion, on the facile idealism characteristic of Western Marxism – a Marxism which seemed at times to have no clear content, as cultural forces were often considered to determine or be part of the base. Still more important was the realization that Marxism had left in its wake a series of interesting questions that Western anthropology had come to ignore. The evolutionist character of Marxism made it sensitive to questions concerning origins and destinations, and to the need to produce a clear typology of social forms. Gellner did not for a moment retreat from the need to explain transitions between different types – he remained critical of naïve serialism – but there is no doubt that his long-standing desire to offer an account of human history was stimulated by thinkers who shared this concern. The second element is the data provided by this particular corner of Soviet life for his research on liberalization. Gellner's essay discussed L. V. Danilova's assessment of the state of scholarship dealing with pre-capitalist society. What impressed him most was the ability of Soviet scholars to make arguments that went well beyond Marxist orthodoxy. Danilova argued that economic factors only gained full salience in capitalist society, with power factors otherwise having primacy. Exactly the same point was made in a careful analysis of L. E. Kubbel's *Songhai Empire*, an account of African feudalism's genesis that argued, with subtlety and attention to empirical material, that developments in the political form created a mode of production – rather than, as Marxism would seem to dictate, the economic mode preceding and generating its political form.

Gellner was clearly fascinated in purely philosophical terms with an entirely different aspect of the work of his Soviet colleagues, namely their attempt to save Marxist theory from obvious objections, and to fill in gaps left by the founding fathers. The great ideologist in this regard was Yuri Semenov, some of whose work Gellner himself translated. Gellner's attention lent great status to Semenov, until that time seen as something of an outsider.[75] Semenov maintained that Marxism had no need to assert that every society went through every stage – thankfully so, given that such unilinealism was clearly empirically false. Marxism could be saved by insisting that class factors mattered in the transition to a new mode of production made first, so to speak, by a single society – that society thereafter

---

75   Gellner's enthusiasm for his work was not shared by some of his Soviet friends, as is made clear in Kabo, *The Road to Australia*, pp. 211–2.

providing an example that allowed other societies to 'skip' stages, aware of a leading model whose example and aid might speed up historical processes. Even greater ingenuity was shown by Semenov in writing, as Gellner put it, the Marxist Book of Genesis. What mattered here was the need to explain the creation of nothing less than a human cooperative essence, the existence of which would ground a Marxist morality. Semenov produced a deductive argument to the effect that food–sharing, which allowed specialists in tool creation and use to flourish, must have given an evolutionary advantage. But, if the sophistication of this account was impressive, it faced problems of its own. If an evolutionary advantage lay in cooperation, how was it possible that its potential was lost for so long during the course of class societies? At several points in the collection, Gellner observed arguments trying to explain the origin of exploitation, making fun of the fact that, to a non–Marxist, this required no explanation whatsoever. Semenov's account, for all its Darwinist flavour, ultimately sinned against the evolutionary paradigm by positing an unchanging essence.

Such questions were nothing compared to two issues which seemed fundamentally to disprove Marxism. Pastoralists are an anomaly in Marxist terms for several reasons: the social form itself was complex, combining communal ownership of pasture with private property in herds, but it proved capable, despite its limits, of creating sometimes huge imperial superstructures – which did not then lead, as noted, to any higher social formation or mode of production. Gellner traced the attempts to force pastoralism into one of the canonical stages, recounting that this had led to the elimination of nomadic groups – and of scholars who had chosen the wrong side in the debate over the proper classification of nomads. It was still dangerous to be on the wrong side of this debate concerning the Asiatic mode of production, about which Gellner wrote his most powerful essay, 'The Asiatic Trauma'.[76] He noted that this was an area of dispute amongst Soviet anthropologists, but he nonetheless used the work of V. N. Nikiforov as a vehicle to demonstrate that this was an insoluble problem for Marxism. A fork existed, either side of which was sufficient to destroy central Marxist tenets. On the one hand, Asiatic societies could be interpreted, as was common in Western thought, as wholly dominated by despotic states – a domination seen in the absence of private property in

---

76 This is the title in *State and Society in Soviet Thought*. The original title was 'Soviets Against Wittfogel, or the Anthropological Preconditions of Marxism'. He was utterly delighted – in the days when secretaries still typed manuscripts – to have his work 'improved' in this area by receiving an early draft corrected throughout to read 'Asiatic Motor Production' ('The Kathmandu Option', p. 354).

land, and perhaps explained, as in the later work of the renegade Marxist Karl August Wittfogel, by the provision of water control services on the part of the state. Nikiforov's work rejected this view, as it had to, in Gellner's view, if Marxism was to be saved. For to accept the idea of an autonomous – indeed even a functionalist – state would be to deprive Marxism of perhaps its central promise to mankind: that there is but one source of oppression in recorded history, that of economic exploitation, the removal of which would allow for harmonious salvation to be restored as the state withered away. Differently put, if political, military and coercive power is autonomous, it too could bring evil into the world, as Gellner as a liberal clearly believed. On the other hand, if Asiatic states were seen as emerging from a particular set of class relations, as Nikiforov believed Marx himself to have stressed in his later years under the influence of the American anthropologist Morgan, an alternative problem emerged which undermined an equally important tenet of Marxist thought. Class societies are supposed to be unstable, tending towards higher stages ultimately allowing human beings to return to their cooperative essence. But this second way of looking at Asiatic societies seemed to suggest that class oppression might continue to exist forever.

Two final general comments need to be made about the book's conclusion.[77] First, there is an interesting attempt to assess the state of the Soviet Union by reflecting on the issues that seemed most troublesome at the time. Ethnic conflict seemed likely to become a serious problem, whilst dealing with the effective autonomy of political power was an ever-present task. Secondly, in a very short space, Gellner offers one of the most considered reflections on the nature of Marxism that has ever been developed. That doctrine must maintain, in Gellner's view, five core concepts: a view of the human essence which serves to ground morality, an insistence that power is derivative, the belief that change is inscribed into the historical process, a privileging of class as the key social bond throughout recorded history, and a limited typology of societies which allows us to see our place in history. Soviet Marxism may have become a thing of the past, but this engagement with it richly deserves our continuing attention.

This is also an appropriate moment to evaluate Gellner's theory of liberalization, so vital to his intellectual project. He presents a politics of insiders, of the persistent rather than the brave. The expectation that they will succeed is deeply functionalist, at times irritatingly so in its teleological presumption that the very existence of a societal need will somehow cause that need to eventually be met. But Gellner's position often deviates from

---

77   Ibid., 'Postface'.

this, and certainly need not be understood in this narrow way. Rather, Gellner can be seen as recognizing the emergence of a social base upon which intelligent political leadership, sooner or later, can build a softer and more successful society. We have here a variation (because of its stress on specialists, favouring real knowledge over ideological dogma) of Barrington Moore's celebrated claim that there can be no democracy without a bourgeoisie.[78]

Gellner's position should be treated with a measure of caution. The Soviet Union did not decompress as he had hoped, in large part because its lack of civil society groups made it impossible for political leaders to find partners in liberalization.[79] But the spread of democracy has rarely been the result of middle-class pressures – the most sophisticated accounts stress the actions of working classes, unsurprising given that they were the social strata likely to benefit most from political change.[80] In a sense, this last point matters little because Gellner is concerned with the forces of late industrialism. But the point about middle classes is that they have been fickle – at times pressing for change, at times prepared to live with parties of order when threatened from below. The question that arises about late industrial society is whether the new middle-class elements that Gellner has in mind are brave enough to bring about fundamental change. The danger is that they too might accommodate themselves to power, provided that their immediate interests are served. There is some evidence from China that this is a possibility.[81] Nonetheless, Gellner makes a striking case, with a clear rationale. There are certainly many examples – Spain, South

---

78 B. Moore, *Social Origins of Dictatorship and Democracy*, Boston, 1966. Gellner's case was re-stated in the *Economist*, 12 February 2009. Introducing a special report on the middle class in emerging markets, its leader highlighted the emergence of new styles of thought.

> As people emerge into the middle class, they do not merely create a new market. They think and behave differently. They are more open-minded, more concerned about their children's future, more influenced by abstract values than traditional mores. In the words of David Riesman, an American sociologist, their minds work like radar, taking in signals from near and far, not like a gyroscope, pivoting on a point. Ideologically they lean towards free markets and democracy, which tend to be better than other systems at balancing out varied and conflicting interests.

79 R. Bova, 'Political Dynamics of Post-communist Transitions: A Comparative Perspective', *World Politics*, vol. 44, 1991.

80 D. Rueschmeyer, E. Stephens and J. Stephens, *Capitalist Development and Democracy*, Oxford, 1992.

81 D. Wank, 'Civil Society in Communist China? Private Business and Political Alliance, 1989', in Hall, *Civil Society*.

Korea, Hungary, Brazil, even contemporary Iran – of the social forces he identified playing some role in the opening up of political life. In this regard a particularly clear contrast can be drawn between the leaders of late-twentieth-century Hungary and Yugoslavia. The skills and expertise of the Hungarian elite led them to abandon the Communist Party well before 1989, aware that social mobility could best be secured by engaging with the wider world. The alternate route is best represented by Yugoslavian elites under Slobodan Miloševic – less skilled, and therefore 'caged in' and prone to play the nationalist card. In general, there is certainly something to the view that contemporary elites often wish to be part of a globalized world, even at the cost of detaching themselves somewhat from their home societies. But there is, of course, a negative outcome to this: that the character of nationalism might change yet again, making it more of a nativist movement appealing to those who are left behind.

7

Knowledge and Illusion

While the title of this chapter suggests a dual focus, it has in fact a single theme. It deals with a set of conceptual tools which, like a coin, have two opposite but complementary faces. The general framework was already present in *Thought and Change*, in the insistence that science undermines received morals as it brings technological innovation. But Gellner's later analysis is more detailed and sophisticated. The most obvious development is an explanation of how science actually works. This account draws upon an inquiry into the implications of work by Noam Chomsky and Thomas Kuhn. Their views were studied by Gellner with the greatest care, his engagement with Kuhn occasioning a complete interpretation of the work of Karl Popper. But a further prefatory comment is in order. Gellner was at once secure and insecure in his feelings about modern rational science. The security rests in the conviction that science works, that it has changed the world, and that there is a need to explain its mechanics. Insecurity derived from the equally strong conviction that there are not, and cannot ever be, foundational philosophical groundings for modern science that are so solid that they can replace the certainties of the past with some contemporary equivalent. It is this that leads to the second element in the title of this chapter, the other side of modern cognitive practices. The fact that science lacks grounding and cannot provide moral certainty creates space for theories designed to make us feel at ease. Gellner does not follow Popper in simply dismissing such theories as pseudo-science. He exhibits a much higher level of understanding, especially of the social roots of particular theories, while nevertheless retaining a great hostility toward them. Gellner was the scourge of re-enchantment theorists precisely because he understood them so well.

Ethics of Cognition

The core of Gellner's philosophy of science is found in *Legitimation of Belief*, begun during his 1968 sabbatical in California and published in 1974. It is one of Gellner's most important books, and was certainly seen as such by the author. It is polished, funny and powerful. The book is a mapping of modern epistemology, primarily a sociological analysis of how cognition actually functions. If it puzzled philosophers, social scientists were equally confused by the depth of philosophical understanding on display, and by the insistence that these problems had real relevance for our understanding of social reality. Accordingly, though it was well-received, it did not – in fact or in the eyes of its author – have a truly major impact, that is, it did not change the terms of intellectual debate.[1] The book simply did not fit into any established genre. Gellner realized this himself, lamenting that his work resembled that of the philosopher

---

1   Alan Ryan reviewed the book respectfully, though he understandably drew attention to the lack of proper copy-editing, in the *New Statesman* (24 January 1975). Bernard Crick was enthusiastic in the *Observer* (9 February 1975). Peter Mew, 'Wot Not Who We Are?', *Inquiry*, vol. 19, 1975, obviously enjoyed the book, but accused it (p. 125) of political irresponsibility on the grounds of excessive quietism:

'Reading Gellner you could be forgiven for thinking that all that is needed, following a general injection of rationality, is a contrite and quiescent return to the mainstream of Western society under the pure guidance of science and technology. This goes deeper than nonsense; it is the disingenuous solution of a swashbuckling liberal who has succeeded in our society and wishes to re-endorse it, who ignores the fact that science and technology are not simply there to be used for the benefit of all. In this connection, it is capitalism which "transcends cultural boundaries" and effectively decides what course science and technology will take . . . The alternative to opting out is, of course, to channel one's energies into the struggle to break the fetters of capitalism . . . '. Alasdair MacIntyre seemed to seek payback in his review for *The British Journal for the Philosophy of Science*, vol. 29, 1978, for Gellner's varied criticisms of his own work – most notably Gellner's 1971 attack on 'The Belief Machine', reprinted in *The Devil in Modern Philosophy*, London, 1974. MacIntyre's main point was that Gellner did not offer enough of a positive philosophy, being content to proceed by analyzing the errors of other thinkers. He was clearly out to wound, mocking the style, indeed going so far as to suggest (p. 108) that 'jokes and sneers are often symptoms of status anxiety and ambivalence . . . '. In contrast, Jürgen Habermas was deeply impressed by the book. He did not review it, but told me that he recommended, without success, that it be translated by Suhrkamp. An indication of Gellner's disappointment was immediate. Paul Stirling was staying with the Gellners in Hampshire on the weekend that the Sunday papers had the book to review. 'I remember him going to buy them all, and that he seemed disappointed' ('Ménage à Trois on a Raft', *Cambridge Anthropology*, vol. 19, 1996/7).

and historian R. G. Collingwood, praised as a philosopher by historians and as an historian by philosophers.[2]

The book begins in a now-familiar manner, announcing that it is necessary to find a general orientation given that we are lost, that our traditional beliefs are open to question.[3] This call for orientation is held to be idiosyncratic given the veritable chorus of pluralist theorists arguing against monistic rationalism, from William James in the past to Gellner's contemporaries Oakeshott, the later Wittgenstein, H. L. A. Hart, Bernard Crick, Quine, Berlin and Toulmin. Gellner defends his monistic urge as critical and limited, claiming that it seeks a minimum of intellectual orientation and is bereft of any desire to abolish social pluralism or to impose monism in political affairs.

The mapping exercise then begins by making a binary distinction between 'selectors' and 're-endorsers', amusingly characterized as the difference between 'hanging' and 'all-too-benign' judges. The latter will be considered later, as part of the analysis of the attractions of false theoretical trails, but they can at least be named at the outset: relativism, naïve evolutionism, and *carte blanche* theories (that is, theories which say that truth is attainable once obstacles to seeing it are removed).[4] Each of these have various manifestations, and they can, moreover, be found in hybrid forms. They stand in stark contrast to the three selectors identified by Gellner.[5] Skeletalism, the search for logical form carried out by Russell and the early Wittgenstein, is judged a rather technical strategy of philosophers; one feels that it is introduced partly so that Gellner can then recount the shift in Wittgenstein's thought towards the sort of relativism that Gellner criticized so ruthlessly in *Words and Things*. It is different with the two other selectors, empiricism and mechanism, identified more or less closely with Hume and Kant respectively. The fifty-odd pages which detail the weaknesses of these selectors, along with an account of their differences and followed by an explanation of their compatibilities, are amongst the most important that Gellner ever wrote.[6] His whole position, mixing sociology and philosophy, is encapsulated here, in a lucid, even simple form. Let us follow the logic of his argument.

---

2   Steven Lukes interviewed by Brendan O'Leary, 27 February 2001. Gellner had considerable admiration for Collingwood, comparing him favourably to Wittgenstein: the relativism of the former was troubled, that of the latter merely complaisant ('Thought and time, or the reluctant relativist', in his *The Devil in Modern Philosophy,* London, 1974).

3   *Legitimation of Belief,* Cambridge, 1974, chapter 1.

4   Ibid., chapter 3.

5   Ibid., chapter 4.

6   Ibid., pp. 71–127.

Gellner echoes Ryle's view of empiricism as 'the ghost in the machine'.[7] But his analysis of this selector points in an entirely different direction from that of his Oxford teacher. A preliminary technical discussion seeks to undermine the moral flavour of Ryle's account by disassociating the ghost-like quality of empiricism from the notion of 'spooks' up to no good. What matters about the view that nothing exists outside of sensation, and that human beings are simply bundles of such sensations, is its severe puritanism. Much customary belief goes out the window if we can find no evidence for it by our senses. Gellner will seek to defend this element of empiricism at all costs. But the defence is subtle, drawing attention to the weaknesses of empiricism rather than ignoring them.

A first general weakness of empiricism follows precisely from the puritanism: we are left with very little ground on which to stand. This problem was clearly stated by Hume, who noted the despair into which philosophy had driven him. Empiricism gives no guarantee of the world's existence, and no faith in a concept as crucial as that of causation. It was the realization of this complete uncertainty that moved Kant to philosophize in the first place. Kant restored order using a very particular move, namely by insisting that our mental structures require order and select information accordingly. If this solution is the best available, it remains a desperate one: the solution depends more on us than on the world outside of us.

The second weakness of empiricism is just as great, and is now much better known. Empiricism as a selector stands accused of impurity, of not even being capable of doing what it promises. The argument here is simple. We live amid a million impressions, and pay attention only to some of them – because they make sense to us, fitting within some schema that we already possess. This point has been made most strikingly in recent thought by Thomas Kuhn.[8] Our conceptual apparatus is what allows us to see facts, indeed to find those that will support what he termed a paradigm. Kuhn goes still further, suggesting that any fact that seems to disconfirm a powerful paradigm is likely to be ignored or explained away. The charge then is bluntly that this philosophy has no capacity to select information after all.

There is a final weakness. In the years before writing *Legitimation of Belief*, Gellner had been enormously impressed by the work of Noam Chomsky, writing on more than one occasion to introduce and explain his work – and corresponding frequently with Chomsky himself to get news

7   G. Ryle, *The Concept of Mind*, London, 1949.
8   T. Kuhn, *The Structure of Scientific Revolutions*, Chicago, 1962.

of his latest publications.[9] In the early 1970s, Gellner was wont to refer to Chomsky as the greatest living philosopher.[10] Gellner admired behaviourists' attempt to develop Hume's psychological insights into a genuine model of the workings of the human mind: at least they took their own arguments seriously. Nonetheless, that attempt was judged to be an absolute failure. The definitive destruction of this model was Chomsky's 1957 review of B. F. Skinner's *Verbal Behavior*.[11] Skinner's model of the mind as a stimulus–response device led him to suggest that the sentences we utter in life repeat those that we learned in our childhood. Chomsky demonstrated, conclusively, that this was nonsense, that our verbal repertoire is far greater and that we have the capacity to invent new sentences rather than simply to repeat ones that have been heard before. The charge against behaviourism is that its self-proclaimed toughness is a façade; its inner core explains nothing. Empiricism is mere mentalism, bereft of cognitive power.

Gellner's survey can be understood by distinguishing between two different meanings of the word 'reduction'. Behaviourist accounts of the human mind can be seen as reductive in the sense of being cheap. These accounts fail to account for the complexity of human consciousness, and ought therefore to be rejected. Chomsky's research programme is concerned with capturing the complexity of linguistic use specifically, but the larger analytic point also applies to other areas of mental activity. Here, reductionism has a different meaning, namely that implied by the notion of a mechanism. Appropriate reduction seeks to locate and to specify the mechanisms by which nature works.[12] Insofar as human behaviour is seen naturalistically in this way, it is bound to be morally repulsive, for this approach takes what we feel to be personal, idiosyncratic and unique and

---

9   There are various letters from Chomsky in the Gellner Archive between 1968 and 1971, discussing Wittgenstein, Ryle and Descartes, providing references that had been requested, and seemingly endorsing some of Gellner's interpretations of his work. Gellner seems to have sent him his 'On Chomsky', *New Society*, vol. 13, 1969. He continued to review Chomsky's books in later years. Their more tendentious exchange on political matters is described below in chapter 11.

10   Probably he meant something more specific, namely the greatest living 'active' philosopher. For Popper was still alive, and his impact on Gellner's work, and Gellner's admiration of Popperian ideas, was unrivalled. Doubts about Chomsky's research programme are by now quite widespread. But this does not affect Gellner's argument – which concerns the nature of explanation in general rather than Chomskian linguistics in particular.

11   Chomsky's review is widely available, for example in J. Fodor and J. D. Katz, (eds), *The Structure of Language*, Englewood Cliffs, 1964.

12   Much the same position is later taken by Jon Elster, *Nuts and Bolts for the Social Sciences,* Cambridge, 1989; *Solomonic Judgments: Studies in the Limitations of Rationality*, Cambridge, 1989, and *Alchemies of the Mind: Rationality and the Emotions*, Cambridge, 1998.

makes it generally explicable. In a certain sense, this is *the* weakness of
the concept of mechanism, namely that it undermines autonomy. Before
commenting more on this, it is useful to spell out further elements of
Chomsky's position which Gellner wishes to elucidate. Most immediately,
it is vital to realize that Chomsky's attack on the cheap reductionism of
behaviourism does not mean that he is some sort of soft humanist, happy
to leave matters at a level where human powers are simply celebrated
– as might be assumed given his radical politics. To the contrary, the
Chomskian programme is hard and cold in its attempt to explain human
behaviour. It opposes cheap reduction, but is wholly in favour of 'hard'
reduction. Gellner recognized that casual remarks by Chomsky occasionally gave the impression that empiricism was to be dismissed, but claimed
that this impression was misleading, for Chomsky was well aware of the
importance of empiricism for testing scientific hypotheses.

Gellner posits here an alternative view regarding humanity. To cele-
brate human uniqueness is to bask in warmth, but it is also to remain
without knowledge; in contrast, explanation must be cold, for it explains
us to ourselves. Gellner sympathizes more with the latter position, as two
examples make clear. Gellner observes – as did Chomsky in correspondence with him – the facility of Ryle's position.[13] Ryle's suggestion that
psychology is only called for in the case of breakdown led him to say:

> Let the psychologist tell us why we are deceived; but we can tell
> ourselves and him why we are not deceived. The . . . diagnosis of our
> mental impotences requires special research methods. The explanation
> of the exhibition of our mental competences often requires nothing but
> ordinary good sense.[14]

Such crude mentalism obscures the fact that much remains to be explained,
and it earns only scorn from Gellner. He showed greater sympathy,
however, to Arthur Koestler's attempt, in a book whose title derived from
Ryle's quip about empiricism, to identify some element of human creativity
which makes us more than mere machines.[15] What strikes Gellner here is

---

13   Chomsky to Gellner, 21 October 1968. Gellner also cited (*Legitimation of Belief*,
p. 90) the judgement made by Chomsky in his *Cartesian Linguistics* (New York, 1966,
pp. 12 and 81): 'Ryle is content simply to cite the fact that "intelligent behaviour" has
certain properties . . . these are characterized in terms of "powers", "propensities" and
"dispositions" which are characterized only through scattered examples. These constitute a
new myth as mysterious and poorly understood as Descartes' "mental substance"'.
14   Ryle, *The Concept of Mind*, p. 326, cited in *Legitimation of Belief*, p. 102.
15   A. Koestler, *The Ghost in the Machine*, London, 1967.

that this programme is logically bound to be self-defeating. Were such an element found, it could then be publicly available, thereby ruling out its capacity to serve as a bastion for humanity.[16]

Before turning to the ways in which the two selectors converge, we should describe Gellner's own position. At the end of *Legitimation of Belief*, Kant is described as 'the greatest philosopher of them all'.[17] This is justified by the claim that Kant saved us from the misery described by Hume, by arguing that our mental structures are such that we must see the world in causal, mechanical terms – the perceived regularity of nature thereby being assured. What then remains of our humanity? Gellner argues that Kant preserves an element of humanity in what he describes as a 'left-handed way': a philosophy which avoids exceptions makes one on this occasion, arguing that the schemata on which it rests can be ignored precisely because it is one that we have ourselves created. Gellner endorses the Kantian position because it is limited. The bare minimum – validation, obligation, validity of thought, freedom – is saved. His dispute is with theories, such as that of the later Wittgenstein, which save far too much. Many philosophers question the success of Kant's argument. Gellner did not provide any sustained defence of Kant's position, perhaps for subjective reasons: his world is Kant's, cold and marked by tension at all times.

Gellner's exam papers at the LSE often asked students questions about whether Kant and Hume were, so to speak, friends rather than enemies. His own preliminary justification for a positive answer was that both thinkers stressed the dangers inherent in religious authority. More important was the division of labour: mechanism shows us the form that explanation must take, whilst empiricism – useless in that regard – remains vital as a selector of evidence by which theories can be tested.[18] But Gellner has admitted the impurity of empiricism. How then can he continue to insist upon its efficacy?

The answer to this question lies in sociology. Both mechanism and empiricism are cognitive ethics. They are norms, telling us how we should proceed to gain understanding. An important passage puts the matter clearly:

No-one who writes a book on method thinks he is merely replicating the precepts of consistency, non-contradiction and so forth. So, a methodology must have some meat which is not merely logic. But if it asserts,

---

16   *Legitimation of Belief*, pp. 105–6.
17   Ibid., pp. 184–88.
18   Ibid., p. 108.

or presupposes, something over and above the formal requirements of logic, will not that *something else*, whatever it may be, have some implications concerning *the world*? And if so, can one not imagine or construct a possible world within which those implications are false, and within which consequently those recommendations are misguided? And if such a world is conceivable, obviously we cannot say, in advance of all inquiry, that such a world is not the *real* world. But what use is a methodology which prejudges the nature of the world we are in, before we have investigated the matter, and before we have any right to an opinion about it? So we cannot use it *before* we inquire, as a tool of investigation, or as a guide to what tools to use. And we certainly do not wish to use it *after* our inquiry is over. For one thing, it is too late by then; for another, by then we can presumably enjoy some much more meaty conclusions, and will hardly have much time for the relatively thin and abstract doctrines of methodology, even if, from another viewpoint, they evidently were not thin and abstract enough.[19]

This is to say, in the contemporary idiom, that there is no firm foundation, no utterly reliable basis for our epistemological positions. In the case of empiricism, what matters is the *a priori* assumption of atomism, that is, the belief that large packages can be separated into component pieces.

It enjoins, above all, a sensitivity to the distinction between that which is publicly verifiable by experiential evidence and that which is not, a sensitivity which is low or even systematically obscured in traditional culture. It creates a distinction where it barely existed . . . Thus the really important social impact of the ghost philosophy is the injunction 'Be sensitive to the boundary, and impose consistency with respect to it'; the secondary injunction, 'Down with the transcendent' (*Burn the books containing it* according to Hume, or *Call it technical nonsense* according to Ayer) does not matter much. If the first injunction is well observed and implemented, for all practical purposes the second is already performed and prejudged. In social contexts in which the first is well diffused and respected, it is perfectly possible to play down and, at a superficial level, ignore the second in the interests of courtesy, kindness, tact or antiquarianism. It hardly matters.[20]

---

19   'An Ethic of Cognition', in *Spectacles and Predicaments: Essays in Social Theory*, Cambridge, 1979, p. 164. This essay, which appeared in 1976 in a volume memorializing Imre Lakatos, should really be read in tandem with *Legitimation of Belief* – for it highlights the latter's central claims with particular power.

20   *Legitimation of Belief*, p. 122.

The atomic presumption may, in some ultimate sense, be unjustified. In political life, Burke insisted that removing the smallest element of the social order could lead the whole to fall – for each part was connected to every other. The possibility that our moral world might be some sort of cozy, meaningful unity clearly appalled Gellner, partly based on the Kantian argument that this would downplay human agency.[21] Of course, Kantian principles are as normative as those of empiricism. The world may not be a marvel of engineering, some sort of Rolls Royce engine which runs flawlessly and smoothly like a machine. This can be put differently by saying that Hume and Kant do not describe some essence of the human mind in and of itself. To the contrary, they suggested ways in which we should conduct ourselves in cognitive terms. And these cognitive norms seem to work: they produce world-transforming knowledge, and the sheer fact of the technical consequences of organized science gives us hope that the reality does indeed operate along mechanical lines.

The sociological character of epistemological assumptions further helps explain the ways in which Hume and Kant – or rather the principles that they represent – can best be seen as working in concert rather than separately. At an epistemic level, the most obvious logical conclusions to draw from sensationalism are unlikely to aid the growth of knowledge. One option in the face of the insubstantiality of the ghost is to passively withdraw from the world, on the grounds that all is illusion. This 'Indian' solution had a distinguished representative in Western philosophy in the person of Arthur Schopenhauer.[22] This route never gained general support, seeming esoteric at best given the obviousness of science's practical success. A second option is active rather than passive: if all we have is our sensations, then we may as well make the most of them.[23] But this route was also avoided because the British empiricists were centrally concerned with a desire to understand the structure of things.[24] Thus David Hume, in spite of his sensationalist view of the mind, was attracted by a nearly Kantian view of structure:

---

21 'Perhaps, who knows, the world is a Big Cosy Meaningful Unity after all, only we haven't hit on it yet: or perhaps – excuse my shudder – one of the existing faiths is the true one' ('An Ethic of Cognition', p. 179).

22 *Legitimation of Belief*, pp. 114–5. This characterization of Schopenhauer is amplified later in his *Reason and Culture*, Oxford, 1992, especially pp. 84–7.

23 The quotation immediately above comparing Hume and Ayer points to Gellner's belief that the logic of the positions of both was radical. But both had settled into the world, rather too comfortably for Gellner's taste.

24 *Legitimation of Belief*, p. 115.

Could men anatomise nature, according to the most probable, or at least
the most intelligible philosophy, they would find, that . . . causes are
nothing but the particular fabric and structure of the minute parts of their
own bodies and of external objects; and that, by a regular and constant
machinery, all the events are produced, about which they are so much
concerned.[25]

Equally, La Mettrie's *L'Homme machine*, to which Gellner had devoted
sustained and admiring analysis in 1964, contains a defence of both empiricism *and* materialism – indeed, empiricism is seen as the best route to
materialism.[26]

Attempts to synthesize empiricism and causal mechanisms can also be
made at the ethical level. Here too the obvious consequence of associa-
tionism might well be the choice to enjoy the finer things in life rather
than attempt in any way to change the world. But the empiricist tradition did not succumb to such passivity. Its great theorists, above all the
philosophical radicals, lived within a reforming world; they sought to
contribute to progressive change through the rigorous application of their
ideas. Formally, it might seem that the utilitarians would have been unable
to do much good because happiness, as critics point out, was used simply
to mean 'whatever men in fact desire', thereby making the ethic vacuous,
and incapable of distinguishing between one policy and another.

Not at all: one of the most important ways in which vacuity was avoided
was precisely at this point. The utilitarian vision, in terms of which this
ethic was articulated, was thoroughly permeated by the sensationalist-
atomistic manner of seeing the world, which consists of seeing the world
made up of our experience, and the experience as broken up into its
elements. From this followed a powerful and most discriminating, non-
vacuous injunction – when assessing important policies, institutions and
codes, before you work out the felicific accounts, break up the items on
the balance sheet into their ultimate constituents. The accountancy must
not be in terms of the old package-deals; all items must be broken up.
And this is enormously important: for the manner in which traditional
ethics convey and maintain their values is precisely by looking at experience through those package deals . . . [27]

---

25   D. Hume, *The Natural History of Religion* [1777], London, 1976, section III, cited in
Legitimation of Belief, p. 57.
26   'French Eighteenth-Century Materialism', in his *The Devil in Modern Philosophy*.
27   *Legitimation of Belief*, p.118.

Gellner encapsulates the puritanism at work in the utilitarian tradition in the quip that it is 'unlikely that any orgy was ever graced by the body of John Stuart Mill'.[28] The same point is made negatively with reference to G. E. Moore, the standard-bearer for Bloomsbury longings for higher states of mind. The legacy of Moore did far less to reform society, at least in Gellner's view, because it undermined the atomic postulate, thereby allowing belief systems to enter in as 'package deals'.[29]

Everything said here about the pillars of modern cognition is high-lighted by consideration of pre-scientific modes of thought. Gellner's portrait of the latter returns us to his early insistence that absurdity and contradiction can help to produce social control.[30] The contrast between the 'modern' and the 'savage' mind depends upon a close reading of an impressive article by Gellner's friend Robin Horton, an anthropologist of sub-Saharan African belief systems.[31] Gellner rejects some elements of Horton's account, notably its claim that there are no alternatives found within traditional belief systems, and its concentration on the situation of isolated individuals. There are in fact many alternatives within traditional systems of thought, but it is difficult to judge between them in a way that would add to the society's shared knowledge. Too many concepts available in these contexts are at the same time descriptive and evaluative, and their cultural entrenchment makes it impossible to challenge them. No generally accepted standard can be used to judge on claims of any sort because the cognitive division of labour is underdeveloped, without a distinction made between these descriptive and evaluative functions. The contrast he draws between traditional and modern thought is rather abstract, and was later reframed in a more effective way at the start of *Plough, Sword, and Book*, his philosophical history of humanity. Nonetheless, in spite of the account's abstraction, this framework allows for the dazzling passages at the end of *Legitimation of Belief* that contrast the philosophies of science of Kuhn and Popper and highlight Gellner's own position.[32]

The standard interpretation of Kuhn and Popper sees them as utterly opposed, unsurprising given the celebrated clash that took place between them at the LSE in the late 1960s.[33] For Popper, what matters most is

---

28   Ibid.
29   Probably Gellner exaggerated here – but in a way that in fact helps his own case. Keynes produced a very great deal of social reform because his puritanism was so deeply engrained.
30   *Legitimation of Belief*, chapter 8.
31   R. Horton, 'African Traditional Thought and Western Science', *Africa*, vol. 37, 1967.
32   *Legitimation of Belief*, pp. 168–84.
33   I. Lakatos and A. Musgrave, (eds), *Criticism and the Growth of Knowledge*, Cambridge, 1970.

openness and criticism, the bravery to make one's ideas as clear as possible
so that knowledge can advance through the openness of theories to refutation. Such a condition of permanent revolution utterly appalled Kuhn,
reminding him of the chaotic intellectual lives of the social scientists he
famously encountered whilst spending a year at the Institute for Advanced
Studies in Princeton – who argued endlessly about the very nature of their
enterprise, to the detriment of the production of actual results. What matters
for Kuhn is a shared set of understandings, a paradigm, within which high-
level research can be conducted and knowledge is accumulated by means
of mutual interaction. The fact that such paradigms are held to be incom-
mensurable makes Kuhn a relativist, but it was the cowardice of the normal
science he approved of that drew Popper's fiercest ire. And the field was
not by any means left to Popper. Kuhn demonstrated that scientists do not
in fact abandon their theories in the face of disconfirming evidence: they
tend to introduce *ad hoc* clauses which immunize theories from refutation
as necessary, for a clean slate would deprive them of the comforts of their
paradigm.

Gellner's interpretation of these two figures is both original and
powerful. Against the current of critical commentary, he insisted that these
thinkers, seemingly opposed to each other, shared a common error. They
had different ways of overlooking the importance of the revolution that
made us what we are, and so it was best to consider each of them in turn.

Gellner begins his overview of Popper's position by noting contradiction and confusion, which he will seek to explain and to resolve. The
contradiction, generally acknowledged and admitted by Popper himself, is
between the bravery he commends in scientific research and his praise of
piecemeal engineering in social affairs.[34] Confusion surrounds the question
of whether Popper should be seen as a positivist. He was accused of this
by members of the Frankfurt School, but went to considerable lengths to
insist that this characterization was unfair.[35] Popper's position on this point
became increasingly important to him, so much so that Gellner felt it
appropriate to distinguish between the views of the early and late Popper.

---

34 Popper has a defence for this, namely that piecemeal changes in society allow us to
calculate the impact of change. This scarcely removes the contradiction. Anyway Gellner
ruthlessly criticizes the defence in *Legitimation of Belief*, p. 172, principally on the grounds
that small changes can be swamped by the sheer remaining bulk of a society's institutions.

35 R. Dahrendorf, 'Remarks on the Discussion', in T. W. Adorno, H. Albert, R.
Dahrendorf, J. Habermas, H. Pilot and K. R. Popper, *The Positivist Dispute in German
Sociology*, London, 1976, and 'Positivism against Hegelianism', in his *Relativism and the
Social Sciences*, Cambridge, 1985, pp. 6–7. There is a sense in which 'Positivism against
Hegelianism' is Gellner's attempt to articulate the debate that never really took place.

What came to matter more and more to Popper was a quasi-Darwinian view that life itself is a process of trial and error, and that progress depends upon the critical spirit which allows this process the maximum space in which to operate.

Gellner's interpretation of Popper rests on the revolution that brings the two great selectors into play. One element of Popper's thought that can be elucidated by these means is his supposed contradiction between the praise of revolution in cognitive but not in social affairs. Gellner suggests that there is no real contradiction here at all. Scientific progress takes place on the side of the great divide marked by the impact and working of the two great selectors. That great divide is a real revolution, but the changes that take place thereafter are really piecemeal cognitive reforms. Einstein's view of the universe did not change everything; rather it incorporated the theories of Newton. The fact that, say, bridges built before 1905 do not require demolition as soon as new bridge-building technologies are developed neatly illustrates the symmetry of the Popperian universe: changes within the realm of knowledge parallel those that are possible in relatively open liberal democracies.

Gellner has harsher words about other elements of Popper's system of thought. Most importantly, he insists that Popper *must* have an allegiance to positivism if the key tenets of his thought are to work. This is most obviously true of the early Popper's insistence on falsifiability. For this principle to function it must be possible to imagine refutation by reference to empirical material. It should again be emphasized that this does not mean that Gellner believes that facts somehow exist unproblematically in a neutral world. The way in which falsifiability works is rather different:

> If we insist that a theory only deserves respect if it is falsifiable, we force anyone who accepts this criterion, to visualize a world in which the theory *can* be falsified. And to do this is to impose a most dreadful and extremely salutary humiliation on that theory. What world-visions, ideologies, most characteristically do, is to construct a world within which their own falsification is quite inconceivable and in which the preliminary steps necessary for such a falsification are blasphemous, and in some way disqualify him who would set them up . . . Insistence on genuine falsifiability deprives the theory or world-outlook of this capacity to be a judge of its own truth. The real importance of the criterion lies in this power to take them down a peg.[36]

---

36   *Legitimation of Belief*, p. 111.

But the same point also applies to the late Popper. For it is mere naïvety on Popper's part, Gellner insists, to imagine that the critical spirit can in and of itself guarantee intellectual progress. This optimism simply fails to take seriously the long periods of intellectual stagnation that have marked human history, and grossly underestimates the difficulties in moving beyond them. In one sense this naïvety is surprising in Popper, given that he also has a psychologistic theory according to which human beings are all too easily attracted to the comfort and cosiness of stable, closed intellectual and social worlds. In any case, Gellner suggests that there are cogent objections to be made against applying natural selection or trial and error methods to human social life.[37]

Kuhn fails in a rather different way to appreciate the great revolution that introduced the cognitive ethics on which we depend. The point about thought before the scientific revolution is not that it was anarchic, but rather that paradigms were so very rigid. The failure to recognize this undermined Kuhn's position in at least two ways. First, normal science itself depends upon a measure of empiricism. Second, it is quite obvious that Kuhn prefers Einstein to Newton, and so would like to escape the relativism inherent to his position. What this suggests is that his paradigm changes take place within the world defined by the great selectors. He has failed, in other words, to distinguish the great scientific revolution that allowed these selectors to work in the first place from the changes that then take place following and within the context of this revolution.

Gellner states that his concern is 'with how the arena came to be set up at all, and not with the rules that govern its internal procedures'.[38] But this is not yet the case, for it is only in *Plough, Sword, and Book*, considered in the next chapter, that he offered an explanation of how the field itself came to be established. Rather *Legitimation of Belief* offers a contrast between two worlds, asserting that there is a 'big ditch' between them. He insists that there are no final proofs of causation, the sufficiency of reason or the orderliness of the world – and that there can never be such proofs. But if we want to acquire powerful knowledge, we must act on the assumption that the world is regulated by cold, orderly, impersonal laws.

This is the only 'proof' which, in the end, is available. We choose a style of knowing and a kind of society jointly. All in all, mankind has already made its choice, or been propelled into it in truly Faustian manner, by

---

37 'Positivism against Hegelianism', pp. 52–3.
38 *Legitimation of Belief*, p. 184.

a greed for wealth, power, and by mutual rivalry. We can only try to understand what has happened.[39]

The formulation that he seems to have found most satisfying, for he would use it often after he came up with it, was that 'positivism is right, for Hegelian reasons'.

The Cunning of Unreason

Appreciation of Gellner's philosophical position as a whole would be incomplete if it rested merely on his defence of the actual workings of these two cognitive ethics: empiricism and mechanism, the 'selectors'. For one thing, there was still no sense of how science emerged. In this area Gellner was, so to speak, a model of logical correctness, in that he offered a causal account that differed from his functional explanation of the actual workings of science. This causal account is addressed in the next chapter. We must deal with a more general consideration now.

Gellner claims, in effect, that there are three modern schools of thought. One of them, broadly speaking liberal, rational and empiricist, has just been described, and another which 're-enchants' the modern world is treated at the end of this chapter. The remaining framework is that of Nietzsche and Freud. Gellner's admiration for Nietzsche was as great as his respect for Hume and Kant, and his occasional treatments of this thinker were subtle. He tended to see Nietzsche as seeking to complete the Enlightenment project, thereby showing us that our principles are not well grounded, rather than pointing in some clear way towards fascism. This is not to say that he accepts that Nietzsche's position is itself firmly grounded. If what we really want instinctually is satisfaction, how was it ever possible for conscience, so clearly at the heart of Christianity, to unman us?

The influence of Nietzsche is apparent in Gellner's response to Hume's claim that reason is and ought to be nothing but the slave of the passions.

Anyone not familiar with Hume's thought might well suppose, on reading this remark out of context, that Hume's vision of man was something like that of Dostoevsky, that he saw man as possessed by dark, tortuous, mysterious, perverse and uncontrollable passions. Not a bit of it. To understand properly the true nature of the famous Humean enslavement to passion, you must conjure up a different picture altogether. Imagine yourself floating in a boat on an artificial landscaped

---

39   Ibid., p. 127.

park, say one designed by Capability Brown. The currents of the lake are the passions, and you are indeed their slave, for the boat has neither oars nor rudder. If reason be the captain, it is a totally powerless one. The vessel will follow the currents, for there simply are no other forces that can impel or impede it.

Will they propel the boat to its destruction, in some maelstrom or cataract? Not at all. These currents are mild, the shores of the lake are rounded and slope gently. The currents may take you to a picnic on an island with a grotto, or, alternatively, to a musical performance of Handel on one of the shores . . . With such passions, who would not gladly be their slave?[40]

If Kant's philosophy was utterly dependent on puritan assumptions, Hume's was as dependent on civility and refinement, so much admired by the Scottish moralists of eighteenth-century Edinburgh. But, says Gellner, our lives are neither restrained nor angelic, and we learn from situations of trauma, from the whole of our experience rather than from a careful sifting and evaluation of a multitude of sensations, all of equal worth.

The above passage – exemplifying Gellner's talent as a stylist – comes from the opening pages of 1985's *The Psychoanalytic Movement*. This title was more or less mandated by the nature of the series in which it appeared, but his own intent was clearly evident in the subtitle he chose for the book: 'the cunning of unreason'. That the first print run of the book mistakenly had 'the coming of unreason' as the subtitle utterly infuriated him – he spent half a morning correcting the mistake in copies that had been sent to him.[41] Despite this hiccough, the book itself was extremely well received.[42] Perry Anderson claimed that it was arguably Gellner's best book, and there is

---

40   *The Psychoanalytic Movement: The Cunning of Unreason*, 2nd Edn, Oxford, 1993, pp. 12–13.
41   With time he learnt to joke about it, imagining Freud chuckling in his grave at such a Freudian misprint ('Psychoanalysis as a Social Institution: An Anthropological Perspective', in E. Timms and N. Segal, (eds), *Freud in Exile*, New Haven, 1988, p. 223).
42   Anthony Clare praised 'a stylish, witty and deceptive readable book' (*Nature*, 14 November 1985); Hans Eysenck welcomed and found plausible the sociological attempt to explain the social success of a faulty theory (*Institute of Psychiatry Journal*, 15 January 1986), whilst the *New Statesman* saw it as 'one of those iconoclastic masterpieces of sceptical good sense and fine intelligence that you might come across once in ten years if you're lucky' (*New Statesman*, 31 January 1986). The most sustained treatment of the book (in which a direct comparison, aware of their Jewish roots, is made between Freud and Gellner) was offered by Jose Brunner, in his 'Foreword' to the re-issue of the second edition of the book by Blackwell in 2003. Brunner's doctoral dissertation, supervised by Leszek Kolakowski, was examined by Gellner and G. A. Cohen. It appeared as *Freud and the Politics of Psychoanalysis*, Oxford, 1995.

certainly a feeling of polish and completeness about it that some of his later books lacked – characteristics that can only really be appreciated by reading the book in its entirety.[43] This is not at all surprising. Gellner's interest in psychoanalysis dated back to the 1950s, and there exists an outline for a book on the subject dated 1961. Further, in the mid-1960s he returned to his earlier plan to conduct fieldwork amongst psychoanalysts. This involved interviews with Donald Winnicott, then president of the British Psycho-Analytical Society. Gellner later recalled a discussion about sex which gave the impression that Winnicott found the act itself to be incredibly difficult, 'as if', in Gellner's words, 'climbing the North face of the Eiger on every occasion' – a view with which Gellner had no sympathy. Perhaps unsurprisingly, Winnicott declined to allow Gellner's proposed investigation but promised to organize research at a later date – a commitment that he would not keep.[44]

Gellner's sympathy for the hard-headedness of the psychoanalytic tradition, one that ascribes to human beings a more realistic, Darwinian-tinged nature, is manifest in the early pages of the book – from which the passage quoted is drawn – in which he describes the 'Nietzschean Minimum'.[45] He makes much of the deviousness of our instincts, and states with some abruptness that in his view clear evidence is not needed on a matter so obviously true, namely that our mental life is at the mercy of unconscious forces. More generally, Nietzsche's positing of a 'will to power', suggesting that there is pleasure to be had in ruling over others, is seen as a dreadful challenge to liberal society. This is contrasted with Freud's habitual, more limited concern with sexual matters. Late Hapsburg society had a highly ambivalent attitude towards sex, at times licentious, at times puritanical. To speak about sex openly then was to challenge social norms in a striking manner. But Gellner suggests that sex presents no real challenge to contemporary liberal society – to the contrary, endless gratification is seen as a possibility soon to be realized. This sets the terms of Gellner's account of psychoanalysis and its offshoots. Therapy is seen as wholly compatible

43   P. Anderson, 'Science, Politics, Enchantment', in J. A. Hall and I. C. Jarvie, (eds), *Transition to Modernity: Essays on Power, Wealth and Belief*, Cambridge, 1992, p. 204.
44   Winnicott to Gellner, 17 May 1966. Gellner had kept this letter for a purpose. Suspecting that he would be accused, as he had been when attacking linguistic philosophy, of a basic lack of knowledge, he intended to produce the letter to show that his attempt at research had been blocked. But he could not find the letter, while the book met with more approval than condemnation. The Gellner Archive also contains a letter from A. H. Williams, the business secretary of the British Psycho-Analytical Society, to Mrs. A. Hayley, 27 October 1965, in which exactly the same arguments as those of Winnicott were made.
45   *The Psychoanalytic Movement*, pp. 17–23.

with liberal society, largely because the radicalism of Nietzsche is diminished through the putative offer of a cure. Roughly speaking, his view is
that what is powerful in psychoanalysis derives from Nietzsche, while the
Freudian contribution is thoroughly question-begging. An example, not
cited by Gellner, makes the point clearly: Freud is thoroughly Nietzschean
when considering marriage as a struggle between wills until death.

The book's main purpose is to offer a sociological explanation for an
astonishing ideological success story. For personal life in advanced liberal
societies has come to be seen in terms derived from Freud, with vast
amounts of money accordingly spent on therapies of one sort or another.
It may well be that our instinctual life is always best seen in Nietzschean
terms. Nonetheless, major changes in society exacerbate our insecurities
and fears, vastly increasing the demand for care and consolation. The
core of Gellner's hypothesis – for the argument had no basis in sustained
research – rests on the view that in late industrial society life depends,
for the vast majority, on relations with people rather than on any brute
interaction with nature. Hell is no longer nature but, as Sartre had it,
other people. Human relations are all too often difficult, competitive,
noisy and troubled. If one pays a therapist, at least one is listened to, and
without interruption. This is but one of the ways in which therapy has a
central role in providing pastoral care. Beyond this, however, is a more
specific account of the way in which therapies, perhaps especially the
costlier, more personalized ones, 'hook' their clients. Gellner here returns
to the analytical framework he had used when dealing with linguistic
philosophy.[46] Passionate adherence to doctrine comes less from plausibility, necessary though that is, than from threats – from the insistence
that severe problems will follow if allegiance is less than total. And there is
a further element to which he devotes a great deal of attention. Roughly
speaking, for most people for most of the time, reality is the result of the
continual affirmation of our selves by others – as was famously argued
by Erving Goffman, perhaps the most brilliant American sociologist of
the postwar period.[47] Gellner argues that analytic sessions become almost
addictive because they sin against the habitual courtesies of social life;
therapists can withhold confirmation for long periods, thereby making
their eventual interventions all the more powerful. Gellner claims that the
truly novel finding of psychoanalysis – the reality of transference – derives
from these circumstances. The fact that analysts control affirmation gives

---

46   Ibid., chapter 2.
47   E. Goffman, *Interaction Ritual: Essays on Face-to-Face Behavior*, New York, 1967, and
Relations in Public: Microstudies of the Public Order, New York, 1971.

them enormous power, making them – as Freud wished – a modern version of Plato's Guardians.[48]

A good deal of the book's interest and power resides in the way that this current of thought is placed within the history of philosophy as a whole. In this spirit, the success of the psychoanalytic movement is partly explained by the philosophical problems that it solves, all of which deserve cursory listing.[49] First, it finds a way to build an ethics that corresponds to our greatest needs, an achievement beyond Nietzsche's powers. The ethics in question are not generalizable, but specific to particular individuals, and all the more powerful for that. Second, the portrait of our troubled and erratic inner life is far more realistic than the calmer portraits offered by Hume and Descartes. Third, the psychoanalytic movement solves the Cartesian problem of the trustworthiness of knowledge by insisting that the curing of neuroses will allow the truth to shine forth. Fourth, the tension within Kant that comes from seeing humans as at once determined and autonomous is replaced by a more sequential view, in which freedom is established once determinant neuroses have been removed. Fifth, psychoanalysis gives us a Durkheimian sense of the sacred, again at the individual level, and surrounds it with ritual. Finally, Weber's insistence that modernity is cold and disenchanted is countered by a doctrine which offers the hope of personal salvation.

Gellner admits that description is unlikely ever to be entirely neutral, and clearly spells out his own view of the scientific standing of therapeutic analysis. Psychoanalysis fits clearly within his general schema of cognition. It is perhaps the classic case of a *carte blanche* theory, taking for granted that truth will simply be apparent once errors derived from neuroses have been resolved. This position is termed conditional realism, and it is quite as bad as naïve realism. For facts do not speak for themselves; they are rather found as the result of questions shaped by theories – which is not, as has been noted, to gainsay the merits of factual investigation in testing theoretical assertions. Further, naïve realism is closely linked to naïve mentalism. The point was strikingly put in *Legitimation of Belief*:

Any explanation of human conduct or competence in terms of a genuine structure is morally offensive – for a genuine structure is impersonal, it is an 'it', not an 'I'. Chomskian structures are also known to be, in part, well hidden from consciousness; he himself lays great stress on this. If this be the correct strategy in the study of man, then the *I* is ultimately to be explained by an *it* (alas). The Freudian *id* was beastly but, when

48 *The Psychoanalytic Movement*, chapter 7.
49 Ibid., pp. 182–6.

all is said and done, it was cosily human in its un-housetrained way; at worst you could say it was all too human: it was human nature seen in the image of conscious man, but with gloves off. (Like us, but without the advantages we've had, if you know what I mean.) The explanation of our unthinking, quasi-automatic competence into explanatory schemata, outlining structures which are not normally accessible to us at all, is far more sinister. This kind of *id* is not violent, sexy and murderous, it is just totally indifferent to us.[50]

This side of the Freudian world view is strikingly humanistic, presuming that we can easily understand ourselves in hermeneutic terms, far removed from any Chomskian sense of competences that need to be explained. But there is another side to Freud's theories, termed by Gellner 'psycho-hydraulics'.[51] This is primarily the Freud of the early years, but always present thereafter to some degree, insisting that mental life is material, and subject to mechanical explanation. But Gellner sees this model of the mind as wholly sloppy and unspecific – he is especially amusing when discussing 'cathexis', that is, the ability of libido to fly around the place, attaching itself to different objects at will. Gellner cuttingly observes that commentators have often thought it possible to clean up Freud, to make his work internally consistent – either as hermeneutics or as materialism. Gellner insists that this can never be done, that the theory tends both ways, gaining from the prestige of science whilst seeing our behaviour in all too comprehensible human terms.[52]

Although there is much more to the book than a Popperian account of the defects of psychoanalysis, that element is present. Much is made, naturally, of the way that the concept of 'resistance' is used to evade falsification – by insisting that there is something psychologically wrong with critics, that they require therapy in order to see the error of their ways and recognize the truth of the psychoanalytic perspective. A very specialized passage amounts to an argument in Popperian terms.[53] Gellner had cordial relations with Adolf Grünbaum, a Popperian philosopher of science, but disagreed with him nonetheless.[54] Grünbaum's claim was that psychoanalytical theory could be stated clearly enough that it would open itself to falsification in principle – though this had not yet been done. In contrast, Gellner insists

50   *Legitimation of Belief*, p. 99.
51   *The Psychoanalytic Movement*, pp. 94–7.
52   Ibid., pp. 95–7.
53   Ibid., pp. 156–67.
54   Grünbaum wrote to Gellner, 18 November 1976, after their first meeting, thanking him for his interest in one of his papers, and expressing a desire to meet again soon.

that the theory can never be formally tested because evidence is controlled by therapists. There is, however, one general exception. Psychoanalysis and therapies offer the promise of a cure, albeit haltingly at times, often claiming merely that misery will be reduced. Such evidence as has been marshalled in this area did not, in Gellner's view, suggest that the promise had been kept. Rather there seemed to be a three-horse race, between psychoanalysis, spontaneous remission, and alternative therapies, in which no contender seemed to have a clear lead.[55] Gellner was amused by the way in which the threat of the unconscious was seen as somehow not too serious. This made little sense to him. If the unconscious could control everything, the idea that it would allow itself to be interpreted was very unconvincing, even comical.[56] The book ends with a clear and distinct view: 'C'est la thérapie, et non pas la maladie, qui est imaginaire'.[57]

He continued to write in this area. For one thing, there was some engagement with the psychoanalytic community itself. John Bowlby wrote warmly, endorsing a good deal of what Gellner had said, but insisting that genuine empirical work had been done on childhood development.[58] Then Gellner entered the lion's den itself. He debated his claims with Charles Rycroft at the Institute of Contemporary Arts. He insisted that analysts were bound to be secular priests, even if they wished to reject that role, for the simplest of reasons: the demand for consolation services was so great that this fate would always be forced upon them.[59] He also engaged in direct debate with Stephen Frosh, interestingly defending his view that science is less impure than psychoanalysis.[60] He sharpened his position in a number of ways. He encapsulated his view of Freudianism's key element in a nice formula stressing that its originality lay not in the idea that the mind has an unconscious, but rather that the unconscious has a mind.[61] In this vein, he cited a comment of Chomsky's that we might never be able to understand human behaviour, even if we unlock the secret of how we are able to learn complex grammar with the greatest of ease.[62] Gellner did not defend Chomsky's view, but emphasized the achievements of psychoanalysis in

55   *The Psychoanalytic Movement*, pp. 171–3.

56   Ibid., p. 140.

57   Ibid., p. 193.

58   Bowlby to Gellner, 21 November 1985.

59   'Psychiatry and Salvation: Discussion Paper', *Journal of the Royal Society of Medicine*, vol. 80, 1987, p. 760.

60   'Psychoanalysis, Social Role and Testability', in W. Dryden and C. Feltham, (eds), *Psychotherapy and Its Discontents*, Buckingham, 1992, chapter 3.

61   Ibid., p. 44.

62   'Psychoanalysis as a Social Institution', p. 227.

pointing to the place in which dark drives met with semantic complexities.[63] In general he stressed that something like instinctual forces must be present, for they made sense of Darwin — whose general viewpoint was held to be true.[64] Finally, he doubted the extent to which counsellors truly endorsed the emotions uncovered by depth psychology, suggesting that they habitually arranged some sort of compromise between deeper feelings and traditional values, thereby continuing in their traditional role as guardians of moral values.[65]

His last writings on psychoanalysis stressed the force of the Nietzschean position. Along these lines, he attacked Jonathan Lear's *Love and Its Place in Nature*, objecting to its view of love as gentle and considerate rather than as 'blind, ravenous, possessive, destructive and tormenting', and to its attempt to build a new epistemology based on love. In Lear's world 'a healthy sexuality is covered by an anodyne account of the world in which all problems disappear. Snow White is furtively curvaceous but she is credited with a saccharine purity'.[66] Similar points were made against Freud's late notion of the 'pleasure principle', held by Gellner to contradict the central Freudian idea — that we have the capacity to make ourselves unhappy. This critique occurs in an introduction to *Civilization and Its Discontents* comparing Freud with other social contract theorists.[67] Freud finds the origin of society in the killing of the father by a band of brothers, and suggests that memories of this primal act then hold society together. Gellner suggests that Durkheim's view of conceptual constraint through ritual makes more sense of society's origin, and objects, on Malinowskian grounds, to the view that legacies of the past have such force — insisting on the need to analyse the present purpose and function of any purported legacy. But even if Freud's general view of the demanding nature of morality is true in some cases — in Shi'ism and Judaism perhaps above all — it makes no sense, as it should, of Hinduism and Buddhism, or of Confucianism, which all lack the rigour characteristic of the three great Abrahamic religions. Still, Gellner's final note stresses how well it fits with our own self-indulgent consumerist society. The fact that the demands of conscience are softened at an individual level is contrasted with Marxism's attempt to create a new public morality.

---

63   Ibid., p. 226.
64   Ibid., p. 225.
65   'Reflections on Depth Psychology and the New Counselling', unpublished paper, July 1985, Gellner Archive.
66   'Vicious Circles of the Psyche', *Guardian*, 23 April, 1992, p. 29.
67   'Freud's Social Contract', in his *Anthropology and Politics: Revolutions in the Sacred Grove*, Oxford, 1995.

Marxism over-extended itself; Freudianism in its various forms lives on, exemplifying Mies van der Rohe's dictum that less is more.[68]

The World Warmed Up

Gellner's understanding and account of modern cognition were profoundly Weberian. The great cognitive practices do not represent the human mind per se, but rather a style of cognition that came into being in a particular place at a particular time. The next chapter describes Gellner's own explanation for this fortuitous opening. But just as important for Gellner is the other side of the rationalization and disenchantment combination that characterizes Weber's thought. In this matter one can claim that he is more Weberian than Weber himself. To justify this evaluation it is necessary to begin by recalling Weber's position.

In 'Science as a Vocation', the important lecture given in Munich shortly before his death, Weber claimed that disenchantment was the ineluctable fate of our times. If there was a technical aspect to Weber's explanation of this phenomenon, it was in a passage comparing modern science to magic − 'disenchantment' is the translation of a term which literally means 'de-magification'. Weber insisted that knowledge comes at the cost of meaning. The world was once seen in anthropomorphic terms, and this made it seem warm and sympathetic: one might believe that sticks and stones are possessed of spirits, thereby making them appear as meaningful entities. In contrast, modern science is rendered morally empty by its presupposition that everything is in principle explicable.[69] Weber makes clear that 'primitive man' is not somehow less capable than a modern urban resident; that is distinctly not the case, given that the former has survival skills which the latter lacks.[70] Nonetheless, the city-dweller does live in a technically sophisticated milieu which now dominates the world. There is an opportunity cost to modernity: the price of technical and cognitive power is a certain moral void, a loss of comforting illusions. Further, our world becomes disenchanted by the nature of its social organization. As bureaucracy and legality characterize industrial society, there is little room for genuine collective fervour of any kind. The world in which we live must be cold rather than warm. At a crucial juncture of his lecture, Weber made a comment about the sociology of death. The modern world sees

---

68 'Introduction to the Second Edition', *The Psychoanalytic Movement*.

69 M. Weber, 'Science as a Vocation' in H. H. Gerth and C. W. Mills, (eds), *From Max Weber: Essays in Sociology*, New York, 1946, p. 139.

70 Ibid.

such rapid change that death now becomes meaningless. Where 'some peasant of the past' could gain wisdom with age because everything had been experienced in this world and salvation was promised in the next, an old person today is 'past it', their death rendered more pointless by the absence of religious legitimation.[71] Weber insisted that science could not answer Tolstoy's question about how one should live; modern knowledge is technically powerful but morally empty.

Weber wobbled when analysing disenchantment. The clear thrust of his argument is that this fate is inevitable, that it cannot be escaped. This led him to harsh words which Gellner quotes in *Legitimation of Belief* with marked approbation:

> Never as yet has a new prophecy emerged . . . by way of the need of some modern intellectuals to furnish their souls with . . . guaranteed genuine antiques . . . they produce surrogates . . . which they peddle in the book market. This is plain humbug or self-deception.[72]

Weber distinguished between thinkers who invent new beliefs on the grounds that they would be good for us, and those who believe in the reality of a deity.[73] He has great respect for the sincerity of the latter, though he does not think that the option is generally available, but he completely condemns the facile instrumentalism of the former. Weber was not, however, above considering the need for religious belief. He claimed that emergent modernity was 'an iron cage', and endlessly worried that it might lead to social stagnation. Egypt had been bureaucratized and rule-bound and this had led to decline, and he worried that this fate might also strike Germany. But the fact that one could choose one's beliefs, that science could not tell us what to do, meant that room was left for human freedom. Weber argued in similar terms in the philosophy of science: rather like Kuhn, he argued that theoretical approaches involve pre-commitments that made them invulnerable to refutation. His position was, therefore, relativist, effectively existentialist, and thereby close to mere 'decisionism'. The position is potentially repulsive, for there seem to be no rational grounds by means of which one position can be chosen above another.

---

71   Ibid., p. 140.
72   Ibid., pp. 154–5.
73   There are of course many examples of the former, perhaps most interestingly in recent years D. Bell, 'The Return of the Sacred? The Argument on the Future of Religion', *British Journal of Sociology*, vol. 28, 1977.

Weber's own politics showed precisely how this capacity for repulsiveness could be made actual. Mere wealth and social integration mattered little for Weber, given his Nietzschean background. His plans for political reform after the First World War privileged a party system in which a clash between charismatic leaders would ensure dramatic, dynamic change within society. There was little sense here of controlling the exercise of power; to the contrary, power was to be given to the elite so that they might move society forward.[74]

Modern social theory is haunted by the ghost of Max Weber. This is especially true of the Frankfurt School. The famous address of Jürgen Habermas when receiving the Hegel Prize in 1974 simply asked 'Can complex societies build a rational identity?'[75] Herein lies the whole programme of one of the most celebrated social philosophers of the age. Much the same is true of the social philosophy of Charles Taylor. His various works have suggested that modern life presently suffers from a malaise because insufficient attention has been paid to ways of creating the communal life necessary for healthy individuals to thrive. Taylor likes to encourage as much as to scare, and so reassures us that the politics of recognition together with an appreciation of our civilization's inherent values will allow for the malaise to be managed.[76] Habermas and Taylor suggest that modernity can allow us a new and solid identity. Gellner is their absolute opponent.

He stands very close to Weber, but adds to his position. He shared the same views on the practical knowledge of 'primitive men', and systematically

---

74   In a celebrated meeting with General Ludendorff in 1919, Weber described his view of democracy in these terms: 'In a democracy the people choose a leader whom they trust. Then the chosen man says, "Now shut your mouths and obey me. The people and the parties are no longer free to interfere in the leader's business"'. Ludendorff felt that he could live with such a system (Marianne Weber, *Max Weber: A Biography*, New York, 1975, p. 653). Weber's political views were first fully discussed by W. Mommsen, whose *Max Weber and German Politics 1890–1920*, Chicago, 1984, contains a discussion of Weber's wartime views on what should be done with territories conquered to the East – views which justify the use of the word 'repulsive' in this paragraph. Brendan O'Leary has pointed out to me that Weber's views were consistent only in their decisionistic character – for he wobbled between proposing party competition to generate good parliamentary leaders and enhancing presidential power.

75   A part of his address was translated and published as J. Habermas, 'On Social Identity', *Telos*, vol. 19, 1974.

76   C. Taylor, *The Malaise of Modernity*, Concord, 1991, and *The Sources of the Self: The Making of the Modern Identity*, Cambridge (MA), 1989. The latter volume, and the later *A Secular Age*, Cambridge (MA), 2007, suggest in places that the underwriting of a solidary self can most securely be achieved through religious belief.

showed that modern cognition has presuppositions that rule out by fiat anthropomorphic self-understanding,[77] and his analysis of the reduction involved in mechanistic explanations adds to Weber's account. Further, a brilliant essay – 'A Bundle of Hypotheses, or, the Gaffe-Avoiding Animal' – partly explains the curious fact that Weber's description of the modern world included two types of rational action, based on values and aims respectively. Gellner argues that the former is devoured by the latter; our constant capital, to adopt Marxist terminology, is continually diminished, leaving us merely with variable capital.[78] This matters enormously. Only relatively small matters can be dealt with by means of rational calculation. Any truly large decision – divorce, death, a change in occupation – cannot be subject to a rational decision, for the simplest of reasons: one's identity will change as the result of the decision. Thus rationality is useful when it is least needed, but hopeless when dealing with crucial issues. Human beings thus change from being a bundle of sensations to being a bundle of hypotheses. In these circumstances, life is much more about finding ways to fit in, by avoiding gaffes, than it is about easy and calm rational calculation. This sort of existentialist understanding, typical of Gellner, does not for a moment lead him to follow Weber in calling for a return to heroic politics. The background assumption is, again, that a choice has already been made. Our style of cognition gives us a higher standard of living, and it is accordingly endorsed by Gellner for social democratic reasons.

The contrast between Weber and Gellner was accurately noted and described by Perry Anderson, as that between the high politics of Wilhelmine Germany and the low, social democratic politics of Masaryk's Czechoslovak Republic.[79] Gellner's own response to the problem identified by Weber is to allow strictly limited commitment to society:

> [T]he acceptance of 'forms of life', from styles of food, handshakes and wallpapers to political rituals or personal relationships – but an acceptance which no longer endows anything with an aura of the absolute, but is ironic, tentative, optional, and above all discontinuous

---

77   *Plough, Sword, and Book*, London, 1988, p. 41.

78   This paper (now in his *Relativism and the Social Sciences*), given at a small conference on rationality in Paris in 1979 organized by Jon Elster, apparently made a large impression on the participants, including Raymond Aron, Bernard Williams, Brian Barry, Gerry Cohen and Donald Davidson. Aron criticized the 'severity' of Gellner's view, as did both Cohen and Davidson. Gellner's response to Davidson's remarks is considered below. After he gave his paper, Patricia Williams remarked that the paper showed to many that he was really a continental philosopher.

79   Anderson, 'Science, Politics, Enchantment', p. 200.

with serious knowledge and real conviction. In this limited sphere of 'culture', relativism is indeed valid. In the sphere of serious conviction, on the other hand, relativism is not an option open to us *at all*.[80]

This passage comes from the section of *Legitimation of Belief* concerned with 'ironic cultural nationalism'. It is not just that one needs irony about one's self; just as important is a much more tentative allegiance to one's nation than a nationalist such as Weber would like.

Gellner criticized numerous theories which sought to re-endorse the world. *Legitimation of Belief* noted three great types. There is no need to consider again the two great *carte blanche* theories that exercised him so much, namely Wittgensteinianism and Freudianism. Similarly, little needs to be said about relativism given the earlier extended discussion of the work of Peter Winch, as well as his attack on Isaiah Berlin – though it is important to remember the two elements of his critique, namely that relativism can be deeply intolerant, and that social change makes epistemic relativism inoperative in contemporary circumstances. The criticisms made against naïve evolutionary theory in the first chapter of *Thought and Change* are likewise maintained throughout his work – as is the claim that a more limited idea of evolution, namely evolution to an affluent world respecting the nationalist principle, deserves our support. The crucial world growth story is, of course, Marxism, and his views here again need not be repeated. But a short list of thinkers seeking to 'warm up' the world can begin with a consideration of theorists indebted to benign views of social evolution.

Pragmatism

Gellner's application to study in Harvard in the early 1950s emphasized the importance of the work of Quine, and there is evidence that he was engaged in critical discussions of his work at that time. Nonetheless, a full two decades passed before Gellner offered an account of Quine's work in two closely related essays.[81] The key theme echoed his charge against the late work of Popper, namely that of an excessive confidence in the continuity of human success in terms of cognitive endeavours. The taken-for-granted confidence at the back of Quine's position is derived, in Gellner's view, from his pragmatism – from the belief that trial and error

---

80 *Legitimation of Belief*, p. 207.
81 'The Last Pragmatist, or the Behaviourist Platonist' and 'Pragmatism and the Importance of Being Earnest', both in his *Spectacles and Predicaments*. One of the papers was given at Harvard, with Quine in the audience.

methods will continue to work, as they have done in prior human history. Two elements are seen as lending support to this view. First, Darwinism is seen rather benignly as suggesting that the best practices are indeed the ones that are selected, that we make our way in nature without much difficulty. Second, the striking success of the American economy in the nineteenth and twentieth centuries is taken as the normal condition of humanity.

Gellner has several objections to this position. He stresses that there have been long periods of stagnation in human history, and that a breakthrough to unfettered economic growth was the result of a very curious concatenation of circumstances. Quine at times invokes a background assumption – 'our scientific method' – that allows him to feel secure in the selections that have been made, and further to take for granted that consensuses reached are less biased than veridical.[82] But this is exactly like Popper, to act within a world which takes our cognitive practices for granted. Quine's accurate and amusing attack on the impossibility that any 'cosmic exile' can exist does not undermine the fact that empiricism in particular remains potent as an epistemological norm. Lastly, Gellner is critical of Quine's reference to natural selection. For one thing, the period over which selection works may be that of millennia, thereby placing it on a different time scale to the sudden and dramatic jumps of human history.[83] For another, natural selection can be rather specific; in contrast, the great selectors on which Gellner insists that we rely are general and puritanical. It is this feature that allows them to deal with crises of meaning and morality, that is, to deal with the situation faced by the originators of our epistemological tradition.

Gellner's admiration for the elegance of Quine's style, and deep appreciation for his technical skill as a logician, does not prevent him from making two further criticisms. He echoes the criticism made directly by Chomsky, to the effect that Quine's allegiance to behaviourism is enough to convict him of mentalism. That we are able to succeed cognitively tells us nothing about the mental competences which allow us to do so.[84] Secondly, he makes a more specialized argument about how Quine seeks to support his position by means of very different arguments, some general, others technical – none convincing on its own, and no more so when taken together.[85]

---

82   'The Last Pragmatist', p. 211.
83   'Pragmatism', p. 253. But neo-Darwinists differ between gradualists and those who believe in punctuated equilibrium – differing both in theoretical reasoning and on the data in the fossil record.
84   'The Last Pragmatist', pp. 227–33.
85   Ibid., pp. 221-40.

Quine was considered as effectively a second-generation pragmatist, far less individualist than William James, lacking any avowed interest in creating an American philosophy, and more or less representative of the rather different America of the 1950s, when his most brilliant work was done.[86] Gellner, by contrast, offered no generational picture of Richard Rorty, whom he came to know, and very much liked, in the last years of his life – perhaps first meeting him when Rorty attended Gellner's opening lecture at the Central European University in Prague in 1991. He socialized with him again after the two men were brought together in Cambridge by Quentin Skinner. Gellner repeated the arguments about pragmatism's excessive confidence in our ability to know the world in a public debate in Brazil, and when moderating a debate between Habermas and Rorty in Warsaw in 1994.[87]

Expressivism

Gellner viewed Hegel as something of a master of obfuscation, suggesting that the triumph of reason may or may not be a sign of the presence of the divine. But he defended Hegel against the interpretation offered by Charles Taylor, arguing that the German philosopher had a much more realistic view of the powers of coercion than did Marx. Taylor, a philosopher of the Canadian New Left, used Hegel to call for the creation of an 'expressivist' politics going beyond 'the end of ideology', to allow for some sort of unity between self and society. Gellner would have none of this when reviewing Taylor's treatment of Hegel:

> Unlike Taylor, I do not take the year 1968 too seriously; a shadow of a shadow, *ersatz* of *ersatz*, it re-enacted 1848, which in turn had re-enacted 1789. But the 1970s scare me stiff. The expressivists never made the *Financial Times* index tremble. The miners and the oil sheikhs, who do have that power, are not activated by expressivist yearnings. All they want is a much bigger share of those post-Enlightenment goodies which expressivism spurns. Furthermore, it is not clear to me how advanced, large-scale societies can fulfil the requirements of expressivism, other

---

86   Ibid., pp. 220, 235.
87   J. Habermas, R. Rorty and E. A. Gellner, 'Enlightenment – Yes or No?', in J. Niznik and J. T. Sanders, (eds), *Debating the State of Philosophy*, Westport, 1996. Gellner died before his text was revised, and it accordingly gives a vivid sense of his speaking style. On this occasion Gellner drew a distinction between the admirable clarity of Quine and Rorty and the deliberate obscurity of Derrida and Foucault, deeming the latter 'countercultural clowns', unworthy of rational opposition.

than by holding Nuremberg rallies. I'd rather do without. What on earth is wrong with having one's expression at home (paperbacks, classic, hi-fi) and leaving the public sphere to soulless pragmatism?[88]

This review was a prelude to a more sustained confrontation between the two, in a 1984 television debate chaired by Michael Ignatieff.[89] Gellner repeated the charge made above in greater detail, insisting that a solid identity was incompatible with modern science, and going on to praise the egalitarianism of industrialism and its ability to diminish conflict – leading to a simple charge: 'Don't live on it and then spit on it'.[90] Taylor argued in contrast that disenchantment was much overrated, and that the self could somehow be anchored in a renewed sense of community.

Anarchism

Gellner maintained cordial relations with Charles Taylor, though he once remarked privately that he wondered if Taylor realized the extent to which Gellner disliked hermeneutics, Marxism and Catholicism, in Gellner's view the pillars of Taylor's thought. His attitude to Paul Feyerabend's *Against Method* was very different, the scathing and brutal character of his criticism perhaps linked to their shared background in Central Europe. The quietness of Canada's past might be some excuse for Taylor's naïvety; the historical record of Central Europe meant that Feyerabend ought to have known better.

Feyerabend's position developed from a central claim, namely that the philosophy of science had been unable to successfully locate *the* scientific method. Gellner had no problem with this premise, going even further and suggesting that it is unlikely that there will ever be a successful theory of this sort.[91] All that we can do is to look at styles of thought, and to specify the one which has led to successful discoveries. But that was not Feyerabend's reaction. Rather than following Gellner's line, or remaining a mere sceptic, he proposed 'methodological anarchism' on the rather paradoxical grounds that no particular method works, and that therefore allowing everything

---

88 'The Absolute in Braces', in *Spectacles and Predicaments*, p. 39.
89 M. Ignatieff, with Ernest Gellner and Charles Taylor, 'The Tough and the Tender', in M. Ignatieff, B. Bourne, S. Bellow, E. Eichler and D. Herman, (eds). (*Voices: Modernity and Its Discontents*, Nottingham, 1987.
90 Ibid., p. 32.
91 'Beyond Truth and Falsehood, or No Method in My Madness', in *Spectacles and Predicaments*, p. 186.

will lead us to something like the truth.[92] The recommendation that 'anything goes' was combined with a series of attitudes that Gellner clearly loathed. It was ignorant, referring to the non-Western world as tribal, seemingly unaware of the character of the very different civilizations of the pre-industrial world; it was facile, pretending that consistency in outlook did not matter; it was delusional, in imagining that normal physical laws did not exist; and it was deeply unattractive in suggesting that violence was justified given the rigidities of organized society.[93]

In a sense, existentialism is not, despite itself, very far removed from anarchism. The premium placed on authenticity makes the establishment of morality impossible, as Sartre's failure to produce his promised treatise on ethics effectively demonstrated, because what one values one day might well be replaced on the next by a different object of affection, endorsed with equal passion. An element of Sartre's reaction to the infinite openness of life, recognized by Gellner in a review of the *Critique of Dialectical Reason*, is that the urge to commit fully can lead to the endorsement of violence.[94] The review itself was a coming to terms with Sartre, considering him as a figure from a particular period, but pointing out, accurately, that the attempt to marry Marxism and existentialism does not really work. Gellner encapsulated the book's essence in an aphorism: 'History is the story of class struggle, but in the idiom of *Huis Clos* [*No Exit*]'.[95]

The *Lebenswelt*

At various points in *Legitimation of Belief*, Gellner approvingly quoted Gaston Bachelard's quip that the world in which we think is not the same as the one in which we live.[96] This view of the power of science, so pithily expressed, led to an attack on phenomenology's attempt to confirm the taken-for-granted meanings of our daily world, our *Lebenswelt*:

> In the days when the *Lebenswelt* was simply the world, *die Welt*, no one felt much need to demonstrate its existence and importance . . . To make that *Lebenswelt* ultimate is, ironically, to violate real common sense, or to give a false phenomenology of our world . . . In the course

---

92   Ibid., p. 185.
93   Ibid., pp. 196, 197, 197, 195.
94   'Period piece', in *Spectacles and Predicaments*.
95   Ibid., p. 110. Gellner discussed Sartre in passing in *Legitimation of Belief*, p. 199, noting the facility of his sense of freedom, characterized by J. F. Revel in a phrase in which Gellner delighted: 'le self service de sa conscience libre'.
96   *Legitimation of Belief*, pp. 101, 194.

of claiming to 'suspend' it, the phenomenologists have in effect done quite the reverse. The alleged suspension constitutes a kind of vindication, a justification of the ordinary world as such, leading it to be treated as ultimate in its own sphere, and no longer treated as a rival or dated scientific theory.[97]

If we want to know what a table really is, especially if we plan to manufacture tables, we should, and more importantly do, turn our attention to the cognitive norms Gellner identified in *Legitimation of Belief*.

> For the ghost, the table is a bundle of actual sensations. For the machine, the table is a congeries of whirling particles. Either of these views deserves respect. The one view which cannot be taken seriously, except as an affectation in the philosopher's study, is that the table is a table.[98]

It is not surprising that Gellner's sabbatical year in California directed his attention towards ethnomethodology, then at the height of its power and influence. This branch of sociology had as its object the authentication of everyday life, the desire to demonstrate that quotidian social practices allow society to be created and maintained. Gellner's appraisal of what he considered to be the Californian way of subjectivity was given as a paper to a conference of ethnomethodologists in Edinburgh in the early 1970s. The paper included anthropological asides on the movement's style of exposition, and it caused great offence. But the attack was deadly serious. Underneath his jokes about accountability, indexicality and reflexivity, Gellner pointed to both idealism and indifference to genuine science – or, rather, a lack of means by which real knowledge could be created or explained. He then amplified his earlier view about the sloppiness of countercultural thought, criticizing Daniel Bell's claim that countercultural ideals represented nothing less than a challenge to capitalism.

> A really advanced industrial society does not any longer require cold rationality from its consumers; at most, it may demand it of its producers. But as it gets more advanced, the ratio both of personnel and of their time is tilted progressively more and more in favour of consumption, as against production. More consumers, fewer producers; less time at work, more at leisure. And in consumption, all tends towards ease and facility of manipulation rather than rigour and coldness. A modern piece

---

97   Ibid., pp. 195–7.
98   Ibid.

of machinery may be a marvel of sustained, abstract, rigorous engineering thought; but its operating controls must be such that they can rapidly and easily be internalised by the average user, without arduousness or strain. So the user lives in a world in which most things have an air of easy, 'natural', 'spontaneous' manipulability. And why should not the world itself be conceived in this manner?[99]

Modernist Theology

Gellner was a constant critic of religion. He resembled Weber in having a certain respect for 'genuine' monotheistic belief, hoping that at least someone would remain faithful to established doctrines just in case they did ultimately prove to be true. But he had complete scorn for modernist theology. He disliked Wittgensteinians who justified religion on the grounds that it was but one way of life amongst others, self-perpetuated via its own practices. But this justification was part of a larger argument. Religious belief could be justified on the grounds that it was functional, and it could be maintained if its practitioners hold, in effect, 'double citizenship' – in both religious and general society. This was only possible, however, because the cognitive claims of religion, so vital to authentic believers, had been downplayed or ignored.[100] These manoeuvres were condemned by Gellner as facile.

Western Marxism

Gellner made rather similar points against Western Marxism. Noting the tortuousness of Althusserian epistemology, he remarked: 'like the man who could hardly watch the play for watching his reactions to it, these men seem to theorize not so much about society and reality as about their own theorizing about society'.[101] In this vein, he liked to cite David Downes's quip that praxis makes perfect.[102] Something of a *reductio ad absurdum* of this style of thought was reached, Gellner wrote, in the account of the Asiatic mode of production offered by Barry Hindess and Paul Hirst in their Althusserian phase. The categories of Marxist theory were expounded

---

99 'Ethnomethodology: The Re-enchantment Industry or the Californian Way of Subjectivity', in *Spectacles and Predicaments*, pp. 61–2.
100 'The Rubber Cage: Disenchantment with Disenchantment', in *Culture, Identity and Politics*, Cambridge, 1987, pp. 159–61.
101 Ibid, pp. 161–2.
102 'Period Piece', p. 108.

in a manner which established that this particular mode could not have existed. Their later reference to empirical reality, that is, their examination of the historical record, was but an afterthought.[103]

Conclusion

Gellner's overall philosophy is nuanced with regard to epistemology, but severe toward thinkers offering more moral warmth and harmony than they can deliver. Let us reconsider both sides of this epistemological coin.

Gellner's view of modern rational science rested on normative foundations which can be underlined by an analogy with liberalism, properly understood. Liberals who simply describe others as ideological, as is far too often the case, naïvely presume that their position is neutral, preordained, even somehow inscribed in the heart of humanity. This is not the case. Liberalism is an ideology amongst others. It is a peculiar one, for it does not seek to control every bit of reality, to claim authority over every part of life, public and private. It is not, to use a Sartrean expression, a totalizing ideology. Only with this in mind can liberalism be defended – as a world view which is rather empty morally, enabling technological development and innovation but also, in my own view, sufficient powers of constraint to sometimes prevent catastrophe. Gellner wrote about the 'end of ideology' school in this way. But the point here is that his account of rational science is subtle because it is similarly self-conscious. There is no excuse for complacency, because neither mechanism nor empiricism is fully grounded. We can imagine different worlds. Nonetheless, these approaches have a measure of effectiveness which keep us in their thrall. It is indeed very difficult to imagine politics in the advanced world managing without the prospect of economic growth created by modern science.[104] Furthermore, Gellner's concern for the details of ordinary life, for improved standards of living and increased life expectancies, has much to recommend it.

Gellner's criticisms of the 're-enchanters' can only be understood by introducing some complexities to the discussion. Why were these polemics so important to him? Why spend so much time on thinkers he regarded as essentially trivial? When explicitly asked this question he once replied on a postcard: 'Envy. Why should they be in the warmth when I am in the cold'.

---

103   B. Hindess and P. Q. Hirst, *Pre-Capitalist Modes of Production*, London, 1975.

104   This sentence reflects my own view. In the next chapter we will see that Gellner does try to imagine social life without ever-increasing growth. One should remember that his theory of nationalism suggests that deep conflict will arise only when social inequality is combined with an ethnic marker.

It is certainly easy to detect a personal element at work here: the view of humans as seeking to avoid 'gaffes' surely came naturally to an immigrant, whose Jewish background, in his own view, made it hard to avoid making *faux pas* of one sort or another. Linked to this is his insistence that no position is fully grounded. At the Paris presentation of his paper on the 'gaffe-avoiding' character of human beings Gellner was criticized for, in Aron's words, the austerity of his view of rationality. An unpublished postscript began by insisting that his view of rationality derived from an interpretation of our situation, and not from his own predilections which may or may not, he insisted, be austere. But he directed his attention towards a view of rationality proposed by Donald Davidson, which centred on the idea of personal development. Gellner would have none of it. After doubting that different cultures shared the same set of values, he then described the situation facing an individual.

> [T]he succession of states frequently does not have a 'progressive' form of A', A'', A''', etc., but rather, an oscillating form of A', A'', A', A'', etc. Everyone knows that this is characteristically the case in inner conflicts within the breast of a single individual, but it is also liable to happen in politics, science, and no doubt elsewhere. And once this is so, then of course there simply is no overall direction which could bring us normative salvation.[105]

With this in mind, he directly attacked Davidson's position:

> The idea that a change from A to A', where the two successive conditions differ in their norms or values as well as in other ways, is 'rational', can only make sense if some meta-world or meta-value is assumed, in terms of which they can be compared, so that the later one be declared superior.[106]

Meta-values needed to be discussed openly, rather than assumed or smuggled into the equation when no one is looking.

Gellner's comments here, and in the debate with Charles Taylor discussed above, allow us to draw distinctions between descriptive and prescriptive aspects of his thinking. Descriptively, we can surely question his insistence that there is little that we can really believe in, that scientific knowledge has left us disenchanted. Are our lives so empty? How 'warm' really were people's lives in the past? Significant victories over disease and early death, perhaps especially over infant mortality, can support the argument that the

---

105   'Postscript to the paper for Jon Elster's Conference', Gellner Archive, p. 5.
106   Ibid., p. 6.

advanced world is far from disenchanted, even taking into account the obvious diminution in religious belief. As it happens, Gellner was quite keen to make this argument himself. His insistence on a measure of stoicism is sometimes stressed so insistently that it obscures his more positive appraisal of this disenchanted world – that it privileges material progress.[107] But a second question must be asked of his position. If disenchantment is inevitable, what should we make of the many re-enchanting creeds that are professed? Gellner's general explanation for the fact that we do not inhabit a Weberian 'iron cage' but rather a more permissive 'rubber' alternative has been noted already: only production requires cold logic, while consumption is free from this constraint. Still, he insists that disenchantment ought to mark our attitudes toward the world. One element of this position is aesthetic, an extreme dislike on his part for sloppy, question-begging thought. But more importantly, he contradicts his own frequent charge that re-enchanters of one sort or another are trivial, the mere providers of cultural entertainment. When pushed, Gellner was prone to argue that the desire to re-enchant the world was in fact dangerous. He made this particularly clear in his television debate with Charles Taylor, attacking at length the latter's desire 'for a self more at peace with the community':

> [T]he only way to do it in the large anonymous mass society is by major . . . political theatre productions, such as are in effect typical of the authoritarian regimes of the thirties . . . where belongingness, to some extent hierarchy, but certainly belongingness – incidentally, exclusion of the outsider – were all deeply symbolized so that their affective life and their political life dovetailed precisely in the kind of way you seem to desire . . . The romantic Left and the romantic Right do sometimes meet.[108]

Gellner went on to question Taylor's claim that liberal democracy expresses our values. He refused to believe this. There had been widespread accommodation to the Nazi order, and that order was entirely compatible with one significant strand in European thought. The romanticism of 'roots', when joined with social Darwinism, was, he argued in his critique of Hannah Arendt, as much a retreat from reason as was the worship of historical forces.[109] He continued to press his attack on Taylor:

---

107 Ignatieff, Gellner and Taylor, 'The Tough and the Tender', pp. 36–7.
108 Ibid., p. 33.
109 'Accounting for the Horror', *Times Literary Supplement*, 6 August 1982, reprinted as 'From Königsberg to Manhattan (or Hannah, Rahel, Martin and Elfriede or Thy Neighbour's *Gemeinschaft*)', in *Culture, Identity and Politics*, pp. 86–90.

[T]he main Nazi critique of Weimar was that the outward institutions and the inner feelings didn't cohere. They used language which overlaps with yours: that the purely instrumental, technical outer world didn't correspond to deep inner feelings. And the justification of this new romanticism was precisely to broaden the congruence. Well you can't have it both ways. If this is what you want, if your complaint against excessive modernity is the insulation of the self, I'm not quite clear in the name of what you reject some versions which are very full-blooded and, alas, gave the participants an enormous amount of satisfaction . . . .[110]

Gellner admitted that he could not fully ground his own liberal leanings. Modern, affluent liberal democratic society seemed to him to rest on fragile foundations. The right strategy was to analyse its character, allowing us to confront its essential problems and to consider the options that remain. What was needed was a coherent philosophy of history.

---

110   Ignatieff, Gellner and Taylor, 'The Tough and the Tender', p. 34.

8

The Shape of History

In the early 1980s, Gellner planned a major cooperative publication that would deal with our present understanding of the ideas and institutions of the history of mankind. Several short essays were commissioned by Gellner, but the project as a whole was not completed. Instead, Gellner wrote *Plough, Sword, and Book*, a monograph that was enormously important to him. The book is dedicated to his children, and it is clearly intended as a statement of his fundamental views. Its content overlaps with that of *Thought and Change*, and it does not disavow the theses of that earlier work. This is a strength and a weakness: some points are restated with greater clarity, but others – notably, the analysis of nationalism – are skimmed over very quickly indeed. But the book's arguments about cognitive growth draw as much from *Legitimation of Belief*'s reconstruction of modern epistemology. This makes the book extremely dense, and in the final analysis less than successful.[1] Gellner realized this himself when he came to read Patricia Crone's *Pre-Industrial Societies*, commenting that the fabulous clarity of that book is what he

---

1   The book was, however, well received. Eugen Weber (*Times Literary Supplement*, 28 October–3 November 1988) and W. G. Runciman (*London Review of Books*, 27 October 1988) outlined the main theses, found the argument interesting, but doubted that it conclusively demonstrated its case. Frank Kermode (*Weekend Telegraph*, 19 November 1988), Adam Kuper (*New Statesman*, 26 August 1988), David Levy ('Political Order', *Times Higher Educational Supplement*, 22 April 1988) and R. A. D. Grant (*Times Educational Supplement*, 14 October 1988) were united in their praise – the last author noting, however, that the book was less for the general reader than for the scholar. A longer reaction came from Michael Meeker (*Cultural Anthropology*, vol. 6, 1991), admiring the model-building skills but arguing that a normative position had been smuggled into an account that claimed to be strictly objective. Gellner himself was most pleased when the book was mentioned favourably by King Hussein of Jordan in a speech to the Calgary Chamber of Commerce, 13 October 1989.

had sought to achieve.[2] But the particular interest of his book lies in its three novel elements, the introduction, as it were, of new cards in his intellectual deck. Each novelty derives from what might be termed a pre-commitment to the work of Max Weber.

The premise of the book is simply that we should be explicit about our place in history. We always harbour background assumptions of this sort; much is to be gained from examining them in order to better understand our situation and the options it allows us. Gellner's starting point is based on his analyses of the Soviet debates about stages of historical development. His own approach is Weberian. He insists that there are three stages of human history – pre-agrarian, agrarian and industrial – and that their workings are best understood with reference to the three sources of social power – economic, political and ideological – whose autonomous character had been recognized and elucidated by Weber.[3]

Second, Gellner fills in a gap noted in the earlier discussion of *Thought and Change*, namely the lack of any account of the origins of the modern world. His version is, again, Weberian in spirit. Gellner had no time for views of an inevitable progression from simple to complex societies, rejecting at all times this 'acorn to oak tree' approach. His account of the transition from agrarian to industrial society stresses its accidental, fortuitous nature. What needs explaining is the fact that a transition was possible at all. The language used to describe it therefore talks of 'escape', the removal of 'blocks', and even of a 'miracle'.[4]

The third innovation concerns the realm of ideas. The most intellectually engaged pages of the book discuss cognitive evolution. These passages offer a causal account of science's origins, complementing the argument for its importance in *Thought and Change* and the account of its functioning in *Legitimation of Belief*. That cognition plays such a large role in his account of modernity's creation is surprising, given that belief is seen as only one of three sources of social power – and it is perhaps unfortunate, too, as it is one of the factors that make the book feel unbalanced. If Gellner is clearly Weberian in stressing the autonomy of political power, he is quite as much

---

2   P. Crone, *Pre-Industrial Societies: Anatomy of the Pre-Modern World*, Oxford, 2003. Her review of Gellner's book, 'Getting the Conceptual Handles', appeared in *Government and Opposition*, vol. 24, 1989.

3   *Plough, Sword, and Book: The Structure of Human History*, London, 1988, chapter 1.

4   Gellner chose his words with care. In his 'Introduction' to a volume of conference proceedings dealing with 'the European miracle' (J. Baechler, J. A. Hall and M. Mann [eds], *Europe and the Rise of Capitalism*, Oxford, 1988) he distinguished between 'the *European* miracle' and 'the European *miracle*' – that is, he disavowed any European moral self-congratulation, asserting further that the miracle could be extended to the rest of the world.

so in this context. Weber wished to argue for something stronger than what might be termed 'reflectivism', present in both Marx and Durkheim, according to which ideas derive from and, so to speak, do the work of more basic social processes. Gellner remains opposed, as one would expect, to a general idealism according to which ideas alone drive reality, but he accepts that ideas can sometimes have that effect. Rational science, once unleashed, has the capacity to endlessly change the social arrangements of advanced liberal industrialism.

The method of the book is philosophical. Gellner stresses at the start that the account is deductive, that a specification of key features of particular social orders leads to arguments dealing with both stability and change. But one should not underestimate the background knowledge in comparative historical and anthropological analysis on which he draws when stating modestly his belief that his argument does not at least contradict known facts.[5] His personal experience of urbanization in the Czechoslovakia of his youth underpins an awareness of different worlds, of Islamic and Marxist societies as well as the European *anciens régimes* that faced Enlightenment thinkers.

The Very Possibility of Society

Interest in the origins of human society had been apparent in Gellner's writings about Soviet Marxism, and seems to have been further encouraged by his move to the University of Cambridge's Department of Social Anthropology, where he was asked to address this issue as part of a lecture series on the subject, hosted appropriately enough by Darwin College.[6] Gellner felt it necessary to address the problem of how society is possible at all. The reasoning behind this formulation is simple. Human beings are not genetically determined in a way that results in a single form of social life. To the contrary, what is most clear from the historical record is the astonishing diversity of human societies. But herein lies the problem, at least for those – including James Frazer – who take empiricism seriously. Why shouldn't the ability to create new associations, as is posited by the sensationalist psychology of David Hume, lead to an endless free-flowing recombination of social life? Why should there be any limits to human expressiveness and diversity? Such a view has, after all, been recommended by various thinkers on the left – by Sartre, whose notion of authenticity allows one to change one's mind at will, and more recently by Roberto

---

5   *Plough, Sword, and Book*, p. 13.
6   'Origins of Society', in his *Anthropology and Politics*, Oxford, 1995.

Unger, keen to restore movement to 'blocked' societies.[7] But Gellner insists that social life does not at all conform to these hopes or expectations; diversity is, so to speak, orderly. Humans genetics permit cultural variation, but life within particular cultures is bounded and predictable.

The thinker who had sensed this problem most clearly was, in Gellner's eyes, Durkheim. The empiricists failed to realize that our concepts are compulsive, forcing us to see the world in particular ways. Kant realized this, but was criticized by Durkheim for failing to see that the character of our concepts, and the compulsion that attaches to them, is the gift of society rather than a property inherent in every human mind.[8] Durkheim's account is well known: moments of collective effervescence are responsible for the creation of social norms. Aided by drugs and alcohol, by the night, by music and by dance, heightened collective awareness is achieved. This is remembered in the sober light of morning, and it is recreated time and again by ritual. Gellner returned to his long-standing view as to what was original in Durkheim, avoiding the now rather hackneyed view that religion is society's self-worship. Even if Durkheim's account of ritual's origins proves insufficient – and there is some degree of irony in Gellner's rendering of drunken dancing round camp fires – we still need to explain the compulsiveness of our concepts.

A great deal of attention is given to the ritualized cognition of this Durkheimian world. Gellner returns here to his earlier work, particularly the 1960s essays on anthropological method and the discussion of pre-modern and scientific thought styles in *Legitimation of Belief*. But he highlights his argument with a new and striking metaphor: a multi-periscope submarine. He presents a picture of active human beings unable to change a social formation because of its circular, self-serving protective devices. His starting point is the simultaneous presence of referential and non-referential statements.

> [S]ensitivity to some external natural feature . . . is normally blended in with other controls, internal to the system. In this way the external reporting is not 'pure', and the pure 'empirical' element can mostly be overridden by the other controls or dimensions. If the leader of the hunt is ritually impure, then conditions for hunting are impropitious – never mind the 'real' natural circumstances. Moreover, the various periscopes, or sensitivities, are diversely constructed; hence their elements do not, and *cannot*, 'add up' with each other.[9]

---

7   R. M. Unger, *False Necessity: Anti-Necessitarian Social Theory in the Service of Radical Democracy*, Cambridge, 1987.
8   E. Durkheim, *The Elementary Forms of the Religious Life*, New York, 1995, introduction.
9   *Plough, Sword, and Book*, p. 52.

The lack of a single, universally applicable criterion for judging claims and beliefs makes cognitive development impossible in early societies. This system is at once rational and non-progressive.

What is the intellectual source of this model? In a letter to Dr Oruç Aruoba, who had translated some of his work into Turkish, he acknowledged that his model of primitive language had been inspired by Wittgenstein.

> The multi-purpose and semi-autonomous subsistence of meaning which makes up the primitive use of language (and much use of language amongst us outside science) is indeed inspired by Wittgenstein's ideal of language games, and his restatement of it.
>
> The reason why I didn't acknowledge it in the book is not, as you suggest in your notes, prejudices perpetuated from *Words and Things*. At least not consciously. The point is this: I think the 'language games' approach to language is a valid account of the non-scientific use of language but not of science. Wittgenstein wrongly generalized it for all language, and considered this idea to be the solution, or rather the dissolution, of philosophic problems. It is nothing of the kind. Most of the philosophical problems arise from the fact that a different use of language emerged, namely the single currency, united, single purpose and referentially exclusive use of language . . . so I used Wittgenstein's idea, but for exactly the opposite purpose for which he intended it. Perhaps I was wrong in not admitting it. I thought it would confuse the issue if I did.[10]

It is as important to recognize another shift in his thought, influenced perhaps by his engagements with Soviet Marxism. Gellner's earlier writings drew a straightforward binary contrast between pre-modern and modern systems of thought. His philosophy of history complicated matters, identifying three major stages in human history, each of which allowed for considerable internal variation.

Gellner's treatment of 'foragia' merits attention. The low population density of primitive life, together with the lack of any division of labour and the absence of material surplus, is described in graphic terms. He is amused by the way in which ideological presuppositions have determined the ways that this mode of production has been characterized. The view from the right is that of Friedrich Hayek, who sees primitive hunters and foragers as so obsessively communitarian that economic growth and social development are completely ruled out.[11] This view is dubbed 'Viennese'

---

10   Gellner to Oruç Aruoba, 30 January 1990.
11   F. A. Hayek, *The Three Sources of Human Values*, London, 1978.

by Gellner, on the grounds that the cosmopolitan, 'open' liberalism associated with that city was threatened – or, rather, felt itself to be threatened – by the arrival of large numbers of poor, kin-bound Balkan migrants in the aftermath of the First World War. At the opposite extreme stands the American anthropologist Marshall Sahlins, who emphasizes that this mode of subsistence requires little 'work' as sufficient food can be found within a rather limited time. Sahlins then expresses admiration for the absence of any bourgeois spirit among primitives who do not produce beyond their basic needs – theirs is the first affluent society.[12] In this view history is not at all progressive: as Gellner puts it, at first nobody worked very hard, then most worked, and now all work far too much.

Gellner does not offer a dogmatic assessment of the Stone Age, noting that it is hard to do so given that data drawn from surviving primitive societies is probably tainted by contact with more advanced civilizations.[13] However, at least two possibilities are taken seriously. Gellner cites the work of James Woodburn on the Hadza of East Africa, which observes a difference between immediate gratification and delayed return, the implication being that this element of social organization might have led to settled agricultural production.[14] But Gellner was well aware, based on his knowledge of pastoral nomadic societies, that Sahlins's position is at least consistent with archaeological findings showing that the cultivation of crops was already familiar to primitives – that is, that the Neolithic Revolution did not result from a sudden technological discovery. For pastoralists are exemplars of a widespread desire to escape the workings of the state. They are fiercely egalitarian, highly mobile, relatively affluent, militarily precocious, and stateless. The last of these conditions is explained to some extent by their mobility. Tribesmen are poor fodder for states. It would be worthwhile in principle to tax the resources of pastoralists but the practical difficulty of doing so means that the effort is rarely made, and even more rarely successful. A tax gatherer who meets with nomads is unlikely to find them in the same place twice. The North African Berber tribesmen Gellner knew were wont to keep jewels hidden inside their clothes so that, if their sheep were stolen, they would have the capital to re-establish themselves elsewhere. Agrarian society results less from a technological discovery or a

---

12   M. Sahlins, *Stone Age Economics*, London, 1974.
13   He also discusses (*Plough, Sword, and Book*, pp. 29–32) a middle position, that of Veblen, in which primitives are seen as sociable and work-addicted; this view of history gets rather short shrift as it says nothing about the importance of the state.
14   J. Woodburn, 'Egalitarian Societies', *Man*, vol. 17, 1982. Woodburn had been a colleague at LSE for many years, and he contributed to Gellner (ed.), *Soviet and Western Anthropology*, London, 1980.

disposition to delay returns than from the presence of agricultural producers who are unable to move around. This is archetypically the case with those whose means of subsistence depend upon irrigation agriculture.

No Exit

Whatever explains the transition to agrarian life, there can be no doubt that a new form of society was created on the back of the surplus generated by a growing population of peasant producers. The presence of experts in coercion and in knowledge, swordsmen and clerks, demonstrated that the division of labour had arrived. Accordingly, Gellner charges Durkheim – and, one might add, most occidental social theory – with being terribly wrong to offer a binary contrast between mechanical and organic societies, the former lacking but the latter wholly marked by the division of labour. High agrarian society exhibits a significant division of labour, about which Gellner writes with great power.

It is obvious that a surplus can be extracted from peasants by means of coercion. But Gellner makes other interesting observations. Life in the agrarian age was lived in a pure Malthusian condition of perennial scarcity. Hunters and foragers could face disastrous ecological conditions, but low population density combined with the ability to travel incredibly long distances and rejoin others with whom social ties are shared meant that survival rates were rather high. Peasants cannot travel in this way, and normally belong to no larger culture. In these circumstances coercive capacity plays a role; defence of the storehouse can ensure survival.[15] But this is only one explanation for power's tendency to become concentrated. More obvious is the sheer logic of competition. Given that a rival is likely to seize every advantage, it makes sense to do the same at the earliest possible opportunity.[16] And a further consideration follows: once a powerful concentration has led to the creation of a single state, other groups are forced, if they are to avoid being exploited, to form secondary states. But Gellner's thought is very sophisticated on this point, stressing that agrarian states habitually do not possess the absolute power that they often claim for themselves. A measure of central coordination often goes hand in hand with effective decentralization; rulers, variously comprised of warriors, clerks, burghers and bureaucrats, often sit on top of laterally insulated peasant 'societies', based on distinctive cultures within which order

---

15   *Plough, Sword, and Book*, pp. 129–31.
16   Ibid., p. 147.

is provided on a self-help basis, often through kinship linkages.[17] This is clearly true of the pastoral tribes in the classic heartland of Islam. The inability of states to penetrate and organize the 'societies' on which they rest was made obvious to Gellner as the result of his fieldwork amongst the pastoral hill tribes of Morocco. [18]

If the sword is mightier than the plough, it does not however exist in isolation. For the agrarian mode of production was not, so to speak, so closed that it allowed for only one ideological superstructure. To the contrary, the period between about 600 BC and 700 AD sees the emergence of the world religions and ethics. At issue in what Karl Jaspers had called 'the axial age' is, in Gellner's eyes, a fundamental change in ideology between a world of ritual and one of concepts.[19] Writing and literacy allow experts in meaning to specify doctrines. Such a crucial development in world history needs explanation, and Gellner suggests that the increasingly abstract way of understanding the world probably appealed because of greater social complexity due to urbanization and an associated development of crafts.[20] The absolute exemplar of such a conceptualist theorist is Plato. The attempt in *The Republic* to sacralize concepts, to give them a purity of form that would ensure obedience to them, is seen as a blueprint for the maximally effective way of ruling agrarian society. But Plato had been wrong, Gellner suggests, in presuming that conceptual purity would have generalized appeal.[21] Far more potent are the personal stories at the heart of the world religions, together with their ability to offer promises of salvation to all. But the key point about conceptual Platonism and the world religions is that they tend to be, despite their tidiness and purity, at once descriptive and normative. Differently put, they characteristically underwrite social orders in the same manner as did the ritualistic thought described by Durkheim.

Relations between social power and intellectual life are likely to be complex. A distinction can be drawn between tensions that result from the specificities of organization and those that result from the logic of cognition. The former help us understand variety within the agrarian

---

17   Ibid, pp. 149–50.
18   *Nations and Nationalism*, Oxford, 1983, p. 9.
19   Gellner had admiration for the way in which Shmuel Eisenstadt developed the insights of Jaspers, and pressed for one of Eisenstadt's papers to be published in the *European Journal of Sociology*.
20   *Plough, Sword, and Book*, pp. 79–83. Gellner adds to this 'demand' side of the equation comments about the 'supply' side – noting in particular the importance of geometry and astronomy, citing E. A. Burtt, *The Metaphysical Foundations of Modern Science*, London, 1925.
21   Ibid., pp. 86–90.

world, the latter suggest an entirely different social formation. Let us take each in turn.

Specialists in coercion will seek to regularize and simplify their lives by adding legitimacy to brute strength. A measure of obedience can be created by convincing people that the social order is just, and that there is no alternative to it. Power utilizes experts in such legitimation, hoping to achieve what became known in the West as 'Caesaropapism', that is, a system firmly uniting political power and religious authority. But this sort of marriage does not always take place. Conflict can result when these types of power do not combine neatly. In *Nations and Nationalism*, Gellner offered a suggestive scheme of binary oppositions, seeking to distinguish varieties within agrarian political structures. First, warriors and clerks could be centralized or uncentralized, with the former position represented by the papacy among clerks, the latter by the diffuse social organization of Muslim *ulama*.[22] Second, rulers could be gelded – literally, of course, in the case of eunuchs – or they could remain stallions, as was overwhelmingly true of the warrior aristocracy of feudal Europe. Third, membership of the elite could be open or closed. The former position was that of Confucianism, the latter that of the principle of heredity enshrined in the Hindu caste order. The final contrast concerned political-religious fusion, present at times in the military orders of Latin Christendom, but more usually absent, as in Hinduism and Confucianism.[23] *Plough, Sword, and Book* paints the same picture in less abstract terms.[24] One characteristic pattern, that of the Latin West, presents a division of labour according to which some rule, others pray and the rest work. But just as important is the fact that a military chief's legitimacy may well enable him to overcome challenges from within the military elite. Hereditary rulers may depend on clerks to authenticate the blood line on which their power formally depends. A second pattern is that of the classical heartland of the Islamic world. Here the continual circulation of elites based on the interaction between town and tribe is at the heart of Gellner's sociology of Islam, described and analyzed in the next chapter. A third pattern is that of Hindu politics, 'the collective snobbery between unequal groups, carried on in the idiom of purity'.[25]

Agrarian society is likely to be stable. Most of human history is far better understood, Gellner often remarked, through Talcott Parsons rather than Marx: stability is the norm, fundamental change the exception. There are

22 Cf. ibid., pp. 98–100.
23 *Nations and Nationalism*, pp. 14–16.
24 *Plough, Sword, and Book*, pp. 94–8.
25 Ibid., p. 98.

multiple reasons for this. It is very unlikely that traders or merchants can bring into being a new mode of production, even though their activities might lead us to predict this. Merchants are marginalized, either in status terms or by delegating their role to a particular ethnicity, as 'middlemen'. Any visible wealth they have is likely to be seized by the powerful. In this context, Gellner liked to cite Montesquieu's account of King John extracting seven teeth of a Jewish merchant, one a day, until on the eighth day the merchant gave up ten thousand marks of silver.[26] Knowing this, merchants have two rational options before them. The most obvious is seeking to join forces with the predators themselves, that is, by converting their own resources, usually through marriage strategies, into power. A second route is that of protecting wealth by placing it where it cannot be touched, as occurred widely in Islamic *awqaf* as well as in the huge temple economies of South India, in the hope that the grantor might derive some regular income from such a move. But a strategy which increases the power of the clerks is equally unlikely to occasion social change. Specialists in belief are unable to take on the specialists in coercion by themselves.

Gellner does not limit his analysis to this static situation. The world religions and ethics are important not just because they give systematic variety to the agrarian world in the form of different civilizations. They also build a bridge to modern knowledge, and to modern production. Before outlining his account of the transition to the modern world, it makes sense, given its density, to discuss its character. We are offered an ingenious intellectual exercise, akin in spirit to the solving of a chess problem. Three elements are involved – protestantism, a new style of production and the balance of power – none of which could alone have managed to effect an exit from agrarian conditions. This is one reason for following Gellner in considering his second, ideological source of tension between power and belief within this section, concerned with the stability of the agrarian world – even though this element, together with the potential for a change in style of production, later proved *in different circumstances* to be part of the explanation for social evolutionary transformation. Two further points about the argument need to be made. On the one hand, the three elements mentioned intermingle, polymorphously related to each other: this is the world of 'elective affinities', the notion made famous in social science by Max Weber, drawing from Goethe's great novel in which chemical elements mixed together interact to produce something entirely new. On the other hand, it should be made clear that Gellner does not simply

---

26 Montesquieu, *The Spirit of the Laws* [1748], Cambridge, 1988, p. 388, cited in 'The Withering Away of the Dentistry State' in *Spectacles and Predicaments*, Cambridge, 1980, p. 311.

repeat Weber's argument about the relationship between the Protestant ethic and capitalism, though he does not dismiss it and certainly endorses the view that a new society was created for non-rational reasons. Rather, what matters for Gellner about protestantism is its effect on cognition, and thereby on production. His contribution here is one of the most original insights in the whole of his thought.

A passage towards the end of the book encapsulates his view of the importance of the world religions. Referring to the disconnected senses of all traditional thought, at once empirical and normative, he stresses the cognitive potential inherent in the orderly, conceptually unified worldview of the world religions:

> These disconnected sensibilities owe their first unification not to being made more referential, but to being made *less* so. Literacy; scholastic unification into a system; exclusive and jealous monotheism; the shining model of truth-maintaining rigorous inference in geometry, logic and perhaps in law; a centralization of the clerisy; a strict delimitation of revelation and a narrowing of its source, excluding easy accretion, a monopolization and bureaucratization of magic by the clerical guild – all these jointly somehow gave rise to a unified, centrally managed, single-apex system. At any rate, something close enough to such an ideal emerges, causing it to become familiar and normative. It only required the apex of the system to let it be known that He did not interfere in the detailed manifestations of His creation, but preferred to maintain its lawlike pattern, and to withdraw into an infinitely distant hiding, for some of his devotees to seek for His design in the regularity of His creation, rather than by privileged short cuts, and to fuse this endeavour with the deployment of precise and content-preserving mathematics – and an objective, referential, world-unifying science was born.[27]

The central claim in this passage – a subsidiary one will be noted below – is that intellectual traditions that are based on concepts often call for reformation. Gellner cited *Religion and the Decline of Magic*, historian Keith Thomas's important account of the attack by reformist intellectuals in the Christian world on the *ad hoc*, occasional practices of traditional magic.[28] Of course, this call nearly always arises because clerics of the world religions have hands that are sullied with contact with the daily workings of political power. Although reformation may be justified as a return to some earlier

27   *Plough, Sword, and Book*, pp. 197–8.
28   K. Thomas, *Religion and the Decline of Magic*, London, 1971.

purity, its importance lies in its suggesting the creation of a new world. Gellner refers to the classic Weberian thesis. He offers no judgement as to its veracity, insisting instead that this is not the only way in which protestantism matters.[29] It is generic protestantism that is relevant, rather than the specific religious movements of early modern Europe. The cognitive change involved is described in these terms:

> [A]n inscrutable, inaccessible, unappeasable, anti-rational yet orderly deity might in effect strongly encourage scientific method. It would do so by turning the orderly facts of its creation into the only evidence of its own design. Such a rigid and austere deity had no cognitive favourites, and would not disclose its secrets capriciously to some. Patient investigation of its rules, as revealed in its creation, would be the only path towards enlightenment.[30]

This accurately describes no less a figure than Isaac Newton, whose religious musings were directly related to what we normally describe as his scientific endeavours.[31] At this point, the subsidiary claim in the above passage becomes relevant. The emphasis on God's refusal to interfere in his creation refers to the intellectual world created by Judaism and the Greeks, which posits a physical universe running according to 'laws' of nature.[32] In contrast, the late appearance and 'completeness' of Islam – further analysed in the next chapter – encouraged the view that everything is caused by God, who is able to interfere in our lives at will. Such a viewpoint seems to have placed limits on scientific inquiry.[33]

The characterization of this new epistemological outlook is familiar to us, for it is based on Gellner's interpretation of the views of Hume and Kant, which stood at the heart of *Legitimation of Belief*.

> The basic contrast is between a concept-implementing society – whose concepts (inevitably endowed with contested and ambiguous edges) are systematically implemented, form a system within which *both* men and nature have their prescribed places, and are sanctified by ritual and doctrine

---

29 *Plough, Sword, and Book*, p. 105.
30 Ibid., p. 101.
31 Ibid., p. 199.
32 Gellner very much liked, and was perhaps influenced by, the work of John Milton. One of his papers making these points was published in the *European Journal of Sociology*: 'The Origin of the Concept "Laws of Nature"', vol. 22, 1982.
33 P. Crone and M. Cook, *Hagarism: The Making of the Islamic World*, Cambridge, 1977, p. 128 and chapter 14.

– and a society in which concepts are at least tacitly de-sacralized, where their application is in some measure based on single, isolated criteria, and within which isolated men face an orderly, 'mechanical' nature.[34]

Where change was stymied by the semi-referential nature of most thought within simple and agrarian societies, this new situation, ruled by shared reference to an external world, allows endless 'turnover' of facts and values. Metaphorically, the change is seen as one from the multi-periscope submarine to 'jaws', that is, to a world in which a single principle could gobble up anything in its way. If this is familiar, the concerns of *Plough, Sword, and Book* allow for a slightly different characterization of what is involved. First, there is the careful identification of a paradox of modern cognition. On the one hand, knowledge is separated from social life, thereby gaining a measure of autonomy. On the other hand, the old division of labour, that is, a world where specialists monopolize literacy, is replaced by a world of standardized knowledge which can be accessed by all. 'Orderly conduct throughout, the like treatment of like cases, and the recognition of symmetrical obligations contained in rules', Gellner argued, 'replace differential awe restricted to ritually heightened situations, and an ethic of uneven loyalty'.[35] Second, he makes use here of a comparison between Durkheim and Weber that would mark his thought thereafter.[36] Where Durkheim explains why all men are rational, Weber offers an account of the adoption of key background assumptions which led some men to become more rational than others – that is, to create and adopt a rational-scientific style of thought.

An innovation of Gellner's account is the argument that a single-stranded approach to facts helps free up economic life.

[A] Protestant world is one in which the sacred is absent (hidden) or, if you prefer, in which it is evenly diffused . . . Existing practices, and the combination of elements which they embody, cease to be hallowed. So the way is free to innovation and growth by means of new devices, by new combinations of elements. Instrumental rationality becomes more common and acceptable.[37]

Individuals who stand, so to speak, naked before the facts will create a world in which economic growth becomes as possible as the growth of

34 *Plough, Sword, and Book*, p. 133.
35 Ibid, p. 110.
36 Ibid., pp. 111, 128.
37 Ibid., p. 106.

knowledge; both come to be seen in practical and instrumental terms, free from the sacralizing cage of tradition. And generic protestantism works in a whole series of other ways as well. What matters most is a new type of personality.

> If a man's motive for economic activity is the desire to demonstrate his saved status and to fulfil his calling, he is less likely to cheat than if he is activated by the desire for gain. His rectitude is not at the mercy of his anticipation of the rectitude of others. Thus Protestantism has a double (and somewhat contradictory) role: it makes men instrumentally rational in handling things, and non-instrumentally honest in their dealings with each other.[38]

If this comes close to endorsing the classic Weberian thesis, it is still the case that much more is at issue. First, higher levels of trust make for ease in productive activity. Second, the self-contained, inwardly-directed character of the actors involved makes it possible to move from a system of pure coercion to one that is gentler and more restrained. Finally, generic protestantism introduced the notion of a calling in life, powerful enough that mercantile activities hitherto shunned as base were now seen as respectable.

Nonetheless, Gellner suggests that generic protestantism does not guarantee in and of itself the emergence of a new world. For one thing, protestantism of this sort is not seen in every world religion, with Hinduism being likely to rule out the egalitarianism implicit in generic protestant-ism.[39] For another, the complete success of a protestant creed is capable of so totally affirming concepts as to prevent the emergence of any new ideas. Gellner suggests that this was as true of the Counter-Reformation's effects on the world from which he came, as it was of Calvinism and of Islam – whose deity, as noted, was held to be quite capable of interfering directly in the world.[40] But the more general point is that new ideas and practices of cognition and of production are not sufficient on their own to prompt a transition to a new social order. Imperial China is held to have been sufficiently aware of its own interests to smother challenges of this sort,

---

38   Ibid., p. 106.
39   Ibid., pp. 121–2.
40   The architecture of Prague is dominated by the Counter-Reformation, with important strands of Czech thought seeing it as having blocked developments that would otherwise have taken place. Gellner shared this perception, and was accordingly drawn to H. Trevor-Roper, 'Religion, the Reformation and Social Change', *Historical Studies*, vol. 4, 1965.

aware that their threat was very great.[41] Just as important is the vital matter of timing. Had there been too great a move from agriculture to mercantile activities early on, it would have put the whole society at risk in the face of harvest failure.[42] Such a move had to be, so to speak, properly timed, made at the moment when an increase in technological power was beginning to bring forth some surplus. But such knowledge, itself characteristic, as noted, of a particular intellectual tradition, depended upon favourable political circumstances in order to operate and triumph. Let us consider now the rise of such circumstances, against the odds, in a particular place and time.

A Curious Concatenation of Circumstances

Gellner admits that no account of the West's ascent is ever likely to be generally agreed upon. This is surely true, given the host of causal variables present within the single case which then had universal impact. The fact that he cites fifteen different possible causes might seem to be a statement of intellectual despair. Nothing could be further from the truth. We will later note all fifteen explanations that he mentions, but it must be emphasized that he offers his own account, hybrid in character and integrating most of the factors he adduces. He sees the rise of the West as the result of a fortuitous opening – and not, as Marx and other evolutionists would have it, the consequence of any logic inherent to some grand process of social evolution.

> What did happen was that a miraculous political and ideological balance of power in the non-economic parts of society made the expansion possible, at a time when the technological potential was also available. Just as miraculously, the impulse to make use of the uniquely favourable concatenation of cognitive, ideological and political circumstances was also present in some at least of the producers.[43]

Let us try to unpack this terse formulation.

The keystone of the explanation is provided by a reflection on David Hume's sociology of religion. On the one hand, Hume had insisted in *A Natural History of Religion* that scripturalist monotheisms are enemies

---

41 *Plough, Sword, and Book*, p. 132.
42 Ibid., pp. 109, 130.
43 Ibid., p. 132.

of civility when they are in enthusiastic reformation mode.[44] Gellner effectively agreed, as noted, insisting that a protestant reformation does not necessarily lead to economic growth. Tawney had stressed this against Weber, insisting that Calvinism had been rigorous, having no truck with easy money-making.[45] Gellner reinforces the analytic point on the basis of his knowledge of Islam. This religion came after Christianity, and its monotheism was more logical and pure: nonetheless, its rigour did not lead to the first breakthrough precisely because the *ulama* in power were so intolerant. But ideological coherence does matter, as Hume seemed to realize when stressing in his essay 'Of Superstition and Enthusiasm' that 'superstition is an enemy to civil liberty, and enthusiasm a friend to it'.[46] To say this, of course, makes for an absolute contradiction within Hume's own position, and it is one for which he has no resolution. But Gellner offers his own explanation.

> The real answer would seem to be that it is important for the zealous enthusiasts to be defeated but not crushed. Their defeat converts them to toleration (in any case consonant with the view that truth can only come from an inner light and not from an external enforcement). The fact that their defeat is not total helps them secure toleration. A spiritual as well as political balance of power helps maintain a situation in which central coercion is not exercised to the full. The societies in which this has occurred in due course demonstrated, by their own wealth and power, the astonishing economic and military advantages which can follow this compromise.[47]

At issue here is the full working out of the generic protestant ethic. The fact that toleration gave protestant intellectuals autonomy without the ability to dominate allowed and encouraged them to concentrate their attention on mundane affairs. Gellner restates his position in these words:

> One, but only one, precondition of the emergence of such instrumental rationality is indeed the availability of a large and expanding surplus,

---

44 D. Hume, *A Natural History of Religion* [1777], London, 1976, chapter 12. We will see that this reading of Hume had first appeared a few years earlier in *Muslim Society*, Cambridge, 1981; it was to be used again later, for a slightly different purpose, in *Conditions of Liberty: Civil Society and Its Rivals*, London, 1993.

45 R. H. Tawney, *Religion and the Rise of Capitalism*, London, 1926.

46 D. Hume, 'Of Superstition and Enthusiasm', in his *Essays Moral, Political and Literary* [1777], Oxford, 1963, cited in *Plough, Sword, and Book*, p. 114.

47 *Plough, Sword, and Book*, pp. 114–5.

which creates a situation in which there is no longer the need for storing and protecting the major part of what is produced. The expanding surplus does, of course, depend on sustained innovation. This, if it is indeed to be persistent and continuous, depends not on any one discovery or even set of discoveries, but rather on a sense of the intelligibility and manipulability of nature. In other words, it calls for a secular, unified, single-conceptual-currency vision of nature.

So, the instrumental spirit in the economy (which, jointly with politically independent producers, helps set up the market), is paralleled by the unified and instrumental attitude to nature. The fusion of data and explanation into a single ideal currency, subordinated to the single aims of explanation and prediction, is essential. The two are parallel, and mutually constitute each other's condition.[48]

The subtle interactions at work here need underlining. Growth in one area does much to occasion it in another. And much hangs on the fact of sustained innovation. Such innovation must not be too great at the start, for if it were, the state would likely wish to control it. But innovation must produce at the right time a continuous stream of technological goods, for this has a crucial role as a bribery fund that ensures social stability, especially in transitional moments. Such innovation can first be seen in city-states, and thereafter in the rather particular circumstances of seventeenth-century Holland and eighteenth-century Britain. An external balance of power allowed city-states a measure of autonomy in which the logic of innovation could take its course. Holland and Britain benefited from an external balance quite as much, but to this was added an internal balance based on political stalemate.

Gellner's argument is abstract and deserves encapsulation. The account offered is not idealist. Gellner is Weberian both in according ideology some causal role and in offering a narrative in which different sources of social power mutually condition each other. Ideological innovation was present and did matter. The generic protestantism seen in several civilizations took on a particularly benign form in the West because a prior balance of power prevented it from seizing power; it abandoned dreams of theocracy, embraced toleration and chose to investigate nature and to perform economically. This, in turn, makes it easier for restraints to be placed on the coercive order, giving still more room for cognitive and economic growth in a process of benign mutual interaction. It is tempting to say that the balance of power in early European civilization made puritans into friends

---

48   Ibid., p. 131.

of liberty and civility. But Gellner will not accept this, noting that political fragmentation can often be found, but sometimes as mere anarchy rather than as an enabling condition for social, economic and political progress.[49]

Rather than offering an encapsulation of this sort, Gellner simply noted the impact of fifteen factors, each of which had been proposed as an explanation for the spectacular development of Europe.[50] The factors are worth citing, since commentary upon them will once again highlight the nature of his account.

1. European feudalism is sometimes seen as a matrix of capitalism, for at least two reasons. Though Gellner insists that feudal society is based on status rather than contract, the fact that there is some market in loyalty at least suggests a world of contract. Far more important is the balance of power that feudalism encourages. 'The central ruler allies himself with the burghers who have acquired a weight of their own, breaks the power of local barons, and effectively centralizes the society'.[51] This is the classic explanation offered by Adam Smith in Book III of *The Wealth of Nations*, a text Gellner knew well.[52] Though appealing, the argument failed to explain why a ruler, once assured of his situation, did not then re-establish his power over the newly created sources of wealth?

2. Church and state are clearly separated in the Occident, and curtail each other's ambitions. But this factor, like most of the others, cannot work alone, not least as the Counter-Reformation joined ideological and political power together again.

3. European states may have had a measure of restraint forced upon them because of competition with other states. 'Presiding as it does over a partly commercial society, [the state's] fiscal income is greater if the subjects prosper. Prosperity depends on a measure of security and liberty. Excessive tax demands or arbitrariness are counter-productive . . . '.[53]

4. The burghers are, for Weberian reasons, self-contained, and this diminishes the intensity of struggles for power. Particular attention

---

49   Ibid., p. 170.

50   Ibid., pp. 158–71.

51   Ibid., p. 159.

52   Smith is discussed in his Radcliffe-Brown Lecture at the British Academy, 'Nationalism and the two forms of cohesion in complex societies', reprinted in *Culture, Identity and Politics*, Cambridge, 1987.

53   *Plough, Sword, and Book*, pp. 159–60, drawing at this point on A. O. Hirschman, *The Passions and the Interests: Political Arguments for Capitalism Before Its Triumph*, Princeton, 1977.

is paid to the English case, in which the defeat of an ideological revolution then led, through political stalemate, to the emergence of toleration.

5. Gellner cites the work of Lawrence and Jeanne Stone, making the Tocquevillian argument that the British aristocracy may have been relatively permeable, a class rather than a caste, thereby allowing a good deal of accommodation with new wealth.[54]

6. The presence of a surplus was necessary, at first to bribe rulers and later to buy off discontent from below.

7. This fund was the result of innovation – as noted, not so great at the outset as to either threaten members of the *ancien régime* or to make it worthwhile for them to seek to control it.[55]

8. Peasant life in general does not encourage specialization and development. Gellner noted the thesis of Alan Macfarlane according to which English society lost its peasantry in the Middle Ages, thereby becoming uniquely individualist.[56]

9. An important religious factor may have been, as Louis Dumont argued, the manner in which monasticism created disciplined and orderly conduct.[57]

10. A second possible religious factor was the way in which the Christian church destroyed extended kinship links, as explained brilliantly by Jack Goody, thereby making people, bereft of their own means of self-help, that much better as fodder for state-building.[58]

11. Gellner suggests that the direct thesis of Max Weber – that the economic ethic of occidental Protestantism created a powerful work ethic – may have some truth to it.

12. Negatively, it may be that all that is needed to explain the difference between northern and southern Europe is the malign influence of the Counter-Reformation.[59]

13. A plural state system built competition into the core of European life, thereby making any return to stagnation impossible.

14. An internal and external balance of power seems to have been crucial. The two may be connected, as noted, in so far as decent

---

54   Ibid, p. 160, citing L. and J. Stone, *An Open Elite? England, 1540–1880*, Oxford, 1984.

55   Ibid., pp. 161–2.

56   A. Macfarlane, *The Origins of English Individualism*, Oxford, 1978.

57   L. Dumont, *Essais sur l'individualisme*, Paris, 1983.

58   Gellner is here adding an interpretation to J. Goody, *The Development of the Family and Marriage in Europe*, Cambridge, 1983.

59   Trevor-Roper, 'Religion, the Reformation and Social Change'.

internal behaviour might augment tax revenues needed for military competition.

15. The presence of a national bourgeoisie, rather than the specialized bourgeoisies of city-states, was crucial, and reinforced many of the factors mentioned. Such a bourgeoisie characterized English history, partly by the early establishment of centralized estates.

Gellner's own account draws to a greater or lesser extent on most of these factors, some of them of his own invention, with others so closely linked to each other as to scarcely be distinct analytically.[60] Exceptions to this generalization are the explanations offered in 5, 8, and 9, which seem to be mentioned mostly out of respect for their authors. Gellner's argument as a whole can be seen as one in which kinship's 'caging' of productive possibilities is escaped, allowing for the emergence of socially mobile individualism, and to that extent explanation 10 can be seen as a summary of his whole position. But one suspects that the purpose in citing this explanation was rather different. The brilliant work of the Cambridge school of historical demography, inspired by John Hajnal and Peter Laslett, led by Tony Wrigley and with a decisive contribution from Jack Goody, had shown kinship links in Europe as a whole to be limited.[61] Gellner found this work to be deeply suggestive, and was therefore somewhat irritated by these scholars' refusal to step beyond their immediate empirical findings. There is a sense in which he was pushing them to theorize their findings.

Two final points about Gellner's own position need to be stressed. First, no single factor explains the transition: it is the combination of elements – indeed the way in which the elements are changed by combination – that matters. Second, resuming the theme of *Thought and Change*, the process as a whole was unconscious, indeed running very much counter to the obvious norms of rationality of the agrarian age. There was no social contract creating this world:

It would have gone against the grain, against the rational interests of participants, who were not yet imbued with the spirit of this order. The logic of the situation in which men found themselves precluded them from subscribing freely and rationally to such a contract (or, in most

---

60   This is most obviously true of the interrelations between 3, 13 and 14; equally the argument of 12 is the limitation mentioned in 2.

61   The fundamental contribution is A. M. Wrigley and R. Schofield, *The Population History of England, 1541–1871: A Reconstruction*, London, 1981.

cases, from finding it intelligible). *We had to be tricked into it.* We may see this as the cunning of reason or as a concatenation of accidents.[62]

The implication here is that others will have to be tricked into it as well. 'Fundamental changes transform identities', he argued once again, going on to insist that consent only made sense within an established world.[63] There were but two reasons for accepting the argument he was putting forward, namely 'the internal plausibility of our own model of how, fundamentally, cognition works, and the external consideration that it leads to great control, power, and hence, pragmatically, that it prevails'.[64]

Consequences

Although industrial society marks a step forward in social evolution it resembles the agrarian world in one way. Neither mode of production is so dominant as to allow only a single political superstructure. Gellner's general view of the world of advanced liberal capitalism is by now familiar: it is a relatively open world in which science prospers, bringing both affluence and diminished moral certainty – with Danegeld doing a good deal to secure social cohesion. Marxist regimes present another social context, still seen as a social world that had lost ideological rigour, accordingly ripe for liberalization – but Gellner now showed some awareness of Aron's argument that left-wing dictatorships were less likely to liberalize than those of the right.[65] This was not true of a third social formation, that of Muslim societies. His claim here – that Islam has the capacity to adapt itself to modernity, thereby resisting secularization – forms the core of the next chapter. The fourth world is that of alternative forms of imitative industrialization. Gellner stresses less the inevitable loss of democracy when centralized power forces development than he does a measure of ideological schizophrenia. Science and technology in the initial breakthrough had at their base the non-rational desire to understand the divine order, and perhaps to bring it about on earth. In contrast, late-developing societies have the option of adopting the fruits of science in a purely instrumental manner, such that 'the computer and the shrine may be compatible'.[66] However, a distinction needed to be drawn amongst the paternalistic

---

62   *Plough, Sword, and Book*, p. 257.
63   Ibid., p. 193.
64   Ibid, pp. 201–2. He cautioned (p. 204) that the pragmatism involved was, so to speak, one-off rather than generic.
65   Ibid., p. 271.
66   Ibid., p. 222.

modernizers-from-above, between those who genuinely believe in the tolerated folk tradition and those who politely ignore it.[67] A final type of society is that of the backward, in which 'relatively strong states dominate weak civil societies, and where ideological life is opportunist and largely a function of utilizing the international competition between blocs. *Cuius military aid, eius religio*'.[68]

This analysis was rather conventional, but more striking were Gellner's sustained ruminations on the character of the sources of power under conditions of modernity. There were difficulties within each realm.

The background condition for the cognitive realm was provided by Gellner's interesting characterization of the modern character of the division of labour. He saw it as vastly increased on the one hand, yet much diminished on the other, essentially because of the generic training in modern societies, all members of which need to acquire the ability to act as clerks within a changing industrial world. The complex specialization of the few disappears as a new world is created, in which all have distinct tasks, most of which are, however, carried out in the same way. Gellner is here repeating a central contention of *Thought and Change*, namely that we are entering into an age of culture – a world in which literacy is available for all given that communication skills are so necessary in modern society. It is at this point that one can see some difficulty arising. Gellner was keen to stress that cognitive power looks set for continual growth, making the underwriting of morals ever less likely. He drew a distinction between the vulgar and the serious Enlightenment, the latter illustrated once again by the spare worlds of Kant and Hume. The conclusions drawn are familiar: identity must be considered with irony, given that true cognitive power lies in a separate realm, causing change and instability to which we must then adapt. Rationality was better for making small decisions than large ones. It worked within a single social world rather than serving as much of a guide between them, a consequence of which was that very important decisions, characteristically made by those occupying key positions of power, will be made less by reason than by intuition.[69] But there is another difficulty that needs to be stressed. Some of the mechanisms by which high culture is provided for a society are far from restrained or limited. The next two chapters consider Islam and nationalism in turn, with a key question in each being whether these ideological principles can ever allow identities to be held ironically.

---

67 Ibid., p. 221.
68 Ibid., p. 223.
69 Ibid., pp. 209–10.

Two sets of comments are offered on the economy. First, the social infrastructure of modern society is so extensive that the idea that matters can be left entirely to the market are rendered nothing less than ridiculous.[70] Differently put, the economy is inevitably politicized, making some sort of corporatist bargaining, whether public or hidden from view, inevitable. The second set of comments is wholly new, and clearly deeply felt. The meaning of wealth is held to have changed. A minor critical comment concerning social mobility was addressed to his Cambridge colleague Chris Hann, the anthropologist of Central Europe.

> I am sceptical about the alleged data denying social mobility. The main gimmick seems to be to say that if you hold social structure constant, then there is not much mobility. But the whole point is that the social structure is totally inconstant, and that the amount of mobility there is, and which has great consequence, is itself a consequence of the changed social structure. No doubt, if we discount all the people who have left the working class, because the working class itself has diminished, and pretend that the proportion of the working class remains the same, then the mobility figures cease to be very impressive, or perhaps there is not much mobility at all. But that totally distorts the reality of the situation. Incidentally, I am not unaware of the tremendous amount of inequality. The point is, it is a different *kind* of inequality.[71]

Still, endless competitive consumerism might end up by destroying the planet on which we live. Of course, the desire for wealth did make sense insofar as material needs had not been satisfied, and it was certainly understandable in those still haunted by recollections of genuine scarcity. But he felt it was possible to imagine the satisfaction of material needs, going on to say that much competition for material goods was ridiculous given that there was often little real difference between an expensive claret and a good supermarket Rioja. He drew an analogy with classical Rome, wondering why a political procedure had not been found for 'dispensing with a useless consumption city, leaving farmers on the land, and not importing slaves'.[72] His hopes of avoiding a similar fate for consumer society rested on an awareness that money mattered less on

---

70   Ibid., p. 189.
71   Gellner to Hann, 5 December 1994. Gellner dictated a good deal of his correspondence, overwhelmingly so in the last years of his life. Accordingly, I have corrected an obvious grammatical mistake that appeared in the original.
72   *Plough, Sword, and Book*, p. 231.

objective grounds than because it brought status. Perhaps it might be possible to divorce emolument from status, as the economist Fred Hirsch had argued in *Social Limits to Growth*, a pioneering book that Gellner much admired.[73]

> In a thoroughly anonymous and mobile suburb . . . how can one convey status other than by material symbols which do waste resources and cause pollution? Would it be conceivable for local councils to confer, let us say, municipal mini-knighthoods? Of course, it is conceivable, but would they be taken seriously enough to dissuade both the recipients of the Borough Ks, *and* their unsuccessful rivals, from purchasing unnecessarily large cars?[74]

The area in which there was the greatest difficulty, in Gellner's view, was that of politics. Orders tended to be obeyed where bureaucracy was well established, as had been so strikingly true in Nazi Germany. Further, the argument that one should not kick against the pricks 'lest worse befall' had the capacity to disable liberal opposition to repulsive regimes, as had been true of the politics of normalization in much of the socialist bloc.[75] Little comfort could be taken from such weak and passive support for liberty. And there was worse. Marxist societies continued to suffer from their ideology's lack of any means to control political power. Gellner devoted several interesting pages to the full-blooded 'right wing alternative'. Fascism had been defeated, but Gellner in his later years came to feel that the desire for community might yet again gain teeth, perhaps linked to an ethos of survival of the fittest.[76] His concluding questions revealed gnawing doubts:

> Will the need to counteract the discontent of a swollen, leisure-endowed but status-less class bring about the revival of a new central faith, centrally enforced? Will this be facilitated by the decline in that instrumental rationality which had brought about the new world, but is no longer required when that world is fully developed? The same solution need not prevail everywhere.[77]

---

73 F. Hirsch, *Social Limits to Growth*, London, 1977.
74 *Plough, Sword, and Book*, p. 231.
75 Ibid., p. 235.
76 Ibid., pp. 242–7.
77 Ibid., p. 272.

Assessment

Plough, Sword, and Book does succeed in offering a striking view of our place in the world. Its sociology of agrarian life has much to recommend it, while the account of the transition to the modern world is subtle and ingenious, perhaps most of all in its claims about the character of generic protestantism. No philosophical history can ever be wholly correct; the genre's utility is rather in providing a model which can help to evaluate the significance of empirical findings. Thus Gellner's model highlights as important the recent discovery in Anatolia of the complex religious monuments of Gobelki Tepe, since these were erected before the emergence of agriculture – a development seen increasingly by archaeologists as the result of desperation rather than of desire. But it is necessary to go beyond this pragmatic view to offer critique – defensive at first, then negative – of Gellner's argument.

Major assaults have been launched against 'Eurocentrism'.[78] One element of this offensive concentrates on European self-congratulation, the belief that special merit of some sort accounts for historical European successes. This is indeed true of some accounts of the rise of the West, the recent work of the historian Anthony Pagden being a prominent example.[79] But this certainly does not apply to Gellner in any immediate or complete sense. For one thing, he was careful to speak of a miracle that happened *in* Europe, rather than uncritically assert that there was a *European* miracle.[80] For another, his account is careful and limited. Accidents are stressed, as are difficulties. He admits that Greek rationality had nothing to do with monotheism, and goes so far as to highlight the interest in magic of members of the late seventeenth-century Royal Society, including Newton himself.[81] Further, political liberty is seen as the result more of accident than of design.

But we can leave the moral issue to one side for a moment, and turn to a second, purely descriptive element of this critique, namely that there was nothing truly special about Western society before roughly 1800. Until

78 J. Goody, *The East in the West*, Cambridge, 1998; R. B. Wong, *China Transformed: Historical Change and the Limits of European Experience*, Ithaca, 1997; K. Pomeranz, *The Great Divergence: China, Europe, and the Making of the Modern World Economy*, Princeton, 2000; J. M. Hobson, *The Eastern Origins of Western Civilization*, Cambridge, 2004.

79 A. Pagden, *Worlds at War: The 2,500-Year Struggle between East and West*, New York, 2008, subject to powerful critical analysis by C. J. Tyerman, 'How Wonderful We Are', *Times Literary Supplement*, 23 May 2008.

80 'Introduction', in Baecher, Hall and Mann, *Europe and the Rise of Capitalism*.

81 *Plough, Sword, and Book*, p. 199.

that time, the major civilizations, perhaps especially China, are held to have been roughly at the same developmental level, all exemplars of Smithian growth. There are very good reasons to object to this view, as is made clear by recent revisions of the revisionists themselves.[82] For one thing, development does seem to have taken place earlier in Europe than elsewhere. Malthusian crises continued to affect China long after they had been dealt with in Europe.[83] Crucially, productivity levels were higher in England than in China by 1700.[84] For another, there remains much to be said for the view that this development depended on prior institutional differences. One aspect of Gellner's work that seems especially solid is his writing on science.[85] Further, his argument about the contribution of warfare – driving emulation, and thereby occasioning restraint on the part of states needing to protect their tax bases – does not seem to have been undermined by recent research.[86]

Direct criticism of Gellner's views of development came from Alan Macfarlane, arguing above all that the concept of transition was overdone, given that the seeds of modernity were present in the European feudal past, albeit sadly blocked in continental Europe by the rise of absolutism.[87] Gellner replied to this just before his death in a spirited manner, accusing Macfarlane of being an English Narodnik unable to truly appreciate the

---

82 J. M. Bryant, 'The West and the Rest Revisited: Debating Capitalist Origins, European Colonialism, and the Advent of Modernity', *Canadian Journal of Sociology*, vol. 31, 2006; M. Mann, 'The Sources of Social Power Revisited: A Response to Criticism', in J. A. Hall and R. Schroeder (eds), *An Anatomy of Power: The Social Theory of Michael Mann*, Cambridge, 2006, and 'Predation and Production in European Imperialism', in S. Malešević and M. Haugaard (eds), *Ernest Gellner and Contemporary Social Thought*, Cambridge, 2007; P. Huang, 'Development or Involution in Eighteenth-Century Britain and China: A Review of Kenneth Pomeranz's *The Great Divergence: China, Europe and the Making of the Modern World Economy*', *Journal of Asian Studies*, vol. 61, 2002.

83 K. Deng, *Fact or Fiction? Re-examination of Chinese Premodern Population Statistics*, LSE Economic History Working Papers 76, London, 2003.

84 R. Brenner and C. Isett, 'England's Divergence from China's Yangzi Delta: Property Relations, Macroeconomics, and Patterns of Development', *Journal of Asian Studies*, vol. 61, 2002.

85 M. Jacobs, *Scientific Culture and the Making of the Modern West*, New York, 1997, and 'Commerce, Industry and the Laws of Newtonian Science: Weber Revisited and Revised', *Canadian Journal of History*, vol. 35, 2000; J. Goldstone, 'Efflorescences and Economic Growth in World History: Rethinking the Rise of the West and the British Industrial Revolution', *Journal of World History*, vol. 13, 2002.

86 J. A. Hall, 'Confessions of a Eurocentric', *International Sociology*, vol. 63, 2001.

87 A. Macfarlane, 'Ernest Gellner and the Escape to Modernity', in J. A. Hall and I. C. Jarvie (eds), *The Social Philosophy of Ernest Gellner*, Amsterdam, 1996, p. 213.

difficulties of escaping the agrarian condition.[88] Macfarlane returned to the
argument after Gellner's death in his sophisticated account of 'the riddle of
the modern world', in which Gellner's philosophy of history is compared
with the views of Montesquieu, Smith and Tocqueville.[89]

We must not foreclose discussion of the moral evaluation of European
development. An interesting argument in this area has recently been
made by Michael Mann, a thinker indebted and sympathetic to Gellner.[90]
Europe may have been liberal internally, Mann suggests, but it was far from
being so externally. It is important to distinguish here between the fact of
viciousness and the more controversial claim that European development
depended upon such viciousness.[91] Gellner was well aware of this violence,
but offered an account in which European development was essentially
endogenous. And he noted that some peripheral countries had benefited
from direct rule.

> An ideal fate of a 'backward' territory might well be the following: a colo-
> nial occupation which provides some schools and the 'infrastructure', and
> undermines the power of the traditional and backward-looking ruling
> class; followed by a struggle for independence which generates a united
> and determined leadership with a good mass organization; followed by
> independence in which these tools can be used for growth.[92]

This is a view upheld by a good deal of modern scholarship.[93] But beyond
this, Gellner did make positive moral points. The initial developmental
breakthrough had depended upon liberal political conditions, and the
resulting model at least provided a model for liberalizing societies to emulate.
A far more important consideration concerned rational science. The moral

---

88   'Reply to Critics', in Hall and Jarvie, *The Social Philosophy of Ernest Gellner*, pp. 661–6.
89   A. Macfarlane, *The Riddle of the Modern World: Of Liberty, Wealth and Equality*,
Basingstoke, 1995.
90   Mann, 'Predation and production in European imperialism'.
91   The most striking attempt to quantify the extent to which predation was responsible
for European economic development remains P. O'Brien, 'European Economic
Development', *Economic History Review*, vol. 35, 1982, which insists that the contribution
was rather small, with most growth coming from the development of home markets.
92   *Thought and Change*, London, 1964, pp. 176–7.
93   M. Lange, for example, argues that areas within the British empire that had experienced
direct rule tended to have the capacity for development (*Lineages of Despotism and Development:
British Colonialism and State Power*, Chicago, 2009). Similar points about the impact of Japanese
imperialism in South Korea are made by A. Kohli, *State-Directed Development: Political Power
and Industrialization in the Global Periphery*, Cambridge, 2004. Cf. D. Acemoglu and J. A.
Robinson, *Economic Origins of Dictatorship and Democracy*, Cambridge, 2005.

contribution of diminished mortality rates and decent living standards resulting from our ability to transform nature was a constant centrepiece of his thought.

Gellner's view of the workings of contemporary society is open to negative critique, however, on two different but related counts. Let me begin with his insistence that the search for wealth has become self-defeating. One cannot avoid seeing here the persona of the thinker, sitting happily in Moscow with a glass of champagne and a piece of excellent black bread – convinced that affluence had been attained, as was indeed the case if one compared the Soviet Union to Tsarist Russia. Temperamentally, I fully endorse such simplicity, even with a measure of frugality. So too did Adam Smith in 1759:

> [Riches] are immense fabrics, which it requires the labour of a life to raise, which threaten every moment to overwhelm the person that dwells in them, and which while they stand, though they may save him from some smaller inconveniences, can protect him from none of the severer inclemencies of the season. They keep off the summer shower, not the winter storm, but leave him always as much, and sometimes more exposed than before, to anxiety, to fear, and to sorrow; to diseases, to danger and to death.[94]

Nonetheless, Smith endorses commercial society. The illusion that wealth would bring happiness – and illusion it was, utterly dominant in the vulgar for all that the wise could see through it – was beneficial: it created not just industriousness but political stability. What matters for human beings, in Smith's eyes, is the approval of one's fellows, and this is most often gained through the possession of riches. Social life resembles, to use a modern metaphor, an escalator: distinction is gained by possessing something that those below lack. Smith's world is one of jealousy, rather than one of envy – that is, in which it is normal to try to catch up with the person above, rather than to create policies designed to level the field, or to change the rules of the game. Of course, Gellner was well aware that monies were only important insofar as they bestowed status – that is, he had reached the conclusions of *The Theory of Moral Sentiments* himself, albeit by a different route.

So the questions that face us become very precise. Has this mechanism come to an end? Or, rather, is it the case that this mechanism now ought to come to an end? What merit, finally, is there to Gellner's contention

---

94   A. Smith, *The Theory of Moral Sentiments* [1759], Oxford, 1976, p. 183.

that the scramble for money can be replaced by the sharing out of status goods? The possibility of ecological disaster naturally entails respect for Gellner's concern, lending his ideas from two decades ago an immediate contemporary relevance. Further, ingenuity may allow for some splitting between reward and status; jobs of inherent interest and status may well attract even if they no longer return the greatest reward. Still, it is hard to follow him very far in this direction. A logical consideration is simply that Gellner's argument does tend to an illicit, teleological functionalism at this point: the 'necessity' for change does not mean that this need will be met. Further, a precondition of Gellner's recommendation – that genuine poverty be abolished – has most certainly not been met. His puritanical view is a poor guide in a fundamental sense: the rich can always find pursuits or possessions which serve as means to distinguish them from those below. The escalator quality of capitalist society most certainly remains in effect, with its ignoble contribution to political stability as strong as ever. If one extends Gellner's argument from a capitalist country to capitalist society as a whole, difficulties increase. Enormous growth is simply necessary if the needs, let alone desires, of the vast majority of humankind are to be met. The possibility of redistribution on a world scale is surely infinitesimal. There is no need to go further, for here undoubtably is one of the major problems facing modernity. Scepticism as to Gellner's suggested reform leads to a wholly unsceptical and fervent hope that scientific breakthroughs will occur, above all in order to create new sources of clean energy.

A larger and more important negative critique is also in order. The traces of Saint-Simonianism that seem present in Gellner's thought, perhaps derived from Masaryk with reinforcement from Aron, suggest a potential for modern industrialized society to stabilize, to find some point of rest. There is a great deal to be said for the notion that the modern era is industrial, and that many social characteristics – bureaucracy, literacy, education – rest on this fact. A Weberian approach to liberal capitalism and to the socialist bloc in the postwar years had a very great deal to recommend it. One might further defend Gellner by remembering that his understanding of modern society stressed that instability would only become truly serious – despite his fears of the stagflation that gripped Britain the in 1970s – when inequality was joined with an ethnic marker. Perhaps Japan points to a possible future in that its homogeneity allowed it to survive a decade bereft of economic growth – but also free from social instability.

Nonetheless, the modern world cannot be understood without recognizing the dynamics of capitalist society. One consideration here is internal. Gellner tends to take for granted that corporatist arrangements are necessary, claiming that at times their absence impairs economic success. Matters are much more complex. To begin with, corporatism is often ill-defined. Countries classified as corporatist have often owed their success partly to the non-corporatist elements in their political econo- mies – to reliance on international markets in the Danish case, and to non-Keynesian monetary policy in postwar Germany. Further, the great postwar inflation probably had little to do with the absence – or presence – of corporatist arrangements: what mattered most was the refusal of the United States to tax its citizens to pay for the simultaneous burdens of the war in Vietnam and 'Great Society' social programmes – with its hegemonic power allowing it to print money, and so to spread inflation throughout the advanced capitalist world.[95] Finally, it is by no means clear that corporatist arrangements are, at least at all times and in all countries, easy to manage.[96]

A second consideration is much more important. Capitalist society creates permanent instability. If the entry of new countries into the devel- oped world makes this obvious at present, change will remain capitalism's essence even if the whole world is industrialized. The single greatest analysis of this process – Karl Polanyi's *The Great Transformation* – was quite as much a product of the Hapsburg world, but Gellner did not consider this work in the context of his analyses of the works of Hayek, Wittgenstein, Popper and Malinowski.[97] Polanyi argued that the endless change brought about by capitalism would eventually lead society to protect itself, a view offered as explanation for international trade rivalry at the end of the nineteenth century, leading in turn to geopolitical conflict in the twentieth century. As it happens, Polanyi's explanation for Europe's disastrous twentieth century is probably incorrect: capital- ists were able to adapt to change, as were their societies, with disaster resulting much more from foreign policy mistakes on the parts of elites.[98] But two points follow from this. First, geopolitics and capitalism most certainly can intertwine, as in protectionist policies, and these may yet lend dynamics, perhaps of an undesirable sort, to contemporary world

---

95 For brilliant analyses along these lines see M. Smith, *Power, Norms and Inflation*, New York, 1992, discussed in J. A. Hall, *Coercion and Consent*, Oxford, 1994, chapter 2.
96 K. Bradley and A. Gelb, 'The Radical Potential of Cash Nexus Breaks', *British Journal of Sociology*, vol. 31, 1980.
97 An intellectual biography of Polanyi is desperately needed. His trajectory has its specificities, notably in having a Russian mother with populist sympathy, a Budapest childhood and experience of interwar 'Red Vienna'.
98 J. A. Hall, *International Orders*, Oxford, 1996.

politics. Second, Gellner's philosophy of history does not really comment on the causes of Europe's twentieth-century wars, thereby failing to give us an account of the autonomy of geopolitics. There are requisite elements, most obviously a theory of international relations, missing from his account of the taming of the forces of coercion.

9

The Sociology of Islam

Gellner devoted a very large part of his considerable energies to the study of Islam. The great labour which went into *Saints of the Atlas* was the mere tip of an iceberg, for his interest in Islam fanned out thereafter in many directions. This led to an engagement with French intellectual life, narrow at first but later with implications for his general social theory. As a teacher – at the LSE, as co-organizer, first with Ioan Lewis and then with Michael Gilsenan, of a postgraduate seminar for London University, and later at Cambridge – Gellner trained, as has been noted, a large number of researchers, the impact of whose work is only now being felt. He tirelessly supported research on Islamic societies. He served as president of the Maghreb Society, wrote two influential and widely cited books and more than thirty articles, reviewed more than fifty books, wrote prefaces for many monographs, fought for articles on Islam to be published in journals where he had influence, spoke at countless conferences and edited four collections of articles. He showed great interest in a series of Muslim societies, visiting and lecturing in Morocco, Algeria, Tunisia, Turkey and Lebanon, most notably, and took shorter trips to West Africa, Egypt, Jordan and Kazakhstan. His occasional pieces on some of these societies had a decisive intellectual impact.[1] All of this led to the synoptic essay 'Flux and Reflux in the Faith of Men' that forms the core of his *Muslim Society*. This was nothing less than a general theory of the workings of a whole civilization, that of the arid Mediterranean heartland of Islam – and in modern as well as pre-modern circumstances.[2] The political circumstances

---

1 Recent examples include H. Roberts, 'Ernest Gellner and the Algerian Army: The Intellectual Origins of the Problem of Algerian Studies in Britain', *The Journal of Algerian Studies*, vol. 2, 1997, and *The Battlefield: Algeria, 1988–2002, Studies in a Broken Polity*, Verso, 2002; D. Shankland, 'Integrating the Rural: Gellner and the Study of Anatolia', *Middle Eastern Studies*, vol. 35, 1999.

2 This is a careful formulation. Gellner insisted that his generalizations only applied to the arid zone of the classical core in which pastoralism played a major role; he suspected

of the time, most notably the revolution in Iran and the apparent 'revival' of Islam elsewhere, led to the book receiving considerable attention – and this fact also accounts in part for the hostility it provoked in some quarters. Finally, he sought to generalize about the condition of nomads in the rest of the world. The most obvious expression of this was his analysis of the way in which this mode of production had been treated by Soviet Marxist thinkers. At the time of his death, he was actively planning a conference on neglected Orientalist questions, including that of the role played by nomads from the East when moving into the West.

This is an impressive record of engagement, clear indication of both the importance in itself of Gellner's study of Islam, and as part of his general social theory. A contrast should be drawn here with his work in the sociology of nationalism. The constant fine-tuning of his view of nationalism is not matched in his work on Islam. Rather, his extensive writings mostly involve the spelling out of a single position; one has the feeling of a consistent theory rather than one replete with internal tensions.[3] This chapter begins by concentrating on Gellner's general theory of the workings of Islam, then considers the ways in which he sought to defend himself against his critics, and finally turns to an assessment of his contribution to this area of study. That review will consider his fieldwork in Morocco, as a standard charge against his general theory is that it is far too heavily based on the situation in North Africa.

The Pendulum Unhinged

'Flux and Reflux in the Faith of Men', the long synoptic essay that opens *Muslim Society*, offers a general theory of the classic core of the Islamic world.[4] In a sense it is curious that the formal presentation of this model came so late. *Saints of the Atlas* shows keen awareness of key elements of the social formation in question. More importantly, as early as 1964 David Hume's sociology of religion was part of Gellner's thinking as the key device

---

that Islam in Africa and Asia ran on entirely different lines. We will see that he sometimes ignored this careful specification.

3   It is thus possible to recognize the core of his general treatment of traditional Islam in the opening pages of *Saints of the Atlas*, London, 1969. This is not to deny the impact of his appropriation of David Hume's sociology of religion, merely to stress that this was a tool allowing for the construction of a particularly elegant model of traditional Muslim civilization. Equally, his early work shows awareness of the impact of reform within Islam, though here sustained attention to Algerian history clearly deepened his analysis of Islam's encounter with the social conditions of modernity.

4   *Muslim Society*, Cambridge, 1981.

for both understanding and presenting the nature of Islam. 'A Pendulum Swing Theory of Islam', published in 1969, served as a first version of the fully fledged theory published twelve years later.[5] The fact that Hume is not even mentioned in *Saints of the Atlas* perhaps indicates Gellner's desire to separate the particular from the general, his fieldwork from his more ambitious theorizing. The period after the publication of his first book – and particularly the academic year 1979–1980 at the Centre de Recherche et d'Études sur les Sociétés Méditerranéennes in Aix-en-Provence – was well spent, allowing for considerable deepening of his position. He absorbed many anthropological (but fewer historical) works on the Muslim world.[6] Still more important were the lessons learned from studying the reformist movement in Algeria, a topic that occupied Gellner a great deal in the early 1970s. We will see in a moment how this affected his account of Islam in the modern world. But before looking at how the pendulum became unhinged, it is necessary to understand the way in which allusion to this piece of machinery helps us, in Gellner's view, to understand pre-modern Islamic civilization.

We have already seen how important the work of David Hume was for Gellner's analysis of knowledge and social development. At the core of Gellner's ingenious use of Hume in the context of Islam is the view put forward in *A Natural History of Religion* of a ceaseless movement between monotheism and polytheism.[7] The rigour of monotheism gives rise to the mediations of polytheism, the excessive corruption of which then makes the purity of monotheism attractive again – but only for a while, of course, before the pendulum swings back again. This notion fits with the binary opposition between doctor and saint, and with the sociological principles of Ibn Khaldun, allowing Gellner a particular theory of oscillation within pre-modern Islam. But let us also recall the way that Gellner explores a tension in Hume's mind. On the one hand, Hume, as a member of the Enlightenment, admires polytheism, which is so close to paganism, on the grounds that it encourages toleration. On the other hand, he cannot bring himself, a Protestant Scot, to accept what he felt to be the corrupt polytheism of Catholicism, his own theory of knowledge resting upon an utterly rigorous, inner-directed sifting of impressions. Hume tried to find a way around this conflict when seeking to explain a certain anomaly – the fact

---

5 'Hume and North African Islam', in Centre of African Studies, University of Edinburgh, *Religion in Africa*, Edinburgh, 1964, and 'A Pendulum Swing Theory of Islam', in R. Robertson, *The Sociology of Religion*, London, 1969.

6 *Muslim Society*, p. vii.

7 'Flux and Reflux in the Faith of Men', pp. 7–16.

that the puritanical enthusiasm of the English and the Dutch did not lead to political intolerance.[8] Gellner refuses to accept Hume's view that this was due to the 'steady resolution of the civil magistrate'.[9] He turns instead to 'Of Superstition and Enthusiasm' for guidance, not least because Hume was himself ill at ease with his initial argument. The key phrase in Hume's essay contrasting enthusiastic monotheism with pluralist superstition is, as we have seen, that 'superstition is an enemy to civil liberty, and enthusiasm a friend to it'.[10] This, of course, directly and absolutely contradicts the earlier view, not least by suggesting that much more is involved than the attitude of the state. Gellner proposes a resolution to this dilemma, never discovered by Hume, which depends upon knowing the context within which enthusiasts are set: their views are labile, so to speak – they take on different political complexions according to different circumstances.

> [A]n 'enthusiastic' (monistic, puritan, scripturalistic) bourgeoisie may indeed be an enemy of liberty and a friend to the state, when caught between the state and tribesmen; while it may become a friend of liberty when it is weak enough to abandon hopes of imposing its forcible views on others, and yet has nothing other than the state monopoly of religion to fear, when the state has tamed or eliminated both baron and tribesman. It was perhaps this specific constellation which converted European enthusiasts to the value of liberty.[11]

A lack of this opposition at the level of social structure meant that the only movement within Islam was cyclical rather than developmental.[12]

'Flux and Reflux in the Faith of Men' joins together Hume's pendulum swing theory with the political sociology of Ibn Khaldun. The great fourteenth-century Muslim diplomat and scholar had noted a circulation of elites, such that a tribe, blessed with the solidarity that resulted from

---

8   Irish Catholics might well find this view complacent.

9   D. Hume, *A Natural History of Religion* [1777], Oxford, 1976, chapter 12.

10   D. Hume, 'Of Superstition and Enthusiasm', in *Essays Moral, Political and Literary* [1777], Oxford, 1963. Gellner notes accurately that the ideas of this essay also inform Hume's *A History of England*, Chicago, 1975.

11   'Flux and Reflux in the Faith of Men', p. 15.

12   Gellner's model of stagnation was consciously designed as an equivalent to the Marxist notion of the Asiatic mode of production. Gellner was very clear indeed that Muslim societies could not themselves be explained in terms of Wittfogel's hydraulic society thesis – making his point on several occasions with reference to R. Fernea, *Shaykh and Effendi*, Cambridge (MA), 1970 – which he reviewed in *Sociology*, vol. 5, 1971. See also 'Introduction', in B. O'Leary, *The Asiatic Mode of Production: Oriental Despotism, Historical Materialism and Indian History*, Oxford, 1989.

the rigours of pastoral life, was able to resist the selfish asociality of urban life – but only for about three generations, before it too succumbed to corruption. Still, this circulation of elites was not fully explained in *The Muqaddimah*, despite occasional perceptive comments about the role of religion. A ruling house becomes vulnerable when it is weak and corrupt, but it is only doomed when it comes to be seen as impious.[13] An unending political cycle gains its dynamic from the swing between religious styles. A learned doctor, revolted by the moral laxity of a city's rulers, can go out to the tribes, shame them into abandoning their ecstatic rituals, and so unite them.[14] If feuding is put aside, the united tribesmen become an impressive military force capable of attacking the city's rulers, and commanded to do so for religious reasons. A single tribe can then take over the urban government. But the social solidarity engendered by the harshness of desert and mountain life cannot be maintained in the city – nor can education serve to inculcate equivalent virtue. Thus the stagnant cycle of Muslim politics is set to begin once again.

Gellner sums up his position by saying, accurately, that the formula of Islamic civilization is that of a culture which is stronger, more extensive and more continuous than the political life of any state within it. He sought to explain the strength of that culture, especially in light of its surprisingly strong hold over tribesmen with entrenched heterodox practices. If one element at work here was the fact that Islamic norms were purportedly fixed once and for all, that the 'gates of interpretation' had been closed in such a way as to make the doctrine non-manipulable for political purposes, Gellner nonetheless stressed that sociological factors best explained the situation. A minor factor was the centrality of the pilgrimage. But the major sociological variable, in Gellner's eyes, was that the circulation of elites perpetually renewed the norms central to Islam. Certainly the cycle

---

13   Gellner admits ('Flux and Reflux in the Faith of Men', pp. 31–2) that oscillation between tribes and cities characterized the pre-Islamic world of North Africa, and he noted that the Soviet anthropologists Khazanov and Markov, whose work is discussed below, felt that this was also true for parts of Central Asia and Iran. But he insisted (p. 32) that the possession of a shared moral language mattered: 'One might say that Islam provided a common language and thus a certain kind of smoothness for a process which, in a more mute and brutalistic way, had been taking place anyway'. On this point, see P. Crone, 'The Tribe and the State', in J. A. Hall (ed.), *The State: Limited Concept*, vol. 1, London, 1993, pp. 472–3, footnote 128, for an argument that tribes had not had much impact before Islam, and could do so thereafter because the idiom of this religion originated in a tribal context and remained suitable for tribal use – suggesting that the impact of Islam was much greater than Gellner allows.

14   Gellner notes complexities to the picture ('Flux and Reflux in the Faith of Men', p. 49). Just as an urban cleric can become a missionary to the tribes, so a successful rural thaumaturge may acquire urban followers.

discouraged political interference with the *ulama* – so, of course, rein-forcing their authority.[15] The main form of social change that existed in the Muslim context helped to renew rather than to challenge its central normative tenets.

Gellner was well aware that the principles of Ibn Khaldun and Hume did not describe every social formation that existed within the traditional world of classical Islam.[16] The Ottoman Empire was long-lived, stable and powerful. This was made possible by a system of rule that had nothing to do with the solidarity of a particular ruling kin group. To the contrary, the rulers of society, both military and bureaucratic, were specially recruited and trained, and they were in theory cut off from their kin backgrounds as slaves recruited by a special levy, the *devshirme*, from the Christian commu-nities within the empire.[17] Gellner suggests an explanation for this curious system of rule by slaves, anticipated by the Mamluks and still symboli-cally practised in the French Protectorate when Gellner first travelled to Morocco. Bluntly, this system of rule does not refute the model that he had sketched. Ibn Khaldun had noted that government could work in a rather different way in the absence of tribesmen. Differently put, states developed real capacity when they were able to gain stable tax revenues from peasants tied to the land.[18] Indeed, the Ottomans had a political theory wholly different from that stressed by Ibn Khaldun. The 'Circle of Equity' stressed the importance of paying taxes so that the state could establish order – the essential precondition for the creation of the prosperity upon which taxa-tion rested. The point about this theory was that tribesmen did not feature at all, whereas peasants were its very essence. All of this is to say that Gellner recognized the presence of an alternative model within Islam. But this did not mean that he felt it to be dominant. He rejected both Perry Anderson's view that Ottoman-style rule replaced the imperfect system described by Ibn Khaldun, and Marshall Hodgson's view that the Khaldunian system was confined to the middle periods of Islamic history, that is, that it was a mere

15 'Flux and Reflux in the Faith of Men', pp. 79–80.

16 This paragraph draws on the discussion in ibid., pp. 73–7.

17 'Flux and Reflux in the Faith of Men' is structured around a discussion of Platonism, the key tenets of which were noted in chapter 3. Platonism 1 is the worship of pure concepts, and Platonism 2 the worship of concepts given substance by codification in a world religion. The Ottomans are seen as Platonism 3: here education and training rather than loyalty to concepts was the base of social cohesion.

18 Gellner notes ('Flux and Reflux in the Faith of Men', p. 75) that this factor helps explain this type of rule's success in the Fertile Crescent, in Anatolia, in Egypt and Tunisia. But he also noted that this rendered the success of Ottoman rule in Algeria all the harder to explain.

interlude between more settled periods of imperial rule.[19] The Ottoman system was unusual, but serious investigation often uncovered Khaldunian principles at work just beneath a veneer of stability.

This understanding of traditional Islam comprises only half of Gellner's general theory. Given that his work as a whole is best seen as an interpretation of modernity, it is scarcely surprising to find that his views – themselves partly the product of his experience in North Africa – are systematic about the relationship of Islam to modernity. Let us examine the evolution of those views, before turning to their treatment in *Muslim Society*.

From the start, Gellner's work expressed the realization that the puritanical option might be the more fruitful one in modern conditions, that the doctor might have a better hand to play than the saint. One crucial change was the greater effectiveness of the state: blessed with new military and transportation techniques, genuine penetration and control of an entire territory became a real possibility for the first time.[20] The second important change was ideological. He had witnessed the impact of Egypt's reform movement whilst undertaking his fieldwork in Morocco.[21] A long 1963 review essay considered the life and times of an urban saint, Shaikh Ahmed al-'Alawi (1869–1934), who witnessed epochal social change.[22] Al-'Alawi was under intense pressure to become more puritanical. The most significant source of this pressure was the fact that opposition to the French came to be led by puritanical *ulama*, whose nationalism included the idea that traditionalist, superstitious Islam should be reformed.

This is not to say that Gellner felt that the transition to modernity had only a single character. In 'Post-traditional Forms in Islam' he suggested that Islam itself comprised an ideological spectrum with strict adherence to the book at one end, and personal charisma at the other. In the early period of Islam, the puritanical extreme had been exemplified by the Kharejites, personal rule by the Shi'ites. In time, these extreme heresies were avoided, the tension between them represented by the contrast between *ulama* and sufi or saint. When addressing Islam in modern circumstances, Gellner's general concentration was on the legalistic and puritanical end of the spectrum, as we shall see, but the essay in question explored two successful

19 P. Anderson, *Lineages of the Absolutist State*, London, 1974, pp. 496–520 and M. Hodgson, *The Venture of Islam*, Chicago, 1974, discussed in 'Flux and Reflux in the Faith of Men', p. 77 and pp. 84–5 respectively.

20 But Gellner drew on the work of his research student Shelagh Weir to note an exception ('Flux and Reflux in the Faith of Men', p. 57). The power of the state in Yemen declined as outside parties provided arms and finance to competing tribes.

21 *Saints of the Atlas*, p. 17, where he cites J. Abun-Nasr, *The Tijaniyya*, Oxford, 1965.

22 'Sanctity, Puritanism, Secularisation and Nationalism', reprinted in *Muslim Society*.

versions of personal leadership within Islam. The economic success of the
Shi'a Ismailis is explained in terms of the political connections established
by the Aga Khans through mixing with upper-class British society. In
contrast, the success of the sufi-led Mourides of Senegal owed everything
to the political vacuum which allowed a group blessed with strong leadership to take advantage of particular economic opportunities.[23]

Nor did Gellner suggest that the triumph of puritanism was inevitable.
He argued in 1962's 'Patterns of rural rebellion in Morocco during the
early years of independence' that the oddity of rural movements – the speed
with which they collapsed, the leniency with which they were treated,
and the fact that they were often directed against a leader who the rebels
approved – could only be understood as posturing prior to a decisive battle
that would determine who would take power and transform society.[24] This
is, of course, a prime example of the general thesis that forced modernization has an elective affinity with non-democratic regimes.[25] But after
seven years of Moroccan independence, it was clear that a decisive outcome
was not imminent. Royal patronage was so skilfully handled that the forces
of opposition were neutralized.[26] Tunisia was equally an exception to the
general notion that modernity would lead to a clear and final victory for
the puritan and reformed end of the spectrum.[27] Like Morocco, Tunisia had
been a protectorate rather than a colony of France, and it scarcely had to
struggle for its independence. In consequence, its atmosphere was relatively
liberal. The middle class managed to survive the transition between regimes,
and this continuity set the tone for society as a whole. Even the trial of

---

23 'Post-traditional forms in Islam: the turf and trade, and votes and peanuts' (published
in 1973 and reprinted in *Muslim Society*) – in effect a review article of H. S. Morris, *The
Indians in Uganda*, London, 1968, and D. B. Cruise O'Brien, *The Mourides of Senegal*,
Oxford, 1970. Gellner's Weberian assumption was of course that the urban and legalistic
end of the spectrum was most conducive to economic success. This led him to review,
with great interest, J. Waterbury, *North for the Trade: The Life and Times of a Berber Merchant*,
Berkeley, 1972 in *Middle Eastern Studies*, vol. 13, 1977. The economic success of the Swasa
confounded his view in that they were tribesmen – although they were at least attracted to
the reformist end of the continuum.
24 This essay – but, curiously, not the self-critical companion piece 'The Great Patron'
(*European Journal of Sociology*, vol. 10, 1969) – was reprinted in *Muslim Society*.
25 *Thought and Change*, London, 1964, and 'Democracy and Industrialization', in
Contemporary Thought and Politics, London, 1974. Gellner's argument on this point is noted
above, in chapter 5.
26 'The Great Patron'.
27 'A Tunisian Visit', *New Society*, vol. 1, 1963. This essay suggests that Tunisia might
become the Denmark of the Maghreb. It contrasts the relaxed style of the Kerkennah
islands with the Weberian puritanism characteristic of the sectarian Ibadis of Djerba.

Ahmed Ben Salah, the leftist politician in charge of socialist experiments in the countryside, was seen by Gellner as insufficient to qualify the regime, for all the effectiveness of its one-party rule, as genuinely totalitarian. The sentence handed down was lenient, whilst there was irony – especially in comparison to the contemporaneous trial of Dubček in Czechoslovakia – in the fact that laissez-faire rather than socialist policies were inaugurated by a show trial.[28] In general, Gellner considered Tunisia to be effectively Kemalist and secular. He felt that Tunisians were at ease with their own identity, a condition that might well help bring about the eventual liberalization of their society.[29]

But these cases were seen as exceptional. The relations of Islam to modernity were better illustrated by developments in Algeria – which he visited on several occasions, taking care also to maintain contact with officials of the newly independent country who were posted abroad. Recording his initial impression of independent Algeria, Gellner noted that the state was bound to dominate society given the huge exodus of the *pied-noirs* and the resulting need to nationalize much of industry.[30] A decade later, Gellner found that Algeria was still marked by the brutality of its independence struggle. In contrast to Tunisia, the single-party regime was relatively weak, and the tone of society set by the *ulama* – still benefiting from the fact that they had played a crucial role in national liberation. Two broad interest groups could be identified, a capitalist middle class and a military-industrial complex, but curiously these did not seem to come into conflict. This suggested to Gellner a continuation of the historic pattern, with the army comprising a new form of Mamluk rule. Beyond this he noted that the programme of forced Arabization faced a considerable difficulty in that those members of the elite who could afford it made sure that their children became fluent in French.[31] These considerations, combined with a further visit and reflections on recent historical research, led to an important article on 'The Unknown Apollo of Biskra'. It begins with an account of André Gide's visit to a decidedly non-puritanical saintly shrine in Biskra, but rapidly shifts its attention to the Islamic reform movement in Algeria. If the intellectual leader of this movement was Ben Badis, a considerable role was also played by Tayyib Uqbi. This firebrand began his career preaching against the very laxity of morals in Biskra that Gide had so much enjoyed.

28 Gellner (as 'Philip Peters'), 'Tunisia: A System on Trial?', *New Society*, vol. 16, 1970.
29 'Cohesion and Identity: the Maghreb from Ibn Khaldun to Emile Durkheim', in *Muslim Society*, p. 95.
30 'Thy Neighbour's Revolution', *New Society*, vol. 1, 1963.
31 Gellner (as 'Philip Peters'), 'Algeria after Independence', *New Society*, vol. 20, 1972.

Gellner sought to explain why the reform movement succeeded. The fact that the saints were implicated in colonial rule certainly helped turn the tide against them, but this was scarcely the key consideration – political opportunism was also evident amongst the reformers. Equally, the fact that more than a century of colonial rule had destroyed local elites enhanced the position of the *ulama*: they filled a social vacuum.[32] But most important was a change in the social function of religious leaders. Tribesmen had respected saints when their activities – from mediation to the protection of the market, and in combination with a relative lack of puritanism – had been useful in their daily lives. Colonial rule left the saints with privileges whilst depriving them of their social function – thereby replicating the resentment directed, at least in the eyes of Tocqueville, at the aristocrats of late-eighteenth-century France.[33] In these circumstances the heterodox and lax style of the saints became generally offensive, not least as the colonialists themselves made fun at their expense. Further, the fact that saints were locally based means that they were incapable of creating any sort of national consciousness. But that is exactly what the *ulama* could provide. Further, they could inspire pride by pointing to the dignity of a great civilization, and make it clear that its general ethic not only is not backward, but is eminently suited to modernity.

> The obligatory prayers and the fast may be a bit of a nuisance, but, unlike ecstatic festivals or reliance on saintly intercession, they do teach a man a bit of discipline, which is a most desirable trait in an industrial worker. They teach him that rules in books are there to be obeyed, and that bringing donations to shrines will get him nowhere. Why not try orderly *literate* prayer and work, instead? For good Weberian reasons, it seems that modernisation may just as well be done with Islam as against it – provided it is the right kind of Islam . . . [34]

Gellner concludes that Algeria has become a modern society, but insists that it is modern in its Islamism, not in its secularization. He liked to illustrate the key general change with reference to the position of women, veiled more often in urban than in rural conditions.[35] This view of Algerian

32 'The Unknown Apollo of Biskra', in *Muslim Society*, p. 166.
33 Ibid., p. 161. Tocqueville's analysis is in *The Old Regime and the French Revolution*, New York, 1955. Cf. H. Arendt, *The Origins of Totalitarianism*, New York, 1958, 'Part One: Anti-Semitism'.
34 'The Unknown Apollo of Biskra', p. 170.
35 Ibid., p. 173. He made continual use of V. Maher, *Women and Property in Morocco*, Cambridge, 1974, not least in this essay, pp. 162–5.

developments has been challenged by Hugh Roberts, as will be seen later in this chapter.

These cases demonstrate that Gellner's theorizing was not always conducted at an abstract level. In the case of Islam, this was most certainly not the case: he knew North African societies extremely well, and we will see in a moment that he made striking guesses about other Muslim societies.[36] Still, *Muslim Society* does cite the findings from Algeria in order to underline a series of abstract considerations. It does so essentially by reference to the classical difficulties of later modernizers – difficulties he had first encountered when dealing with the ideology of the earliest Moroccan nationalists. The desire to catch up in developmental terms creates a terrible dilemma. Those who choose to Westernize can find their own feelings of inferiority enhanced by the fact that they adopt so much from the world they rebelled against. But the alternative populist position, seeking roots internal to the native tradition, has the dreadful drawbacks of implausibility and inefficacy.[37] Islam, in Gellner's view, avoids this dilemma. Adoption of the high tradition of law, literacy and discipline is seen as a route to modernity. Muslims can be modern since their religion serves as a superb protestant ethic. Gellner puts the matter in the strongest possible terms:

> The distinctive pattern of distribution of scripturalist puritanism and of hierarchical ecstatic mediationist styles in Islam may help to explain *both* why industrial society failed to be born within it, *and* why Islam may be in the end so adaptable to industrial society, perhaps more so than the faith which provided it with its historical matrix. Egalitarian scripturalism is more suited to a mobile technical society than ascriptive, mediationist, manipulative spiritual brokerage. To *engender* industrialisation, it is presumably best if the scripturalism is insulated and protected in a more or less peripheral part of the older society, within which a new world can emerge in a relatively undisturbed way. But to *survive* in conditions of emulative industrialisation, it may be better if the scripturalism is at the very centre rather than at the periphery, and can slough off the peripheral styles as superstitions and unworthy accretions – thereby simultaneously affirming its own continuity and local roots *and* explaining away its political and economic retardation. It can then simultaneously affirm an ancient identity *and* justify a strenuous Leap Forward.[38]

---

36 He claimed a sense of ease when dealing with Muslim societies (J. Davis, 'An Interview with Ernest Gellner', *Current Anthropology*, vol. 32, 1991, p. 70).

37 In this context he notes that the populists of Islam are not Muslim city-dwellers, but Westerners admiring 'noble' tribesmen ('Flux and Reflux in the Faith of Men', p. 63).

38 Ibid., p. 65.

The success of Marxism had been explained by its capacity to act as a modern Weberian ethic; the survival and transformation of Islam is equally explained by its capacity to act as a protestant ethic suited to modernity.

Gellner's claim is that the puritanical option is dominant within Islam, thereby making Islam, alone amongst the world religions, secularization-resistant. A series of observations followed from this framework. To begin with, a contrast is drawn between the fundamentalism of traditional elites and that of social radicals. In the former camp belong both Saudi Arabia and Northern Nigeria, unsurprisingly since both regimes were created as a result of the last turn of the Khaldunian cycle.[39] He thought that the latter camp was exemplified by the Libya of Muammar Gaddafi, whose power is seen as resulting from a combination of the old regime's collapse and the availability of oil monies.[40] The key point that Gellner makes about the Libyan situation is that it is potentially very radical indeed. Despite the fact that in the traditional world the *ulama* had been dependent on tribes, their role as sole representatives of the law and their ability to call in tribesmen meant that they provided some counterbalance to the state. In Libya, this may no longer be the case: the attempt to undermine the tribes in the name of the people might lead to the state becoming utterly pre-eminent. Gellner suggests a different character for each of these two versions of fundamentalism – the one more confident as the result of indirect rule, the other born of powerlessness as the result of direct colonial rule; the former may be more obviously political, but the latter is likely to be more austere and inwardly-directed.[41] He made a final, theoretical suggestion, perhaps as a reaction to the Iranian revolution: there may be two stages to the fundamentalism of those countries that had experienced direct colonial rule. If the first was nationalist in its opposition to foreign domination and against lax traditional Islam, the second may be a genuine and altogether less restrained movement of the dispossessed directed against internal enemies.[42]

All of this is set against the awareness that there were indeed Westernizers within the Muslim world. Here again, there is a distinction that must be made. Morocco represents, of course, less Westernization than a moderate version of Islam – but its traditionalist dislike of social radicalism makes it

---

39   Ibid., pp. 65–6.
40   Ibid., pp. 63–4 and 'Revolution and Revelation' (a review of L. Anderson, *The State and Social Transformation in Tunisia and Libya, 1830–1980*), *New Republic*, vol. 195, 1986.
41   'Flux and Reflux in the Faith of Men', pp. 65–6.
42   Gellner notes that class conflict only turns revolutionary if it can conceptualize itself in ethnic or religious terms (ibid., pp. 66–7). Iran had not formally been colonized, but Gellner argued that the cosmopolitan and Westernizing style of the Persian ruling class made it seem as if this had been the case.

otherwise akin to Saudi Arabia. The fate of the Ottomans was very different. Unlike in other parts of the Islamic world, religion had been shackled to the imperial state: this meant that religion could not drive nationalism. But nationalist questions remained vital. The communities preserved by Ottoman rule were able to secede and thereafter to nationalize their own territories – with the Lebanon proving to be an exception in that rival communities destroyed the state and faced each other in perpetual conflict.[43] Kemalist Turkey itself was led by a state strengthened in military victory; in consequence, it was able to combine social radicalism (changing the alphabet and the position of women) with an insistence on secularism – or at least a determination to make religious belief a private matter. Gellner stressed that the Turkish attempt to combine democracy with secularism seemed doomed to instability, at least until a full transition to industrial society had been made. If elections led to the success of Muslim parties, the army was prepared to step in and secure Turkey's secular route to modernity. He noted with amusement that Nur Yalman, a particularly sophisticated Turkish anthropologist, was prepared to consider rural and permissive Islam as a progressive alternative to the military. This was akin to the urban middle classes wearing traditional costume, for 'refined, urban-apartment Sufism is no longer the same as the annual pilgrimage/festival of a tribal segment'.[44]

Additional Writings and Replies to Critics

Gellner did not undertake more fieldwork in North Africa after the early 1960s, in part due to health reasons and in part because permission to undertake such anthropological research became more difficult to obtain. His continuing interest in Muslim societies was largely expressed through exercises in intellectual history and through vigorous attempts to defend his views.

He showed particular and long-standing interest in debates about the nature of pastoral nomadism – going back to the distinction drawn in *Saints of the Atlas* between marginal and primitive tribalism, that is, between those with and those without knowledge of an alternative social world.[45] He pleaded for comparative studies of nomadism, and especially for particular

---

43   Ibid., p. 59.
44   Ibid., p. 60. The analysis of the Ottoman exception and of Kemalism is spelled out in more detail in 'Kemalism', in *Encounters with Nationalism*, Oxford, 1994, and 'The Turkish Option in Comparative Perspective', in S. Bozdogan and R. Kesaba (eds), *Rethinking Modernity and National Identity in Turkey*, Seattle, 1997.
45   *Saints of the Atlas*, pp. 1–2.

attention to be paid to the history of the Far East.[46] All of this guaranteed that Gellner's research on Soviet thought would include attention to the place of pastoral nomadism in the Marxist scheme of historical development.[47] His particular focus was on those writers who were examining pre-modern Central Asia, massively transformed under Soviet rule. Pastoral nomads present a problem for Marxism in possessing private property in herds whilst at the same time sharing pasture land and professing basic egalitarian attitudes. Moreover, their political organization presents a further problem in being either too small (stateless even though private property exists) or far too large (the empire of Genghis Khan can scarcely be explained by examining settled property relations). Finally, relatively brief moments of imperial activity are often reversed, leaving no trace in the historical record; the conundrum for Marxism is that empires rose and fell without much development taking place.

Gellner noted various stages to the debate. B. Y. Vladimirtsov's classic position saw pastoral nomadism as a combination of patriarchalism and feudalism. There were considerable difficulties with this view: the stage was seen as transitional between modes of production without much speci-fication of those modes, let alone of the mechanisms of transition involved. Accordingly, the work of L. P. Potapov was more impressive to him as a piece of Marxist scholarship. Nomads were here seen as passing through three clearly specified stages, with the transitions between each of them resting securely on material factors. This was a political position, especially in light of how the barbaric Soviet treatment of nomads was justified in terms of the necessities of historical progress. As it happens, dissenting views that were more intellectually interesting did not prove to be as dangerous as had been the case in the debates on the Asiatic mode of production.[48] This allowed S. E. Tolybekov to produce various studies of Kazakh nomads which made a permanent contribution to the literature. At the heart of Tolybekov's work was a reiteration of the way in which nomads combined some private property with fierce egalitarianism, together with a realization that this mode of production was not 'progressive' in the requisite Marxist

---

46   'Introduction: Approaches to Nomadism', in C. Nelson, *The Desert and the Sown*, Berkeley, 1973, notes the book's lack of consideration of the work of Owen Lattimore. Gellner followed the work of many scholars of nomadism, amongst them G. Dahl and A. Hjort on East Africa, T. Ingold on the herding of reindeer, and, most importantly, the Soviet scholars to whom our attention now turns.

47   Discussion of Gellner's untangling of this debate is drawn from his 'Introduction' to A. M. Khazanov, *Nomads and the Outside World*, Cambridge, 1984 (reprinted as 'The Nomadism Debate' in *State and Society in Soviet Thought*, Oxford, 1988).

48   'The Nomadism Debate', p. 104.

sense – something which justified, for Tolybekov, benign intervention by Soviet authorities. This view would become mainstream, even though it could not – given its essential contradiction of Marxist doctrine – be much bruited about. It is present in the work of G. E. Markov and especially in that of A. M. Khazanov, first in his book on the Scythians and then in his later *Nomads and the Outside World*. This pleased Gellner, but it would be a mistake to see his involvement with Soviet scholars on this issue as merely a search for confirmation of his own views. He was deeply impressed with Khazanov's scholarship, and delighted by the Malinowski Memorial Lecture in which Khazanov compared Muhammad with Genghis Khan.[49] The 1994 conference on the Muslim states of Central Asia was to have been followed by a more ambitious undertaking dealing with the other Orientalism – that is, the impact of nomads on the polities of Eastern and Central Europe.

A second work of intellectual history was that of establishing the proper genealogy of ideas which were crucial to understanding the study of North Africa. He had read Masqueray's *Formation des cités chez les populations séden-taires de l'Algérie* as the result of Montagne's generous acknowledgement of this work, but *Saints of the Atlas* shows no sign of any fully developed tracing of his own intellectual ancestors. The republication of Masqueray's book in 1983, nearly a century after its first appearance and with a preface by Gellner's friend Fanny Colonna, a historical sociologist of Algeria, led him to this genealogical exercise.[50] Masqueray provides superb evidence of the swings between fusion and fission in Berber tribal life in North Africa, but he did not fully theorize his own observations. Nonetheless, his work opened up a path to such theorization. One route from Masqueray led to Durkheim, whose *Division of Labour in Society* makes a distinction between basic lateral segmentation, in which clans are formed of similar groups which happen to be juxtaposed to each other, and vertical segmentation, a more advanced form in which cohesion is created by joining together units of different size. Durkheim was less interested in this second form, but it provided the core of Evans-Pritchard's theory of segmentation. If that connection was underplayed because of Evans-Pritchard's opposition to Durkheimian principles, so too was a second lineage – which led from Masqueray to Montagne and thence to Berque and to Raymond Jamous, and, in America, to Carleton Coon and to David Hart. Here the problem was twofold. Intellectually, Montagne's obsession with the role of *leffs*, noted in chapter two, underplayed the importance of balance by use of the principles of segmentary organization. Politically, Montagne came to be discredited as the French retreated from empire, especially as new fashions in anthropology were either abstract (the structuralism of Lévi-Strauss) or so convinced of Marxist categories that the Maghreb was deemed feudal.

Establishing this much of a genealogy was simple. Gellner's full intellectual powers were brought to bear on a matter of much greater complexity, namely that of the relation between Masqueray, the analyst of Berber community, and Fustel de Coulanges, the theorist of ancient Greek and Roman communities in his *The Ancient City* (1864). Both were alumni of the École Normale Supérieure, but only Fustel returned to teach at that institution (from which position he influenced Durkheim). Despite all this, Masqueray never referred to Fustel. Gellner suggests that he rejected Fustel's view that the birth of political forms had anything to do with religious development – in this going even further than Durkheim. 'Fustel had made religion essential *and* primary. Durkheim had made it essential but not primary. For Masqueray, it was *neither*'.[51] If this view underwrote the secularism of French administration of the Algerian Berbers, with which Masqueray was involved, his work allowed for the possibility that French policy might preserve local Berber culture. Where Fustel's view that each community had its own system of meaning would have had difficulty with the fact of tribesmen and urban dwellers sharing a religious idiom, Masqueray's position made it possible to at least recognize the basic two-in-one character of North African Islam. Masqueray could of course have used this material for a direct onslaught on Fustel, but he did not do so – perhaps because of his peripheral position in French intellectual life.[52]

Another exercise in intellectual history concerned Islam and the nature

---

51 'The Roots of Cohesion', p. 39.

52 Hugh Roberts, an LSE colleague, challenged Gellner on this point, to the latter's considerable irritation, when the first of his two papers was read in 1991 at a meeting of the Society of Moroccan Studies at the School of Oriental and Africa Studies, chaired by Gellner who was then the president of the society. See H. Roberts, 'Perspectives on Berber Politics: On Gellner and Masqueray, or Durkheim's Mistake', *Journal of the Royal Anthropological Institute*, vol. 8, 2002, and '*De la segmentarité á l'opacité: Á propos de Gellner et Bourdieu et les approches théoriques à l'analyse du champ politique algérien*', *Insāniyāt: Revue algérienne d'anthropologie et de sciences sociales*, vol. 8, 2003. Roberts endorsed Gellner's findings on Morocco, including its explanatory base in the theory of segmentation. But he felt that these did not apply to Algeria. These papers argue that the Berbers of Algeria had a political culture that allowed for the provision of order and stability, that is, that segmentary theory did not apply to the Kabyles. Crucially, he felt that the tradition that went from Masqueray to Montagne was aware of Kabyle political culture, making Gellner's account of Masqueray's work misguided.

of civil society. Gellner began by contrasting Machiavelli and Tocqueville.[53] Machiavelli noted the ease with which a European feudal kingdom could be conquered, in large part because powerful barons might ally with an invader; but such a kingdom would be difficult to rule precisely because of the continuing sources of resistance in the localities. The situation was reversed in the Ottoman Empire: conquest was made difficult by the greater power of the central state, but rule – should conquest be achieved – was rendered unproblematic by the absence of secondary sources of power. Tocqueville made the exact opposite argument. The removal of the Ottomans from Algeria did not make administration after 1830 easy, for the French faced the prolonged tribal rebellion led by Amir Abd el-Kader. Gellner was delighted by the paradoxical answer that he was able to give – that both had been correct – when seeking to explain the contradiction between the two thinkers, for it supported his key contentions about Islam. Machiavelli was correct because he was writing about the Ottomans, who had indeed created systematic central rule; but Tocqueville's insights were equally true because they referred to the Khaldunian world, whose centrality to – and mode of operation within – classical Islam he had sought to explain. This interpretation led him to make two interesting points about Islam and the nature of civil society. First, he drew a contrast between, in effect, absolutism and despotism – that is, between the powers of states in the Occident and in the Orient. European absolutism was essentially rule-bound, and so eventually permitted civil society to emerge. In contrast, the altogether more arbitrary rule of Islamic states, whether long-lasting or transient, did much to atomize social relations. This consideration is liable to lead to error unless it is linked to a second one. Traditional Muslim society was not in fact completely bereft of the power of self-organization. Very much to the contrary, extended kinship played a role, and was perhaps necessary due to both the fact that states were not rule-bound and lacked capacity to provide much order in large parts of the territory they supposedly ruled. But the caging quality of the 'republic of cousins' was as much a danger to civil society as was despotism. Even the slight check to political power caused by the rotation of the elite did not lead to genuine social innovation. So civil society was different, resting on a particular sort of group – open and elective – whose operations could then balance the state. A corollary of this general view was that Gellner stood apart from many recent theorists of liberalism (such as Berlin) in refusing to give much weight to Benjamin Constant's essay on 'The Liberty of the Ancients compared with that of the Moderns'.[54]

---

53 *Conditions of Liberty: Civil Society and Its Rivals*, London, 1994, pp. 81–6.
54 B. Constant, *Political Writings*, Cambridge, 1988.

Constant only stressed that ancient liberty was not *individual* liberty, and in fact opposed such liberty; but he did not specify the role of social sub-groups and their heavy ritualization in the process *both* of depriving the individual of freedom *and* of maintaining social order in the absence of a strong coercive centre. It is *this* perception which makes Fustel the ancestor of modern 'segmentary' theory, of the understanding of a society which *is* plural, but *not*, in our required sense, 'civil'.[55]

In his last years, Gellner drew a further and related contrast between Marxism and Islam. If both ideologies were suited for modernity in their capacity as ersatz protestant ethics, the way that they created moral codes, capable of offering complete guidance for the conduct of social life, was just as important. This view was contested by Talal Asad on the grounds that traditional Islam did not have the capacity, present in most modern states, to actually put its moral project into effect.[56] Gellner accepted this point – as he was bound to do given his awareness of the weakness of pre-industrial rule, and his acceptance of a Khaldunian view of loss of moral virtue – but then sought to specify his charge:

> But the crucial point is: can one usefully compare the modern socialist state with the traditional Muslim one? One must compare a modern socialist state with a modern Muslim one. Then the comparison becomes more illuminating. In both cases there is an atomised civil society, a strong and moralistic state, committed to the implementation of an overall vision, which is justified as the agency which implements that vision and is charged with leading mankind to a true fulfilment. It has a bias in favour of substantive, rather than merely procedural justice.[57]

We have already seen that Gellner noted variety within the Islamic world once the pendulum was unhinged: the power of the *ulama* looked set to be completely undermined in Libya, whilst even in Algeria they did not actually run the state. But the point in question was utterly exemplified for him by the rule of clerics in Iran. If part of the explanation for the success of Khomeini lay in the way that the particular Shi'ite myth of martyrdom could mobilize the people, Gellner's interpretation stressed that the views of

55   'The Importance of Being Modular', in J. A. Hall (ed.), *Civil Society: Theory, History, Comparison*, Cambridge, 1995, p. 54.
56   T. Asad, 'The Idea of an Anthropology of Islam', reprinted in J. A. Hall and I. C. Jarvie (eds), *The Social Philosophy of Ernest Gellner*, Amsterdam, 1996, p. 396.
57   'Human Rights and the New Circle of Equity', in F. D'Agostino and I. C. Jarvie (eds), *Freedom and Rationality*, Dordrecht, 1989, p. 139.

the Ayatollah represented a move within Shi'ism towards a more standard Sunni Islamic position.[58] Legitimacy in Shi'ism had been held in abeyance, whilst waiting for the appearance of a hidden Imam. The writings of Khomeini suggested to Gellner that legitimacy had now come to be seen in terms of the implementation of the law; such implementation was possible *now*, and the arrival of an Imam would simply transfer power rather than change the terms of reference entirely.[59] All of this underwrote Gellner's view of Islam's strength in the modern world.[60] On the one hand, the fact that it was a moral *Weltanschauung* meant it made no sense of the notion of universal human rights – for here was a civilization which conceptualized morality in terms which were not our own.[61] On the other hand, reformed Islam in general looked set to weather those social changes of modernity that had destroyed the Soviet Union. The trouble with Marxism was perhaps not so much its sense of the sacred but rather its lack of any sense of the profane. Differently put, Marxism asked to be judged by its role in this world, and so could be found wanting by means of a clear and absolute test. Islam had not tied its hands in this way, and hence could not be so easily defeated.[62]

The ingenuity apparent in these extensions of his views on Islam was just as present in his attempts to defend himself against his critics. A first defence concerned the historical record. Gellner admitted that he paid more attention to the social anthropology than to the history of Muslim societies, but he nonetheless sought to defend himself against the charge that his views lacked historical sense.[63] One general accusation was that

---

58 'Inside Khomeini's Mind', *New Republic*, vol. 190, 1984 (reprinted in *Culture, Identity and Politics*) and 'Human Rights and the New Circle of Equity'.

59 The most powerful critique of Gellner's sociology of Islam – S. Zubaida, 'Is There a Muslim Society? Ernest Gellner's Sociology of Islam', *Economy and Society*, vol. 24, 1995 – argued that Gellner was absolutely wrong in this matter, stressing instead the personalism of Khomeini's claim to power.

60 It is impossible to resist a moment's digression to compare Gellner's response to Khomeini with Foucault's. Gellner opened his article with a series of quotes, many of them anti-Semitic, designed to show that the force of Khomeini was allied to vicious intolerance. Foucault's articles for *Corriere della sera*, *Le Monde* and *Le Nouvel Observateur* (collected in J. Afary and K. B. Anderson, *Foucault and the Iranian Revolution: Gender and the Seductions of Islamism*, Chicago, 2005) show by contrast a dreadful – and orientalist! – naïvety.

61 'Human Rights and the New Circle of Equity', p. 140.

62 This point was made several times in Gellner's late writings, e.g., 'Islam and Marxism: Some Comparisons', *International Affairs*, vol. 67, 1991; 'Homeland of the Unrevolution', *Daedalus*, vol. 122, 1993; *Conditions of Liberty*, London, 1996; and 'Fundamentalism as a Comprehensive System: Soviet Marxism and Islamic Fundamentalism Compared', in S. Appleby and M. Marty (eds), *Fundamentalisms Compared*, Chicago, 1995.

63 *Muslim Society*, p. vii.

his model depended too much on his North African data, and that he was insufficiently aware of historical diversity within Islam.[64] Gellner's response to this – admitting the Ottomans as an exception, suggesting that Khaldunian features were only just below the surface elsewhere – has already been noted. A more particular matter concerned the history of the saints of the Moroccan Atlas. Historical material was provided by Berque's important book on the seventeenth-century saint Al-Youssi, and by Magali Morsy's discovery of an English renegade's account of early-eighteenth-century Moroccan saints' political activities – all of which was supplemented by the Moroccan historian Abdallah Hammoudi who drew attention to a series of neglected documents.[65] According to Gellner this was a welcome and valuable 're-historicisation of the ethnography'.[66] This was not really an adequate response; Hammoudi in particular had stressed that the saintly centres came to prominence less as mediators than, so to speak, by favour of one particular tribe, together with the fact that their history showed them to have been at times very far from pacific. As it happens, Gellner could have replied to these specific points. On the one hand, the social origin of the saintly centres by no means necessarily undermined his account of their eventual social role, given that they did not continually favour a single tribe: in this matter, cause and function can be properly distinguished. On the other hand, Gellner always affirmed that the saints were putatively pacifist – which is to say that he knew there had been exceptions, and in any case stressed that unity between the different tribes was sometimes created by a rural saint rather than an urban reformer. A second and more sustained response was forthcoming, however, when dealing with Clifford Geertz's periodization of Moroccan religious history, particularly when this came to be accepted as established lore.[67] Geertz suggested that 'the maraboutic

---

64   This was a very general charge, as in the reviews of *Muslim Society* by Berque, 'The popular and the purified', *Times Literary Supplement*, 11 December 1981, and F. Halliday, 'Muslim Society's Model World', *Manchester Guardian Weekly*, 26 July 1981.

65   M. Morsy, *Les Ahansala*, Paris, 1972 (reviewed by Gellner in *L'Annuaire de l'Afrique du Nord*, vol. 11, 1972), J. Berque, *Al-Yousi: Problèmes de la culture marocaine au XVIIeme siècle*, Paris, 1958 and A. Hammoudi, 'Segmentarity, Social Stratification, Political Power and Sainthood: Reflections on Gellner's Theses', reprinted in Hall and Jarvie, *The Social Philosophy of Ernest Gellner*.

66   'Reply to Critics', in Hall and Jarvie, *The Social Philosophy of Ernest Gellner*, p. 656.

67   Gellner, 'Saints and Their Descendants', in *Muslim Society*. This piece is largely a review of P. Rabinow, *Symbolic Domination: Cultural Form and Historical Change in Morocco*, Chicago, 1975, a book which Gellner considered to have uncritically accepted Geertz's position. Further comments on the dangers of 'culture-talk' are contained in an unpublished piece in the Gellner Archive entitled '*L'Année dernière à Meknes*'. This piece is of especial interest in that the author of whom Gellner is critical, Vincent Crapanzo, had – in his *Tuhami,*

crisis' of the seventeenth century, that is, the period marked by charismatic revivals in which one dynasty collapsed and a new one was born, led to fundamental change: pure, miraculous charisma came to be replaced by routinized, hereditary charisma.[68] This was a view that Gellner could not accept:

> [I]t seems to me most doubtful whether the seventeenth century was such a watershed, whether there is any such tension, whether magic and ancestry were opposed, and whether indeed either of them could, for any length of time, operate on its own. Ancestry alone either overproduces leadership and thus brings about an inflationary devaluation of its currency (as often happens), or, in conjunction with primogeniture or some other form of restrictive rule . . . becomes too rigid. Magic on its own is too liberal: by permitting free entry into the market . . . it leads to excessive instability and goes against the grain of a kinship-oriented society. The most viable mix is a judicious blend . . . [69]

Gellner also noted how illegitimate it is to draw conclusions about saints in general from evidence derived from Morocco – a corollary of which is that evidence of saintly behaviour elsewhere may allow particular Moroccan events to be put into a larger context.[70] This is not to say that Gellner was unprepared to accept that a change in idiom, in terms of a stress on descent from the Prophet, was datable. 'But this change of idiom of genealogy is something quite different from the alleged confluence of previously separate magical and genealogical principles, an idea which seems both implausible and speculative'.

Gellner spent the most time defending segmentary theory as the essential tool for understanding the sociology of Berber tribal society. There seems to be agreement that Gellner became devoted to segmentary theory at the moment when it was losing its salience within social anthropology in general.[71] This did not diminish the vigour of his defence. In order to

---

Portrait of a Moroccan, London, 1980 – relied on the assistant formerly employed by Gellner and by David Hart. Gellner drew a contrast between the Moroccan's love of clarity and the narcissistic epistemological cloudiness of the Western anthropologist.

68 C. Geertz, *Islam Observed: Religious Development in Morocco and Indonesia*, Chicago, 1969, p. 44.

69 'Saints and Their Descendants', p. 210.

70 'The Marabouts in the Marketplace', in *Muslim Society*, p. 217.

71 W. Kraus, 'Contestable Identities: Tribal Structures in the Moroccan High Atlas', *Journal of the Royal Anthropological Society*, vol. 4, 1998, and the various works of Munson cited below, make this point. Gellner did not cite nor address the criticism of segmentary theory made by Emrys Peters – 'Some structural aspects of the feud among the camel-herding Bedouin of Cyrenaica', *Africa*, vol. 37, 1967 – even though this appeared before the publication of *Saints of the Atlas*.

see what is involved, it is necessary to draw a distinction here, for Gellner rightly felt himself to be assailed from two rather different quarters.

One line of attack was launched by Clifford Geertz in his review of *Saints of the Atlas*.[72] In Geertz's view, kinship alliance was a mere idiom, an ideological superstructure explaining little about the social reality of North African society. Gellner made at least three counter-arguments. First, he objected strongly to the vague and ineffable 'cloud-culture-talk' to which the Geertzian school of anthropologists of Morocco was prone.[73] Second, he drew a distinction between a world in which kinship ruled and one in which dyadic patronage relations did indeed come to the fore – and insisted that the latter principle was related to modernity's increase in the power of the state. The point here was that the very notion of segmentation as mere idiom depended upon the ability to contrast it with a world in which it had once been the dominant form of social organization.[74] Third, Gellner noted that the rule of Ahmad Bey in nineteenth-century Tunisia depended upon insulating rulers from contacts outside their own circle. This suggested that segmentation must have been a reality rather than cover for a patronage system. 'Had optimal, dyadic patronage been the norm, the system as a whole would have been highly unstable and unpredictable, and the insulation of the top ruling group could not have worked at all'.[75] It should also be noted that a powerful justification for using the concept of 'tribe' is now available; it will stand at the back of the discussion in the rest of this chapter.[76]

---

72   C. Geertz, 'In Search of North Africa', *New York Review of Books*, vol. 16, 1971, p. 20. It is not at all clear why Geertz's praise for Gellner's work in *Islam Observed* – which cites Gellner's doctoral thesis (p. 51) and refers to it as 'a fine study of a saint cult in action' (p. 124) – had been abandoned a mere two years later, especially since there was no fundamental difference between Gellner's doctorate and *Saints of the Atlas*. For the review was essentially hostile, considering Gellner 'an old believer' in some simple view of the facticity of external reality, possessed of a finished theory of segmentation that he sought to apply mechanically. The review rankled, and Gellner later fought back ('Reply to Critics', pp. 640, 645), insisting that there was, contrary to 'subjectivist-relativist fads', an external reality to be investigated and that he had not gone into the field possessed of any pre-conceived theory.

73   'The Marabouts in the Marketplace', p. 218. He clearly enjoyed pointing to an inconsistency within this school's attack on the notion of social structure ('Reply to Critics', p. 654). The varied works of L. Rosen paint a picture of clever individuals making up their world as they go along; this sits uneasily with 'the culturalism which dismisses structure altogether as the invention of the conceptually imperialist anthropologist unwittingly serving, abetting and even aiding colonialism' – not least, it might be added, since the latter view sees human beings as passive concept-fodder for systems of meaning.

74   'The Marabouts in the Marketplace', p. 216.

75   'Trousers in Tunisia', in *Muslim Society*, p. 176.

76   Crone, 'The Tribe and the State' and (partly in response to critics of that essay) 'Tribes and States in the Middle East', *Journal of the Royal Asiatic Society*, vol. 3, 1993.

Gellner took much more seriously a second line of attack, initiated by Hammoudi but expressed most forcefully by Munson.[77] Argument here was empirical rather than epistemological, the general claim being that segmentary balance had never characterized the tribes of the Central High Atlas. Munson claimed that a re-analysis of the ethnography of the Ait 'Atta failed to find either a clear tree-like structure at work or any sign of balanced opposition by means of kinship – with a good deal of evidence coming to light of mafia-style behaviour and of alliances born of interest rather than kinship. Gellner objected to this at great length on three counts, after noting that his attention had been concentrated on the saints rather than on the tribes.[78] First, he drew attention to Munson's description of the Ait 'Atta, pointing out that the strategic location of pastures in different ecological zones was exactly the sort of structural base for social organiza-tion by means of kinship that his model would have predicted. Secondly, a series of institutions – above all, collective oaths and feuding – only made sense if a segmentary system was in operation. This was not to say that the system always operated smoothly. Leaders did sometimes accrue consider-able power – although it remained the case, in Gellner's view, that they were unable to cement their advantage. Thirdly, a negative argument was forcefully made. Given that there was relative order in the absence of the state, some principle must have been at work. Gellner suggested that this favoured an endorsement of the principle of segmentation. All that Munson had done was to note practices likely to lead to very violent conflict, without offering any explanation for the maintenance of order.[79]

A third issue which provoked Gellner to defend himself was occasioned

---

77 Hammoudi, 'Segmentarity, Social Stratification, Political Power and Sainthood'. Munson began his assaults on the segmentary theory in 'On the Irrelevance of the Segmentary Lineage Model in the Moroccan Rif' (*American Anthropologist*, vol. 91, 1989) – which made use of the ethnography of D. Hart, *The Aith Waryaghar of the Moroccan Rif*, Tucson, 1976, to disprove that book's theoretical underpinning. Hart broadly accepted Munson's charges in 'Rejoinder to Henry Munson, Jr., "On the Segmentary Lineage Model in the Moroccan Rif"' (*American Anthropologist*, vol. 91, no. 3, September 1989). Munson's attack on Gellner's use of segmentation, 'Rethinking Gellner's Segmentary Analysis of Morocco's Ait 'Atta' appeared in *Man*, vol. 28, 1993. Gellner responded to this in 'Reply to Critics', the section mostly devoted to segmentation also appearing as 'Segmentation: Reality or Myth?' (*Man*, vol. 1, 1995) – with a brief response by Munson in the same issue.

78 More particularly, Gellner stressed that he had no detailed knowledge of the Ait 'Atta – having tested his general views by examining the behaviour of the Ait Sokhman ('Reply to Critics', p. 641).

79 Munson's comment in 1995 (p. 831) on Gellner's third and negative point was sharp: 'If he had a calculator that consistently gave wrong answers, would he keep using it simply because he did not have a better one?'

by the notion of Orientalism as pioneered by Edward Said. We will see later, in chapter eleven, that Gellner would attack Said for the use of double standards, for endorsing the views of the politically correct and damning the views of those whose politics he did not like. But his principal earlier comments concerned a different aspect of Said's critique of 'Orientalism', namely its claim that Islamic development had been blocked by Western power. These views were particularly present in the work of his former student Bryan Turner.[80] Turner, together with Talal Asad, was a key member for some years of an intellectual cenacle centred in Hull and devoted to the rather dizzying task of combating Orientalism while furthering the concepts of Althusserian Marxism. Gellner was very amused by the fact that many Marxists and Muslims were held to be Orientalists – as was the early work of Turner himself. But he remained critical of the recommended position. Most obviously, he was loath to accept the view that Muslim societies might have developed economically and politically but for the incursions of the West – though those incursions most certainly changed the terms under which development takes place.[81] 'Stagnation' was historically normal, and so probably not the result of imperialism. Beyond this, Gellner was suspicious of the purportedly Marxist categories favoured by these scholars, not least as conceptual exercises looked set to replace the study of actual societies.

A fourth defensive argument was mounted against Charles Lindholm, the social theorist and anthropologist of the Middle East, who offered a view of the relationship between Islam and civil society that subtly differed from that of Gellner.[82] For one thing, Lindholm stresses – following the pioneering work of Patricia Crone[83] – that the early history of Islam inscribed in it a deep distrust of political power. This complements Gellner

---

80   Gellner wrote an admiring review of Turner's thesis when it appeared as *Weber and Islam*, London, 1974, in *Population Studies*, vol. 29, 1974. He was fascinated by Turner's *Marx and the End of Orientalism*, London, 1978, as can be seen in his very lively review article, 'In Defence of Orientalism', *Sociology*, vol. 14, 1980. But he became impatient with Turner's *Capitalism and Class in the Middle East* (London, 1984), which he reviewed in *British Journal of Sociology*, vol. 36, 1985.

81   He noted ('In Defence of Orientalism') a key contradiction at work in Turner's position. A defining characteristic of Orientalism was held to be the belief that development occurs endogenously, but some such notion underlay the view that Muslim societies might have developed without external interference.

82   C. Lindholm, 'Despotism and Democracy: State and Society in the Pre-Modern Middle East', in Hall and Jarvie, *The Social Philosophy of Ernest Gellner* – a view expanded in his *The Muslim Middle East*, Oxford, 1995.

83   See especially P. Crone, *Slaves on Horses: The Evolution of the Islamic Polity*, Cambridge, 1980.

more than it contradicts him. He argues that the weakness of the state inside the classical heartland of Islam results both from doctrine and from the presence of tribes. Accordingly, the belief system is held to have an autonomous impact not just, as Gellner stressed, because of its puritanical and closed scripturalism, but also because of the details of its political theory. Secondly, Lindholm suggests that communities within the city are essentially civic, indeed Tocquevillian in character, but he admits that civil society is as yet impossible because of the generalized distrust of the state. Gellner was unable to accept either point. Drawing on his Moroccan experience, he doubted the absolute hostility to the state, noting instead a curious co-existence of disobedience and religious respect.[84] More importantly, he firmly rejected the notion that Tocquevillian ideas helped us understand the urban population within Islam. If one reason for this was his continued belief that the cohesion of tribes contrasted with the atomism of fearful city-dwellers, he also stressed different historical backgrounds. Where the puritans in America sought toleration, having abandoned the idea of imposing righteousness on a whole society, Islamic reformers feel themselves in possession of a truth they are obliged to spread.[85]

Perry Anderson's analysis of Islam was one of the influences that had led Gellner, as noted, to consider the place of the Ottomans within his general theory. But Anderson's sparkling general review of Gellner's intellectual position as a whole added an insistence that Islam was at once less egalitarian and less secularization-resistant than Gellner imagined.[86] Gellner's rebuttal was straightforward. He insisted that the evidence so far – notably the tendency of fundamentalists to triumph over nationalists – suggests that science and consumerism have not undermined Islam:

> Peace in the Middle East has made advances in part just because two nationalisms prefer each other to the fundamentalists waiting in the wings. The fundamentalist option, in a chaotic world, has to be taken seriously, and Islam exemplifies the most powerful form of it. I do find Khomeini's thought impressive . . . The fact that an apostate can be hounded strikes me as a sign of strength, not weakness.[87]

---

84 'Reply to Critics', p. 657.
85 Ibid., pp. 659–60. Gellner's formulation here is a little facile. Some puritan groups, famously those in Salem, wanted the freedom to impose their own doctrine. Nonetheless, it remains true that no attempt to impose uniform beliefs on the whole society was successful.
86 P. Anderson, 'Science, Politics and Enchantment' in Hall and Jarvie, *The Social Philosophy of Ernest Gellner*, p. 421.
87 'Reply to Critics', p. 660.

Assessment

Gellner admitted that he had a penchant for neat, crisp models – and was indeed well known for his skill at producing them.[88] The central charge that has been directed against Gellner's work on the sociology of Islam is that it is clearer than the truth. His close friend Paul Pascon complained of the functionalism that he felt marred *Saints of the Atlas*.[89] Clifford Geertz stressed the 'mechanical' quality of *Saints of the Atlas*, and his praise for *Muslim Society* as 'the boldest and most ingenious' treatise on Islam was quickly followed by the caustic statement that 'it reminds one of nothing so much as the hidden-hand clockworks of classical economics – all motions and no movers'.[90] This charge was echoed by others. Talal Asad queried the very notion of undertaking an anthropology of Islam, a viewpoint that underlay Zubaida's important assessment of Gellner's position; both suggested that Gellner 'essentialized' Islam to such an extent as to cause harm rather than to encourage enlightenment.[91] All of this suggests that assessment must concentrate on what it means to produce a model – turning in this case from the North African to the more general material.

The most striking appreciation of *Saints of the Atlas*, and to some extent of Gellner's work on Islam in general, appears in 'Tribes without Saints', a brilliant, sadly unpublished paper by Patricia Crone.[92] Before turning to some of the main lines of criticism in that paper, its conclusion can usefully be cited.

> But this does not mean that Gellner's theory should be abandoned, for one would hardly expect a *theory* pertaining to human societies to have precise predictive value. The relationship between abstract theory and concrete reality in the social sciences is not in fact unlike that in medicine. Medical textbooks describe the equivalent of ideal types. The causal connections they propose differ from those of the social sciences in

---

88   Davis, 'An Interview with Ernest Gellner', p. 70.

89   P. Pascon, *Capitalism: Agriculture in the Haouz of Marrakesh*, London, 1987.

90   C. Geertz, 'In Search of North Africa', and 'Conjuring with Islam', *New York Review of Books*, 27 May 1982, p. 25.

91   Asad, 'The Idea of an Anthropology of Islam' (which criticizes Geertz as much as Gellner) and Zubaida, 'Is There a Muslim Society?'

92   A version of this paper was first given to the Anthropology Department Seminar at Cambridge. It provoked little reaction, to Gellner's dismay, leading him to remark that his colleagues simply did not understand how brilliant was the material presented. The version of the paper that I am using was presented to the Mellon Seminar at Princeton in 1991. I am grateful to Patricia Crone for providing me with a copy.

that they can be tested by repeated experiments, formulated with mathematical precision and based on examples so numerous that statistical
predictions are possible; but like the theories of social scientists, they lose
their precision when they are applied to individual cases; once again too
many factors are involved, too many of them historical and too many
of them unknown; in order fully to explain the disease patterns exhibited by individual patients one would need a separate account for every
one of them. This does not however mean that the patients in question
cannot be suffering from the same disease, or that the disease itself has
been wrongly identified; it merely means that medicine is not a science.
The social sciences are not sciences either, but one would not wish to
abandon the search for regularities on that ground. Gellner is surely right
that all the holy men of the tribal Middle East should be classified as
manifestations of a single syndrome and that this syndrome arises from
the dispersal of power characteristic of segmentary organization.

The claim here, that models are useful if they capture a basic phenomenon
but then move us to further specification, seems absolutely right as a matter
of epistemological protocol. Does Gellner's work encourage such intellectual
growth? Crone's paper suggests a positive answer. To begin with it is possible
to find a fair number of saintly mediators in the Middle East resembling
those studied by Gellner. But there are tribes without saints. The Bedouin
of Northern Arabia lack saintly mediators – and, incidentally, are puritanical
in style for all their illiteracy, thereby casting doubt on another of Gellner's
central assumptions. Disputes amongst these Bedouin are managed without
the creation of Hobbesian anarchy. Crone's suggestion is that the absolute
simplicity of life as lived by these tribes may allow segmentation to produce
order entirely by itself. Mediation becomes more important once tribes
become semi-nomadic or even settled, for this change in status creates many
more issues that require resolution. This insight helps us better understand
the particular Berber saints that Gellner studied himself.
  Crone's paper is, in a sense, close to Gellner in specifying the social
conditions that give rise to saintly mediation, as well as in allowing a very
positive role for segmentation in general. Rather different research can also
be seen as inspired by Gellner's early work, whilst correcting it in a wholly
different direction. The single most striking example is the research of
Shelagh Weir on the settled tribes of a remote massif of northern Yemen.
Order is provided here by entirely different means than those specified
by Gellner. Weir discovered many documents, going back for centuries,
showing treaties and agreements between different tribes. Weir was one
of Gellner's last students, and he constantly argued with her, suggesting

that order must have come from the segmentary principle. But her portrait of political culture as a means to order is convincingly laid out in a book destined to become a classic in its own right.[93]

The fact that order can be maintained between tribes through mechanisms other than saintly mediators is one consideration that makes us realize that Gellner's reply to Munson's critique, clever though it is, does not really convince. In this matter, there is justification in the claim of the Austrian anthropologist Wolfgang Kraus that 'on the level of generality the model had arrived at in his thinking, it has become immune to empirical refutation, despite his confessed respect for empirical reality'.[94] As it happens, there is much to be said for the general notion of segmentation as a pillar of Gellner's thought, notably that it gave some clear sense of the weakness of pre-modern states – a vital and helpful piece of sociological understanding. But Kraus makes his negative comment only in order to distinguish the later work from the earlier fieldwork, held to be fertile and suggestive.[95] He notes that the model of segmentation in *Saints of the Atlas* is a philosopher's construct, albeit one hedged with so many qualifications noting likely divergences from reality as to invalidate Munson's critique. Kraus was clearly inspired by Gellner's model, but came to realize, through his own fieldwork in the Central High Atlas, that systematic modification was necessary.[96] The fact that segmentation did not always explain events did not mean that it could be dismissed entirely. The language of segmentation matters enormously to tribesmen, making it much more than a false view of the world. Accordingly, Salzman's theoretical position achieves a conceptual advance by seeing ideology as a resource:

> [S]egmentation is an organizational ideology that is capable of regulating practical social relations but is only under specific conditions realized in behaviour. When conditions favour other kinds of social relations, different models which may coexist with segmentation come to the fore, but segmentation is nevertheless ideologically reproduced as 'a social structure in reserve' to be reactivated when conditions change again.[97]

---

93 S. Weir, *A Tribal Order: Politics and Law in the Mountains of Yemen*, Austin, 2007.

94 W. Kraus, 'Unpublished Postscript' to *Contestable Identities*. I am grateful for having been shown this short text.

95 Kraus, 'Contestable Identities', p. 5.

96 W. Kraus, *Die Ayt Hdiddu: Wirtschaft und Gesellschaft in zentralen Hohen Atlas*, Vienna, 1991 (reviewed by Gellner in *Social Anthropology*, vol. 1, 1993); 'Contestable Identities'; and *Islamische Stammesgesellschaften: Tribale Identitaten im Vorderen Orient in socialanthropologischer Perspektive*, Vienna, 2004, especially pp. 145–51.

97 Kraus, 'Contestable Identities', p. 4, referring to P. C. Salzman, 'Does Complementary Opposition Exist?', *American Anthropologist*, vol. 80, 1978.

With this in mind, Kraus supplies, as Munson did not, a mechanism of order.

> Political relations are described by informants as a rather stable structural disposition of segmented groups. A segment's position in this structure is considered decisive for its collective action, above all in fighting, but it is understood that segments may strategically diverge in action from the given arrangement. Nevertheless, the structure itself is held to be made up of 'actual' relations between segments, but these relations themselves may be rearranged. In contrast, genealogical relations are understood as being the 'original' and immutable relations between segments. Expectations of individual and collective behaviour tend to follow 'actual' political relations, but a plea for support or assistance may also be voiced in terms of an 'original' relation, for instance of brotherhood.[98]

The ability of tribesmen to manipulate their concepts in a manner that improves the workings of their society conveys exactly the image of human behaviour central to most of Gellner's work. Moreover, the ability to distinguish political alliances from kinship links depends upon a clear sense of the latter's nature as an objective physical fact rather than a mere cultural construct.

Let us turn to the general model. The cyclical view of pre-modern Islamic politics does work in some places and some periods, not least outside the Mediterranean world which concerned Gellner most – amongst the Pathans, for example, who straddle the border between Pakistan and Afghanistan.[99] Nonetheless, Gellner does overgeneralize. The Nile allowed for a measure of state strength absent in pastoral areas, and the same is true of the peasant bases of states beyond the Anatolian case that he had acknowledged. Zubaida correctly points out that the *ulama* were not necessarily puritanical, whilst tribes could be friends rather than enemies of the state.[100] One is tempted to say at this point that Zubaida's interesting comments are precisely the result of his elaborating on Gellner's general model! But his central contention cannot be dismissed so easily.

What then about the unhinging of the pendulum? Shankland makes a strong case for the usefulness of Gellner's ideas as an aid to understanding

---

98 Kraus, 'Contestable Identities', p. 10.

99 F. Barth, *Political Leadership Among Swat Pathans*, London, 1985; C. Lindholm, *Generosity and Jealousy: The Swat Pukhtun of Northern Pakistan*, New York, 1982. In the early 1950s Gellner had thought of undertaking a comparative study, wishing to compare the situation in the High Central Atlas with that in Waziristan.

100 Zubaida, 'Is there a Muslim Society?'.

the situation in the Turkish countryside.[101] Perhaps the main claim that one can make is that Gellner was characteristically insightful in recognizing so very early that Islam would not fade away but rather become a major force in the modern world. Then there is surely a good deal to be said for his view that high culture is an aspect of modernity, and that Islam has capacities in this regard. Nonetheless, his model of non-secularizable modern Islam does deserve to be challenged. One must follow Perry Anderson, to begin with, in noting the contradiction to Gellner's general view of the world that follows from his insistence on the ability of Islam to avoid secularization.[102] Economic success seems to be possible in this case, even while a total ideology maintains its power. There is no sense that science will undermine traditional belief, indeed no real sense that science is necessary for economic growth in modern Islamic societies. The best that can be said for Gellner here is that he wished to hang on to his central insight, that fundamentalist Islam had real power, even if this led him to contradict some positions that he generally held. The revival of Islam had first helped nation-building, but thereafter became so powerful as to supplant it. What one senses here is fear, of the emergence of a social formation immune to dialogue.

It is still more important to point out that Gellner's position has serious empirical defects. It is hard to see Islamism as the child of industrialization, as seems to be suggested when he argues that modern Islam is a functional equivalent of nationalism – whose origins he insists lie in industrialization. Further, the view that Islam has replaced national differentiation most certainly deserves to be challenged. To some extent, this is simply because his later work put to one side his earlier careful qualification, that his knowledge was restricted to the classical heartland of Islam. Shared Islamic faith was not enough to prevent the break-up of Pakistan in 1971. Indonesia and Malaysia show that the national principle can triumph over that of the world religion.[103] The same point can be made about some countries even

---

101   Shankland, 'Integrating the Rural'.

102   Anderson, 'Science, Politics, Enchantment', p. 421.

103   T. J. Mabry, 'Modernization, Nationalism and Islam: An Examination of Ernest Gellner's Writings on Muslim Society with Reference to Indonesia and Malaysia', *Ethnic and Racial Studies*, vol. 21, 1998. This powerful paper makes a further point (p. 84), namely that the high tradition in Java was heterodox in Islamic terms, joining together elements of animism, Hinduism and the worship of Muslim saints. My own limited, tourist exposure to Indonesia mostly gave the firm impression of a world utterly different from that of the Middle East. But one cannot entirely dismiss Gellner's concerns. For some madrasahs did seem puritanical, not least because modern communication systems allowed religious material to be imported for the first time, from Saudi Arabia.

within the world with which Gellner was most familiar. Turkey retains its national distinctiveness. Roberts was clearly stimulated by Gellner, but argues convincingly that *ulama* only had power over the army in Algeria – considered as very different from Morocco – for one short and very particular period.[104] Further, severe criticism is surely necessary, given the poor economic performance of many Muslim states, of the idea that modern Islam is serving as a functional equivalent to the protestant ethic. In general, there is justice in the charge that Gellner essentializes modern Islam. Democratization has been more limited in Arab states, for example, than in the Muslim world as a whole, in part because the geopolitical instabilities of that region have produced military regimes, fiscally stretched and prone to suppress their civil societies.[105] The same point can be made regarding the central claim that Islam cannot be secularized. Many Muslims are clearly secular in wishing to maintain their religious beliefs as a form of private consolation whilst allowing political matters to be decided on instrumental rather than religious grounds.[106] Of course, against this there are powerful revivalist movements seeking to establish godly rule. Gellner implies that the force of such movements derives from the core components of Islam as a belief system. An alternative explanation would suggest that fundamentalism has triumphed in some places because of the failure, in turn, of Arab nationalism and of the nation-building efforts of particular states. This provides a simple and convincing basis for the charge that Gellner essentializes Islam: his account excludes the impact of politics.

Gellner's explanations for many phenomena are based on his understanding of social structures. There is a great deal to be said for this, though his basic materialism can become crude – as perhaps when he effectively insisted that the ecological circumstances of pastoral life determined tribal politics. But this approach tends to miss the ways in which the character of social movements is derived from the nature of the states with which they interact. An explanation for this claim is in order. An example of this sociological principle is that of working-class movements before 1914. Workers became ever more politicized along the continuum that goes from the United States to Britain, and then from Imperial Germany to Tsarist

104 Roberts, 'Ernest Gellner and the Algerian Army'.

105 A. Stepan and G. B. Robertson, 'An "Arab" more than "Muslim" Electoral Gap', *Journal of Democracy*, vol. 14, 2003.

106 B. Turam, *Between Islam and the State: The Politics of Engagement*, Stanford, 2007; D. F. Eickelman, 'From Here to Modernity: Ernest Gellner on Nationalism and Islamic Fundamentalism', in J. A. Hall (ed.), *The State of the Nation*, Cambridge, 1998; D. F. Eickelman and J. Piscatori, *Muslim Politics*, Princeton, 1996; Sadik J. al-Azm, 'Is Islam Secularizable?', *Jahrbuch fur Philosophie des Forschungsinstitut fur Philosophie Hannover*, vol. 7, 1996.

Russia. The structure of capitalism cannot explain this, but comparative historical sociology can.[107] American workers acted at an industrial level rather than against the state for the simplest of reasons: the state was their own, and it permitted union activity. In contrast, workers in Russia gained political consciousness and 'took on' the state precisely because unionization was forbidden: they had no choice. Strong political feelings result from exclusion, with liberal integration doing much to diffuse conflict through society. Another example of the same point concerns modern revolutions. A mass of evidence shows that only when there is 'no other way out' do actors turn from reformism to risking their lives on barricades.[108] One can highlight the general point by saying simply that the social movements with which we concern ourselves are usually those that are effectively political movements.

That this principle seems to apply within the Islamic world is suggested by a brilliant comparison between Iran and Egypt.[109] Fundamentalist Islamism does not necessarily follow from some conceptual core of the religion itself. Rather, states that are at once over-mighty in their despotism and weak in their ability to deliver services, obviously two sides of a single coin, push reform movements in the direction of greater radicalism. This does not bring much comfort, for identities created by exclusion are often resistant to change. More striking still is the difficulty of reforming many regimes in the Middle East, exacerbated by the fact of their oil wealth. Engineering such change from the outside is extremely difficult, though the transformations of Kurdistan and Iraq may yet be consolidated, with consequences that would surely then be felt within Iran.

---

107   M. Mann, *The Sources of Social Power. Volume Two: The Rise of Classes and Nation-States, 1760–1914*, Cambridge, 1993, chapters 15, 17 and 18.

108   J. Goodwin, *No Other Way Out: States and Revolutionary Movements, 1945–91*, Cambridge, 2001.

109   A. Bayat, *Making Islam Democratic: Social Movements and the Post-Islamic Turn*, Stanford, 2007.

10

A General Theory of Nationalism

Shortly after *Nations and Nationalism* was published, Gellner made one of his then frequent trips to Moscow. Handing a copy of the book to his friend Anatoly Khazanov, he remarked that the book contained his life. Khazanov devoured the book that very night, met Gellner the next day, and asked if he had been referring to the long parable about the relations between the Ruritanians and the Empire of Megalomania. Gellner replied in the negative, stressing that it was the book as a whole that held within it his experiences.[1] There are passages where this is obviously true. Modernity obviates the state's need to rely on specialized middlemen, Gellner claimed, where it had hitherto acted as their guardian. Much discontent is therefore defused by dispossessing such groups, in 'a pathetic theatre of humiliation . . . to the delectation of the majority'. In no case was this more true than in that of European Jews.

> These persecutions illustrate, better than any others, the kind of fate which is likely to befall culturally distinguishable, economically privileged and politically defenceless communities, at a time when the age of specialized communities, of the traditional form of organic division of labour, is over.[2]

Just as importantly, the book deploys Gellner's full intellectual repertoire. He draws from Hume and Kant when seeking to explain the nature of the modern self, but relies just as much on his philosophy of history. And the book is clearly that of an anthropologist, distinguishing between structure and culture and acknowledging the character of pre-industrial societies, and offering particularly interesting insights about the relationship between

---

1   Interview with Khazanov, 2 January 1999.
2   *Nations and Nationalism*, Oxford, 1983, p. 107.

Islam and nationalism. Finally, one should note that the book is written, so to speak, from the inside, allowing for varied staccato comments on multiple issues – the struggles of states over peoples, the reasons for the unlikelihood that pan-Arab nationalism's defeat would be reversed, the behaviour of empires, the mythical character of much nationalist ideology – that were further developed by later theorists. Each re-reading reveals new insights.

Nations and Nationalism was declared one of the hundred most influential books since the war.[3] It is extremely ambitious, offering nothing less than a general theory, and it was generally very well received – it would become his best-selling work, widely read the world over.[4] More was involved here than the sheer intellectual merits of his case – which had, after all, appeared previously, at least in essence, two decades earlier in *Thought and Change*.[5] What mattered was the revival of nationalist movements in the world, most obviously following the collapse of Soviet hegemony.[6] In the last decade of Gellner's life, he attended a huge number of conferences on nationalism, his theory often the subject of discussion and criticism. This led him to further develop his position, and to offer prescriptive comments; he also replied to his critics.[7] Two comments from his last rebuttal should be borne

---

3   'The Hundred Most Influential Books Since the War', *Times Literary Supplement*, 30 December 2008.

4   B. Barry, 'Review of Ernest Gellner's *Nations and Nationalism*', *Ethics*, vol. 95, 1984; J. Kellas, 'Review of *Nations and Nationalism*', *International Affairs*, vol. 60, 1984; A. D. Smith, 'Book review: Ernest Gellner, *Nations and Nationalism*', *Millennium*, vol. 13, 1983; B. Crick, 'The Gad-fly and the Eagle', *New Statesman*, 16 September 1983; W. Johnson, 'State Power', *New Society*, 25 August 1983; J. Breuilly, 'Reflections on Nationalism', *Philosophy of the Social Sciences*, vol. 15, 1985 and J. Dunn, 'For the Good of the Country', *Times Higher Educational Supplement*, 21 October 1983. It is very noticeable, in contrast, that the book's publication in the United States passed almost without comment.

5   We shall see that *Nations and Nationalism* found a way to incorporate key elements of the earlier treatment of nationalism, heavily based on the experience of decolonization, within the more general theory.

6   J. Breuilly, 'Introduction' to *Nations and Nationalism*, 2nd Edition, Oxford, 2007, pp. xix–xx. Breuilly argues convincingly that Gellner had been something of a voice in the wilderness in regard to nationalism in the years after the publication of *Thought and Change*. He believes that the field was dominated by Elie Kedourie's *Nationalism* – a book which loathed nationalism, making much of its anti-rational character. (Breuilly is a little parochial here: it was Karl Deutsch rather than Kedourie who dominated the field in the United States.) It would be nice, but probably mistaken, to think that it was the rationality of Gellner's structural account of nationalism that led to its sudden prominence.

7   Gellner replied to papers criticizing his view of nationalism by Perry Anderson, Kenneth Minogue, Michael Mann, Anthony Smith, Brendan O'Leary and Nicholas Stargardt in 'Reply to Critics', in J. A. Hall and I. C. Jarvie (eds), *The Social Philosophy of Ernest*

in mind as we proceed, for they address the criticisms that he most often faced. The first comment – noting his love of Czech folk songs – was cited above, in chapter one. Gellner insisted that he was sensitive to the appeal of nationalism, refusing to accept the charge that his account of nationalist motivation was merely instrumental.[8] His second comment sought to refute the charge that his theory was functionalist in the illicit, teleological sense of lacking causal agency.

> I accept entirely this repudiation of teleological explanation: I have many needs which, whatever their urgency or intensity, nature has not deemed fit to satisfy. Bitter experience, quite apart from the canons of scientific propriety, have taught me this unpalatable truth. Needs engender no realities. But my theory does not sin against this. It is straightforwardly causal. Political and economic forces, the aspirations of governments for greater power and of individuals for greater wealth, have in certain circumstances produced a world in which the division of labour is very advanced, the occupational structure highly unstable, and most work is semantic and communicative rather than physical. This situation in turn leads to the adoption of a standard and codified, literacy-linked ('High') idiom, requires business of all kinds to be conducted in its terms, and reduces persons who are not masters of that idiom (or not acceptable to its practitioners) to the status of humiliated second-class members, a condition from which one plausible and much-frequented escape route led through nationalist politics.[9]

Gellner can and should be upheld on both these counts. But our concluding assessment of his theory argues that his claim that it is causal is neither complete nor entirely correct. In particular, his entirely proper functionalist account of nationalism – that homogeneity is a prerequisite for the success of society – needs to be treated with caution. In this matter one can follow Gellner himself, in a sense: for, in this crucial area, he changed his mind, or at least wobbled in an important way.

Gellner, Amsterdam, 1996. O'Leary revised his paper in light of these criticisms, to the new version forming part of J. A. Hall (ed.), *The State of the Nation: Ernest Gellner and the Theory of Nationalism*, Cambridge, 1998. The papers mentioned, together with those in *The State of the Nation* and Breuilly's 'Introduction', present the main criticisms directed at Gellner's theory. But these papers are only the tip of a large iceberg of critical commentary.

8 'Reply to Critics', pp. 624–5. He is replying in this instance to P. Anderson, 'Science, Politics, Enchantment', in Hall and Jarvie, *The Social Philosophy of Ernest Gellner*. The same point is made in Dunn, 'For the Good of the Country'.

9 Ibid., pp. 627–8.

Nations and Nationalism

It is not often appreciated that the logic of the book's argument is very similar, for all its varied and interesting asides, to that of the treatment of nationalism found in *Thought and Change*, with such novelties as there are appearing only towards the end of the monograph. This is certainly true of the set of definitions which open the book. These spell out the implications of the earlier claim in *Thought and Change* that the national principle meant rule by one's co-culturals. Both sentiment and movement are seen within the terms of this principle, now expressed as the principle of political legitimacy asserting that polity and nation should coincide.[10] Gellner makes much of the difficulty of defining the nation, noting that both cultural and voluntarist definitions are often inadequate – for each can apply to many social relations other than the national. But the book overcomes the difficulty, asserting that modern circumstances prioritize a national culture which is willed because it provides the only framework within which a decent life is possible.[11]

The circumstances in question are explained in terms both of his philosophy of history and his interpretation of modern epistemology. Gellner considers nationalism to be modern because agro-literate polities were not societies in the modern sense. Rather, specialized elites ruled over communities, as we have seen, which characteristically managed their own affairs, a situation exemplified by the millet system of the Ottoman Empire. Industrial society is held to be utterly different. A scintillating restatement of the ideas of Hume and Kant spells out the character of life under this mode of production in a new and suggestive manner. Just as fact is freed from value, so too is role freed from social structure. Social mobility is enabled by the spread of generic education – that is, educational training which is often less specialized than that of the clerical elite of agrarian societies. Such training allows for movement between jobs during a single lifetime, thereby creating a baseline egalitarianism that characterizes modern life.[12]

---

10 *Nations and Nationalism*, chapter 1.

11 Ibid., pp. 7, 53–5 .

12 Breuilly's excellent 'Introduction' cites papers written in the years between the appearance of *Thought and Change* and *Nations and Nationalism*, but unaccountably misses the 1973 paper 'Scale and Nation', in *Contemporary Thought and Politics*, London, 1974. This important paper spells out more thoroughly than had *Thought and Change* the precise character of work in industrial societies. A further point can be made about the second edition in which Breuilly's introduction appears. The earliest printing of the book's first edition was fronted by three quotations, one of them – 'Our politics however was a rather

The fundamental reason that Gellner felt so sure of his theory was the fact that virtually every state in the modern world, whatever their political beliefs, pays obeisance to the deity of education.[13] But far more than that is involved.

> The employability, dignity, security and self-respect of individuals, typically, and for the majority of men now hinges on their *education*; and the limits of the culture within which they were educated are also the limits of the world within which they can, morally and professionally, breathe. A man's education is by far his most precious investment, and in effect confers his identity on him.[14]

The key sentiment here needs immediate highlighting. A powerful retort to the charge that his account of nationalist motivation is thin, bloodless and instrumental is that the feeling on which nationalism is based is that of the desire to avoid humiliation. A more subtle answer is that the desire to work should not be seen in purely economic terms. This is how critics coming from an established community, taking its character for granted, see employment. But Gellner writes from the position of an outsider, knowing that a job symbolizes the ability to gain admission into a society in the first place.

The chapter that follows the discussion of the modern self builds on his earlier claim that nationalism, properly understood, is not about the expression of prior national identities but rather the actual creation of these very identities.

> It is not the case that nationalism imposes homogeneity out of a willful cultural *Machtbedürfniss*; it is the objective need for homogeneity which is reflected in nationalism.[15]

> The great, but valid, paradox is this: nations can be defined only in terms of the age of nationalism, rather than, as you might expect, the other way round.[16]

---

less daring form of culture' – was written by J. Sládaček, and then circulated in Prague in *samizdat* form before later publication in *Index*. In printings of the book in the 1990s Gellner took care to identify Sládaček as Petr Pithart, 'subsequently prime minister of the Czech lands'. This correction is missing from the second edition of the book.

13   *Nations and Nationalism*, p. 28.
14   Ibid., p. 36.
15   Ibid., p. 46.
16   Ibid., p. 55.

It is phrases such as these which seem to posit history as the unfolding of
a mechanistic process, leading many to raise against Gellner the charge of
illicit functionalism.[17] Gellner's views are certainly expressed so forcefully
that one can understand why this indictment has so often been made. But it
should be rejected. One consideration to bear in mind is that the forceful-
ness derives from Gellner's determined rejection of nationalist ideology, of
nationalists' self-understanding which declares that the nation was always
there, ready, as their favoured metaphor has it, to be awakened by a kiss.[18]
He insists that this will not do, pointing to the fact that so very often a new
world, of literacy and shared belonging, is created by nationalists for the
first time. Just as importantly, the social engineering involved very often
leads to the destruction of other potential nations, at least when measured
in terms of linguistic variety – there being something like 8,000 languages
and a mere 200 or so states. A key principle for Gellner is accordingly that
nationalism is rather weak: many cultural units assimilate to larger ethnic
groups, and it is impossible to predict in advance which ones will eventually manage to turn themselves into nation-states.[19] But the most significant
consideration is the undoubted fact that he does indeed offer a causal
account of the origins of the nationalist principle. This is necessary, for
insisting that the sharing of a literate high culture is necessary for modern
social life does not for a moment explain why there need to be so many
different cultures. Why was it that the culture of specialized elites sitting
atop the self-help communities of agrarian society could not be accepted by
everyone under their control?

---

17   Illicit functionalist statements are even more apparent in *Language and Solitude:
Wittgenstein, Malinowski and the Habsburg Dilemma*, Cambridge, 1998, chapters 6 and 7.

18   The force of his argument led Benedict Anderson to chastise him (*Imagined
Communities*, London, 1983, p. 15) for seeing in nationalist statements falsity rather than the
act of creation. One imagines that Gellner's 'ferocity' in this matter derives in part from his
Jewish background, given that so much nationalist ideology included so many false claims
about Jews.

19   B. O'Leary, 'Ernest Gellner's Diagnoses of Nationalism: A Critical Overview, or,
What Is Living and What Is Dead in Ernest Gellner's Philosophy of Nationalism', in Hall,
The State of the Nation, pp. 49–51, argued against Gellner on this point outlining mechanisms
allowing for prediction – or retrodiction. We will see that Gellner felt that O'Leary had a
tendency to take national feeling for granted. (In fact, O'Leary recognizes that tribal societies
are not national, claiming rather that once national sentiment is created it is unlikely to
disappear). O'Leary is a very distinguished descendant of Gellner, but on the latter point
another such, David Laitin, stands closer – for he makes much of the mutability of national
feeling (*Nations, States and Violence*, New York, 2008). Both political scientists depart from
Gellner's habitual insistence on the inevitability of the one-to-one correspondence between
nation and state.

Gellner essentially repeats his account of industrialization's uneven spread from *Thought and Change*, this time using a new parable: the relations between the backward peasants of Ruritania and the Empire of Megalomania – the former quite properly seen as Czechs and Slovaks, the latter as the German-speakers of Vienna. The presupposition of the whole argument is simple:

> Early industrialism means population explosion, rapid urbanization, labour migration, and also the economic and political penetration of previously more or less inward-turned communities, by a global economy and a centralizing polity.[20]

The subtle composite portrait that follows concentrates on intellectuals and peasants-turned-workers, omitting the traditional tribal chiefs who had played some role in the argument of *Thought and Change*. Concentration on Central Europe rather than North Africa also means that the intellectuals are seen in a slightly different light. The few Ruritanian peasants who become intellectuals, fluent in both the language of court and of church (that is, at least in the Austrian case, German and Latin respectively), became influenced by liberal ideas, thereby ending up as teachers and professors rather than priests. Gellner stressed that a large proportion of this group chose to assimilate into the dominant political culture, as was possible given that no identifiable trait, religious or otherwise, prevented this from happening. To become German was, after all, to join a world civilization and rise in the social hierarchy. But not every intellectual took this path. Many were moved by the sufferings of the Ruritanian peasants who had arrived in urban areas. No explanation is given as to why intellectuals preferred one path to the other.[21] In contrast, the position facing peasants arriving in towns is all too clear. It was not just that the effects of early industrialization were harsh. Rather, the need to operate in a language other than their own led to the sense of humiliation already noted, that is, the fear that one might permanently remain a second-class citizen. So here was the raw material for a nationalist movement – intellectuals feeling empathy for their fellows, their affinity often wedded to romantic notions of folk community, and peasants-turned-workers suddenly aware of how much easier it is to deal with officials in one's own language. Gellner issued a caveat at this point, anticipating even at this early stage a

---

20   *Nations and Nationalism*, p. 42.
21   *Language and Solitude*, p. 23, notes the lack of a proper explanation, but suggests that late entrants to the dominant group are likely to be disadvantaged.

criticism that had been made of his earlier work on nationalism. He drew a distinction between the actual motives of actors, and motives that they might have had if they had calculated their interests in purely materialist terms. The motives that they might have had – but didn't – would have included career advancement for the intellectuals (opportunities might be greater in Megalomania but the competition was stiffer) and the possibility of economic development for the workers.[22] But these motives did not drive the process: what mattered was the generosity of the intellectuals and the humiliation of those forced to deal with bureaucrats steeped in a different linguistic and cultural code.

A particular but only partial innovation of the book is the distinction made between the situation just described, that is, one in which fission may or may not take place due to communication barriers, and a more deterministic situation in which the creation of social homogeneity is made more difficult by the entropy-resistant features of certain groups. Gellner makes the point in abstract terms to begin with, by imagining some people possessed of an ineradicable blueness. The difference is then simple: 'Ruritanian culture can be shed; blueness cannot'.[23] This has been seen as a major change from his earlier work: human beings, or rather some of them, are now seen as less malleable than was implied in the initial formulation of Gellner's views.[24] But this is not quite right. The theory in *Thought and Change* is redefined here and incorporated within a larger frame. The causal agency in the initial formulation was, so to speak, obvious and absolute: intellectuals had no choice but to play the nationalist card because their social mobility was blocked. The monograph makes the point brutally with regard to sub-Saharan Africa. 'The nationalism that this engendered was simply the summation of all the blacks, the non-whites of a given historically accidental territory, now unified by the new administrative machinery'.[25] This account of the region's situation continued by noting the remarkable immutability of African borders, suggesting, however, that it was still too soon to know whether nation-building would take place via the use of a colonial language or through the choice of a native tongue. But Gellner did feel that nationalism in Africa was more likely to be effective, that is, successful in nation-building, when it could ally itself with a world religion. In this context, he offered an account of developments in the Horn of Africa, noting with bitter irony that the declaration of equality

---

22 Ibid., pp. 61–2.
23 Ibid., p. 69.
24 O'Leary, 'Ernest Gellner's Diagnoses of Nationalism', p. 50.
25 *Nations and Nationalism*, p. 83.

for all ethnic groups in Ethiopia was 'followed fairly soon by a systematic liquidation of intellectuals drawn from the non-Amharic group, a regrettably rational policy from the viewpoint of preventing the emergence of rival nationalisms within the empire'.[26]

The discussion of entropy-resistant traits goes somewhat further, in a slightly speculative manner. For when Gellner moves from the abstract to the concrete, often matters are not at all straightforward. He argued that the 'pervasive values and attitudes . . . linked to religion . . . have a limpet-like persistence . . . for the populations that carry them', citing both the situation in Ulster and the difficulties facing Kabyles in metropolitan France – and noting in both cases that the fissure between the groups involved was cultural, not physical.[27] However, consider this passage:

If, however, the hypothetical blues possess no territorial base in which they can plausibly hope to establish an independent blue land, (or alternatively, if they do have one, but this blue homeland is, for one reason or another, too exiguous and unattractive to secure the return to it of the blues dispersed in other regions), then the plight of the blues is serious indeed.[28]

It is not clear to whom this refers. Perhaps Gellner had in mind African-Americans in the United States, identifiable in physical terms, thereby being subject to racial prejudice.[29] But the reference might as easily apply to European Jews. Whilst some Jews at the end of the nineteenth century were recognizable 'physically', others clearly were not. It was this latter group that Hitler so disliked. In this case, what mattered was the determination of the majority to exclude a minority – or, rather, to weed

---

26 Ibid., p. 85. Gellner is here drawing on the work of Ioan Lewis. Gellner offered initial comments about the relationship between Islam and nationalism at this point; these are considered in the next section of this chapter.

27 Ibid., p. 71. The language here is slightly strange, at least when considering the Irish case, for it dismisses entirely the legitimate grievances that were involved.

28 Ibid., p. 69. Gellner went on to contrast this situation with that of Ruritanians, who might benefit from a federalism giving them regional autonomy in combination with the ability to move unhindered within the larger state. He suggested that different groups might accept less than total independence voluntarily, and cited Quebec, somewhat against the spirit of the comments made about that nation in *Thought and Change*, as an example. In contrast, others – notably the Ibos in Nigeria – had been deprived of the federal option by force.

29 Brendan O'Leary suggests this, stating that Gellner sees race as more entropy-resistant than culture or language – thereby rightly avoiding racism while again insisting, as in his early anthropology, that a cultural story might have a foundation in physical reality.

them out.[30] Often traits that had been shed were again made real by the
actions of others. Of course this situation can change, as was the case with
the slow erosion of the Catholic and Protestant pillars of Dutch society in
recent years. But this scarcely dents Gellner's case which concerns, after all,
entropy-*resistance* rather than, so to speak, entropy-impossibility.

If the thoughts on entropy-resistance do most to add consistency to his
work on nationalism as a whole, the creation of a typology of nationalism-
engendering and nationalism-thwarting situations was innovative. Eight
potential situations are created by means of three variables – access or the
lack of it to both power and education, and the presence or absence of a
shared cultural background.

The typology of nationalism-engendering and nationalism-thwarting situations

	P	~P	
	E	~E	
1	A	A	early industrialism without ethnic catalyst
2	A	B	'Habsburg' (and points east and south) nationalism
	E	E	
3	A	A	mature homogeneous industrialism
4	A	B	classical liberal Western nationalism
	~E	E	
5	A	A	Decembrist revolutionary but not nationalist
6	A	B	diaspora nationalism
	~E	~E	
7	A	A	untypical pre-nationalist situation
8	A	B	typical pre-nationalist situation

Here, ~ stands for negation, absence; P stands for power; E for access to
modern-style education; and A and B for names of individual cultures.
Each numbered line represents one possible situation; a line containing

30   The distinction between a group caging its own members and a majority refusing to
allow a minority to assimilate is made particularly fruitfully by D. Laitin, 'Nationalism and
Language: A Post-Soviet Perspective', in Hall, *The State of the Nation*. Laitin suggests that
theorizing these factors can usefully add to Gellner's more economistic account. Gellner's
position is not really, as argued, economistic, and he was well aware of Laitin's factors, even
if he did not formally place them at the centre of his theory.

both A and B shows a situation in which two cultures co-exist within a single territory, and a line with A and A stands for cultural homogeneity within a similar territory. If A and B stand under an E and/or a P, then the cultural group in question does have access to education or power; if it stands under an ~E or ~P, it lacks such access. The situation of any group is indicated by the nearest E and P above it.[31]

Five scenarios generated by the scheme do not create nationalism. Line one refers to a world in which state preceded nation, that is, in which national homogeneity had, at least to some extent, been established early on. This social world saw class conflict but little change of borders, for class without an ethnic catalyst is held to be relatively powerless. Once educational standards are more broadly shared, societies of this type move to line three. Lines seven and eight refer to the agrarian world, in which nationalism is by definition ruled out. In contrast line five sees a situation in which some of the powerless are educated at a higher level than their rulers, though both belong to the same cultural pool. This situation can lead to revolution, but not to nationalism. With these cases out of the way, it can be seen that there are three nationalism-prone situations, a fact which pleased Gellner since it improved upon the binary opposition between Western and Eastern forms of nationalism proposed by John Plamenatz.[32] He is in fact very close to Plamenatz in the way that he describes lines four and two, respectively 'classical Western liberal nationalism' and "Habsburg" (and points east and south) nationalism'. Western nationalism in effect unites culturally advanced areas hitherto lacking a single political system – in large part securing this by expelling alien rulers. The classic instances of this type are nineteenth-century Germany and Italy, both so prominently possessing high literate culture that the possibility of liberalism is present precisely because rather little social engineering is involved. Line two requires social engineering. Here, the culture in question is bereft of a high tradition, thereby demanding much effort to create one out of a folk tradition. This most certainly applied to the Ruritanians of Central Europe, not least the Czechs. But it applies just as much and possibly more so to the south, on which the discussion of nationalism in *Thought and Change* had concentrated. Ruritanians and the colonized belong to the same category of Gellner's scheme.

These first two nationalism-creating situations are recognizable from

---

31   Ibid., p. 94, and chapter 7 passim.
32   J. Plamenatz, 'Two Types of Nationalism', in E. Kamenka, (ed.), *Nationalism, The Nature and Evolution of an Idea*, London, 1973 – deemed by Gellner to be 'the Sad Reflections of a Montenegrin in Oxford' (*Nations and Nationalism*, p. 99).

Thought and Change, although their character is more clearly described thanks to the new typology. But the nationalism of line six is identified and characterized in the monograph for the first time. Diaspora nationalism is that of a cultural group different from the majority ethnicity, bereft of power but possessing high education and skills. Such groups were almost essential to traditional empires, with the British for example making particular use of South Asians in Africa and the West Indies. Members of these diasporas can serve as palace guards, financiers or bureaucrats – roles which, when handled by locals tied into kinship networks, can be used as positions from which to attack the state. The occupants of these positions have included Greeks, Armenians, Jews, Chinese and Indians. Many are treated as pariahs, excluded from mainstream society by status considerations.

> The advantage . . . of dealing with a minority, one with whom you could not eat, marry, or enter into political or military alliance, was that both parties could concentrate on a rational cost-benefit analysis of the actual specific deal in question, and expect, on the whole, to get what they bargained for, neither more nor less. Within the minority community, of course, relationships were once again many-stranded, and hence deals were less rational and reliable, and more many-sided. But in the wider society, those who lack status can honour a contract. [33]

These groups often do very well in a modernizing world. But they are also placed in a very dangerous position, at once militarily weak, conspicuous and successful. The newly created intellectuals of a modernizing society are all too likely to covet positions that guarantee fame and fortune. From this follows either genocide or expulsion. Diaspora members who foresee this have but two choices, that of finding some way to assimilate or that of creating their own state, as was famously true of the Zionists who created Israel.

There are two final novelties to *Nations and Nationalism*. On the one hand, there is an extended discussion about the future of nationalism. National feelings were likely to attenuate once the hump on the road to industrial society had been passed, an important expression of optimism for Gellner given that he straddled the worlds of rationalism and nationalism. This envisions a world already discussed, that of 'ironic cultural nationalism', in which a shared cultural style is necessary even though it does not command our full loyalty. There was a paradox about the world of greater affluence, in which the stakes of conflict seem to be diminished:

---

33 Ibid., p. 104.

'intellectuals, the driving force of initial nationalism, are now, in a world of nation-states, often the ones who move with the greatest ease between states, with the least prejudice, as once they did in the days of an international inter-state clerisy'.[34] Nonetheless, Gellner rejected any facile idea of convergence, though it might well apply at the highest occupational levels:

> [I]t remains difficult to imagine two large, politically viable, independence-worthy cultures cohabiting under a single political roof, and trusting a single political centre to maintain and service both cultures with perfect or even adequate impartiality.[35]

On the other hand, a very powerful short chapter on ideology makes three particular claims.[36] First, Gellner distinguishes his theory from that of Karl Deutsch.[37] He claims that Deutsch saw nationalism as resting on the communication of particular messages, a reassuring doctrine since it suggests that different messages could produce different ideologies. Gellner would have none of this: it was the spread of mass communication media, rather than any particular content that they might deliver, which sustained national identification. Second, he forcefully insisted that Kant's idea of self-determination had no relationship, as Kedourie had claimed, with the principle of national self-determination. Kant's insistence that the self not be based on anything contingent made him the sparest of universalist cosmopolitans, far removed from nationalism's concern with the need for rootedness. Finally, Gellner considered false theories created in order to explain nationalism. Three had been mentioned in *Thought and Change*, namely those theories which saw nationalism as universal, as the result merely of ideas, and as the preserve of the Dark Gods.[38] He now added Marxism to this list.

> Just as extreme Shi'ite Muslims hold that the Archangel Gabriel made a mistake, delivering the Message to Mohamed when it was intended for Ali, so Marxists basically like to think that the spirit of history or

---

34 Ibid., p. 118.

35 Ibid., p. 119.

36 It also replies to criticisms made by Kedourie of *Thought and Change*; these are considered below.

37 K. Deutsch, *Nationalism and Social Communication*, New York, 1966, discussed by Gellner in *Nations and Nationalism*, pp. 126–7.

38 *Nations and Nationalism*, pp. 129–30. His arguments against the first of these positions were repeated on several occasions, not least in 'The Sacred and the National', in *Encounters with Nationalism*, Oxford, 1994 – a striking discussion of C. C. O'Brien, *Godland: Reflections on Religion and Nationalism*, Cambridge (MA), 1988.

human consciousness made a terrible boob. The awakening message was
intended for classes, but by some terrible postal error was delivered to
nations. It is now necessary for revolutionary activists to persuade the
wrongful recipient to hand over the message, and the zeal it engenders,
to the rightful and intended recipient.[39]

It is worth noting that his typology had sought to explain nationalism
without any reference to class, understood as an agent of historical destiny.
This was not to say that he ignored social inequality. Very much to the
contrary, his fully developed position was that neither class nor nation
could be relied upon to act permanently, almost metaphysically, as movers
of the historical process. If class without nation was powerless, so too was
the nation in the absence of social inequality.[40]

---

39   Ibid., p. 129.

40   Ibid. His comments on the relationship between Marxism and nationalism are most
forcefully stated when addressing the work of Tom Nairn and Miroslav Hroch. Gellner
greatly admired the intellectual honesty of Tom Nairn, reviewing favourably his *The
Break-Up of Britain: Crisis and Neo-Nationalism*, London, 1977, in 'Nationalism, or the New
Confessions of a Justified Edinburgh Sinner', in *Spectacles and Predicaments: Essays in Social
Theory*, Cambridge, 1979 – whilst stressing that the arguments marshalled by Nairn did not
sit comfortably with the *New Left Review* stable to which he was attached. Nairn's views
about nationalism were deeply indebted to Gellner's chapter in *Thought and Change*. He
would occasionally tease Gellner about the House of Windsor, earning the reply that the
situation was really not that bad and could be lived with. Gellner certainly had a strong
attachment to Scotland. He did not often comment on the nationalist fringes of Great
Britain, although he did condemn the unnecessary killing in Northern Ireland – refusing at
the same time to condemn terrorists in some places, notably Palestine ('Ruthless Liberalism',
Fortnight, April 1995, p. 28). Nairn wrote an interesting piece – 'The Curse of Rurality:
Limits of Modernization Theory', in Hall (ed.), *The State of the Nation* – shortly after Gellner
died. In it he repeated the charge that Gellner was soft on 'Windsordom', treating it as
equivalent to Austro-Hungary, and suggested that the transition to modernity was proving
to be far less smooth than Gellner had imagined. In contrast, relations with Hroch seem
to have been slightly strained. Gellner admired Hroch's detailed empirical study of small
national movements, *Social Preconditions of National Revival in Europe*, Cambridge, 1985 –
first published in German in 1968. But shortly before his death, and only once communism
had fallen, he made clear his distance from its explanatory argument – in 'The Coming of
Nationalism and Its Interpretation: The Myths of Nation and Class', in G. Balakrishnan
(ed.), *Mapping the Nation*, London, 1996 (his essay was first published in Russian in 1992,
and then in Italian in 1993). If the main argument against Hroch was that class and nation
needed each other to change historical patterns, Gellner added to this a careful dissection
of the Marxist metaphysics that Hroch had employed (or perhaps been forced to employ)
in his book. Hroch contested Gellner's arguments after the latter's death, in 'Real and
Constructed: The Nature of the Nation', in Hall, *The State of the Nation*.

Additional Writings and Replies to Critics

The disintegration and collapse of the Soviet Union, as noted, put nationalism at the centre of world politics and intellectual attention in the last decade of Gellner's life. This resulted in a considerable record of publications: several prefaces to the many translations of *Nations and Nationalism*; interviews, especially in Eastern Europe; various prefaces to books on nationalism; a large number of articles on nationalism, the most original of which were collected in *Encounters with Nationalism* in 1994; the important 'Reply to Critics'; and a posthumously published short book on *Nationalism*.[41] As some of this material was repetitive, it makes most sense to deal with it analytically, by considering in turn the additions to the theory and responses to some of his critics, before turning to the prescriptive turn in his thought occasioned by worries about the collapse of the Soviet Union.

The additions to the basic theory can in turn be divided into three. First, Gellner put forward a new way of classifying nationalism, largely overlapping with the previous typology – with the exception that diaspora nationalism is not specified as a type in its own right, and the sub-Saharan situation drops out of the picture altogether. There are two elements to the new classification, the first concerned with stages and the second with geographic zones. It can be said immediately that the stadial theory is marred by only really considering European history. No such criticism can be levelled against the description of zones, because it was purposely designed as a description of Europe. Let us take each of these categories in turn.[42]

The first stage is held to be exemplified by the Congress of Vienna. At first sight, the most obvious point about the peacemakers at Vienna is that they paid little attention to the nationalist principle. However, Gellner suggested that the world had already changed, and explained why this was so in a passage whose importance resides in the agency it attributes to nineteenth-century European elites.

> [T]he rulers themselves, were part and parcel of the changes and were eager to advance some of them, which were conducive to the enhancement of their own wealth and power. They rationalised administration,

---

41   A near complete bibliography of Gellner's writings on nationalism is available in Hall, *The State of the Nation*, pp. 307–10.

42   Gellner is here close to E. H. Carr's *Nationalism and After*, London, 1945. In a lecture at the end of his life ('Nationalism and the International Order', in *Encounters with Nationalism*), he noted that he had read Carr's book early in his career.

continuing the work of the pre-Napoleonic Enlightened Despots, and
were quite eager to expand education. A centralised orderly bureaucracy,
implementing general rules and appointed by the centre, not selected,
like some Ottoman pasha, in virtue of their local power base, had to use
one language or another to communicate with each other from one end
of the empire to the other. It ceased to be the ethnically neutral Latin,
and became the ethnically divisive German. This in itself, even if the
society governed by the new bureaucracy had not been changing, was
bound to have potent nationalist-type implications: when the bureaucracy becomes more pervasive and intrusive, and employs one vernacular,
the choice of that language become, important for people.[43]

The second stage is that of irredentism, or, more accurately given that not all
nationalist movements sought to bring in peoples left outside their homelands, of the self-styled 'awakeners' of nations. Gellner's attempt to deal
with the exceptions to his theory – that is, Greek and Balkan nationalisms,
both clearly present and powerful before the impact of industrialization
– concerns us below. The central contention is, however, very much in
line with his general theory: nationalist ideas triumphed, but few boundaries were changed – thereby demonstrating that weakness of nationalism
found at the centre of his theory. The fact that the third stage, that of the
Treaty of Versailles and of Woodrow Wilson's call within it for national
self-determination, contributes so much to the growth of nationalism in
effect amounts to a new innovation in Gellner's approach. The role of
geopolitics in the initial theory had been accidental; here it becomes much
more central. And this centrality does not apply only to the creation of
nation-states. The new units were fragile and feeble, haunted by the presence of significant minorities from nearby homelands to which they could
appeal for help. Such internal weakness amounted to a vacuum into which
Nazi Germany and the Soviet Union moved with appalling ease. Their
interventions exemplified the fourth stage, that of ethnic cleansing (and
of mass murder and population transfer) carried out amidst the fog of war.
If the illustrative material for this point is drawn from European experience, a claim to generality is made of the last stage, that of the attenuation
of national feelings. The central idea echoes the discussion of nationalism's future from Gellner's monograph: 'Stable government plus affluence
and the expectation of growth do jointly militate against extremism'.[44] But
Gellner adds to this the claim that a great ideological change has begun to

---

43   *Nationalism*, London, 1997, p. 39.
44   Ibid., p. 48.

have a major generalized impact: 'the brilliant success of the two major defeated nations and the economic malaise of some of the victors have made it plain that what makes you big, important, rich and strong in the modern world is not acreage, but rates of growth'.[45]

The geographical zones described by Gellner are witnesses to differing links between state and culture. The first zone is that of the Atlantic seaboard, in which – with the exception of Ireland (and a critic might add Great Britain, Spain and Belgium) – state and culture were interlinked for centuries, thereby creating sufficient cultural homogeneity to spare this world any severe nationalist conflict. The second and third zones are very familiar, namely those of liberal unification nationalism in Italy and Germany (where the bride of culture was ready, merely awaiting its state) and of the classic nationalism of East and Central Europe. The latter was bound to be illiberal, as Plamenatz (again cited here) had stressed, given the sheer amount of cultural engineering involved due both to their mixed populations and to their need to shape a folk culture into the high culture of a national state. In contrast, the fourth geographical zone Gellner identified represents another innovation in his thought. This is the Soviet Union. This reconstituted empire had no trouble containing nationalism, with later scholarship showing indeed that it affirmed, albeit merely for purposes of transition, some ethnicities – interestingly, as Gellner noted, at the expense of Russians themselves.[46] But once the Soviet Union was defeated in the economic Cold War, nationalism quickly occupied the resulting vacuum. He finished his account by wondering where post-Soviet politics would fit, in terms of his stadial theory. 'Shall we see the proliferation of small, weak, inexperienced and minority-haunted states, or ethnic cleansing, or a diminution of the intensity of the ethnic intrusion into politics?'[47] If Yugoslavia had manifested the worst possible outcome, the situation in Russia was as yet unclear – but it was one which filled Gellner with foreboding.

A final innovation in this zonal system is the introduction of a fifth zone, designed to accommodate Islam. His last thoughts here are novel, for they differ from the argument he made about Islam and nationalism in *Nations and Nationalism*. The monograph had stressed the secularization-resistant capacity of Islam familiar to us from *Muslim Society*, that is, its ability to survive in the modern world by stressing the scripturalism and discipline

---

45   Ibid.
46   T. A. Martin, *The Affirmative Action Empire: Nations and Nationalism in the Soviet Union, 1923–39*, Ithaca, 2001; *Nationalism*, pp. 56–8.
47   *Nationalism*, pp. 57–8.

of its high culture.[48] The dilemma faced by most developing countries was exemplified in Russia, torn between Westernizers and populists, the former tuned in to the needs of modernity at the cost of abandoning their own culture and the latter proud of a native tradition but more or less unable to deal with the task of modernization. In contrast, Muslims could appeal to their roots – for these were the roots of the high tradition rather than of the tribes, so legalistic and rigid as to be eminently suited to the modern age. The situation as a whole was very different from that of Europe, where secularization preceded the age of nationalism. This might seem to suggest that only the power of Islam was important in modernity. However, he stressed the link between Islam and nationalism. In Algeria, the high culture proved a rallying ground against the colonizers. More generally, Gellner suggested that the 'political conjurers could build their patter around the strict theology, while they shuffled the cards dealing with political morality according to their own preference, without attracting too much attention'.[49] We have already seen that his later reflections, after the publication of *Nations and Nationalism*, are very different. He continued to argue that Islam had an enormous advantage when confronting its own backwardness. But he had come to see revived Islam as a force with the potential to go beyond nationalism:

> For a long time, nationalism and even various forms of Marxist–nationalist syncretism were prominent. Islamism and nationalism could also co-exist: it was not clear whether Islam deserved praise for being the social cement of the Arabs, or whether Arabs deserved respect for being the carriers of Islam. Ambiguities of this kind are not uncommon in the ideological life of societies. But by now, much of the ambiguity is dispersed: fundamentalism has emerged as the dominant and victorious trend. Whether this will continue to be so we do not know . . . [50]

His views here have already been criticized. Both Turkey and Algeria see national patterns trumping Islamic norms; it is further evident that Islam has not triumphed over nationalism in Malaysia or Indonesia. And shared Muslim faith was not enough to prevent the break-up of Pakistan in 1971.[51]

---

48 Gellner suggested that Confucianism lacked equivalent power in modern circumstances, and ascribed this to the nature of its doctrine – 'a little too brazenly deferential and inegalitarian for modern taste' (*Nations and Nationalism*, p. 80).
49 Ibid., p. 81. He cited as examples of this flexibility the conservative regimes of Saudi Arabia and Northern Nigeria, and socially radical ones such as Libya, South Yemen and Algeria.
50 *Nationalism*, p. 83.
51 O'Leary, 'Ernest Gellner's Diagnoses of Nationalism', p. 75.

The third and final set of additions is rather more ad hoc. Rather different accounts are offered, to begin with, of Greek and Balkan nationalism, both of which gathered steam well before the impact of industrialization, as already noted. A certain amusement colours Gellner's account of the Greek case; the initial rising took place in Romania, where Greeks were but a rich minority, and aimed at the restoration of Byzantium rather than the creation of a nation-state. But the fact that the Greeks were traders allowed him to argue that some of them were touched by industrialization before it fully arrived. However, this makes no sense of the Balkan cases, above all that of Serbia. The crux of Gellner's explanation revolves around the fact that the rulers were of a different religion than the ruled, allowing for group self-identification that was reminiscent of Algeria. Further, Christianity served as a conductor of the Enlightenment.

> This conductivity must also be part of the reason why the Romanovs modernised faster than the Ottomans, thereby creating a messianic intel-ligentsia whose salvation politics proved fatal in 1917 — a fate Turkey was spared in as far as the Young Turks were pragmatists concerned with state power, not salvation-drunk messianists. Bandit-rebels in Balkan mountains, knowing themselves to be culturally distinct from those they were fighting, and moreover linked, by faith or loss-of-faith, to a new uniquely powerful civilisation, thereby became ideological bandits: in other words, nationalists.[52]

The Balkans also feature in a second set of amendments to his theory, designed to explain the murderous virulence of nationalism, both in general and with more particular reference to the purportedly liberal unifi-cation nationalisms of Italy and Germany. The intense feelings generated by the ills of early industrialization were once again offered as a generic factor. But two further factors, both novel to Gellner's work on nation-alism thus far, were adduced. First, nationalism is likely to be particularly vicious in societies in which the principle of honour and the practice of self-policing are paramount. This certainly applies in the Balkans and in the Caucasus. Gellner cited short stories by Milovan Djilas to make a further point, namely that much of the killing in these cases takes place within the ethnic group concerned. This returns us to a phenomenon noted above, namely the unwillingness of some groups to let their members escape the cage of cohesion. Most attention was given to a second, ideological, factor. The romantic reaction against the cold rationalism of the Enlightenment

---

52   Ibid., p. 42.

gained real bite, that is, moved well beyond the benign position of Herder, when it was joined together with instinctualist, neo-Darwinian views of popularized Nietzschean hue. The community was now to be biologically rather than merely culturally different. It was to affirm its specificity 'politically with an aggressiveness which was more of an end than a means, which was the expression and precondition of true vitality'.[53] Stressing the importance of roots led Gellner to reformulate his comments about middlemen in particularly striking form. 'Superficial smart alecks with a shallow urban cleverness, who can assume any accent and are committed to none, are the very model of a moral pathology'.[54] The fact that these figures can now no longer be clearly identified on the basis of their religion, abandoned as they became cosmopolitan, makes it necessary, if they are to be excluded, to switch from asking them about their faith to asking them about their grandparents.[55] A comment is called for regarding this important late addition. Gellner had once irritated Anthony Smith, as noted, when asserting in general lectures at the LSE that the Holocaust was best seen as an unnecessary mistake of industrial society, leading Smith to characterize Gellner thereafter as a non-Marxist materialist thinker. If there had been truth to this in his earlier years, there is no doubt that in his late and mature thought he was fully aware of cultural forces within modernity.

Gellner constantly engaged with his critics. His most important responses – concerning the motivation of nationalists and the causes that occasion their movements – have been at the centre of this chapter. But his more particular responses to two LSE figures also must be noted. Smith had been Gellner's doctoral student, and Gellner often introduced him at lectures by saying how proud he was to have taught someone who had come to dominate the bibliography of modern research into nationalism. But they did not agree. Gellner felt that Smith's doctoral dissertation had not properly interpreted Gellner's own theory, downplaying its structural content.[56] He became still more sceptical when Smith developed an alternative theory of his own, stressing that an historic ethnic core was essential for any modern nation-state's success and viability.[57] Gellner had always noted that nationalists often used shreds and patches of previous ethnic identities, and he admitted in conversation that he was puzzled by seemingly

53   Ibid., p. 70.
54   Ibid., p. 73.
55   Ibid.
56   A. D. Smith, 'Addendum to Gellner's Theory', in *Theories of Nationalism*, London, 1983, pp. 265–7.
57   A. D. Smith, *The Ethnic Origins of Nations*, Oxford, 1988. Cf. A. D. Smith, 'State-Making and Nation-Building', in J. A. Hall. (ed.), *States in History*, Oxford, 1986.

proto-nationalist language in Shakespeare. But these melanges were only myths, created for modern circumstances. It was this last position that was on view in a celebrated public debate with Smith at Warwick two months before Gellner's death.[58] Wittily drawing a parallel between the question of nationalism's ethnic roots and the celebrated nineteenth-century debate as to whether Adam did or did not have a navel, Gellner stated his position in the bluntest of terms:

> Some nations have navels, some achieve navels, some have navels thrust upon them. Those possessed of genuine ones are probably in a minority, but it matters little. It is the need for navels engendered by modernity that matters.[59]

This passage is taken from *Nationalism*, demonstrating that key ideas were used, polished and then reused. The book cites Estonia as a wholly invented nation; the Czech case showed how much internal conflict there could be in ideas of national self-perception.[60] And underlying this last critique was a very particular view of culture. Cultures could transmit practices over time and yet occasionally change completely, and with speed. Any account of nationalism emphasizing internal culture was doomed to failure, even though there might be a high degree of cultural continuity in any particular case, because of the existence of rival national cultures. Explanation needed to stand outside all national cultures to explain why the principle of nationality had such broad appeal.[61]

Gellner's second set of comments were addressed to his friend Elie Kedourie – whose insistence that nationalism was not a permanent fixture of the historical record had, Gellner always said happily awoken him from his own dogmatic slumbers. Gellner could not accept the idealism of Kedourie's account (nor its view that Kant had provided ideological cover for nationalists), unable to believe that an ideological invention could be so influential unless it somehow fitted with structural conditions. His own causal arguments led to continuing disagreements with Kedourie. First, in Gellner's view nationalism resulted more from the unevenness of industrialism's spread and the humiliation that this involved for some than from the top-down activity of a power-hungry nationalist elite.[62] Second,

---

58   The exchange was reprinted in *Nations and Nationalism*, vol. 10, 1996.
59   *Nationalism*, p. 101.
60   Ibid., chapter 15.
61   Ibid., pp. 93, 95.
62   *Nations and Nationalism*, p. 39. But he also pointed out, against Kedourie, that the educationally privileged of the diaspora could also be driven towards nationalism, essentially

he rejected Kedourie's charge that he was claiming that industry could only arise amongst nationally homogeneous populations: very much to the contrary, it could arise in multinational situations, and it was this very fact that created the tensions that led to nationalism.[63] Finally, Gellner noted that Kedourie's own late work on nationalism made much of the dislocations caused by European imperialism, suggesting a convergence between their two positions.[64]

The Prescriptive Turn

That Gellner was deeply disturbed by nationalist violence in the last years of his life was apparent in the utter seriousness with which he approached the issue.[65] There were two related components to his visceral fear. On the one hand, there was the recollection of 'the sequel to the analogous break-up of the Habsburg empire, which led to a political system so feeble that it fell to Hitler and Stalin with barely a sign of resistance'.[66] On the other hand, his belief that state socialism had atomized society made him fear that the quickest route to independent social organization was likely to be that of ethnic mobilization.[67] He was a strong and open supporter of Gorbachev, endorsing the strategy of using the party as a means to reform itself. The alternative position, that of Yeltsin, scared him stiff, for its desire to counterbalance the party by calling for ethnic mobilization looked set to open a Pandora's box of ethnic conflict. However, he acknowledged after the coup attempt that Yeltsin had been fundamentally right: Gorbachev had not been able to carry the party with him, and only the presence of a countervailing force had prevented some sort of return to the bunker.[68] But this particular outcome did not alleviate his fear, unsurprising given events in the erstwhile Yugoslavia and in Chechnya, and his later fears of conflict in the Caucasus.

It is hard to say whether political events made him more aware of

---

to escape the activities of, so to speak, native nationalist movements.

63   Ibid., pp. 108–9.

64   Ibid., pp. 128–9, referring to Kedourie's long introduction to his edited volume *Nationalism in Asia and Africa*, London, 1970.

65   Steven Lukes attended many of Gellner's lectures over the years, and recalled a complete change in tone in a lecture given in Vienna which addressed the potential that nationalist violence would be unleashed by the collapse of communism (Lukes interview with B. O'Leary, 27 February 2001).

66   'Nationalism in Eastern Europe', *New Left Review*, no. 189, 1991, p. 134.

67   Ibid., p. 133.

68   Ibid., p. 134.

Malinowski's political theory or whether his discovery of the Hapsburg roots of Malinowski's work – as the result of the centenary birthday celebrations held in London and in Cracow in 1984 – had a wholly autonomous effect of their own. But there can be no doubt that his interpretation of Malinowski, on which he was working at the end of his life as we shall see later, provided him with a new way of thinking about nationalism. Of course, in his last debate with Anthony Smith his argument was in effect Malinowskian in saying that our sense of history is based on our current needs. But it is 'The Political Thought of Bronisław Malinowski', a reconsideration of Malinowski's late and wholly neglected *Freedom and Civilization*, that most clearly signals a change in Gellner's theory of nationalism.[69] Gellner's argument is paradoxical, accepting the injustice of inequality between imperialists and colonized, but refusing to accept as a corollary the view that the colonized should gain independence as fast as possible to become like their erstwhile rulers. Rather what is needed is an egalitarianism in which all nations are ruled from the outside. 'No nation is fit to rule itself . . . They fight each other, and they oppress their own minorities and hamper – if not worse – the free expression of their culture'.[70] Indirect rule is necessary, as practised in effect by both the British and Austrian empires, and as to be practised putatively in the future by an international organization such as the League of Nations. A policy of this sort would work well in England.

> The League commissioner, perhaps a minor Habsburg archduke, would work discreetly from some functional but unostentatious secretariat, located in a new edifice in some anonymous London suburb – say Neasden. An architect in the Bauhaus tradition would be commissioned to design it. All ritual and symbolic activities, on the other hand, would continue to be based in Buckingham Palace. Thus the English would be emotionally spared any visible, let alone conspicuous, externalization or expression of their diminished sovereignty.[71]

Gellner highlighted the attractiveness of this option. History had shown that Austro-Hungary in its last years was morally more attractive than the Soviet Union under Stalin – that Franz Joseph, as Gellner liked to quip,

---

69 'The Political Thought of Bronislaw Malinowski', *Current Anthropology*, vol. 28, 1987, reprinted as 'A Non-nationalist Pole' in *Encounters with Nationalism*.
70 'A Non-nationalist Pole', p. 76.
71 Ibid., p. 78.

was preferable to Joseph.[72] Further, the 'universal protection of cultural autonomy, combined with political constraint imposed by a benevolent centre, must clearly appeal to an age such as ours, which suffers from the opposite condition – political independence blended with dreary cultural standardization'.[73]

This enthusiastic endorsement of Malinowski's position is clearly and without question far removed from the main thrust of his prior work on nationalism. It is not wrong to see his main analytical work as arguing that multinational arrangements are doomed, something accentuated at the end of *Nations and Nationalism* when he had argued, as noted above, that it was unlikely that a state would support two cultures within its territory. It was this that led him, in his earliest sustained visits to the Soviet Union, to feel that his theory would apply even more strongly to the socialist world. There were descriptive considerations at work here: the European Union was something like an Austro-Hungary that works, though the causal waters were muddied here by the fact that contemporary European nationalism's virulence had been diminished by the achievement of affluence – and, one might add, by ethnic cleansing. But his new position was very largely prescriptive; it was dictated by sheer fear. The question that must concern us as we proceed is this: is this change of tone a straightforward contradiction within his thought, or merely the expression of a deep but potentially resolvable tension?

Assessment

Gellner finished *Nations and Nationalism* with a metaphor, that of a transition from the world of Kokoschka to that of Modigliani, the former chaotic and the latter more orderly.[74] This captures all too accurately the ethnic homogenization that took place in Europe, properly characterized as the Dark Continent of the twentieth century.[75] That Gellner offered an explanation of this tectonic shift is a huge intellectual achievement. Any complete assessment of the state of the field in the study of nationalism is impossible here, given both the efflorescence of theory and of empirical studies of nationalist movements throughout the world. But some of these developments can be cited in order to assess Gellner's contribution, with particular reference to his causal claims and to his more general view that

---

72   Ibid., p. 77.
73   Ibid., p. 79.
74   *Nations and Nationalism*, p. 139.
75   M. Mazower, *The Dark Continent: Europe's Twentieth Century*, London, 1999.

homogeneity is necessary for societal success. It may be helpful to say at the outset that political considerations must be added to Gellner's important account with its socio-economic causal model. Doing so will allow us to modify his definition of the phenomenon under consideration.

There are clear causal arguments in his work. Active discrimination, exclusion and the possibility of being murdered led many members of diasporas to realize that only the establishment of their own state could provide protection. The theory of nationalism present in *Thought and Change*, restated in the monograph via his analysis of entropy-resistance, stresses a block on social mobility so absolute that the rise of nationalist politics was all but inevitable. In contrast, there seems to be something like flexibility in the parable about the Ruritanians, for there was the opportunity, taken by many, of assimilating to the dominant culture. There is a sense in which this flexibility had to be there, for otherwise Gellner's prescriptive comments would be rendered nonsensical, simple contradictions of all that he had said previously. At issue within his thought is the great tension just described, between the major analytical expectation that multinational polities are doomed and the hope that they might somehow survive. With this thought in mind, let us turn to the European material – and more particularly the Bohemian material – from which he drew. I begin by bracketing his causal account, without challenging its validity.

Some basic historical points need to be made immediately. Gellner's account of the forces operative in the age of nationalism is essentially apolitical.[76] This means that insufficient attention is paid to geopolitical conflict. Some of the mechanisms leading to the worst nationalist excess are best understood within this framework.[77] The most dangerous situations arise when rival national movements claiming the same piece of territory are backed by powerful neighbouring states. The fear that assistance for one's rival may come from abroad encourages pre-emptive cleansing, for those rivals can all too easily be dubbed a fifth column likely to betray the state; equally, the fear that one might be cleansed makes it rational to look to one's homeland for support. And one can go beyond these variables by referring to Max Weber, showing how nationalism was affected by two elements taken to constitute the strength of a state. First, Weber was a Fleet Professor, convinced that imperial possessions were necessary for the well-being of the state. Secure sources of supplies mattered quite as much as markets, for geopolitical autonomy depended upon the ability to feed one's population and to have the raw materials required to produce a full

---

76   This is also the central claim of O'Leary, 'On the Nature of Nationalism'.
77   M. Mann, *The Dark Side of Democracy: Explaining Ethnic Cleansing*, Cambridge, 2005.

complement of weapons. There is, secondly, a less well-known side to Weber's politics, neatly summed up in the nickname used by his friends: 'Polish Max'. This referred to his early research project on Polish labour on the East Elbian Junker estates. The attitude that Weber took to such labour – that it would weaken the fabric of the nation – was entirely typical of the time. The leading edge of power seemed to reside in monolingual nation-states, not least as multinationalism was considered likely to undermine military efficiency. Somewhat in the spirit of Gellner's own desire to distinguish different moods in the history of European nationalism, one can say that this protean force is best seen in Freudian terms as labile, prone to be coloured by its surroundings. In the late nineteenth century nationalism was closely linked to imperialism: a strong state needed – or, rather, in order to be strong its leaders felt that it needed– both a nationally homogeneous people and imperial possessions if it was to survive in a hostile world. It is crucial to highlight here the active role of some of the Megalomanias of the time. Politically conscious movements tend to arise when states act on civil society, whether in terms of taxation, repression, exclusion or conscription. This most certainly applies to nationalism. The earliest demands against many imperial systems were for the simple recognition of historic rights. Exit from the empire became a fully attractive option only when people felt so voiceless that loyalty was destroyed.[78] Secessionist impulses very often resulted from the drive of great powers to homogenize their territories. Differently put, some great powers sought to become nations – a possibility for the Tsarist Empire if the Ukrainians remained 'little Russians' but a permanent impossibility for the Hapsburgs given the absence of a *Staatsvolk* of sufficient size.[79] The analytical point here is the one noted in the previous chapter. Social movements gain their character not just from socio-economic circumstances, but also from the nature of the political environment in which they have to operate.

It might seem as if these historical considerations fit within Gellner's theory. Had he not stressed the unsettling effects of the introduction by the leading power of a single state language?[80] Furthermore, he offered

---

78   These concepts are of course those of A. O. Hirschman, *Exit, Voice and Loyalty*, Cambridge (MA), 1978.

79   D. Lieven, *Empire: The Russian Empire and Its Rivals*, London, 2000.

80   In an interesting response ('Reply to Critics', p. 636. Cf. *Nationalism*, p. 39) to an article by Michael Mann ('The Emergence of Modern European Nationalism', in J. A. Hall and I. C. Jarvie, [eds], *Transition to Modernity*, Cambridge, 1992), Gellner made it clear that state modernization in general, rather than industrialization per se, was responsible for the onset of nationalism. To be fair, Gellner had never treated industrialization as a synonym for the mode of production, rather as a synonym for modernity.

a defence against the politically centred view expressed in the paragraph above:

> Oppression is not some kind of independent and additional factor: cultural differentiation, inoffensive under the old intimate social order, is automatically experienced as oppression in the age of anonymity, mobility, and pervasive bureaucratization with a standardized idiom.[81]

But the phenomenology involved is subtly different, rendering politics autonomous in a way that does not really fit Gellner's theory.[82] The repression involved was not any old repression, not a mere concern to keep order, nor a desire to establish more modern bureaucratic rule. Rather, these great powers sought to become nation-states themselves – a desire which meant not just establishing a state language but banning the languages of other ethnicities. Their leaders felt that forging a national identity was necessary: revolutionary France had shown that national loyalty could generate enormous power, and as Clausewitz, the great Prussian reformer and theorist, stressed, this changed the terms of state competition thereafter.[83] It was this sort of repression that ruled out the possibility of minority-group loyalty, making exit the only viable strategy. But two further implications need to be stressed.

First, Gellner's approach to nationalism is one-sided in that it centres on secession. This is misguided: nationalism could and did involve large states quite as much – indeed one could argue that nationalism has had its greatest effect on the world as the result of French, German and American actions. Second, rulers can themselves be nationalists, seeking to establish a homogenous world. Kedourie was right in this matter, even if the actors really involved were rather different than he had imagined – military leaders such as Clausewitz rather than mere intellectuals. If one takes seriously

81 'Reply to Critics', p. 637 – responding here to O'Leary, 'On the Nature of Nationalism'.

82 One justification for the claim made at the start of this chapter that the key book contains all sorts of comments about nationalism, can be found at this point. Gellner entertains this political oppression theory in *Nations and Nationalism* (p. 57), but rapidly qualifies it by saying that ethnic markers are more often emphasized by romantic members of the middle and upper classes than by 'the lower orders'.

83 Gellner noted ('Reply to Critics', p. 626) that he had not claimed that nationalism was best seen in Listian terms as an ideology designed to force industrialization, stressing instead the causal argument present in the parable of Megalomania and Ruritania. (He had in mind here R. Szporluk, *Communism and Nationalism: Karl Marx versus Friedrich List*, Oxford, 1988, critically discussed in 'Nationalism and Marxism', in *Encounters with Nationalism*.) The claim here is that large states were active, seeking to become nation-states themselves, in order to increase their military and economic power.

the charge of illicit functionalism levelled against Gellner, that is, the charge
that he teleologically suggests that the needs of industrialism will somehow
inevitably be met, a way to save the theory is here – by stressing the agency
of political leaders.[84] The point I wish to make is that such agency has indeed
marked the historical record at times. As such, it must form part of any general
theory of nationalism. This is not to say that Gellner's own genuinely causal
account, socio-economic rather than political in character, should be rejected.
The claim rather is that the theory needs to be complemented.

Gellner was offered this recuperation of his theory and chose not to
accept it, insisting that his own causal account was perfectly adequate.[85] One
reason for his insistence is probably that his theory derives from a consideration of Austro-Hungary. In his last years in Prague he liked to refer,
surely correctly, to the empire as less a prison-house than a kindergarten of
nations. The fact that Vienna could never rule over anything like a German
majority, however defined, meant, as noted, that it was virtually necessary
to accommodate linguistic variety. The state did not seek to destroy other
languages, though at times it promoted the use of German – but promoted
it, most of the time, for reasons of bureaucratic efficiency rather than ethnic
mobilization. It was permissible to teach Czech in primary schools from
the eighteenth century, and this was extended in the nineteenth century
to secondary schools, albeit in a complex and halting process of extension, withdrawal, and further extension. In 1882, the Czechs gained their
own university, and extended their cultural activity in every sphere. One
measure of Vienna's attitude was the Crown Prince's attendance at the
first performance at the Národní Divadlo, surely the greatest symbol of
the Czech national revival. Further, the Czechs made steady progress in
the newly industrializing towns, most importantly Prague, which they
came to dominate culturally by the turn of the century.[86] Equally, the
Bohemian lands became ever more prosperous, providing something like
half of Cisleithania's industrial output in the early years of the century. Very
complex schemes were introduced to allow for greater linguistic equality,
especially at a local level. These were often resisted, sometimes by rioting,
but nonetheless slowly inched forward. Finally, it is worth noting that in
the years before 1914 the Czechs themselves were gaining a significant
number of positions in the central bureaucracy.

---

84 O'Leary suggested saving the theory this way, using Jon Elster's notion of 'filter
explanations', in 'On the Nature of Nationalism'.
85 'Reply to Critics', pp. 627–8.
86 G. Cohen, *The Politics of Ethnic Survival: Germans in Prague, 1861–1914*, Princeton,
1981. A similar story is told of Budweis/Budějovice by J. King, *Budweisers into Czechs and
Germans: A Local History of Bohemian Politics, 1848–1948*, Princeton, 2002.

This largely addresses only one side of the matter, that is, from Vienna's perspective. When one turns to the attitude of the Czechs themselves, the notion that nationalism must involve the campaign for an independent state makes still less sense. Czechs were aware that independence, however conceived, would be dangerous, given the possibility of intervention from either Berlin or St Petersburg. Had Austria not been there, it would have been necessary to invent her! Almost as important for many Czech intellectuals was the realization that some sort of accommodation with the increasingly politically conscious German community was required, especially in light of the geopolitical alliance between Vienna and Berlin. Bluntly put, there was almost no Czech voice at the end of the nineteenth century calling for independence. What Czech leaders sought was a more liberal empire, perhaps a constitutional monarchy, in which their voice could be heard, guaranteeing the protection and flourishing of the identity that they were trying to create. It is particularly revealing in this matter that the very slight beginnings of Masaryk's pro-independence stance came only in the years immediately before 1914, when he felt that the Czechs were gaining strength and solidarity and that Vienna was becoming more intransigent.[87] Masaryk finally opted for independence only during the war, at a moment when Vienna introduced centralist and Germanizing schemes designed to diminish gains that had already been won by the Czechs. The absolutely vital point here concerns Gellner's definition of nationalism. It is erroneous: not every nation seeks its own state. Nationalism is better defined in the simplest terms as the desire for the national group to prosper – a condition that can be achieved inside a larger framework, especially since going it alone often exposes the group to great danger.[88]

This counterfactual debate, of whether Austro-Hungary was doomed as the result of its nationalities problems, has no resolution. The most balanced

---

87 Bugge, *Czech Nation-Building, National Self-Perception, and Politics, 1780–1914*, Doctoral Dissertation, Aarhus University, 1994 (revised edition forthcoming from Harvard University Press), chapter 10.

88 An important general point can be made here by noting a second disagreement with Brendan O'Leary. Johnson ('State Power') had noted in his admiring review that it was hard to imagine how one could refute *Nations and Nationalism*. Indeed the book is full of riches, with occasional comments pointing in directions that differ from the main thrust of the argument. O'Leary suggests that Gellner always felt that nationalists could be satisfied with home rule rather than secession, arguing further that self-government matters more than prosperity – not least as its absence helps occasion nationalist demands. I have no trouble with either claim insofar as they refer to empirical reality. But I still believe that *Nations and Nationalism* is essentially about the end of multinational entities, and less due to the desire for self-government than O'Leary suggests. Only this reading makes sense of the fact that the prescriptive turn of Gellner's later years sees him arguing against his earlier self.

discussion is that of Danish scholar Peter Bugge. That the Czechs did not seek independence at least suggests that the empire might have survived. Hence Bugge's account of its failure differs from that offered by Gellner in his parable of Megalomania and the Ruritanians, in that it is based on a contrast between horizontal and vertical forms of political organization – that is, roughly speaking, between interest-based politics across national groups and nationally delineated political demands. There were signs of horizontal organization in the Bohemian lands by the end of the nineteenth century: bourgeois interests usually took this form, and significant moves in this direction could be detected amongst both industrial and agrarian workers.[89] Factors limiting this horizontal organization often had little to do with national conflict – the desire of the great landowners to divide and rule played a role, for example, in preventing the emergence of a class-based opposition that would have threatened their position. In the end, however, the fundamental factor preventing the consolidation of horizontal political organization was the character of the state.

> [N]ationalism was a residual political phenomenon. The lower social strata's access to political decision-making always lagged behind the national communities' willingness to embrace them, and since the state – the parliament and the government – denied them the possibility of asserting their social interests and maybe even suppressed their (trans-national) attempts to organize, they had only the national to turn to. National radicalism was also stimulated by the political parties' lack of genuine influence on the policies of the executive. The court, the nobility, and the top bureaucracy had an interest in a weak or paralyzed *Reichsrat*, and Austrian parliamentary politics was caught in a vicious circle: the less political influence, the greater the incitement to prove one's importance to the voters with spectacular manifestations of national zeal; and the more the *Reichsrat* was exposed to obstructions and fights, the harder it was to argue for the virtues of a democratic approach.[90]

The state censuses, demanding selection of a single narrowly defined identity, helped to further politicize matters. So too did the constant back and

---

89 An obvious and important related consideration should be borne in mind. The Bohemian economy was booming in the two decades before the First World War. This brute fact provided the background to the behaviour of bourgeois and socialist forces. There was very little sign of bourgeois forces in Bohemia calling for anything like secession. More striking still were arguments made by the socialists to the effect that the imperial territory should be preserved so that modern economies of scale could be protected for the future.

90 Bugge, *Czech Nation-Building*, p. 316.

forth between concession and repression, that is, the inability of the state to make up its mind regarding its treatment of minorities. There is surely an explanation for this. What mattered most to the state was its position in the international arena. A period of quietism, free from geopolitical involvement, would certainly have helped to diminish levels of internal conflict, perhaps by allowing the state to operate in a less unitary manner. But the empire sought power and glory, as its sustained desire to acquire new possessions so obviously demonstrated. A final point can be added. Once national movements gain political consciousness a Pandora's box is opened. Differently put, a reform that might work in one set of circumstances may fail in another. Timing matters. The exceptionally sophisticated cantonization-type principles enshrined in Moravia's pre-First World War compromise did not look set to establish ethnic peace. Very much to the contrary, outright political conflict was replaced with legal arguments about which community children ought to belong to officially, thereby determining which language they would be taught.[91] A comparison with Switzerland suggests itself at this point. Cantons within Switzerland did indeed become cages, albeit cages maintained more by social pressure than by legal edict. But the deep tradition in Switzerland of popular politics and eventually democracy provided a safety valve – the emergence of the same horizontal interest groups that were stymied in the Bohemian case.[92]

These comments aim to correct Gellner by stressing the importance of politics, of the ways in which liberal politics might contain secession. But several additional points – relevant beyond this particular case – should be made. First, Gellner's account of the relations between Ruritania and Megalomania steps back to some extent from its original brilliant insight, namely that nations are claims as much as they are realities, and that social and linguistic engineering was required to turn the Czech from a low into a high culture. To be precise, the parable of Megalomania and the Ruritanians gives the impression that the Czechs were a solid 'Ruritanian' nation unable to advance only because its life chances were limited by a bureaucracy bound to operate in German. But Czechs were a less firmly established community than this suggests. Rather, Czech language activists were often frustrated by the refusal of their would-be 'pure' Czech target group to abandon their multiple identities, which were based on complex linguistic abilities.[93] Secondly, the sociology in Gellner's account concentrates on the

91   T. Zahra, 'Reclaiming Children for the Nation: Germanization, National Ascription, and Democracy in the Bohemian Lands, 1900–1945', *Central European History*, vol. 37, 2005.
92   J. Steinberg, *Why Switzerland?*, Cambridge, 1996.
93   P. Judson, *Guardians of the Nation: Activists on the Language Frontiers of Imperial Austria*,

links between intellectuals and the newly urbanized working class, seeing the latter as the troops set to realize the vision of the former. Matters were more complex. To begin with, Gellner slightly underplays the sheer ideological élan of intellectuals, less driven to sympathize with poor workers than to assiduously copy best practice from elsewhere. More importantly, his sociology of support for nationalism is distinctly amiss. Workers were not really discriminated against linguistically, not least since early industrial work was not especially abstract – it required the use of but few words in a new language, all of them easily learnt. This is not to deny that workers *became* caged nationally, by the end of the century rejecting the courting of Viennese social democrats, nor is it to dispute Gellner's awareness that industrialization dislocates and uproots, with the cult of the nation presenting an obvious new source of meaning – and humiliation certainly a factor in the general equation.[94] Still, the shock troops of the national movement tended to be the newly educated, that is, those individuals whose life chances would immediately be affected should the language of administration, in Bohemia and perhaps even in the bureaucracy's inner core, cease to be conducted solely in German.[95] Finally, it is important to remember that political compromise in Bohemia was always difficult and eventually impossible because of the behaviour of the German community. At best, the Germans were asked to give up their position of dominance, at worst to submerge themselves inside a Czech-speaking community. Formerly dominant minorities are often intransigent.[96] Over time, this group defined itself in increasingly ethnic terms, as noted, and looked for support not just to Vienna but also to Berlin.[97]

Let us now ask whether constitutional design can allow for many nations to live peacefully under a single roof – and thereby approach the related

---

Cambridge (MA), 2006. Criticism can be made of this view (and of the related positions of Bugge's *Czech Nation-Building* and King's *Budweisers into Czechs and Germans*) that there were nationalist actors without widespread nationalist sentiment. These scholars pay great attention to culturally mixed areas, in which language repertoires were complex. Gellner can be defended, at least in part, on the grounds that such mixed areas were by no means the norm. Thus there was a considerable ontic base for Czech nationalism, as Bugge admitted in conversation in Aarhus in November 2007.

94   P. Bugge, *Czech Nation-Building*, pp. 317–18.

95   These social groups have a prominent role in E. Hobsbawm, *Nations and Nationalism since 1780*, Cambridge, 1990, p. 117. The book's arguments are otherwise generally close and indebted to those of Gellner.

96   The last conference that Gellner organized – and spoke at on the day of his death – dealt with groups of this sort.

97   P. Judson, *Exclusive Revolutionaries: Liberal Politics, Social Experience, and National Identity in the Austrian Empire, 1848–1914*, Ann Arbor, 1996.

question of whether national homogeneity is necessary to the smooth workings of a modern industrial society. This is not to suggest that the past should be forgotten. The facts that no European empire was able to decompress successfully, and that liberal political structures in much of Europe were consolidated only on the back of ethnic cleansing, demand that the prospects be considered with humility. Still, might liberalism one day be a solution to the national question, instead of the happy by-product of horror?

It is of course true – indeed it is nothing less than a tautology – that the survival of a society depends on its members sharing a set of expectations. We are indebted to Gellner for making us realize that high culture must be added to the Hobbesian minimum if a modern society is to prosper. Beyond this point, however, a vital distinction needs to be drawn. It is true that national homogeneity helps those countries which possess it. Small, nationally homogeneous states, for example, are amongst the most advanced in the world, exemplars not just of the ability to act flexibly in the world market, but also of consolidated social democracy and high levels of welfare. Denmark and other Scandinavian countries are clear examples here and perhaps Ireland as well.[98] One could add recent cases which seem to support Gellner's position. After the collapse of communism Czechoslovakia looked set for a stalemate, to some extent structurally determined by the large industries of the Slovaks. The Slovaks' needs were very different from the decentralized and smaller-scale industries of the Czechs, the former needing state support, the latter more prepared to compete in international markets. Separation has allowed for two separate strategies, and both groups have benefited.[99]

But all this does *not* mean that countries with diverse populations should try to become nationally homogeneous, although they certainly need a cultural consensus that recognizes difference. There are two sets of reasons to avoid nationalizing homogenization. On the one hand, it may well cause disaster.[100] To insist on the need for total national unity is to encourage pre-emptive ethnic cleansing.[101] The same is true of calls for partition as a means to end ethnic conflict. The separation of Czechs

---

98 J. L. Campbell and J. A. Hall, 'Defending the Gellnerian premise: Denmark in Historical and Comparative Context', *Nations and Nationalism*, vol. 16, 2010.

99 Of course, qualifications to even these generalizations are necessary. Nationally homogeneous states can be divided by class or ideology, even when small – as was true for many years of the Republic of Ireland, and as is still true of Serbia today.

100 Laitin, *Nations, States and Violence*, chapter 5.

101 D. Laitin, *Identity in Formation: The Russian-Speaking Population in the Near Abroad*, Ithaca, 1998, chapter 12.

and Slovaks was peaceable because the border between the two areas was historic and mutually recognized. In contrast, partitions make a fresh cut into territory that had previously been unitary, with dreadful results.[102] On the other hand, national demands can be and sometimes are satisfied by the protection of a minority group's voice and cultural rights. In order to be a complete, fully participating Indian citizen one needs, for example, facility in at least three languages. Two of these languages, Hindi and English, are the official languages of the central state, the latter still present because so many elites resisted its extirpation at the time of independence, given that their fluency gave them a cultural advantage. A third language is that of one's state, and a fourth is that of a minority within such a state. One less language is required if one is a Hindi speaker within a state which has Hindi as its official language. The point is a simple one: by and large, India functions on the basis of this linguistic diversity.[103] And there are other factors making India a state-nation rather than a nation-state, including the unity established as part of a common struggle against the British – and the continuing presence of the Indian army and of a genuinely meritocratic and powerful state bureaucracy, together giving backbone to the state.[104] Of course, this is but an example of the possibilities inherent in federal and consociational arrangements of varied sorts.[105] It may yet prove to be the case that such arrangements can work even in Iraq, that most suffering of states.[106] And one can add to optimism of this sort. The link between imperialism and nationalism has largely been broken, as Gellner stressed: national prosperity does seem to result from participation in leading

---

102   B. O'Leary, 'Analyzing Partition: Definition, Classification and Explanation', *Political Geography*, vol. 8, 2007.

103   D. Laitin, *Language Repertoires and State Construction in Africa*, Cambridge, 1992.

104   A. Stepan, 'Comparative Theory and Political Practice: Do We Need a "State-Nation" Model as Well as a "Nation-State" Model', *Government and Opposition*, vol. 43, 2008. However, in conversation Gellner was wont to insist on a reservation: India had not yet made a complete transition to modern industrial society, making it possible that ethnic mobilization might yet adversely affect its cohesion.

105   For recent reviews of current thinking on these mechanisms see B. O'Leary, 'Debating Consociational Politics: Normative and Explanatory Arguments', and J. McGarry and B. O'Leary, 'Federation as a Method of Ethnic Conflict Regulation', in S. Noel (ed.), *From Power Sharing to Democracy: Post-Conflict Institutions in Ethnically Divided Societies*, Montreal and Kingston, 2005. These excellent papers add to politically prescriptive sociological analysis. At least some of the sociology concerned resembles Gellner's, notably the insistence that these schemes look set to do best in conditions of affluence.

106   This is the case argued with characteristic brilliance by B. O'Leary, *Getting Out of Iraq with Integrity*, Philadelphia, 2009.

markets rather than from the possession of territory.[107] The intensity and stakes of geopolitical competition have accordingly been lowered somewhat, thereby diminishing the compulsion for states to be unitary. Finally, it may be that national homogeneity is better at mimicry than at innovation – it may even be possible that innovation will matter ever more within modern political economy.

Gellner's prescriptive turn entertained hopes of this sort. He feared the consequences of the Soviet Union's collapse, and came, as we shall see, to dislike what he termed the claustrophilia of the Czech Republic in which he died – despite the fact that in a sense the national homogeneity that country achieved fulfilled his theoretical conditions! But the hopes he entertained were limited and cautious, as they should have been.[108] Recent empirical inquiry seems to show that the spread of education is linked to nationalist conflict, as Gellner had argued, in countries as diverse as Sri Lanka, Rwanda and Cyprus.[109] And the link between nationalism and imperialism is not completely broken: Vladimir Putin, to give but one example, is not cognizant of the certain fact that retaining Chechnya will hinder rather than help the Russian economy. Further, there most certainly are areas in the world in which nations fight over the same territory, as was recently the case in the erstwhile Yugoslavia and in Rwanda, making murderous homogenizing drives a potential reality in a significant number of places. Of course, illiberal state policies towards national minorities exist in some abundance – notably in Tibet, Southern Sudan, Kashmir, Chechnya and Kurdistan. In these circumstances, secessionist nationalism is likely to flourish quite as powerfully as it did within European history. Then there is the sad fact that many federal and consociational schemes have failed, leaving open the question of whether the devolution of power appeases or abets secessionist nationalism. Finally, it may be that there are new structural elements within world politics that might reinforce the unpleasant side of nationalism.[110] The neo-liberal economic policies encouraged by the United States do nothing to help state-building, and at worst help to weaken states that had begun to gain capacity. Ethnic mobilization is all

---

107 *Nationalism*, p. 48.

108 The last chapter of *Nationalism* insisted (p. 102) that there is 'no magic formula for calming ethnic conflict and replacing it with sweetness and light'. He cautiously endorsed stability, affluence and continuity, but insisted that no principles of political cartography would ever be available which would allow for complete clarity – for a move, to adapt his metaphor, from Modigliani to Mondrian.

109 I am drawing here on forthcoming work by Matthew Lange of McGill University in Montreal.

110 Mann, *The Dark Side of Democracy*, chapter 17.

too easy in such circumstances, and its suppression well beyond the power of states bereft of bureaucracies and merit-based armies. Secondly, the end of Leninist state socialism means that a major meaning-system which had been an alternative to nationalism is no longer available. Third, the gap left by socialism's decline has been filled, especially in much of the Middle East, by Islamism. If nationalism has changed its character for the better in some places, as the link with imperialism has been broken, it may be that it will mutate once again into a lethal brew linked to religious fundamentalism. Hence we can conclude that Gellner was, so to speak, in the right place, utterly torn between fear and hope, never allowing the latter to replace hard-headed analysis.

Cambridge and Prague

In August 1984, Gellner moved to Cambridge as the William Wyse Professor of Social Anthropology. The appointment had been contentious. Edmund Leach had objected behind the scenes, apparently trying to run another candidate, Anthony Forge, for the position. Rodney Needham, the holder of Oxford's chair in social anthropology, sat – by reason of tradition – on the committee, and objected to the appointment in the strongest terms. But these old enemies did not prevail, and Gellner moved back to anthropology. He gave several reasons for the move in an interview – in addition to something he did not mention, namely the push factor from the LSE due to the manner in which he had been treated over the Martin White chair.[1] He was happier, and felt more useful, when teaching anthropologists rather than philosophers: the latter needed to arrive armed with a sense of what they wanted to say, whilst the former, if properly directed when doing their fieldwork, could nearly always do decent work. The fact that Cambridge is small and easy to get around suited his physical condition, as did the fact that the standards of health care there are exceptionally high. He also spoke of snobbery, the charm of candlelight on the silver in King's, one of the most beautiful colleges in Cambridge. This claim deserves comment. There was nothing snobbish whatsoever about him, traces of the young mountaineer allowing him to live simply at all times. Moreover, he was a slightly uneasy member of the college. For one thing, he dined out on the fact he would have to kneel in front of the Provost to take an oath, with the Provost in question being Bernard Williams, whose origins lay in

---

1   J. Davis, 'An Interview with Ernest Gellner', *Current Anthropology*, vol. 31, 1991, p. 67. The rest of the information in this paragraph comes from this interview. Alan Macfarlane, one of his Cambridge colleagues, doubted that complete acceptance would have suited him, recording Gellner's remark that lack of total involvement in any organization helped him protect his intellectual independence (A. Macfarlane, 'Ernest André Gellner, 1925-1995', *King's College Annual Report*, November 1996).

linguistic philosophy. Williams apparently then abolished this ritual, over Gellner's protest, so as to avoid being mocked – though it was apparently restored at a later date. Further, he was irritated at times by the super-liberal atmosphere of the college, perhaps especially when his attempt to help members achieve their desire for greater gender equity by proposing the brilliant Islamic historian Patricia Crone was rejected. Still, he was often in the college, usually playing chess after lunch, rather enjoying the mild absurdities of meetings to decide who should occupy parishes which the college still controlled.

Despite all this, the years in Cambridge were difficult and troublesome for him in at least one way. The holder of the named chair normally represented the department in a rather wide range of meetings, with most matters in the university decided by academics rather than by administrators. Gellner hated this, accustomed to a professional administration at the LSE and clearly longing to focus on his own work. He felt he was not particularly good at administration. Perhaps this was unsurprising, for his close colleagues included Colin Renfrew and Anthony Giddens, in charge respectively of the archaeology and sociology departments, both of whom he regarded as brilliant administrators. Further, he did not find relations easy with all members of the department. There was considerable conflict at this time with Keith Hart, contrasting with easy relations with Chris Hann – despite the latter's direct opposition to his views on civil society and the nature of changes within postcommunism. He was considerably relieved when the chairmanship passed to others. His frustration surely had a foundation. In the last decade of his life he was in constant motion. For one thing, nationalism rose to the top of the political agenda. For another, during the last two years of his William Wyse professorship, he was also involved in setting up the Prague campus of the Central European University. And it may be the case that an element of personal tragedy stood behind what seemed at times a mad schedule – as when he flew to Brazil for a single day to oppose Richard Rorty in a philosophical debate. His youngest son, whom he adored, had had a nervous breakdown, and one sensed that travel let him escape the difficulties of confronting this on a daily basis.

The Impact of the Sacred Grove

Gellner took his role as social anthropologist with great seriousness. He was active in key institutions, notably as president of the Royal Anthropological Institute between 1991 and 1994. Perhaps more central to his own interests was the new European Association of Social Anthropologists, which he addressed at its founding conference, the talk appearing in the association's

journal, *Social Anthropology*.[2] Further, he attended mainstream anthropological conferences, notably that of the American Anthropological Association,
where discussions were held around *Plough, Sword, and Book*. The occasion
was memorable for many because of his reply, after many careful evasions,
to an insistent line of feminist questioning asking why he had paid no real
attention to the role of women in historical development. His penchant for
speaking his mind – assuring the questioner that he liked women, but that
they had nothing to do with historical development – caused mild uproar.
A different sort of institutional involvement can be seen in the lectures
he gave in the university, particularly those that brought anthropological
material to bear on key social science issues.[3]

Still more important was the desire to justify a particular style of anthropology, to set the discipline on a proper course. He much enjoyed tracing
the intellectual origins of the British tradition of social anthropology, and
this played its part in his passionate argument for the approach against, as
he saw it, a dreadful move towards an overemphasis on meaning. The devil
he felt he had slain in philosophy thus came back to haunt him in anthropology, drawing forth his full critical talents.[4] A good deal of his fire was
concentrated on Clifford Geertz. He liked to claim that his attack on Geertz
in an essay for *The American Scholar* was so welcome to many American
academics that it was responsible for his election as a foreign member of
the American Academy of Arts and Sciences.[5] Finally, it should be stressed
that the possibility of doing sustained fieldwork again attracted him. The
Cambridge years saw him continuing his involvement with Soviet anthro-

---

2 'Anthropology and Europe', *Social Anthropology*, vol. 1, 1993. The address was given
in 1990 at the founding meeting of the association in Coimbra, Portugal. The second
meeting in 1992 was held in the Czech Republic, with Gellner playing an active role in the
proceedings. The essay was reprinted in his *Anthropology and Politics: Revolutions in the Sacred
Grove*, Oxford, 1995.

3 Two examples stand out: 'Origins of Society', in *Anthropology and Politics*, and 'Trust,
Cohesion and the Social Order', in D. Gambetta (ed.), *Trust: Making and Breaking Cooperative
Relations*, Oxford, 1988. The latter, given as part of a lecture series at King's, exemplifies
his habit of speaking his mind. He began by saying that there were too many historians
of political thought, leading to a situation in which Hobbes could be seen as completely
liberal rather than as the theorist of order. This naturally drew a sharp response from John
Dunn, one of the leading lights of an approach to intellectual history best exemplified by
the work of Quentin Skinner, in his paper in the same volume. But sharpness on Dunn's
part went hand in hand with appreciation, not least when noting that 'only' Gellner could
have attacked Berlin as forcefully as he did when reviewing John Gray's book on the Oxford
historian of ideas.

4 Davis, 'An Interview with Ernest Gellner', p. 66.

5 'The Stakes in Anthropology', *American Scholar*, vol. 57, 1988, reprinted in *Anthropology
and Politics*.

pology, trying to work out the extent and limits of intellectual liberalization. The culmination of that work was to have taken place during his sabbatical in Moscow in the academic year 1989–90, but the tectonic shift of that year changed his intellectual agenda. Nonetheless, he regarded the period in Moscow as one in which he was undertaking fieldwork – although the questions with which he had to deal, including the theory of nationalism and the nature of liberal society, necessarily involved drawing on all his intellectual equipment. But despite this concern with social reality, the fact remains that his most prominent contributions whilst at Cambridge were theoretical. Of course, he had his own continuing intellectual interests, with the philosophy of history offered in *Plough, Sword, and Book* appearing whilst he was at Cambridge. But those interests took on a particular form, were indeed influenced by living life amongst the anthropologists. Three particular contributions deserve comment.

He had lectured on rationality to the social anthropology students since at least 1976, at the invitation of Jack Goody. One set of lectures was recorded and bound under the title 'The Roots of Compulsion'.[6] The material from some of the lectures was used in the early sections of *Plough, Sword, and Book* dealing with ritual and conceptual styles of knowledge. But the larger part of the material appeared in 1992 as *Reason and Culture: The Historic Role of Rationality and Rationalism*. This was his second volume for Blackwell's series on 'New Perspectives on the Past', the first being *Nations and Nationalism*, and many of his prior concerns reappear here, at times in striking formulations.

The first part of the book gives the most detailed account in Gellner's work of Descartes, stressing his thought's hard, classical and bourgeois qualities.[7] Thereafter Gellner restates his general epistemological view by means of a confrontation between Descartes, Durkheim and Weber. We have already seen that Gellner accepted Durkheim's view that our concepts are determined by the social rituals that surround them. He then imagined Descartes responding to Durkheim, insisting that no ritual surrounded his own search for clear and reliable ideas, and adding the charge that not all ritual leads to the emergence of powerful cognitive knowledge.[8] But Durkheim's epistemology is saved, selectively, by Gellner's Weberian claim that the ritual of the Jansenists resembled that of the Calvinists in being

6   The lectures are available in the Gellner Archive.
7   Gellner also expressed his views on Descartes in 'The Pure Inquirer', in *Spectacles and Predicaments: Essays in Social Theory*, Cambridge, 1979, a review of Bernard Williams, *Descartes: the Project of Pure Inquiry*, London, 1978.
8   *Reason and Culture: The Historic Role of Rationality and Rationalism*, Oxford, 1992, pp. 38ff.

ascetic, orderly and this-worldly. These amusing pages conclude with Gellner's characteristic claims – that science emerged accidentally, for all the universal impact that it would have thereafter.

Most attention is devoted to the enemies of reason. The best-known enemy is authority backed by faith. It is most effective when it rests on revealed truth, for a rational defence of religion is likely to eventually undermine it – although believers ought to be wary of such a classical defence of religion since it can apply to any and every faith.[9] As one would expect, considerable attention is paid to the two main ways in which the tense dualism between nature and the self in Kant's philosophy is resolved – by claiming on the one hand, as did Hegel and Marx, that historical progress would lead to a higher unity, and by insisting on the other hand, as did Nietzsche, that we should simply follow our instinctual drives. The relativism of those stressing the power of culture – the later Wittgenstein, Isaiah Berlin and Thomas Kuhn – is discussed, again in terms that are now familiar. But there are also novel elements in the text. Chomsky's work appears again as a counter to empiricism's model of man, but sustained attention is given to the philosophical import of competences that seem to work well beneath the surface of human consciousness. This is a far cry from Descartes's hope that thought could be grounded clearly and publicly, at least potentially accommodating the possibility that this might lead to irrational outcomes.[10] Gellner is especially striking, as noted in the preface, when commenting on Julien Benda. A genuine commitment to rationalism means that one must admit that it is poorly grounded, making it necessary to live without complacency.

The final part of the book, concerned with rationality as a way of life, develops this very claim. The history of reason in action leaves us as 'Prometheus perplexed'.[11] Reason does not work equally well in every sphere, reigning supreme in cognition but largely unable to achieve much in cultural terms. He stressed again that reason is not very useful when dealing with the huge choices that change our identity. His account of reason adds to the charge of parricide, that is, the destruction in the West of the monotheism which had done much to give birth to reason in the first place, the secondary charge of suicide – the inability to create or restore a sense of moral autonomy. There is a contrast here with another allegation, that of impotence – the weakness of empiricism, its inability to provide facts free of theoretical trappings. Gellner hardened his position at this point. He

---

9   Ibid., p. 60.
10   Ibid., pp. 124–8.
11   Ibid., chapter 8.

thought the anxiety about this aspect of empiricism was odd given the obvious success of science. He insisted firmly that new facts were able to destroy theories, there being many more consensual refutations within the scientific community than its critics realized. The same point was made more forcibly about politics: prison camps had existed under state socialism and Pol Pot's regime had killed an enormous proportion of its population – these were facts though they had been denied for bizarre reasons by some intellectuals.[12] If the key argument for the absolutist, transcendental quality of science remained historicist and of a limited one-off pragmatist kind – that is, that it worked – Gellner underlined the consideration with especial force. Even if there was a sense in which we constructed science, the odd fact is that the objects discovered by its method are not within our control. They are not made or controlled by us, but discovered. Reality always surprises us.[13]

Very much in contrast to this consolidation in *Reason and Culture* of his key ideas was his continuing work on Malinowski – the result of deep fascination and engagement, it allowed a final coming to terms with his own intellectual trajectory. We have already seen that Malinowski's politics had done a good deal to change Gellner's view of nationalism, allowing him to argue that several nations might live under a single political roof. Behind Malinowski's politics was an escape from the stark either/or contrast that Gellner had earlier drawn between positivism and Hegelianism. The former continued to be seen as linked to the Viennese cosmopolitan world represented by Popper, and the latter, so much the charter for culture, was now seen more fully as the key justification for nationalist revivals – especially for historic nations which possessed their own states.[14] The excitement apparent in Gellner's interpretation of Malinowski resides in the Pole having, as it were, stepped outside the confines of this binary opposition – playing with the dealt cards in a wholly original manner. The key discovery about Malinowski's early years was that his thesis, 'The Principle of Economy of Thought', honoured as *sub auspiciis Imperatoris* in 1908, dealt

---

12   Ibid., p. 168. I think the implicit target here is N. Chomsky and E. Herman, *The Political Economy of Human Rights*, 2 volumes, Boston, 1979.

13   Ibid., p. 164.

14   '*Zeno of Cracow* or *Revolution at Nemi* or *The Polish Revenge*: A Drama in Three Acts', in *Culture, Identity and Politics*, Cambridge, 1987. The paper also appeared in a volume of papers drawn from the Malinowski memorial conferences: R. Ellen, E. A. Gellner, G. Kubica and J. Mucha, (eds), *Malinowski Between Two Worlds: The Polish Roots of an Anthropological Tradition*, Cambridge, 1988. Gellner wrote many papers on the Hapsburg roots of Malinowski's thought, culminating in *Language and Solitude: Wittgenstein, Malinowski and the Habsburg Dilemma*, Cambridge, 1998, discussed below.

with the great Viennese positivist Ernst Mach. The interpretation offered in the thesis stressed both the need to concentrate on observable entities and their adaptive role in knowledge. It was these features that carried over into Malinowski's own anthropological method. The revolution in anthropology associated with Malinowski's name was based on replacing the magpie method of Sir James Frazer's *The Golden Bough*, which had sought to explain social life by the interpretation of 'survivals' of one sort or another.[15] Malinowski's key methodological innovation had been known to Gellner since his time as a doctoral student in anthropology: an institution or belief was to be studied in terms of its current use or function, in terms of the social context of which it formed a part – though Gellner had sought to disconnect the method from the assumption that societies were stable, thereby allowing for historical analysis. Crucially, as has been noted, this position allowed for Malinowski to stress national feelings. The Poles had a national culture even without a state, allowing Malinowski to marry an empirical method with a sense of the importance of culture.[16] It might, after all, be possible for several national cultures to prosper under the rule of a single state, for the vicissitudes of nationalism to be avoided.

One sign of Gellner's status at Cambridge came in the form of an invitation to deliver a sermon to the university.[17] He took this invitation very seriously, and talked about its basic scheme for some time before delivering

---

15   Gellner reviewed recent work on Frazer, then wrote an important essay – 'James Frazer and Cambridge Anthropology', *Anthropology and Politics*, highlighting the associationist character of the method – and treating it as a logical consequence of the empiricism of David Hume. Turner's painting of *The Golden Bough* adorns the cover of *Anthropology and Politics*.

> The sacred grove of Nemi is represented by a single huge tree (the tree of knowledge) under which sits a diminutive figure being hailed by a stranger. A small crowd stands at a distance overlooking a panoramic view complete with misty lake and mountain bluffs. Why would a book called *Anthropology and Politics* be marked by Frazer's primal scene? The subtitle gives us a better guide to what the book is really about: *Revolutions in the Sacred Grove*. The idea of a priest-kind, whose successor must first kill him seems well-suited to academic life in our century; and Gellner's central theme is the intellectual politics of modern anthropology. He clearly thought that Malinowski's slaying of Frazer was the formative act in twentieth-century anthropology (K. Hart, 'Ernest Gellner: Bard with the Killer Touch', *Cambridge Anthropology*, vol. 19, 1996, p. 93).

16   He speculated in an interesting way as to why Westermarck, who knew Central and Eastern Europe, had not been able to achieve Malinowski's revolution before the Pole arrived in London. Both thinkers rejected fully-fledged nationalist ideals, but Malinowski also embraced them – thereby giving him a sense of the need for holistic explanation that Westermarck never achieved. (*Language and Solitude*, pp.129-31).
17   'The Uniqueness of Truth', a sermon before the University of Cambridge, King's College Chapel, 31 May 1992, reprinted in *Anthropology and Politics*.

it, marking a break from his general reticence to discuss ongoing work on the grounds that doing so made it harder for him to concentrate on its completion. At this time, Akbar Ahmad, with whom he shared an interest in Muslim tribal organization, asked him to co-author a book dealing with postmodernism and the condition of Islam – an invitation which he had accepted partly so that a good example might be set by having a non-believer and a practising Muslim discussing important issues in a civil manner. He used the sermon as the structural basis for a long essay describing the ideological options available at that time. The publishers came to feel that the different contributions of Gellner and Ahmad did not fit together, and so arranged for separate publications. Perhaps the decision of the publishers was based on the harsh polemical tone of Gellner's text, published as *Postmodernism, Reason and Religion*. He had come to loathe postmodernism, regarding it as a terrible disease likely to cause real damage in the academy. He liked to ask his friends if they knew about the offer made by a deconstructionist to a member of the Mafia. He was happy to supply the punchline: it was an offer he could not understand.

Gellner claimed that we face three ideological options – religion, post-modernism and reason – all of them circulating around each other in the uncomfortable tension that lies at the heart of Sartre's great play, *Huis Clos*. Religious fundamentalism was illustrated by means of what had become his standard argument about Islam, namely that it was less likely to be secularized than the other world religions, and so certain to have a powerful presence within modernity. He made clear his own distaste for belief based on revelation, but also expressed admiration for fundamental-ists' concern for truth, together with mild envy at the consolation that it gave them.[18] In contrast, derision and scorn were poured on postmodernists in the longest section of the text. It should be admitted, however, that Gellner was not well versed in postmodern theory, although the two essays which he attacked do indeed exemplify the genre.[19] His real enemy

---

18   *Postmodernism, Reason and Religion*, London, 1992.
19   The essays in question were those by Paul Rabinow and George Marcus, the editors of *Writing Culture: The Poetics and Politics of Ethnography*, Berkeley, 1986. Gellner had reviewed rather harshly Rabinow's account in *Symbolic Domination* of the descendants of a Moroccan saint (*Times Literary Supplement*, 13 February 1976). This new attack led to a hostile review by Rabinow in *Man* in which he accused Gellner of fabricating a quotation. Gellner replied ('On Fabrication', *Man*, vol. 1, 1995, p. 631), denying the charge but admitting that the wrong page number had been given. 'But the passage is unquestionably there, and Rabinow, who after all is its author, must have known that it was indeed there when he made this curious and baseless accusation. What is bizarre about this episode is that Rabinow should knowingly affirm a brazen untruth which is so very easy to nail down'.

was the relativism that he felt was at the core of postmodernism. But there is a certain tension here, between the endless flexibility in postmodernism and the sense of collective systems of meaning that characterizes much anthropological relativism. By and large Gellner ignored this, concentrating instead on the dangers of relativism. His central claim was that postmodernism results from a conflation of subjectivism, that is, the loss of belief in standards of objective knowledge, with liberal guilt about imperialism. One could summarize the postmodernist position by saying that the whole idea of objectivity and clarity is simply a cunning trick of dominators. Descartes had simply prepared the ground for Kipling. Descartes, *ergo* Kipling. The latter is rejected – and therefore Descartes along with him.[20]

One source for this argument derived from Gellner's earlier attack on Geertz. The American anthropologist had claimed that the language of Evans-Pritchard was so clear that it prevented understanding, apparently because it imposed occidental conceptual categories on the thoughts of others. This came to form part of Geertz's analysis of the work of several famous anthropologists, leading him to recommend what Gellner termed 'epistemological hypochondria', that is, a deplorable emphasis on the point of view of the author.[21] Gellner's fear was that so much time might be spent studying one's own position that fieldwork would become impossible. Expiation for the sins of imperialism through subjectivist self-analysis might then debilitate the discipline. As it happens, Gellner had very particular views about the relationship of anthropology to imperialism. He doubted that imperialism had been much helped by anthropologists, but argued that imperialism had greatly helped anthropology by making it easier for its practitioners to get into the field. He offered two further explanations for the rise of subjectivism. One source was to be found in the history of Marxism, which first sought to explain away the revolution's failure to occur on the grounds that the working classes were trapped by the commanding heights of capitalist culture, and then attacked via critical theory the putative objectivity of positivism. A second source of subjectivism was to be found in his increasingly pessimistic appraisal of social science. Its lack of genuine cognitive advance, at least in comparison to natural science, meant that academic power and prestige could be achieved by means of ineffable obscurity. And he offered one further speculation. Postmodernism had

---

20 *Postmodernism, Reason and Religion*, p. 30.
21 C. Geertz, 'Evans-Pritchard's African Transparencies', *Raritan*, Fall 1983, reprinted in Geertz's *Works and Lives: The Anthropologist as Author*, Oxford, 1988. Gellner reviewed this work in the *Times Higher Educational Supplement* on 22 April 1988.

gained great support in the United States simply because the universalism of that culture was so hegemonic that the 'discovery' of difference was all too powerful. All this was but a prelude to the attack on relativism. Particular care was taken to characterize Geertz as a relativist, despite his denial, so that attention could then be directed against his claim that there could be no 'knowledge beyond culture'.[22] Gellner insisted that science was precisely knowledge beyond culture, and restated arguments showing that it had totally changed our position in the world. Further, relativism was by no means as nice as it felt itself to be, noticeably leading at times to respect for cultures in which dissenters were often persecuted. Just as important was a fierce reiteration of his argument against idealism. Meaning was not the only thing that made the world go round. To the contrary, meaning sometimes changed as the result of revolution, marking it as a secondary rather than primary source of power. A final blow was directed at Geertz in this regard. *Negara*, his splendid account of the workings of the Balinese state, formally made much of hermeneutic explanation but substantively offered sensible and mundane explanations resting on wholly material factors.

'Enlightenment Rationalist Fundamentalism' was the third figure in the debate, and the one with which he identified. It shared with religion the desire to establish truth, but all that it was able to offer in this regard was a procedure rather than a general morality. This latter point made it, in a sense, close to relativism. But where relativism was a fad, science, ungrounded though it may be, had a sufficient track record, intellectually and practically, to sustain it. And he added one final set of considerations. Two attempts to politicize the Enlightenment, to create heaven on earth, had been made – by the Jacobins and by the Bolsheviks. There should be no repeats. What was needed was an arrangement resembling constitutional monarchy: real power, whether political or cognitive, should be in one place, performance and entertainment elsewhere.

There is a postscript to the story of this book. The leaders of the Erasmus Foundation had become worried – presciently, given later developments in Holland – that social cohesion might be undermined by a withering of shared standards, and so organized a conference around Gellner's volume.[23] Various papers were delivered on religious and ethnic fundamentalism, and there was striking discussion about the erstwhile Yugoslavia between the Yale historian and Croat patriot Ivo Banac and the British journalist

---

22   C. Geertz, 'Anti Anti-Relativism', *American Anthropologist*, vol. 84, 1984.
23   Praemium Erasmianum Foundation, *The Limits of Pluralism: Neo-Absolutisms and Relativism*, Amsterdam, 1994.

Misha Glenny. But the centrepiece of the meeting was a confrontation between Geertz and Gellner. As is so often the case, real engagement on the key relevant issues did not take place. What was noticeable to those who attended, including this author, was the extent to which Gellner had wanted to debate – unsurprisingly, since it was he who had arranged for Geertz to be invited.[24]

Reflections on the Revolution in Russia

Between September 1988 and October 1989 Gellner lived in Moscow, in an unfashionable but relatively self-contained suburb in the south of the city. To have concentrated on Soviet anthropology at the expense of neglecting the death throes of Soviet communism would have been equivalent, he suggested on his return, to studying the Île de France during the French Revolution.[25] He abandoned his formal plans, and learnt as much as he could by talking to as many people in as many walks of life as possible. At one time he had hopes of writing books on *perestroika* or on the intelligentsia, but neither materialized – in the latter case because he had insufficient time to work out exactly what was going on.[26] This is not to say that he was unable to offer striking insights.[27] Still more important, his period in Moscow was both enjoyable and exceptionally stimulating. He gave a large number of talks, and very much enjoyed speaking Russian. There were many reasons for the attraction. Intellectual life was very high-powered, and it had a breadth which mirrored his own interests. He felt that the fate of the region would be determined by events in Moscow. In this matter, he was essentially *parti pris*, worrying that the collapse of the Soviet Union would lead to consequences as dreadful as those that had followed the collapse of the Hapsburg and Ottoman empires. The attachment lasted for the rest of his life: he gladly returned to teach in summer schools organized by his friends Lena and Yura Senokosov, to whom he dedicated the last monograph published in his lifetime.

---

24 Gellner insisted that 'however much I tried to remove personal animosity from disagreement, he simply wasn't capable of responding. If criticized and not treated as a Guru, which is what he is used to, he becomes prickly and touchy and simply cannot take it. I find this a pity . . . ' (Gellner to Patricia Crone, 12 October 1995).

25 Davis, 'An Interview with Ernest Gellner', p 68.

26 Discussions took place with Paladin, the initial publishers of *The Psychoanalytic Movement*, for a book on *glasnost*. His desire to write something more general on the intelligentsia was noted by Anatoly Khazanov, interviewed in January 1999.

27 Several observations of this sort were made, for instance, in an interview with Nikki Keddie, 'A Year in the Soviet Union', *Contention*, vol. 2, 1992.

Gellner kept field notes during his sabbatical year, but these have not survived. Still, there are many anthropological observations to be found in a series of occasional pieces. He noted the desire to establish monuments remembering both the victims and the culprits of repression, an indicator not just of the fact that the culprits themselves were often persecuted but quite as much of a widespread recognition of diffused guilt.[28] Quite as striking was the extent of media freedom, though he noted wryly that this carnival of the intellectuals was dubbed *Telavivenie* – an indication of continuing anti-Semitism.[29] Particularly interesting was the absence of any clear manifesto of the new order, although he judged this fuzziness to be probably desirable. In general, he took particularly seriously the distinction between two periods, namely those of Stalin and stagnation. Curiously, the horrors of Stalinism did not really undermine belief, as he made clear in a very striking review of Sakharov's *Memoirs*.[30] That the heroic romanticism which sought to create a new world caused bloodshed seemed almost necessary, and so excusable. The period of stagnation associated with the Brezhnev years was merely shoddy in comparison. And such shoddiness killed belief.

He was characteristically witty on the ironies of demands from above that civil society should suddenly come into being, and he offered a marvellous portrait of Gorbachev as Harun al-Rashid, able to balance superbly between different factions in the Congress of Deputies in 1989.[31] Further, he had a real sense of the structural constraints on reform: peasants no longer wanted their land back, whilst the workings of the economy depended in fact upon a sort of socialist industrial feudalism.[32] The most striking piece that he wrote was based on field experience. He visited Georgia and Belarus, and additional insights were gained from a rather longer acquaintance with Estonia, for a discussion of 'Ethnicity and Faith in Eastern Europe'.[33] He clearly enjoyed himself enormously, especially when reporting on Belarussian peasants' memories of the Polish gentry who had dominated them in the interwar years. That one such member of the gentry had enjoyed *droit de seigneur* was recalled with admiration rather than resentment by the grandson of the woman involved. What mattered for the future in more general terms was the world of difference between areas that had lived under communism for forty as compared to seventy years.

---

28   'Perestroika Observed', *Government and Opposition*, vol. 25, 1990, p. 4.
29   Ibid., p. 5.
30   'A reformer of the modern world', *Encounters with Nationalism*, Oxford, 1944.
31   'The Congress of Deputies', Gellner Archive.
32   'Perestroika Observed', p. 8.
33   'Ethnicity and Faith in Eastern Europe', *Daedalus*, vol. 119, 1990.

There was the acute moral dilemma of whether charges should be brought against members of the previous regime. In 'To Try or Not to Try. The Liberal's Dilemma' his position is made especially clear.[34] He attended meetings of 'Memorial', a society dedicated to remembering and seeking justice for the victims of Stalinism. He was not at all convinced that it made sense to prosecute those who had perpetrated Stalin's excesses. For one thing, most such perpetrators were very old. For another, Stalinism had been very different from Nazism in that the perpetrators had themselves very often been the subject of hideous cruelty and persecution. But something else was more important. Any set of trials would sooner or later be bound to focus attention on the role of the Party, since it was in the end the single institution of any consequence within Soviet communism. If the Party were to be utterly discredited there would be a complete institutional vacuum. As vacuums tend to become filled, Gellner felt sure that intense nationalisms would come to the fore – with consequences that might well be disastrous.[35] His own hopes were for continued liberalization, a controlled decompression within the Soviet Union allowing for territorial continuity to be maintained. This did not occur. In fact, Yeltsin played the Russian national card, though only after Party leaders had attempted a coup. Nationalism and democratization took the place of liberalization. As noted, Gellner feared that this was a disastrous error and he did not subsequently change his mind. When, in the summer of 1994, he read Anatoly Khazanov's manuscript about the end of the Soviet Union in his Italian summer house, he replied saying that he had almost become a Russian imperialist, and as such was not at all keen to endorse his friend's delight at the end of the Soviet empire.[36] He liked to say that he had became a follower of Jaroslav Hašek, the author of The Good Soldier Švejk, who once stood for the Prague City Council on the ticket of a party he had himself founded, the Party of Mild Progress Within the Limits of the Law.[37] Further, he took to suggesting that the Chinese might do better by reversing Russian policy – that is, by having perestroika before glasnost.

Beyond these occasional pieces stands something more systematic,

---

34 Unpublished paper, Gellner Archive.

35 The dilemma described here was perhaps a subset of something larger. In 1992 Gellner felt very torn in the matter of trials in general. On the one hand, he noted that no trial of Stalinism had taken place anywhere, despite the millions of deaths. On the other hand, he felt that trials might lead those who had lost power to seek a counter-restoration to protect themselves. He noted wryly that he was hard to please.

36 The book appeared the next year as After the Soviet Union: Ethnicity, Nationalism and Politics in the Commonwealth of Independent States, Madison, 1995.

37 This trope was repeated on several occasions, as in 'Reply to Critics', pp. 677–8.

namely his attempt to define the nature of civil society. By the late 1980s Gellner was wont to say that the nature of civil society, and, crucially, the possibility of its extension, was *the* question of the age. In Moscow and later in Prague, he suggested that a key part of the answer was to be found in seventeenth-century English history. What he was doing here was using his thoughts on the contradiction in Hume's sociology of religion to create an original viewpoint on the origin of civility and toleration in Europe. His claim was that stalemate – the inability over time to fully defeat one's rivals – led to a grudging decision to live together, which in turn morphed into a positive appreciation of diversity. The fact that he often spoke about Islam when in Moscow led him to consider civil society not just in contrast to failing Marxism, but also in relation to the power of this revived religion. Accordingly, there is a sense in which this late work pulls together much of his previous thought, and to that extent it is a good introduction to his sociology. And one can go further: this material spells out his liberalism perhaps more clearly than elsewhere, and to that extent is something of a summation of his social philosophy.

His views on civil society gained an early airing when he gave the Tanner Lectures at Harvard University in 1990.[38] The first lecture was rather dense, and hard for the audience to grasp; the second in contrast was highly successful, not least in leading to a debate with Daniel Bell who chaired the meeting. Gellner's presumption, that socialism had failed, was challenged by Bell, playing the devil's advocate, on the grounds that it had never been tried in the conditions which might have allowed it to work – that is, that it had no chance in Russia, a peasant society which had yet to modernize. Gellner refused to accept this, refuting Bell by citing Czechoslovakia, industrialized and affluent in the interwar years, with a sense in Prague thereafter that it had been robbed of its destiny as a second Munich. There were further papers, but all the arguments were drawn together in *Conditions of Liberty: Civil Society and Its Rivals*, which appeared in 1994. Gellner had reservations about the book, or so he professed, on the grounds that it recycled too much of his previous work. But the reception of books is something of a mystery, and this monograph gained wider and more favourable acclaim than any book that he had previously written.[39] It was recognition of the fact that he had become a public intellectual.

---

38   'The Civil and the Sacred', in G. B. Petersen (ed.), *The Tanner Lectures on Human Values XII*, Salt Lake City, 1992.
39   The book was very widely and favourably reviewed, notably by John Gray ('Our Way', *London Review of Books*, 22 September 1994), Francis Fukuyama ('The Mystery Deepens: The Persistence and Fragility of Civil Society', *Times Literary Supplement*, 28 October 1994), and Alan Ryan (*New York Times Book Review*, 1 January 1995).

And the author in any case judged the book too harshly. It is indeed true that key arguments were repeated: one can find in the chapter on Adam Ferguson, for example, a neat summary of his view of the fortuitous opening of Western society.[40] But a good deal in it was new.

The book made a crucial and wholly novel contribution in its opening pages. It is now generally recognized that naïve boosters of civil society, prone to romanticize popular forces, fail to understand that societal self-organization is not necessarily desirable. The mafia is an unattractive model; so too was the high level of societal self-organization in Weimar Germany, most obviously in its communist and Nazi forms.[41] Gellner was the first social theorist engaging in the debate at that time to make this clear, and he did so with reference to tribal society. A society of cousins can be utterly constraining; hence civil society depends on a guarantee of the ability both to enter and to leave groups at will. After making this distinction, Gellner then concentrated on the great ideological communities of Islam and Marxism. If the arguments about Islam are the same as those discussed in chapter nine, genuinely new thought was on offer about the fate of the socialist bloc. Most importantly, Gellner admitted that he had been completely wrong in imagining that Marxism would be an ersatz Weberian ethic allowing for successful late development.[42] There were several elements to his explanation for this failure. The most immediate concerned the nature of social life in communist society. Gellner made much of Marxism as the creator of a moral order, noting again that periods of heroism, even with the vast numbers of dead that they created, could be understood within the terms of that morality. The period of stagnation was wholly different. Life became sleazy and markedly atomized; the lack of trust in socialism, the fear that neighbours might report you, accentuating this well beyond anything seen in capitalism. The crucial consideration was that Marxism had sanctified daily life, including that of the economy, leaving no mundane world to which to retreat: the situation with world religions, including revived Islam, has always been different – allowing belief to be sustained even in difficult times.[43] In a sense, Marxism had been judged by its own standard,

---

40　*Conditions of Liberty: Civil Society and Its Rivals*, London, 1994, chapter 8. The book also repeats arguments about the relative moral emptiness of liberalism, the self-defeating quality of modern wealth production, the incoherence of democratic theory (in an argument asserting that civil society was a superior concept because of its more realistic sociological foundations), and the character, stages and varieties of nationalism.

41　S. Berman, 'Civil Society and the Collapse of the Weimar Republic', *World Politics*, vol. 30, 1997.

42　*Conditions of Liberty*, p. 49.

43　In the last years of his life Gellner often made this argument, not least in frequent

and was found wanting – not so much in itself, for Gellner made much
of the benefits that industrialization had brought, but in comparison with
progress in the advanced capitalist countries of the West.[44] More directly,
Gellner had come to believe that a command administrative hierarchy was
inimical to economic success. Whilst he had little time for Václav Havel
as social theorist, he adored one sociological observation in *The Power of
the Powerless*. The enthusiastic Czech brewer described by Havel, wishing
merely to improve his beer, caused problems for his boss within the political
hierarchy; and it was easier to dismiss him as a troublemaker than work to
improve the product.[45] The point that Gellner is making is simple: loyalty
to two masters, to power as well as to production, creates confusion which
is unlikely to benefit economic life. This led to further interesting thoughts
about the place of the economy in modern life. A measure of autonomy for
enterprises was necessary for the flourishing of civil society, for a reason still
more important than economic efficiency: bluntly put, there was no other
source of power, as Weber had argued before, able to balance the state.[46]
On this basis, Gellner offered some *obiter dicta*: just as Marxism (loosely
seen as an ideology seeking to control the economy) had to be totalitarian,
so any command administrative system had to be Marxist.[47] But he took
especial care not to be misunderstood. A modern economy was like an
elephant in a small boat; it was inevitably politicized because the state was
responsible for providing the infrastructure on which it depended. The
autonomy of enterprises in liberal society could only be relative, a sort of

---

visits to Chicago, then the home of a project dealing with religious fundamentalism. A
particularly striking example of this line of thought is 'Fundamentalism as a Comprehensive
System: Soviet Marxism and Islamic Fundamentalism Compared', in M. Marty and S.
Appleby (eds), *Fundamentalisms Comprehended*, Chicago, 1991.

44   *Conditions of Liberty*, chapter 19. Cf. 'Homeland of the Unrevolution', *Daedalus*, vol.
122, 1993.

45   *Conditions of Liberty*, p. 89, referring to V. Havel, *The Power of the Powerless*, Armonk, 1990.

46   M. Weber, 'Socialism', in W. G. Runciman (ed.), *Weber: Selections*, Cambridge, 1978.

47   This line of thought was continued in 'Coming to Terms', a review of A. Gleason,
Totalitarianism: The Inner History of the Cold War, published in *The New Republic*, 4 December
1995. Gellner suggested that Nazism was in the end less totalitarian than was Bolshevism.

I remember hearing a wartime speech of Goering's over the radio: apart from referring
enviously, with barely hidden admiration, to Soviet toughness – this was, he said, no longer
toughness (*Haerte*) but barbarism, infuriatingly they repaired destroyed railway lines in
severe frost *with their bare hands* – he also said, when we win, we shall live and let live, none
of that dreadful puritanism for us. His sybaritic attitude was personal as well as political.
Had Hitler won and then died about the time Stalin died, Goering might have been a more
successful Krushchev' (p. 45).

reciprocal consent between the parties. Further, he was opposed to the imposition of neo-liberal policy in post-communist society.[48]

The book contains other novelties, perhaps best seen from two angles. On the one hand, some elements of his prior thought gained a new edge as the result of particularly striking new formulations. The stress on generalized education as necessary for repeated occupational change was summed up by referring to modular furniture, in which pieces could be added at will. Humanity in the modern world needed to be modular in just this sense. This in turn allowed him to sum up his view of nationalism in relation to civil society, and more particularly to express his fear as to its role in postcommunism:

> [T]he modularity of man, so intimately tied up with an industrial and growth-oriented society, has two aspects, two principal social corollaries: it makes *possible* Civil Society, the existence of countervailing and plural political associations and economic institutions, which at the same time are not stifling; and it also makes *mandatory* the strength of ethnic identity, arising from the fact that man is no longer tied to a particular social niche, but is instead deeply linked to a culturally defined pool. The one potentiality is a mere option, essential presumably in the long term if the society is to be capable of competing with its rivals, but not always overwhelmingly strong in the short term; the other, however, constitutes an immediately and powerfully felt imperative. This is a fact, whether or not we like it.[49]

On the other hand, there were more innovations as well. One was the hope, generated by the cooperation of the Soviet Union and the United States at the time of the first Gulf War, that increasing governance at the global level was actually coming to the fore – thankfully, in Gellner's view, given that only this could allow for an effective response to ecological disaster and to terrorism. A second innovation concerned the validation of civil society. He thought that 'preaching across cultural boundaries . . . [was] . . . a fairly pointless exercise . . . They are what they are, and we are what we are: if we were them, we would have their values, and if they were us, they would have ours'.[50] This was not for a moment to say that he was a relativist, for he continued to stress the power of modern cognition and to base his own standards upon it – and to stress the power of its

---

48 'Return of a Native', *Political Quarterly*, vol. 67, 1996.
49 *Conditions of Liberty*, pp. 127–8.
50 Ibid., p. 214.

example throughout the world. But there is a slight difference of tone in this late formulation: the eventual spread of science might do less to undermine established beliefs than he had once hoped.

Two challenges were mounted to his views on civil society. The first came from his Cambridge colleague, the anthropologist Chris Hann, who insisted that the collapse of state socialism did more to undermine security than to advance anything like a 'civil' society.[51] There was not in fact much difference between the two, as Gellner himself pointed out.[52] Gellner certainly had no time for pure marketism, and was wont in his last years to worry about the emergence of 'spivvy' capitalism in Russia – though he did feel that the transition in the erstwhile Hapsburg lands was likely to succeed.[53] More interesting was the later criticism of Ashutosh Varshney, who objected to Gellner's view that civil associations must be voluntary, as well as to the implication that this condition can only be reached in modern circumstances.[54] Varshney pointed to the voluntary nature of many civil associations in the past, and went further in arguing that minorities were often protected by communities within which they were more or less caged. Perhaps this shows the fertility of Gellner's model, encouraging as it does social science research on the extent to which traditional pluralisms can take a liberal direction.

Controversies

Gellner's engagement in polemical controversies did not cease in his later years, as is obvious from the disputes with Geertz, Taylor, Rorty, and with postmodernism more generally. There were two further polemics: one conducted with Noam Chomsky in private correspondence preserved in the Gellner Archive, the other, with Edward Said, the subject of considerable publicity. Both reveal a great deal about Gellner's general social philosophy.

---

51   C. Hann and E. Dunn (eds), *Civil Society: Challenging Western Models*, London, 1996, especially C. Hann, 'Introduction: Political Society and Civil Anthropology'.
52   'Reply to Critics', pp. 677–8.
53   'Agenda', January 1993. Gellner was close at this time to Stephen Graubard, the editor of *Daedalus*, and helped plan some excellent issues on the sociology and meaning of the collapse of the Soviet Union. Graubard seems to have asked for guidance regarding the issues of the time. There were four areas to Gellner's 'Agenda': nationalism (and the impossibility of finding clear normative principles to deal with the conflict it created); the problems involved in creating an 'instant bourgeoisie'; Islam as the 'shadow religion' in Central Asia, and the nature of the moral vacuum, at once similar to and different from that faced by the Weimar Republic.
54   A. Varshney, *Ethnic Conflict and Civil Life: Hindus and Muslims in India*, New Haven, 2002, pp. 42–4.

The exchange with Chomsky began as the result of Gellner's review of Bernard Lewis's *Semites and Anti-Semites*. The main purpose of the review was to challenge Lewis's account in two ways: by insisting that anti-Semitic feeling was present in traditional Muslim societies (even if it was less central to that civilization than it was to Christianity), and to suggest that modern circumstances – the ending of strictly specialized occupational niches – were bound to create difficulties for Jews.[55] Chomsky's concern however was with a particular passage in Lewis's book, cited in the review:

[T]he Anglo-American liberal, who claims a monopoly of sin for his country . . . the tortured WASP radical, who sees the Arab-Israeli conflict as ultimately one between Harlem and Scarsdale, and makes a choice determined by his own personal blend of prejudice and guilt.

Gellner had seemed to endorse this description by writing about the 'bizarre . . . fruits of self-hate decried by Lewis'. Chomsky felt that this was a slur, and in effect challenged Gellner to produce evidence of such attitudes.[56] Not one to duck a fight, Gellner said in his reply that the person who best represented the position he had in mind was in fact Chomsky himself. From this starting point, there followed a general discussion of the nature of the political responsibility of intellectuals in the modern world.

Gellner effectively opened the debate by insisting that a Manichean view of the modern world, of a contrast between liberty and pluralism as compared to authoritarianism and oppressiveness, seemed to him correct. He had no wish to deny the crimes and blunders committed by his own side, nor did he think that these should be ignored rather than criticized.

But in criticising . . . one does it in context, never losing sight of the fact, or allowing one's readers to lose sight of the fact, that the survival of freedom and accountable, limited government is an enormously important value even when some of its defenders are occasionally tarnished. If this context is recognised in your political writings, it somehow is totally obscured, and it would be perfectly natural for a reader to feel that it is absent . . . [57]

He went on to say that 'a kind of populist spirit' pervaded Chomsky's political writings, in which good and evil are easily identified. In contrast, Gellner noted that his own scholarly work, whilst also dualistic, had tried

---

55 'Prejudiced Encounters', *Times Literary Supplement*, 22 August 1986.
56 Chomsky to Gellner, 15 September 1986.
57 Gellner to Chomsky, 3 October 1986.

to 'identify the mechanisms with which we operate' rather than to attribute goodness or badness to people. He went on to stress the complexities of the situation in the Middle East. He was well aware that '. . . the Palestinians are in no way connected with what happened to the Jews in Europe, nor are they responsible for the theological documents of the Old Testament, and can reasonably claim that there is no reason why they should suddenly become a minority in their own country'. But if one started from the view that the survival of both communities is legitimate, then castigation of crimes (which had unquestionably occurred) ought to be a bit more symmetrical.

Chomsky replied to this letter at great length and with a candour that Gellner found very moving.[58] There were several elements to his reply. First, he insisted that he had often condemned injustices in the Soviet Union (being perhaps even more critical, he claimed, than was Gellner in this regard) and elsewhere, and pointed out that he had been an anarchist since he was about twelve. Second, he noted – and offered to document – extensive American atrocities in Indochina, Central America and the Caribbean. Third, he objected to Gellner's Manichean view:

> What you call the 'East-West' conflict is not an East-West conflict. That is to a large extent a propaganda construction of elites on both sides. In reality, the Cold War is a much more complex system, in which elites on each side exploit the quite real crimes of the other as a device to control their own populations and to carry out their own crusades in their own domains.

Finally, he insisted that the majority of social critics in the United States were straightforwardly honest, and entirely free of the complex motives that had been ascribed to them. Intellectuals ought to work at all times against repression wherever it is found, without fear or favour. Accordingly, Gellner was held to be failing in his duty as an intellectual.

Gellner's reply was lengthier than his initial letter, and it covered a good deal of sociological ground. He began by trying to explain why he valued the West and felt state socialism to be such a threat:

> The complexity and interdependence of the industrial machine which alone makes possible the overcoming of poverty-inspired oppression, means that our society is bound to have strong central institutions concerned with the maintenance of the shared infrastructure. The nature

---

58   Chomsky to Gellner, 13 October 1986 and Gellner to Chomsky, 27 October 1986.

of the division of labour makes it very unlikely that this society will be endowed with countervailing institutions of a social or political or territorial or kin type. In other words, the only possible countervailing institutions are economic ones. There is *no* anarchist option. Nor, in the long run, is there a classical economic liberal one. The only genuine options are either some form of mixed economy, which is capable of ensuring the rule of law, freedom of information, a measure of checks on government etc., or 'socialism', which means in concrete terms that the political and economic hierarchies are basically identical. There is no third alternative.

Gellner added to this the view that the chances of liberalizing authoritarian rightist regimes were better than those of liberalizing socialist dictatorships. In other words, he had become, as noted, convinced by Aron. The privileged members of the former 'have money, and it is possible to make a deal with them, saying: you can keep your money if you give up power'. By contrast, left-wing regimes cannot voluntarily liberalise beyond a certain point. The important privileges and perks within them do not have the form of 'wealth' but are all so to speak prebendal, they are attached to official positions. If you lose the position, you lose everything. Consequently political struggle within them must be of the winner-take-all or total kind, thereby ruling out the possibility of a liberal outcome.[59]

Gellner again insisted that he did not wish to deny, nor to avoid criticism of, crimes committed by the West. But he insisted that the crimes committed by the two sides were not remotely comparable. Whereas the crimes of the West were a by-product of a conflict situation or of mistakes by individuals,

the systematic oppression which is a part of the rival system is a consequence, not of course of individual wickedness, but of the inevitable structural principles of that kind of social organisation. They are also qualitatively rather larger. Nothing the liberal West has done compares with either Stalin or Pot.

---

59 Nonetheless, he admitted that his own views of the Soviet Union were relatively mild. He was referring here to the fact that a measure of liberalization had already taken place – as in the practice of harassing dissidents by the rule book rather than by gulags. Though he had accepted Aron's point, he had not given up hopes of controlled decompression, and explained that it was on this matter that his current research focused.

On this basis, Gellner then turned to Chomsky's anarchist standard of judgement. 'Why should a man judge his own society by an absurd standard, unless he has the need to use a standard which will then enable him to condemn that society with vehemence? In other words, is this not evidence for Lewis's charge of "self-hatred"?'

Chomsky, in a very long reply, refused to accept any of these arguments. He rejected the notion of two opposing sides altogether (whilst arguing, however, that the West was responsible for the horrors committed by Pol Pot), and repeated his view that intellectuals should stand up against all repression. He felt that his motives had been slandered, and made it clear that he regarded Gellner's position as craven. He felt that there was no point in continuing the correspondence, and there was no further response from Gellner – who was happy, he noted in conversation, to let the matter drop, as he felt that real engagement was not taking place.

Turning to Gellner's other notable polemic of this period, spectacular public fireworks resulted from his review of Edward Said's *Culture and Imperialism*.[60] We have already seen in Gellner's reviews of the work of Bryan Turner a deep scepticism toward the view that the West was responsible for blocking the rise of Muslim societies. His review of Said's book offered a direct critique of the 'bogy of imperialism'. He felt that modern imperialism was made inevitable by the technological lead of one part of the world, and was therefore reluctant to accept the view that Occidental ideological presuppositions had played the crucial role given to them by Said. In any case, Gellner argued that Said's readings of Gide, Camus and Fanon were mistaken. But he was moved to action here less by a long-lasting dislike of the idealism in Said's position than by the *en passant* attack on such serious scholars as Patricia Crone and Michael Cook. The main point of the review was that powerful scholarship of Oriental societies had come from very varied places, some from Western scholars and some from the colonial administrators known to him from his North African work – and errors were equally possible on the part of those of whose ideological position Said approved. Said's reply ignored most of this, accusing Gellner of Orientalism on the grounds that his work on Islam lacked knowledge

---

60 'The Mightier Pen? Edward Said and the Double Standards of Inside-Out Colonialism', *Times Literary Supplement*, 19 February 1993, reprinted in his *Encounters with Nationalism*. Cf. R. Irwin, *For Lust of Knowing: The Orientalists and Their Enemies*, London, 2006, especially chapter 9. Irwin's book provides plentiful evidence in support of Gellner's claims about Said. But Irwin is mistaken in one regard. There is no evidence that Gellner was writing a book about Orientalism at the time of his death – though he was, as we will see in a moment, planning a conference on the subject, conceived however in an original way.

of classical Muslim languages, although he acknowledged 'some fieldwork (without Arabic or Berber) in a part of Morocco', so as to suggest, on the basis of a single quoted sentence, that his work exhibited 'obsessive revulsion for "Islam"'.[61] Gellner replied forcefully, though he refrained from underlining his facility in Berber. One point he made very clearly was that the sentence in question had been torn out of context, and emphasized his obvious and long-standing commitment to understanding Muslim societies. He then returned to his main charge, that Said only took seriously the scholarship of the politically correct. 'I am worried . . . by the attribution of merit and truth in virtue of who one is, or to the political category or group of origin to which one belongs, rather than to the affirmations themselves on merit'.[62] A further letter from Said effectively repeated his original case, whilst denying the charge of political correctness.[63] A final letter from Gellner made fun of Said's insistence that literature had played a key role in imperialism by imagining the viceroy of India worrying about the contents of the latest issue of *Scrutiny*.[64] There is an epilogue to this controversy. In the last months of his life Gellner was planning a conference on a rather different sort of Orientalism, namely the view of Central and Eastern Europeans about the lands to their east, lands which had often bred nomads who had overrun them.[65] The conference mattered to him a great deal, not least as it allowed him to engage with many of the Soviet anthropologists that he knew. It seems that Said had accepted an invitation to attend.[66]

The Central European University

Shortly after his return from Moscow Gellner was visited in Cambridge by Ivan Havel, who brought with him a personal request from his brother Václav to assist in the creation of a Central European University. This was to be funded by George Soros, the Hungarian exile of Jewish background who had become one of the world's great financiers. Soros had already played a significant role in intellectual opening and civil society development in

61   E. Said, 'Letter to the Editor', *Times Literary Supplement*, 19 March 1993.

62   'Letter to the Editor', *Times Literary Supplement*, 9 April 1993.

63   E. Said, 'Letter to the Editor', *Times Literary Supplement*, 4 June 1993.

64   'Letter to the Editor', *Times Literary Supplement*, 11 June 1993.

65   He had insisted on using 'Three Heroes', a painting by V. M. Vasnetsov (1848–1926), as the jacket illustration to his *State and Society in Soviet Thought*, Oxford, 1988 – it showed 'the Russian version of their own traditional states, as an organized force defending Russia from nomadic incursions'.

66   C. Hann to Gellner, 28 November 1994.

Central Europe, and his Open Society Institute now played a major role in the region. Such a university would have campuses in Prague, Warsaw and Budapest, and it would improve the human capital of the region in order to ensure that democratic openings were consolidated. The guiding light of the whole enterprise was liberalism, exemplified for Soros in the work of Karl Popper – who had refused Soros as a research student long ago, but whose ideas led to a special meeting in Prague on 26 May 1994.[67] Václav Havel was very keen on this renewal of cultural capital, and was prepared to loan as the site for the Prague campus a nearly completed trade union conference centre in Táboritská, a street in the heart of Žižkov, the interwar hub of Prague's red working class. Gellner was torn. He faced forced retirement in Cambridge at the end of the 1992/3 academic year, and was already looking for further employment – for it was clear, to his friends and to Gellner himself, that he did not wish to settle down to any sort of quieter life. To that end he was being courted by Boston University, and was at times interested in other openings in North America. But he had always felt relatively ill at ease in the United States, knowing himself to be European; in any case, events in Europe were far more interesting. Yet there was a problem. His great interest was in the former Soviet Union, not least as he felt that developments there would determine the fate of the region. Furthermore, he had reservations about the Czechs, in large part because of the manner in which the Sudeten Germans had been expelled, though he was just as concerned with their capacity for craven subordination. But, in the end, he chose to concentrate his attentions on Prague. He taught there part-time from 1991–3 whilst finishing up at Cambridge, and on a permanent basis for the remainder of his life. He handled his reservations in a characteristic way – by teaching in Russia in the summers, and by eventually looking for a cottage to purchase in the south of Bohemia.

He was decidedly delighted to be back in Prague. When the Café Slavia – next to the Národní Divadlo, both of them sacred sites of Czech nationalism – re-opened, he felt sufficiently moved to suddenly stand and sing a Czech patriotic song, to the bemusement of the clientele. Regular purchases of Bohemian glassware were made, given away to friends as if in a personal attempt to revive the Czech economy. He very much enjoyed speaking Czech on a daily basis, and was amused when told that his figures

---

67 The occasion – which involved a seminar, an Open Society Prize, and the granting of an honorary degree from Charles University – was very carefully handled, much to the amusement of Tom Nairn, a fellow of The Centre for the Study of Nationalism at the time. No smoking was allowed in the building several days in advance, and questions, which had to be asked by Gellner, were pre-prepared.

of speech were dated and were those of a thirteen-year-old schoolboy. And he enjoyed re-reading Czech and Hapsburg literature, appreciating in particular Roth's *The Radetzky March*, Robert Musil's *The Man Without Qualities*, and Hašek's *The Good Soldier Švejk*. Many found great charm in his attachments to Czech culture, and he played a notable role in introducing intellectuals from the West at meetings of one sort or another. He clearly enjoyed showing the city to many visitors, whether academics or family members, and took great pleasure in entertaining them in the city, characteristically plying them with excellent Moravian wine. He sent many visitors to beautiful towns such as Telč, and to the south of Bohemia, especially to Krumlov. He went there himself, recalling German activism in reaction to Czech nationalism; he also returned to Příbram where he had spent much time as a child. His limited free time was often spent exploring parts of Bohemia, notably the spa towns still best known to us as Marienbad and Carlsbad.

The university personnel derived in part from his links to Jiří Musil. In 1990 Gellner attended a conference organized by Musil – who had just become head of the Sociological Institute because, as someone who had never joined the Party, his hands were notably clean. On that occasion, Gellner insisted that the Czechs would prosper, at least in part because they had Prague – correctly predicting that it would soon become a major tourist attraction.[68] Musil, Gellner and Ray Pahl, a sociologist from the University of Kent who shared with Musil an interest in urban sociology, took advantage of the meeting to plan a department of sociology for the Central European University. A short opening summer session took place in 1991, with the full-scale programme – soon including further social science subjects, notably international relations – getting under way in the autumn. One-year courses were offered to students from the whole of Eastern Europe, partly taught by visiting professors, in social theory, stratification, research methods, 'market, state and society', 'nationalism, ethnicity and race', and in postcommunism. These initial years were exciting and extraordinary. For many, this was the first opportunity to talk freely, and with colleagues from different countries, and lives were distinctively changed by this experience. Gellner very much enjoyed the informal atmosphere there (for he lived in the same building as the students), insisted that the students call him Ernest, and was deeply interested in their lives and ideas. There can be no doubt that Gellner made a substantial but incalculable contribution to the intellectual life of the region. Still, the schedule was punishing, and

---

68 But he also had fears at this time, worrying that there might be a communist backlash on the part of the workers of northern Bohemia, a poor, degraded industrial and mining area.

he could not have managed without the constant support of his wife. For he was not just teaching in both Prague and Cambridge but also involved in setting up, from 1992, a Centre for the Study of Nationalism. The desire to have such a centre had been on his mind from the start – because he was so terrified that the collapse of the socialist bloc would lead to the disasters that had followed the ending of Ottoman and Hapsburg power.[69]

But there were considerable frustrations involved in working for the Central European University. Most obviously, there was a complete lack of any organized structure, in large part because decisions for many years were made by Soros himself. A titanic clash of egos soon took place between Soros and Václav Klaus, the free-marketeer who became prime minister in 1992, the immediate result of which was a decision to close down operations in Prague. As it happens, that decision was rescinded, but it created an air of uncertainty that Gellner felt was utterly opposed to the needs of institution-building. His hope was that the appointment of a rector for the university as a whole might change things significantly, especially if such a person were able to persuade Soros to make a large donation so the university could manage its own affairs. But the appointment of Alfred Stepan did not prove to be any sort of administrative cure-all, even though Gellner appreciated the liveliness of his ideas. For one thing, endless discussions about the purchase of a building came to naught, and an unfortunate move was made into a Stalinist building that turned out to be riddled with asbestos. Eventually a small building was purchased on Prokopova, very close to the original site in Žižkov – but this was just at the end of his time in Prague, and only provided a home for his centre. No permanent solution to the funding problem was found whilst Gellner was alive, and he was endlessly irritated at the inability of the central organization to finalize the terms of his own contract. Soros soon became convinced that the Poles, Magyars and Czechs were successfully consolidating their democracies, and so chose to spend more of his money further to the east. This led to the closing of the Prague campus in the summer of 1995, with all subjects moving to the Budapest campus – except for sociology, which went to Warsaw. There was considerable irony in this: Soros's interest in decentralization did not seem to apply to his own university; it became ever more a Magyar monopoly.[70] Gellner would have been prepared to move to

---

69   His concern was so strong that he sought for funding from several sources – from the European Academy in 1991, and from the Nuffield Foundation and the European Union shortly before his death.

70   Relations between Soros and Gellner were not close. Gellner wrote to Soros occasionally, and met him at meetings of the Senate. He tried to convince him that theoretical reflection was necessary rather than a self-indulgent ivory tower activity. On

Warsaw, if need be, but not to Budapest – he felt that the Hungarians were clever, and he did not speak the language. He continued to press for the return of the philosophy department to Prague, and was deeply angered by the move of the philosophy library to Budapest.

Gellner's reputation lent weight to the university as a whole, with his Centre for the Study of Nationalism naturally attracting scholars not just from Central Europe but also from points further east and west, both as visitors and fellows. Amongst their number were Rashid Kaplanov, Victor Shnirelman, Anatoly Khazanov, Petr Pithart, Tom Nairn, Michael Ley, Zdeněk Stary, Charles Taylor, Ron Dore, Shmuel Eisenstadt and Geoffrey Hosking. Most importantly, the centre organized a series of conferences and seminars. A large conference in 1993 brought together a very large number of the world's scholars of nationalism, and Gellner notably organized a programme which involved increasing general awareness of Czech nationalism – by gaining entry into the grand reception rooms in the castle designed for Masaryk by the Slovenian modernist architect Jože Plečnik, by an evening at the Národní Divadlo, and by a performance of Czech folklore. But smaller conferences and seminars dealt with the Czech-Slovak split (one conference on the theme being held in Edinburgh, another in Prague, with comparative material on the potential split between Quebec and the rest of Canada); Philosophy and Westernization (dealing with the elective affinities between different philosophies and particular Central European countries); the filling of the postcommunist vacuum in Russia (co-presented with the Moscow School of Political Studies); the role of ethnography in the formation of national self-images and national ideology; the role of historiography in the construction of national ideologies and self-images; Alois Musil and the Muslim world; and Muslim postcommunist societies.[71] In the autumn of 1995, ten pre-doctoral students were recruited to the centre in Prokopova, to join Gellner and two of the academic visitors. They found the experience remarkable, but one of them, Siniša Malešević (later to

---

one occasion he wrote (Gellner to Soros, 30 October 1995, Gellner Archive) to say that Dr Zahradnik, President of the Czech Academy, had proposed a triangular relationship between the Centre, his Academy and Charles University. 'No doubt important people in the Czech government are hostile to us. But there is also quite a different current, and the letter and initiative from the head of the Czech Academy seems to prove that it is worth aligning oneself with it'. Gellner noted that he had admired a presentation that Soros gave on Popper, and felt that his interpretation of the situation in Russia was particularly impressive.

71 The conference on nationalism led to S. Periwal (ed.), *Notions of Nationalism*, Budapest, 1995, to which Gellner contributed an introduction.

become an established figure in the field of nationalism studies), confessed to feeling unease when Gellner sat down to watch television with him – saying it was as if Max Weber had dropped by.

Reflections on Czechia

Not all of Gellner's life revolved around the university and his centre. Of course, he observed the Velvet Divorce of Czechs and Slovaks with considerable interest. This was a split of which he approved, in large part because he felt that this was the only way in which a perceived inferiority of Slovak intellectuals could be remedied.[72] But he made no public statement endorsing the split, probably because he did not approve of all or perhaps most such splits – noting privately that he thought Quebec's best option was to remain within Canada.[73] Further, he took considerable pleasure from the conflict between Havel and Klaus, the one seen as a representative of the Frankfurt School and the other as an adherent of Milton Friedman.[74] He had enormous admiration for Havel's moral stature and felt that the Czechs were lucky to have him – even though he found his ideas (but not his plays) vague and unrealistic.[75] Nonetheless, he came increasingly to feel that Czechia had become desperately dull. He remembered the multi-cultural Prague of his childhood, and could not help but contrast it with a new Prague bereft of Germans, Jews, and Slovaks. He said frequently in those years that he did not wish Prague to become like Vienna. There was an obvious irony in this. His theory of nationalism insists that homogeneity is the base on which industrial success can be built. Nonetheless, he loathed the lack of diversity, and sought to oppose the claustrophilia of the Klaus government. The conferences he organized were in part designed to add spice to Czech intellectual life, and he sought to establish intellectual links locally. His work on nationalism had an immediate impact in Prague, not

---

72   He had attended a conference on 'Ethics and Politics' in Bratislava in April 1990, and came back convinced that only full independence could remove the chip on the shoulder of the Slovak intellectuals with whom he spoke. The Gellner Archive contains an unpublished essay describing the atmosphere of the conference.

73   The last pages of his *Nationalism*, written during the last summer of his life, are relevant in this context. His argument there was that we do not possess any clear set of principles by means of which to deal with every nationalist claim. Sometimes self-determination was right, sometimes it was better to encourage processes of assimilation.

74   He was acute on Klaus, noting well before it became obvious that his radicalism was largely rhetorical, that is, that little was in fact done to undermine the social safety net to which the Czechs had long been accustomed.

75   'The Price of Velvet: Tomáš Masaryk and Václav Havel', in *Encounters with Nationalism*.

least as he established links with Miroslav Hroch, as well as with academics in different departments at Charles University.

He offered sustained reflections on the way in which the Czech past might affect its future in two essays, and he noted on at least one occasion his intention to write more about Czechia. 'The Price of Velvet' compared Masaryk and Havel. Admiration for both figures was apparent, but so too was bitter criticism at the 'velvety' character of Czech political transitions. The historicism of Masaryk, the sense that one ought to act only in accord with historical developments, was seen as contributing to Czech fatalism in the face of great powers.[76] Gellner later noted that Masaryk might have fought in 1938 had he still been alive, whereas Beneš, despite the desires of his generals, refused to do so; the transition in 1948 was even less contentious. In contrast, Havel stressed the power of the people in ending communism. Gellner simply felt that this was not true, as was apparent from the way in which Havel as president chided the Czechs for political passivity. A much better guide was to be found in the early 1990s in the viewpoint of Petr Pithart. Gellner had long known Pithart's work: he had previously been a communist, but then became a dissident whose *samizdat* writings on the meaning of the 1968 events, under the pen name Sládeček, he had previously analysed.[77] He became the prime minister of the Czech half of Czechoslovakia after 1989, before becoming closely associated with the Central European University.[78] Pithart's argument was simple: there had been no revolution at all, the regime lasting so long because of Czechoslovakia's genius for normalizing itself. This is something that Gellner feared, and it explains his enthusiastic review of a long letter of Jan Patočka's which offered an account of Czech history to a German woman who might well have joined him in Prague.[79] Patočka had little time for Masaryk's view of the Czech past, giving a much smaller role to the Hussites. What mattered for Patočka was the absence of a native aristocracy and the presence of a Catholicism that suppressed Enlightenment thought. The end result in Patočka's eyes was petty-mindedness in tandem with an egalitarianism that undermined human agency. It was for these reasons that Patočka had suggested during the communist period that a dose of Nietzsche might help the Czechs more than continual obeisance to Masaryk. Gellner was sympathetic to this view. But he was not able,

---

76 Not all blame was laid at Masaryk's door, since the handing over of power in 1918 had been equally smooth.

77 See above, chapter 6.

78 Pithart, quoted in Gellner, 'The Price of Velvet', p. 126.

79 'Reborn From Below: The Forgotten Beginnings of the Czech National Revival', in *Encounters with Nationalism*.

as noted, to follow Patočka and Pithart when they seemed to suggest that an alternative Czech foundation story might be found in the non-ethnic patriotic views of the early-nineteenth-century mathematician Bolzano.

The Sense of an Ending

The depth of his political concerns in the final years of his life was apparent to all who visited him in Prague. His concern with Islam and nationalism, with the revival of capitalism and the filling of a moral vacuum, were behind his interest in Russian developments. But his interests involved intellectual history and comparative sociology quite as much. The planned conference on Orientalism was to be matched by another on the Caucasus, likely in his view to become the scene of bitter nationalist conflict, and so deserving considered attention. There were other detailed plans. He wanted to work on the triangle of nationalism, populist ethnography and anthropology.[80] Furthermore, he was interested in the revival of a saint cult in south Bohemia, and hoped to work with Czech colleagues. His complete independence of mind was on display time and again in these years, partic-ularly in a series of reviews, most of which served as essays in their own right. One example was his participation in the debate over Heidegger's philosophy and politics.[81] Where most commentators had written about this in the most sententious terms, Gellner almost shrugged the matter off. For him, Heidegger was a dull opportunist whose prose at times was impen-etrable and whose politics told us little about the moral dilemmas facing intellectuals in the twentieth century. In contrast, Sakharov illuminated those dilemmas, and produced genuinely interesting philosophical ideas.

Still, many friends and observers noted that he was tired. For one thing, there was simply the punishing schedule of travel, publication and teaching that characterized these last years. For another, he did not enjoy being treated as an authority, and was indeed almost irritated at times when asked to repeat himself: this was obvious to those who attended the conference on Muslim postcommunist societies – he came to life only when turning away from his older work to talk about Alois Musil, the T. E. Lawrence of the Hapsburgs.[82] Most noticeable was a considerable dose of pessimism about current intellectual trends. 'Anything Goes' was very representative in this regard. The *fin de siècle* had been genuinely liberating; in contrast,

---

80 Gellner to his former doctoral student Shelagh Weir, 4 July 1995.
81 'Mind Games', *New Republic*, vol. 209, 1992, reprinted as 'The Nazi Jew-Lover', in *Encounters with Nationalism*.
82 The essay he devoted to Musil is reprinted in *Encounters with Nationalism*.

the *fin de millénaire* seemed wilfully self-destructive – self-indulgent, prone to relativism and bereft of much sense of reality. Social constructivism was rampant, and it desperately needed to be replaced with an emphasis on the natural basis for the construction of society – that is, re-emphasis of the way in which science changes our world.[83]

Some of his late writings contained biographical snippets, although he refused to write an autobiographical introduction to a volume of essays assessing his work.[84] His mind was often on the character of his life and career. When in Italy in the summer of 1995 he wrote to Wendy Doniger about one of his closest friends, Richard Olendcki, a Pole who had survived Auschwitz and with whom Gellner would sail when he was in Massachusetts. They had had a final lunch in Warsaw where Gellner for a short period held an appointment as an Erasmus Professor.

> Richard Olendcki dies as he wished to do very peacefully and quickly. He had made arrangements with the doctors to ensure that there was no lingering . . . I admired him very much and there is no man I would rather choose for a companion if I had to be on the mainland of Europe in let us say 1941.[85]

He travelled a great deal that autumn, and arrived in Budapest rather tired in early November to host a conference organized by his Centre for the Study of Nationalism on the role of formerly dominant minorities. The idea was simple – to cast light on the potential behaviour of Russians, especially those 'beached' in areas that they had once dominated. To that end, papers were offered on the Hungarian experience, and on different facets of the Irish situation. The LSE was well represented, with papers being delivered by Brendan O'Leary, Marianne Heiberg, Bill Kissane, George Schöpflin and Dominic Lieven.[86] Gellner gave an impromptu talk on the last day of the conference, 5 November, apparently brilliantly summarizing the proceedings. He then attended a long bureaucratic meeting at which

---

83   'Anything Goes', *Times Literary Supplement*, 16 June 1995, reprinted as 'The Coming *Fin de Millénaire*', in *Anthropology and Politics*.

84   Such autobiographies were a standard feature of the series in which the volume appeared (J. A. Hall and I. C. Jarvie [eds], *The Social Philosophy of Ernest Gellner*, Amsterdam, 1996). He tried on several occasions to sit down to this task but simply could not bring himself to do it.

85   Gellner to Doniger, 2 August 1995, Gellner Archive.

86   Lieven's talk apparently blamed the French Revolution for all the mess that nationalism had caused. Gellner would have none of this, clearly rejecting nostalgia for the world before 1789 (email from Kissane, 17 April 2009).

he finally gained assurances regarding the future of his centre. He then flew back to Prague, went to his rooms in Prokopova, and was felled by a heart attack – sudden, massive and immediately fatal. The letter to Doniger suggests that this is the death that he too had wished for: certainly it is hard to imagine him somehow slowing down.

His students in Prokopova were shattered. Appreciation for their teacher, for his informality and concern for their well-being combined with insistence on the highest intellectual standards, was expressed at a first memorial service in Prague, the comments later published in *Prospect* in December 1995. The leading papers in England featured obituaries, all of them affectionate, some marked by small errors.[87] The *Economist* noted his ability to transcend particular fields, and endorsed this by repeating the boast of Max Weber: 'I am not a donkey and I don't have a field'.[88] Two appreciations went beyond the formalities to capture something of the man. Alan Macfarlane wrote a lengthy and powerful appreciation for his college.

> Something that struck most people was the contradiction between the acerbic and often cruel debater, and the enormously kind and gentle human being. At the personal level, as his numerous friends and pupils could witness, his life was full of little acts 'of kindness and of love'. He was also extremely generous with his time, possessions and support. At times he felt that all this natural kindness might be taken as a sign of weakness, so he used to try to justify it as a Machiavellian strategy.
>
> Memory of his roots made him an extraordinarily modest person, self-depreciating, humble and somewhat shy . . .[89]

Macfarlane stressed his ability to ask the right questions, noting finally that 'in the man and in the writing one felt the touch of genius'.

Tom Nairn had spent a year as a fellow of the Centre for the Study of Nationalism, purportedly working on 'micro-nationalisms' – something which amused Gellner a good deal – and he drew on this experience to express his own sense of loss.

> Gellner's office in Prague looked northwards towards Žižkov Hill, a view of the things that most interested and infuriated him. It was dominated by the Czech National Memorial and the outsize equestrian statue of the

---

87 He did not die at Prague Airport, whilst he was survived by his wife and all four of their children.
88 25 November 1995.
89 Macfarlane, 'Ernest André Gellner, 1929–1995'.

blind Bohemian military hero, General Jan Žižkov . . . The National Memorial had also been used by the Communists to pretend that they were the true inheritors of Czech nationhood. Klement Gottwald, the 'Czech Lenin', was embalmed there for some years after his death in 1953, until the air conditioning failed and the mouldy cadaver had to be furtively smuggled out. So from where Ernest sat . . . there was a daily reminder of another example of how vulgar autocracy, fake ethnicity and Stalin's big stick had fused together to form a uniquely dire parody of modernity.

I always felt that what mattered most about modern history was in that room. The thought of never entering it again, never hearing Ernest's walking stick thumping up the corridor, or the latest low jokes about Socialism, Slovaks or Californian professors, fills me with desolation. One consolation is that he seems to have been irrepressible and in no way diminished, right to the end. Certainly, conversations last year showed the same mixture of disrespect, malicious humour, deep insight and spiky, somewhat conservative, rectitude as 20 years before.[90]

There were three further services. Czech law required that his body be kept for some time before it could be flown home to England. Eventually, the body was cremated after a private but very well-attended service held near Chichester, where he had long kept a boat. David and Deborah Gellner spoke movingly about their father. A memorial meeting was held at the LSE, at which several people spoke, most strikingly Shelagh Weir. The final service was held at King's College on 24 February 1996. Both Ron Dore and John Davis gave formal addresses, and these were interspersed with readings from Weber and Descartes, and from his own *Legitimation of Belief*. The programme contained lines from Fulke Greville's 1609 play *Mustapha*. Gellner loved this passage, and had used it as the legend to *The Psychoanalytic Movement*.

> Oh wearisome condition of Humanity!
> Borne under one Law, to another bound:
> Vainely begot, yet forbidden vanity,
> Created sicke, commanded to be sound:
> What meaneth Nature by these diverse Lawes?
> Passion and Reason, selfe-division cause:

---

90 T. Nairn, 'Nationalism Is Not the Enemy', *Observer*, 12 November 1995.

> Is it the marke, or Majesty of Power
> To make offences that it may forgive?
> Nature herself doth her own selfe defloure,
> To hate those errors she her selfe doth give.

The dual emphasis on passion and reason made these lines a wholly appropriate epitaph for Ernest Gellner.

Epilogue

Gellner left behind two manuscripts at the time of his death.[1] The first was written during his last summer in Italy, at the request of Weidenfeld and Nicolson, and as the result of a very large advance. It was effectively finished, even polished, and it appeared as *Nationalism* in 1997. Its contents have already been noted – the restatement of his views, the debate about the modernity of nationalism, the insistence that normative principles are very hard to come by. David Gellner wrote a preface for *Nationalism*, and he did so for the second manuscript as well – or, rather, manuscripts (one of which was entitled simply 'Meaning'). The book appeared in 1998 as *Language and Solitude: Wittgenstein, Malinowski and the Habsburg Dilemma*, a fine title because the painting by an unknown artist of a single man hunched in misery had been carefully chosen by Gellner himself. The preface suggested that the book was a 'fitting – almost autobiographical – last work'.[2] This is correct. For one thing, the book touched on many of the themes that had preoccupied Gellner all his life, from the philosophy of Wittgenstein to nationalism and to anthropological theory. For another, the book amounts to a final coming to terms with his Central European background.

The book opens with the starkest of contrasts, insisting that there are but two ways, individualism and communitarianism, in which the world can be approached, a binary opposition held to apply to everything, from epistemology to politics. Individualism had initially been characteristic of Viennese politics, long led by German-speaking liberals, proud of a state

---

1 An important third text (whose varied contents have already been noted at various points in the preceding chapters) also appeared shortly after his death, his 'Reply to Critics', in J. A. Hall and I. C. Jarvie, (eds), *The Social Philosophy of Ernest Gellner*, Amsterdam, 1996.
2 D. Gellner, 'Preface', *Language and Solitude: Wittgenstein, Malinowski and the Habsburg Dilemma*, Cambridge, 1998, p. vii. The preface explains in detail the way in which a single volume was drawn out of the numerous manuscripts – drawn out, I might add, with skill and sympathy.

which sought to rise above nations. This progressive view was challenged by ethnonational movements, initially and most obviously from Hungarian speakers, and later from all over the empire, including Czech leaders and, eventually, German speakers as well. This development made life very difficult for those with Jewish backgrounds.

> In this struggle, the new nationalism used to the full, and very effectively, the romantic vision of man, invoking roots and repudiating cosmopolitanism. No doubt it could not have been so effective in this if the social and intellectual climate had not been so favourable – but it was. It ensured that this vision was deeply and powerfully internalised in the hearts and minds of men – those it favoured, but equally, or perhaps even more, those it rejected. It condemned them to self-hatred and self-hatred was their lot: as many of them had very considerable literary talents, they expressed and recorded it with eloquence.[3]

Feelings of difference were continually reiterated for the seemingly endless stream of *Ostjuden*, the unsophisticated and ethnically caged Jews who arrived in Vienna in the years after 1918, ruling out assimilation into the German-speaking community. Further, ethnonationalism had no appeal for those with Jewish backgrounds who were more assimilated, for rising standards of education meant more competition for the skilled jobs that so many of them held. Not surprisingly, in these circumstances loyalty to the empire came to rest on the armed forces, the socialist leadership and the Jews. The most obvious example of the cosmopolitanism of the last of these groups is Karl Popper's *The Open Society and Its Enemies*.

Gellner claims that the young Wittgenstein spells out forcefully the loneliness that is involved in pure individualist cosmopolitanism. His position was overdetermined. A particular source for the young philosopher's loneliness was the emphasis on language, on the limits of what could ever be said. This was joined to the epistemological tradition of Descartes, Hume and Kant – that is, the tradition of thought which sought to establish certainty by stepping outside cultural bounds. The despair to which this tradition could lead was powerfully expressed by Hume – for all that his bluff confidence allowed him to escape it. Wittgenstein had none of the easy being-in-the-world that had marked the Scottish philosopher. He was Jewish, and probably homosexual as well, and had no chance of leaving anxiety behind by easy entry into mainstream society. His desire to escape these circumstances was very great, and he found a way by reversing his

---

3 *Language and Solitude*, p. 38.

view of the nature of language – from an aseptic mirroring of facts, to
nothing less than the provider of a form of life. Gellner stresses that the
Philosophical Investigations does not describe any particular society, in part
because Wittgenstein's own populist move, as a schoolteacher, had been
so very unsuccessful. Nonetheless, the switch from his early to his late
philosophy depended upon the terms of debate available in the society
in which he lived. Gellner summarizes the move as one from a world in
which there is no culture to one in which there is nothing but culture.[4]

Gellner would have none of this, feeling that Wittgenstein had managed
to get it wrong twice. A novel feature of the book is a detailed analysis of
the weaknesses of the young Wittgenstein's view of language, that of a
mirror held up to reality.[5] Language is more than a series of disconnected
and immutable propositions; it rather contains connections and ambiguities
and change. The view of language proposed by the young Wittgenstein was
such as to make social life impossible, neatly illustrated by Gellner imagining a conversation held within the terms proposed.[6] But the alternative
proposed by the later Wittgenstein – that language is culture, and that we
cannot escape its bounds – is rejected quite as firmly, for reasons with which
we are now familiar. Escaping from a particular view of language illicitly
led Wittgenstein to imagine that all attempts to find secure knowledge
were mistaken. It is in this context that Gellner makes a novel observation
about Malinowski.[7]

We have already seen the core of Gellner's understanding and appreciation of Malinowski. The Pole is the perfect foil to the Viennese Jew
in escaping the Hapsburg dilemma. The empiricism of Mach is endorsed
in combination with an appreciation of culture. Politically, this allowed
Malinowski to seek to protect national sentiments without allowing them
any sort of absolutist status. The novel point added here concerns language.
In 1923 Malinowski's 'The Problem of Meaning in Primitive Language'
appeared as a supplement to a book on *The Meaning of Meaning*, co-authored
by C. K. Ogden, the first translator of the young Wittgenstein's *Tractatus
Logico-Philosophicus*.[8] This essay arrived at the same view of language

---

4   *Language and Solitude*, chapter 19, disputed the claims by A. Janik and S. Toulmin
in *Wittgenstein's Vienna*, New York, 1973. Janik and Toulmin argued that Wittgenstein had
sought loneliness; Gellner's argument was that loneliness was exactly the condition that he
sought to escape.

5   Ibid., chapter 11.

6   Ibid., pp. 108–9.

7   Ibid., chapter 29.

8   C. K. Ogden and I. A. Richards, *The Meaning of Meaning: A Study of the Influence of
Language Upon Thought and the Science of Symbolism*, London, 1923.

suggested by the later Wittgenstein, emphasizing in particular that meaning resides in action and use. But Malinowski insists that this is not the only type of language in existence. Such contextual language is clearly dominant in simpler societies, but it has been replaced, at least in the higher reaches of scientific discourse, with linguistic use that is context-free, and accordingly far more malleable. Language is not always a prison; it can also be a tool. This had long been Gellner's view, and he accordingly endorses Malinowki's position with delight – though noting sadly that Malinowski backtracked from this sensible position in later work.[9]

In the last pages of the book, Gellner expands on Malinowski, adding further arguments to explain why the binary choice between communitarianism and individualism is mistaken. Each position has weaknesses as well as strengths. Atomistic individualism is enormously important because when used prescriptively it creates knowledge powerful enough to transform the world, and to bring in its wake the riches on which we depend. But it fails to provide us with a way of life, indeed it fails to account descriptively for the sociability of lived experience. Cultural theorists make this point, correctly, and their position is accordingly indispensable. But that is not for a moment to say that it can be turned into an absolute, presuming that culture is everything, a cocoon from which no escape is possible. Some escape has been made, and our problem is that of seeing how much meaning this then allows us to create for ourselves. This brings us to the distinctiveness of Gellner's position. He was at once the theorist of nationalism and a rationalist enlightenment fundamentalist. How did he manage to combine the two?

Gellner's greatest allegiance was to the fallible world of scientific rationalism, though he felt that its general appeal rested less on its openness that on its brute capacity to provide a high material standard of living. The second principle of the modern social contract, the recognition of nationalism, was also necessary for achieving that high standard of living. And that standard of living could in turn be relied upon to tame nationalism itself. For one thing, the stakes of conflict would be lowered once a high standard of living was generally available – removing from the equation the political gunpowder created by the presence of an ethnic marker in combination with social inequality. In these circumstances, he came to believe late in life, the preservation of cultural difference under the same political roof might, after all, be possible. For another, the dependence of a high living standard upon science meant that in the end the occasional moments of absolutism of nationalist ideology would be undermined – for science

---

9   *Language and Solitude*, chapter 30.

was based on change, doubt, the relative uncertainty of being. This was not to say that there would be any general adoption of Kantian-style views. What mattered was rather that the unfolding logic of industrial society would give greater prominence to new middle-class specialists likely to prefer technical reason to ideological verbiage.

All that could be offered then was ironic cultural nationalism. The need for this limited identity came from the fact that one must have some style, some rules of engagement for social life to take place. This plea for limited identity should not be taken to mean that Gellner is any less rationalist than Popper – who condemned nationalism in all its forms. The difference is really that Gellner's loyalty to rationalism stressed its emptiness, its lack of grounding, in contrast to Popper's rather romantic view that critical rationalism was written into the very nature of life. In that sense, Gellner was much more deeply homeless than Popper. For much of his career, he was sustained by the feeling that technological power would slowly undermine ideocracies. Late in life, he began to doubt that this would be the outcome within the Islamic world. His thought in these areas remains challenging, though my own sense is that his understanding of social life lacks sufficient awareness of politics – both as a cause of discontent and as a practice by means of which conflicts can sometimes be accommodated.

What does all this say about the way in which he came to terms with his own Jewish background? The distinctiveness of his position can be appreciated by referring to the recent brilliant work of Pierre Birnbaum on the varied ways in which social scientists with Jewish backgrounds have confronted their pasts.[10] Complete assimilation can, in Birnbaum's view, be dreadfully misguided since it destroys cultural distinction, with the historical contribution of Jewish culture being very much at the forefront of his own mind as something of great value. This places Birnbaum in the camp of Isaiah Berlin and his follower Charles Taylor, as a proponent of liberal integration – that is, of a culturally pluralist world – though he is fully cognizant that this must not be so exaggerated as to recreate cultural cages from which it is hard to escape. Birnbaum suggests that this line of thought owes much to Montesquieu. I am not so sure. The *Persian Letters* certainly argues for toleration, but does so in a very particular way. There is no doubt at all that Montesquieu has absolute allegiance to a very few universal standards, but beyond those he seems almost a complete sceptic and relativist – not so much praising different ways of life as throwing up his hands at the mild absurdity of every single one of them. In a sense, this is

---

10 P. Birnbaum, *The Geography of Hope: Exile, the Enlightenment, Disassimilation*, Stanford, 2008.

Gellner's ironic cultural nationalism. Certainly, Gellner had no very great Jewish allegiance to return to, his Czech roots being far more central to his identity. He did not hide his Jewish background, but he did not romanticize it either – and certainly did not wish to somehow recreate it. One might say that this makes him a bad Jew, though surely the point is that this was not really his identity, or not at least an important aspect of it. But perhaps he was true to his Jewish background in a very particular way. Consider this comment of Hannah Arendt, writing about Walter Benjamin's generation of thinkers whose background was Jewish:

> [T]hese men did not wish to 'return' to the ranks of the Jewish people or to Judaism, and could not desire to do so – not because . . . they were too 'assimilated' and too alienated from their Jewish heritage, but because all traditions and cultures as well as all 'belonging' had become equally questionable to them.[11]

Of course, this is slightly wrong. The great subtlety of Benjamin as a thinker cannot disguise the fact that he found some sense of belonging in Marxism, while other thinkers from this background found belongings of very varied sorts. The distinctiveness of Gellner is that he was brave enough to do without any complete and guaranteed identity, precisely because every belonging *had* become questionable to him – though his Czech upbringing had given him a real sense of the nature of belonging. Accordingly, Gellner's world is austere. But therein lies its attraction. Not much real comfort for our woes is on offer; the consolations peddled in the market are indeed worthless. What Gellner offered was something more mature and demanding: cold intellectual honesty.

---

11   H. Arendt, 'Walter Benjamin: 1892–1940' in her *Men in Dark Times*, London, 1970, pp.187–8. This passage is cited in Z. Smith's sensitive 'F. Kafka, Everyman', *New York Review of Books*, 17 July 2008.

Index